MW01275487

The Feinberg Edition

A Shot of Torah

Short, fun, deep, and inspiring divrei Torah
for your Shabbos and *Yom Tov* table

Rabbi Aba Wagensberg

L'dor V'dor
Ramot Press

First Printing: 2015

ISBN: 978-0-9965158-5-6

Ramot Press

Jerusalem, Israel

www.RamotPress.com

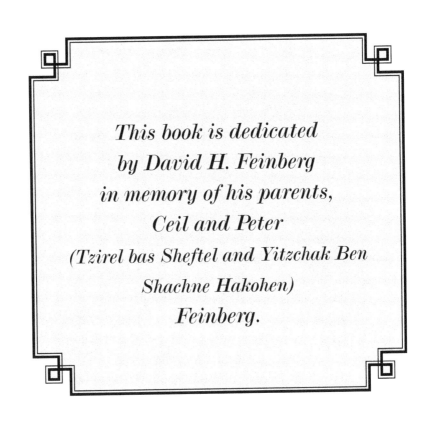

*This book is dedicated
by David H. Feinberg
in memory of his parents,
Ceil and Peter
(Tzirel bas Sheftel and Yitzchak Ben
Shachne Hakohen)
Feinberg.*

This book is dedicated in loving memory of my aunt Helen (Chaya Sarah) Katz who passed away at the age of ninety years old. She was a very special person, filled with optimism even in trying times. She treated everybody with respect and sweetness. We all miss the matriarch of our family. Her passing marks the end of an era. Aunt Helen, may you receive unlimited Nachas from your entire family. We love you and miss you.

ישיבה פרימרי
Yeshiva Primary
80-11 210 St / Jamaica, NY 11427
(718) 217-4700
Fax: (718) 217-8739

Rabbi Aba Wagensberg, Shlit"a

In a way, you are my Rebbe. As the Rambam writes,

הילכות תלמוד תורה פרק ה הלכה י"ב
כשם שהתלמידים חייבין בכבוד הרב כך הרב צריך לכבד את תלמידיו ולקרבן
כך אמרו חכמים (משנה אבות ד-יב) 'יהי כבוד תלמידך חביב עליך כשלך'
The Rambam continues, הלכה י"ג: התלמידים מוסיפין חכמת הרב ומרחיבין לבו.

Aba, you did this as a youngster of 9 years old and continue to do so as an adult through your shiurim, tapes, radio addresses and now with your sefarim.

אמרו חכמים: הרבה חכמה למדתי מרבותי, ויותר מהם מחברי, ומתלמידי יותר מכולם
וכשם שעץ קטן מדליק את העץ הגדול, כך תלמיד קטן מחדד את הרב, עד שיוציא ממני בשאלותיו חכמה מפוארה
Knowing this Rambam, how can I write an approbation?!?

The Chassam Sofer in Parshas Behar, perek gimmel, pesukim 1-2 asks why the Torah chose to teach us the lesson "שכל המלמד בן חבירו תורה כאלו ילדו" by the children of Aharon HaKohen in respect to Moshe Rabeinu? The answer is that Moshe himself attested "עכשיו רואה אני שהם גדולים ממני וממך". Nadav and Avihu were greater than their Rebbe Moshe, yet once one taught a talmid Torah, even upon the talmid's rise to greatness - as you have done Reb Aba - a rebbe who nurtured a talmid remains his rebbe forever.

You attended Yeshiva High School at the Talmudical Academy of Adelphia under the Roshei HaYeshiva Rabbi Yeruchem Shain and the Menahel, Rav Dovid Trenk shlit"a. A mesivta that produced hundreds upon hundreds of bnei Torah and yirei HaShem, literally hanefesh asher asu b'Adelphia.

Upon graduation, you were presented with a fabulous business proposition where they guaranteed fabulous salaries and bonuses, yet after considering the opportunities, you turned it down and you went to Eretz Yisroel to learn under HaRav HaGaon HaRav Chaim Pinchas Sheinberg zt"l at Yeshivas Torah Ohr in Yerushalayim, where you spent many years in Kollel.

In your first sefer published several years ago "Inspiring Change", you elucidate and explain esoteric kabbalistic concepts in a down-to-earth inspirational way.
This new sefer is a parsha/holiday book meant to be user-friendly at the Shabbos/Yom Tov table. There are four divrei Torah for each parsha and for each holiday so that one dvar Torah can be shared at each meal, including melaveh malka.

As usual, you do not miss any detail and included 4 divrei Torah for each Yom Tov for bnei chutz l'aretz who will have 4 Yom Tov meals over their 2 day Yom Tov, thus ensuring that the Shabbos and Yom Tov table be "zeh hashulchan asher lifnei HaShem."

You have z'chus Avos. Your parents from day one have - countless times - emotionally articulated to me their hope that you grow up to be a ben Torah, yirei shamayim and a Rav. Their yearning and tefillos have been answered fully and their son, you Rev Aba, truly personify a ben Torah, yirei shamayim and a marbitz Torah far and wide.

It is with humility that I offer a birkat Kohen; that you be zoche to continue in avodas hakodesh, and that you have nachos from your children, your spiritual children, your talmidim and from yourself as well.

בא"ת פ"ק כפר בחלון לפ"ק
Zalman Dov HaCohen Deutscher

Dean

Rabbi Zev Leff

Rabbi of Moshav Matityahu
Rosh HaYeshiva—Yeshiva Gedola Matityahu

הרב זאב לף

בס"ד

מרא דאתרא מושב מתתיהו
ראש הישיבה—ישיבה גדולה מתתיהו

D.N. Modiin 71917   Tel: 08–976–1138 'טל   Fax: 08–976–5326 'פקס   71917 ד.נ. מודיעין

Dear Friends,

I have read portions of the manuscript "A Shot Of Torah" by my esteemed and illustrious colleague and friend, Rabbi Aba Wagensberg.

The author presents short Divrei Torah on the Parshiyos HaTorah and on the various holidays. As in his previous works the essays are steeped in Torah wisdom and presented in a lucid manner. I found them to be informative, inspiring, and entertaining.

I recommend this work as a source of Torah knowledge and inspiration, as well as an effective tool to enhance one's Shabbos and Yom Tov table with fine Divrei Torah that will be a true Oneg Shabbos (Shabbos delight) and simchas Yom Tov (holiday pleasure).

I commend the author for producing another quality work, and pray that Hashem Yisborach bless his whole family with life, health and the wherewithal to continue to benefit the community in his many and varied ways.

Sincerely,
With Torah blessings

Rabbi Zev Leff

ישיבה מורשת יהושע
YESHIVA MORESHES YEHOSHUA
817 Central Avenue • Lakewood. NJ 08701 • (732) 370-5043 • Fax (732) 370-5044

כד' ניסן תשע"ה

לתלמידי, ידידי אהובי ר' אבא וואגענסברג עמו"ש

שמך הולך לפניך - Your name precedes you, as does your voice!

Tuning in on Thursday nights here in Lakewood, 107.9, to the Rav Aba Wagensberg Experience, The Parsha, is a treat — ten questions, then the joy of simchas HaTorah as the answers pour forth, one by one.

The chevra is treated to... "And that is the answer to question one,"... two, etc. Rav Wagensberg, using as his sources Divrei Chazal - Midrashim, Rishonim, Achronim, Maharal, Reb Tzadok, Zohar, and a sprinkling of Kabalah - leads us, his listeners, on this exhilarating journey.

Enriched, we look forward to Shabbos and the seudos — to delve into, talk about, and give over to family and friends that which we have heard and internalized.

With this sefer we are zocheh to have at hand (and not have to wait till next Thursday) Reb Aba's Divrei Torah in sefer form.

Now every "Aba" (Daddy/Totty) has a chance to prepare a "vort" to say over at the three seudos on Shabbos... and never one to miss a beat, there's a fourth, for Melave Malka!

Plus two for seudos Yom Tov. And two more for us chutz l'aretzniks for Yom Tov sheini!

It is truly a zechus for me to share in your heilige work, by writing these words.

"אשריך ואשרי חלקך"

Sincerely,

Dovid Trenk

9

Table of Contents

Volume 1

Acknowledgements 17
Preface...22
Introduction 26

Bereishis
Three's Company 29
The Transformers..33
From the "Bashes"...36
Body and Soul 39

Noach
Practicing What We Teach 43
Noach Flipped Out 47
Noach "Meats" God 50
A Towering Temptation...53

Lech Lecha
Down to Earth 56
Lead the Way...60
Keep it in Mind 62
Please Sign Below 65

Vayeira
Delayed Reaction 68
For the Greater Good 71
It's No Laughing Matter 73
Keeping the Faith..77

Chayei Sarah
One Foot in Heaven..80
From the Peaks to the Depths 84
Smarty Pants 87
Taking the Oath 90

Volume 2

Acknowledgements

It is with my deepest gratitude to **Hashem** that I present you with my newest publication, "A Shot of Torah." When it comes to thanking Hashem, I do not even know where to begin. However, if I were to begin, I would not know how to stop. Whether it's my family, my friends, my mentors, my students that God has given me, or the circumstances that He created which brought me to this very moment, I cannot even find the words to express my appreciation. So all I will say is: thank you, Hashem, I love you.

I have been incredibly blessed to have been surrounded by numerous good people in my life. My appreciation to these people is unending. In this section I would like to mention those who had a direct hand in this publication.

Spending hours each week to type up these teachings is a challenging undertaking. There are always matters that demand my attention. There is one thing, however, that motivates me to spend the time necessary to make this a reality, and that is you, my dear readers. Many of you were students of mine from seminary, yeshiva or study groups. Others discovered my classes online, and joined. Either way, your loyalty and support have been immeasurable, helpful and appreciated. Your e-mails with positive feedback have served as a tremendous source of *chizuk* for me. Often when typing up the next teaching, I envision your faces and your Shabbos tables, and I then picture these ideas being shared with family and friends. That alone provides me with a desire and fortitude to keep on going. With a heart full of *nachas*, I humbly thank you all.

Although I will discuss my relationship with **Mr. David Feinberg** later on in the Preface, I felt that it was absolutely necessary to mention David again over here. David, thank you for being my *chavrusa*; thank you for supporting this project; and thank you for being my friend. Laura and I are blessed to have you, your wife Carol, your son Daniel and his wife Lauren as our family friends. May you see much *nachas* from this book, and from your entire family.

Researching, collecting, organizing and printing these teachings that spanned many years was a daunting undertaking. There was one person who literally spent hours on this phase of the project. His name is **Yosef Sokol** ("Joey"), my cousin. No matter what glitch got in our way, Joey creatively found a solution ("Sokol Solutions"), and carried it out with efficiency, professionalism and alacrity. Thank you, Joey; I think we make a great team!

It's not often that an author gets the privilege of having his wife edit, proofread and do some of the type setting of his book. I did have that honor. Memories of **Laura** spending countless hours at the table with papers, pens and computers makes my heart swell with appreciation. Thank you Laura for investing so much of your time and energy into this project. Laura, I am forever grateful for your sacrifice and support.

We had a vision for the illustration, and **Mrs. Esther Gnat** delivered. "A picture is worth a thousand words," and that is the amount of words I have to express my gratitude to her for a fantastic job. Thank you, Mrs. Gnat.

Bringing this project across the finish line was done by my precious daughter, **Esther Rochel**, who stepped up to the plate, took initiative, and used her knowledge to complete this process. All I can say is Baruch Hashem, I am filled with so much nachas. Thank you Esther Rochel, I love you.

Thank God, I have been blessed to have Rebbeim in my life who are legends in their own time. I mention some of them here.

When I was a little boy in Hebrew Day School, I was failing terribly. There was one person who changed my direction in a drastically positive way. That person is **Rabbi Zalman Deutscher** *shlit"a*. Rabbi Deutscher's vast knowledge of Torah is matched by his remarkable talent as an educator par excellence. Those two qualities are complemented by his caring heart and kindness. I do not know where I would be today if not for Rabbi Deutscher. I am unaware of other Rebbeim who teach in elementary schools and then keep tabs on their students when they go on to high school, post high school, and even continue to stay in touch with them to be of service for the rest of their lives. Rabbi Deutscher does exactly that. I fondly remember the visits he made to us in Yeshiva High School (always bringing cakes and a little extra cash just in case we needed it). It was you, Rabbi Deutscher, who suggested which path I take in Eretz Yisrael; it has, Baruch Hashem, been successfully continuing until this very day. Moreover you have taken a special interest in my family as well, helping in any way that you can. Rabbi Deutscher, Thank you, Thank you, Thank you. Thank you for all you have done, and thank you for agreeing to pen a beautiful approbation for this publication, my second book. I remain your humble student.

Another legend in his time was my ninth grade Rebbi in Yeshivas Adelphia New Jersey. His name is **Rabbi Dovid Trenk** *shlit"a*. His fire for Torah and love of every Jew made an everlasting impression on me. He not only taught us *gemara*, but he taught us how to be a *mentch*, not just by what he said, but by acting as a role model. Rabbi Trenk is a mechanech par excellence. I will share just one brief story which reveals this. Before inspecting the dormitories for items that the yeshiva forbade, Rabbi Trenk would send one of the boys to the dorm to give us advance warning that he was coming. Anybody who was involved with these forbidden items had a chance to hide them before he came. By the time he arrived, we all looked like nice little boys laying in our beds and reading sifrei kodesh like little angels. What was the point of doing this? He wanted to catch us doing the right thing! This motivated us to do more and more of the right thing, so that we would make Rabbi Trenk proud. Thank you, Rabbi Trenk, for your beautiful approbation to my second book. I remain your humble student.

Another legend in his time that I have been blessed with is **Harav Zev Leff** *shlit"a*. Rav Leff has been an invaluable source of support and sage advice over the years. I am so blessed to have such a *Talmid Chacham* and *Gadol B'Yisrael* as a family friend. Thank you, Rav Leff, for all the time and guidance you have given me over the years, and I also thank you for such a beautiful approbation for my second book. I remain your humble student.

My in-laws **Mr. and Mrs. Roman and Elaine Frayman** have been so instrumental in helping me in general, and specifically with regard to this project. Not only are they avid readers of my weekly articles, but their advice on how to improve them is priceless. Thank you for your constant love, care and kindness, and thank you for taking such an interest in my project. Mom and Dad, I love you.

I cannot thank my parents **Mr. Morris (Moishe) and Mrs. Elaine Wagensberg** enough for all they have done for me throughout the years. They have constantly sacrificed and supported me on my journey through life, during the pleasant times and during the difficult times. Thank you for your love, care and kindness shown in every step I have taken. Thank you for your advice and thank you for always being there for me. Mom and Dad, I love you.

I am so proud of my children; they have all grown up into such fine human beings who are sensitive to others. They have all been excited about this book, and they have all encouraged me along the way. So, to **Esther Rochel, Nachi, Shiffy, Rivky, Shirel, and Aharon Chaim** I say Thank you. I love you all dearly and forever.

Although I have already mentioned her above, before concluding this section of acknowledgements, I must add the feelings that I have for my dear and precious wife **Laura**. Regarding this publication, Laura has spent many hours collecting, organizing and editing these teachings. It was Laura who suggested that I conclude each essay with a practical application that people can walk away with. This idea has been very well-received, to say the least. But Laura's input goes far beyond all of that. Laura has been, and continues to be, my constant source of encouragement and support. The overabundant love that I feel from Laura makes me feel as though I am walking around in Paradise. It is because of Laura that I cherish each and every day that I am blessed to spend with her. There are no words other than thank you. Thank you, Laura, I love you.

Preface

The History

Over the years I have had the privilege of staying in touch with many of my students through the *parshah*/holiday emails that I send out weekly. It is distributed to thousands. Hundreds of people print them out to share at the Shabbos table. Dozens of letters and emails have been sent to me, thanking me for them and describing how greatly these Torah thoughts enhance their Shabbos experience, while also encouraging discussion at the table.

The Idea

Thus, an idea was born. What if we were to collect these weekly publications, modify them, revise them, and add practical applications, and present them as a book? This would give our subscribers easy access to some of their favorite essays, with many new additions. It would also enable us to reach a much wider audience of people who are not yet on our email list.

It Differs

This book, *A Shot of Torah*, differs from my first publication *Inspiring Change* in the following way; *Inspiring Change* is a collection of eight chapters that are a longer and more in-depth analysis of self-improvement going in order from inner-self to outer-self. However, *A Shot of Torah* is a collection of shorter essays, hence the name, *A "Shot" of Torah*.

Each essay has been condensed from the audio/video lecture series that I have given over the years. Each class ranges between an hour to an hour and a half. In an attempt to grab onto the essence of each talk, in shorter form, these articles were created. The chapters are arranged in order of *parshiyos* and holidays. It is designed to be user-friendly for the Shabbos Table, or any other time for that matter. I chose to include four pieces per *parshah*. The reason for this is so that you can share one piece at each meal on Shabbos, including *Melaveh Malkah*. There are four pieces for each holiday as well.

Although in *Eretz Yisrael* there is only one day of *Yom Tov* (excluding *Rosh HaShanah*) and only two pieces would be necessary for the two meals; we have, nevertheless, included four pieces for the four meals since in *Chutz La'Aretz* there are two days of *Yom Tov*.

Title – Illustration

The idea for the cover illustration came from the title and from the concept of this book. As we mentioned, these pieces are shorter versions of longer lectures. These *divrei Torah* are also intended to be shared as the Shabbos/ *Yom Tov* table. At those tables we customarily drink a *l'chaim* between the fish and the meat. Therefore the name my wife suggested, *"A shot of Torah",* is very fitting since it alludes to the small shot-glass of alcohol that is drunk at the Shabbos/ *Yom Tov* table.

The idea for the illustration of wine being poured from the bottle into the Kiddush cup in the shape of Hebrew letters came from my mother. When she suggested it, the following thought came to my mind. The Gemara says *"nichnas yayin yetzei sod"*- (When wine enters, secrets come out, *Rebbi Chiya Eruvin chapter 6 "Hadar" page 65a*). One interpretation of this passage could be that wine is connected to the secrets of the Torah. Both Hebrew words *yayin* and *sod* share the same numerical value of seventy, which refers to the seventy interpretations of the Torah. Moreover wine is actually found hidden within the grapes, hinting to the secrets of Torah that are hidden beneath the surface. This idea is very connected to the *divrei Torah* found within this *sefer* because the teachings tend to cover the four levels of Torah understanding, *pshat, remez, drush* and *sod* (simplistic, code, expounding, and secrets). How fitting it would be then to drink a shot of Torah together with the shot of wine at the festive Shabbos and *Yom Tov* meals.

The Practical

As I mentioned, we have added a practical exercise at the end of each essay in order to be able to actually implement these lessons into our daily living. The motivation behind this came from my wife, Laura. Laura has been editing my *parshah* emails for some time now. She mentioned to me that there seemed to be something missing - a gap between the end of the teaching and the blessing. Laura suggested that we need to find a way of making these teachings concrete in people's lives and not just leave them hanging, thinking of how the lesson can make a difference in their lives. These practical applications would be the necessary ingredient that would serve as the bridge from the Torah to the blessing.

I was thinking that this fits into the *Ramban* in his letter when he says that whenever we get up from studying a *sefer*, we should think about how we can apply what we have learned. Hopefully, we have satisfied this suggestion to some extent.

I cannot begin to tell you how much positive feedback I received from my students when I began suggesting these exercises in my lectures and emails. It has made these lessons so relevant to people's lives. Laura, I am eternally grateful for you! It is my hope that this book will help to further enhance your Shabbos and *Yom Tov* meals, generating holy Torah discussions.

David Feinberg

This book is the Feinberg Edition on account of my dear friend, Mr. David Feinberg. Many years ago, when David's son, Daniel, studied at Darchei Noam Shappells, he suggested that I begin learning with his father. Daniel, I can't thank you enough because this resulted in a close friendship and my longest standing *chavrusah* ever! David and I have studied many things together including *Chumash*, *Halachah*, holidays, prayer and philosophy, but mostly it's been Talmud.

I am very impressed with Mr. Feinberg. He is level-headed, balanced, and filled with a beautiful set of values that he lives by. To David, the study of Torah is not just learning, but rather it is an experience to explore. David savors every word and enjoys breaking the Talmudic code himself. He considers the time spent learning Torah as the highlight of his day. Good people like Mr. Feinberg are hard to come by, and I am proud and thankful to have him as a study partner; but more importantly, I am blessed to have him as a friend. These qualities of David are matched by his generosity, which enabled me the privilege of bringing this publication to fruition.

Thank you, David, for your help; thank you, David, for your support; thank you, David, for your caring; thank you, David, for your warmth; thank you, David, for your listening ear; thank you, David, for your advice. And thank you, David, for being my friend. Thank You, G-d, for bringing David into my life, thank you, Daniel, for making the *shidduch*, and thank you, Carol, for sharing David with me.

May I take out a moment to also thank my students and readers for sharing these thoughts and teachings with your families and friends. In a way, it is as if you have invited me into your homes for Shabbos. For that, I am forever grateful.

Warmest wishes,

Aba Wagensberg

Introduction

In a very complicated and technological world, the Shabbos table may be the only setting for real quality family time. There are no appointments or meetings to attend, and no gadgets beeping and ringing to distract us. The time we spend with our families and friends around the Shabbos table may be the only "shot" we have left to impart our values with them, and create an everlasting bond.

The Shabbos table conversations are the memories that our children will savor, and carry with them throughout their lives. If they have positive feelings when they reflect on those moments, they will want to have Shabbos tables of their own and pass on the message to the next generation.

Shabbos meal time is limited. Typically, people spend just an hour or two on Friday night and Shabbos day meals. The third meal and *Melaveh Malkah* are considerably shorter. Besides catching up with each other, what better way to spend that time together other than Torah conversation. Since the Torah is eternal, the conversation will build an everlasting relationship. This is my hope with this publication - namely, that it generates Torah discussion, bringing us closer to each other and closer to G-d.

In addition, when Torah is shared at a meal, the table is transformed into the Altar, the food we eat is transformed into Offerings, and we are transformed into *Kohanim* (see *Avos* 3:4). Moreover, when Torah is spoken during the meal, then an angel comes down and creates a spiritual image of our table, and brings it up as a present to G-d; as it says, "This is the table that is before G-d" (see *Me'am Lo'ez*, Lv. 2:13; Eze. 41:22).

Sefer Vayikra

Vayikra

Holy Man

"**M**other knows best." This is as true today as it was since the beginning of time.

This week's portion, *Vayikra*, deals with the various offerings brought in the Sanctuary and in the *Beis HaMikdash*.

The opening sentence of this *parshah* is, "*Vayikra el Moshe* - And He called to Moshe" (*Vayikra* 1:1).

The *Ba'al HaTurim* points out that the acronym of these three words consists of *vav, aleph, mem*. When unscrambled, those three letters spell *imo* (his mother).

What message is Hashem trying to convey in this secret code?

The *Midrash Tanchuma* (*Rebbi Tanchuma, Parshas Tzav* # 14), asks, "Why do little children begin their Torah learning with *Sefer Vayikra*?" The answer is given, "It is because all the offerings are contained within *Sefer Vayikra*. The offerings are pure. Little Jewish children, not having experienced the taste of sin, are also pure. Therefore, The Holy One Blessed Be He said that little Jewish children should begin their journey of Torah study with the sacrifices. Let the pure ones occupy themselves with acts of purity."

The *Lekach V'halibuv* asks: who do you think is responsible for the purity of little Jewish children? Obviously it is the power of the Jewish mothers who set the tone of the home in which the little Jewish children grow up.

It is the Jewish mothers that ensure that the atmosphere of the Jewish home is filled with a spirit of purity.

Therefore, how apropos it is that the *Ba'al HaTurim* points out the message coded into the opening words of this *parshah*. *Vayikra el Moshe* contains the acronym of *imo* (his mother). This comes to teach us that a child's spiritual success largely depends on the mother's efforts.

This week I would like to implore the Jewish women of each household to look around the home and see what can be done to improve the spiritual status and holiness of the places in which we live. Any little change in the right direction has tremendous value.

May we all be blessed with holy women in our lives, and subsequently reach the highest levels of purity.

Vayikra

Shoes 4 Sale

In the following piece, we are not being asked to walk a thousand miles in another person's moccasins; nor are we being reminded what it is like when the shoe is on the wrong foot; all we are saying is that wherever we go, it should be with a good pair of shoes on our feet.

Our portion deals with various offerings that were brought in the Sanctuary, and later on, in the Temple. The *Arizal* (*Likutei Torah, Ta'amei Hamitzvos*) explains the *Kabbalistic* mechanics behind the offerings.

He says that there are four levels of Creation. In ascending order, they are:

1) The mineral world

2) The vegetable world

3) The animal kingdom

4) Man

The offerings were meant to fix all four levels of Creation. The offerings were able to achieve this because all four levels of Creation participated in each offering.

The offerings had salt (mineral), wine or oil (vegetable), the animal itself, and the person who confessed. Through the presence of these four levels in an offering, we were able to rectify all four levels of Creation by elevating them spiritually.

The Sh'lah HaKadosh (in his *siddur*, citing his *Rebbe*, the *Maharshal*) points out that each level of Creation nurses from the level underneath it. For example, things which grow receive their nourishment from the minerals of the earth beneath them. Animals are sustained by consuming the vegetation beneath them. People get their sustenance from partaking of the animals beneath them.

The *Arizal* (*Sha'ar HaMitzvos, Parshas Eikev*) adds that when each level nurses off of the level underneath, then that lower level becomes part of the level above it to the point that they are inseparable. Therefore, when a person partakes of animals, the animal becomes a part of man. However, since the levels of vegetation and mineral are already part of the animal, then not only does the animal become part of man, but so do all the other levels.

The point of all this is that man is expected to channel all the energy he receives from the three levels underneath him to serve God. In this way, man harnesses all of Creation, directing it all to God. This brings about the elevation of the entire world.

The *Arizal* teaches that it is for this very reason that only Torah scholars are allowed to eat meat (*Rebbi, Pesachim*, chap. 3, *Eilu Ovrin*, pg. 49b). Only a Torah scholar can be trusted to use all the levels contained in the meat for the right purpose. Everything is elevated through his Torah study and *mitzvah* performance.

A person devoid of Torah, however, may not have the tools to raise all the levels to God. Moreover, a person without Torah and *mitzvos* may abuse the levels of Creation, driving them to the lowest of places, achieving the direct opposite of the purpose of their creation.

This approach in understanding the mechanics behind the offerings will help us understand the importance of wearing shoes. The Talmud teaches that a person should always be prepared, if necessary, to even sell the beams of his home, just in order to buy himself a pair of shoes (*Rav Yehudah* in the name of *Rav, Shabbos*, chap. 18, *Mifanin*, pg. 129a).

Another passage says that one of the types of people that are excommunicated, as far as Heaven is concerned, is one who does not put shoes on his feet (*Pesachim*, chap. 10, *Arvei Pesachim,* pg. 113b).

A third Talmud teaches that when putting shoes on in the morning, one should recite the blessing that says that God has made for me all of my needs (*Berachos*, chap. 9, *Haroeh*, pg. 60b).

All this can make us wonder what is so important about a pair of shoes.

The *Sh'lah* and the *Gr"a* (*Imrei Noam*) explain that when we wear a pair of leather shoes, it becomes absolutely clear that we, mankind, are in charge of the whole world with all of its levels. This is because, by wearing shoes made from animal skin, we are basically walking all over the animal. This demonstrates complete dominion.

A verse that supports this reads, "You give him dominion over Your handiwork, You placed everything under his feet" (*Tehillim* 8:7). Once again, the purpose of this power is actually a responsibility. We have been charged with making all the aspects of Creation more meaningful and more spiritual.

This explains the blessing over shoes that states that "God has given me everything." Are shoes really everything? The answer is yes! This is because shoes from animal skin have the vegetable world and the mineral world wrapped up in them. When man takes all three levels of Creation and puts them on his feet as shoes, he is showing that everything has been given to man. The blessing makes a lot of sense now.

It also becomes clear why a person is excommunicated by Heaven if he does not wear a pair of shoes. It is because such a person is not living up to God's expectation of taking all aspects of Creation and bringing them closer to Hashem. This mission is so important, that one must be prepared to sell the beams of his house in order to buy a pair of shoes.

We will now gain a new appreciation of the Midrash that says that Chanoch was a shoemaker who would say, "Blessed is the Name of His Glorious Kingdom for all eternity," with every stitch he sewed into a shoe (*Yalkut Reuveini, Bereishis, Asarah Ma'amaros L'Rama Mipano*).

The *Shvilei Pinchas* explains that Chanoch wanted to tie together all levels of Creation with each and every stitch. He wanted to supply his fellow citizens with leather shoes in order to publicize the mission on which they were sent by God. This mission was to rule over all Creation, thereby directing and harnessing all things for the higher purpose of serving Hashem. In this way, Chanoch tried to stem the tide of the Great Flood that he saw prophetically was on the way.

Perhaps we could suggest that this is why the verse stresses that, "*Vayehalech Chanoch* - And Chanoch walked" (*Bereishis* 5:24). By fashioning leather shoes for the people of his time, Chanoch wanted to teach people how we are supposed to walk through life in this world by utilizing everything in the service of God.

Maybe we could put this teaching to good use by using it to further improve our Jewish living. From this entire approach it is evident that putting on shoes is a very holy activity.

Each morning we could try the following exercise when putting on shoes and when reciting the blessing that states that "God made everything for me." We should stop and think to ourselves, "I am responsible for this world beneath me, and I want to use all levels of Creation to serve God." This alone might just change the entire direction of our day.

May we all be blessed with a good pair of shoes, and walk proudly around the world, lifting all objects to a higher purpose by harnessing them in the service of God, and thus deserve to be alive when the Temple is rebuilt to witness the bringing of the offerings once again.

Vayikra

"Levelator" Going Up

Maybe it's true what they say about Jewish holidays: "They tried to kill us; we won; let's eat." However, when we sit down at the table, so much more is happening than just filling our bellies.

This week's portion kicks off an entire book that deals primarily with the offerings that were brought in the Sanctuary, and later on, in the Temple itself. Some of the commentaries grapple with the concept of animal sacrifices.

The *Alshich HaKadosh* asks why an animal has to lose its life, when it was a person who sinned. It would seem that the person who sinned should be put to death. Of what crime is the animal guilty that it should substitute for the person at fault?

One approach, offered by the *Arizal* (*Likutei Torah V'Ta'amei HaMitzvos*), shares a deeper dimension of the mechanics behind the scenes. Although, in the previous piece, we mentioned that there are four levels of Creation, we could also look at it in a slightly different way that dictates that there are actually five levels of Creation.

The five levels of Creation, in ascending order, are:

1) Inanimate objects

2) Things which grow

3) Animals

4) People who speak

5) The soul

Kabbalistically speaking, one of our missions in this world is to elevate each level of Creation and bring it closer to the Almighty. When one takes a step back and observes the rituals that took place in the Temple, one will find that this was precisely the goal to be achieved.

The salt used with the sacrifices was intended to elevate the lowest level of inanimate objects, since salt itself is inanimate. The wine and oil that was used in various offerings was meant to raise the"this year"

 level of things which grow, since these ingredients come from grapes and olives that grow.

The animals that were brought as offerings were supposed to lift the level of the animal kingdom. The *vidui* (confession) recited by the person bringing the sacrifice was in order to elevate the level of people who speak. Finally, the thoughts of the *Kohen* (priest) at the time the offerings were brought were intended to elevate the level of the soul.

This is why the Torah states that the offerings that were brought were a "*Korban LaHashem*" - an offering to God (*Vayikra* 1:2). This wording teaches us that, ultimately, all levels should be directed towards Hashem. This is why animals must lose their lives. It is not because they sinned or did anything wrong. Rather, it is a process that must take place in order to raise the animal to greater spiritual heights bringing it closer to Hashem.

Perhaps we could add to this the Ramban's definition of the word "*korban.*" He says that the root of *korban* is *krav*, which means to "get close" (*Ramban Vayikra* 1:9). When we apply this definition to the aforementioned verse, "*Korban LaHashem*," it literally means to get close to God.

Today, in the absence of the Temple and its offerings, we have a powerful substitute, and that is our very homes. Every Jewish home can be a miniature Sanctuary.

Our tables replace the Altar (*Chagigah*, chap. 3, *Chomer BaKodesh*, pg. 27a, the opinion of *Rabbi Yochanan* and *Reish Lakish*); what we eat is a substitute for the sacrificial food; and we are in place of the *Kohanim* (priests), after all, we are called a "*mamleches kohanim*" or a "Kingdom of Priests" (*Shemos* 19:6).

The salt that is supposed to be on our tables (see *Shulchan Aruch*, *Orach Chaim*, *Hilchos Bitziyas Hapas*, chap. 167:5) elevates the level of inanimate objects; the wine we drink lifts the level of things that grow; the meat we eat raises the level of animals; the words of Torah we share increases the level of man (see *Avos* 3:3, the opinion of *Rebbi Shimon*); and the holy thoughts we think advance our souls to untold heights (see the *Tzetel Katan* by the *Rebbe*, Reb Elimelech from Lizensk, paragraph 15).

The truth of the matter is that this elevation process need not be restricted only to eating. Everything with which we come into contact and every activity in which we engage can be harnessed for a higher purpose. All we have to do is ask ourselves, "How can I infuse meaning into this, propelling it to greater plateaus?"

Perhaps the most important area we can apply this lesson to is with regard to the people in our lives. How can we assist our relatives, friends, neighbors, and co-workers to maximize their potential? Of course, we should start with ourselves; however, we should not stop there. This approach to life is what builds great people.

How can we practically apply this to our everyday lives? Perhaps we could offer a few examples. Imagine channeling the energy we get from eating, drinking, sleeping, and exercising towards the service of God. Picture the difference we could make in a person's life with a smile and a kind word of encouragement. These seemingly "small" things go a long way.

May we all be blessed with the inner strength to climb the spiritual ladder of success, and in the process, bring everybody and everything around us closer to God.

Vayikra - Parshas Zachor

A Penny a Day

Nobody ever really offers us a penny for our thoughts; however, what does matter are our thoughts about the penny. What do we think about giving away a coin to somebody else in need? How quick are we to part with our hard-earned money? Our view on this subject may just make all the difference in the world; it may, in fact, determine whether we become givers or takers.

This Shabbos, we begin a new book of the Torah (*Sefer Vayikra*) which opens with the portion of *Vayikra*. Often, we also read an additional passage, *Parshas Zachor*, taken from the book of *Devarim*.

The *Shulchan Aruch* (*Orach Chaim* 685:2) states that *Parshas Zachor* is read on the Shabbos preceding *Purim*. We learn from *Tosefos* in the Talmud (*Berachos* 13a, which the *Shulchan Aruch* cites) that the reading of *Parshas Zachor* is a *mitzvah d'oraisa*, a Torah commandment.

Parshas Zachor opens in *Devarim* 25:17: "Remember what Amalek did to you on the way, when you were leaving Egypt." The end of the passage (v.19) commands us to "blot out the remembrance of Amalek." How do we succeed in fulfilling this command?

The *Emunas Itecha* (citing the *Ya'aros Devash*, *Cheilek* 2, *Drush* 15) provides a novel and insightful approach to answer this question.

In *Megillas Esther* (3:9) we read that Haman gave ten-thousand talents of silver to Achashverosh as a means of convincing him to annihilate the Jews. The *Emunas Itecha* explains that Haman instructed Achashverosh to distribute the money to the poor. Haman, who understood the tremendous power of *tzedakah* (charity), devised this strategy to ensure that his evil plans would succeed.

However, Haman did not realize that God had pre-empted his plot by ensuring that the Jews gained merits by contributing money and materials toward the construction of the Sanctuary. Their merits would serve to counteract and nullify those that Haman gained by donating to the poor.

We learn from this approach about the tremendous power of *tzedakah*, since:

1) Despite his evil motives, Haman nevertheless attained merits for giving charity to the poor.

2) The merits we gain by giving tzedakah are such that they can overturn and nullify any evil decrees against us.

We could suggest that this second idea is hinted at in the chronology of "special" Torah readings, which are read at this time of year.

There are four "special" Torah passages which we read around the month of *Adar*:

1) *Parshas Shekalim* - the Shabbos preceding *Adar*.

2) *Parshas Zachor* - the Shabbos preceding *Purim*.

3) *Parshas Parah* - the Shabbos before *Parshas HaChodesh*.

4) *Parshas HaChodesh* - the Shabbos before the month of *Nissan*.

The first of these portions is *Parshas Shekalim* which discusses the donations given by *Bnei Yisrael* toward the building of the *Mishkan*. The second special reading is *Parshas Zachor* which includes the commandment to wipe out Amalek.

The juxtaposition of these *parshiyos* emphasizes the lesson we mentioned earlier. Through our tzedakah, we will be able to defeat our enemies and overturn their plans, thus succeeding in blotting out Amalek from this world.

At this point, I would like to share with you a few statements from our Sages regarding *tzedakah*. (These statements are based on verses in the Torah and deserve further analysis. See the Talmud, *Bava Basra*, for details.)

1) "*Tzedakah* is equal to all the other *mitzvos*." - *Rabbi Asi, Bava Basra* 9a

2) "One who gives charity anonymously is even greater than Moshe Rabbeinu!" - *Rabbi Elazar, Bava Basra* 9b

3) "If one gives a coin to a pauper, he is blessed with six blessings. If one also adds a *kind word when giving his donation, he is blessed with eleven blessings.*" - *Rabbi Yitzchak, Bava Basra* 9b

4) "If one pursues [to give] *tzedakah*, God will provide him with enough money to continue giving charity." - *Rabbi Yitzchak, Bava Basra* 9b

5) "If a person gives charity regularly, he will merit having wise and wealthy children who will also be masters of the Aggadic passages!" - *Rabbi Yehoshua ben Levi, Bava Basra* 9b

6) "If someone criticizes God by questioning why He does not support the people He makes destitute, you must respond by explaining that God created a system whereby those who give to charity are, in fact, the ones who benefit - as they are saved from the judgment of purgatory." (In other words, one must realize who is doing whom a favor!) - *Rabbi Meir, Bava Basra* 10a

7) "Great is *tzedakah* in that it hastens the redemption." - *Rabbi Yosi, Bava Basra* 10a

8) "Charity saves from death." - *Mishlei* 10:2

9) "One who gives a coin to a pauper will merit receiving the countenance of the Divine presence." - *Rabbi Dustoi*, in the name of *Rabbi Yannai, Bava Basra* 10a

What a wonderful practice it would be to get a *tzedakah* box in our hands, and twice a day, drop a coin in it. Once in the morning before praying to help our prayers be accepted (see *Tehillim* 17:15 and *Bava Basra* 10a, *Rabbi Elazar*) and once at night prior to going to sleep to help us wake up in the morning, because sleep is a sixtieth of death (*Berachos* 57B), and charity saves from death (*Mishlei* 10:2).

Another propitious time to give charity for women is right before lighting the Shabbos candles. This is because lighting the candles atones for the sin of Eve, who extinguished God's light (a person's soul) by bringing death into the world. Lighting candles is part of the process of bringing that light back into the world. Therefore, charity at that time helps achieve atonement. (See *Ben Ish Chai, Bereishis* #31, and *Shabbos* 119B, and *Kitzur Shulchan Aruch* chapter 72:2.)

May we be blessed with the strength and patience to give our money to *tzedakah*, and have compassion on our brothers and sisters, so that we deserve to greet the *Moshiach*, who will gather in the dispersed, destroy Amalek, and rebuild the Temple.

Tzav - Shabbos HaGadol

Going the Distance

Strength is not determined so much by the power that we have today, but by the stamina we maintain for long periods of time. This is precisely how the Jewish people's strength has been measured over the ages.

In this weeks portion, *Tzav*, it says that Hashem tells Moshe to command Aharon and his sons saying, "*Zos Toras ha'olah hee ha'olah...* - this is the law of the burnt offering; this is the burnt offering on the fire of the Altar..." (6:2). *Rabbeinu Bachya* says that this burnt offering is the most honored of all the sacrifices we have. This is hinted to in the text of the aforementioned verse which seems to repeat itself superfluously. First, it says, "*Zos Toras ha'olah* - this is the law of the burnt offering," and it continues, "*hee ha'olah* - this is the burnt offering." The verse already says it is the law of the burnt offering; why then, does it say for a second time that it is a burnt offering?

Rabbeinu Bachya suggests that the latter words do not define it as the burnt offering, but rather *hee ha'olah* means that it is the highest and most important of the offerings. One support for this idea is the striking difference between the burnt offerings and all the other offerings. All the other *korbanos* have parts that are consumed by the owners and the priests; whereas the burnt offerings are consumed totally by the fire and God.

Why did the Torah wait to teach us this in the portion of *Tzav*. In last week's portion, *Vayikra*, this should have already been mentioned, because the burnt offering and its halachic requirements were introduced there. For example, the fact that it has to be a male animal and faultless (without blemish) and that the owners would traditionally designate the animals as *korbanos* by placing their hands on the head of the *beheimah*. So, when we introduced the burnt offering, it would have been appropriate to mention its exalted status straight away. Why, then, the delay until this week's portion, *Tzav*?

The question is greater when one considers the fact that in the portion of *Tzav*, we only deal with the secondary aspects of this offering. For example, if there wasn't enough time during the day for the Altar's fire to consume the limbs and fats of the offering, then those limbs and fats may be burned on the Altar all night long, *bedi'eved* (in a secondary fashion) (see *Ramban Tzav* 6:2). Why would the Torah mention such a fundamental aspect of the burnt, and most supreme, offering in a portion that discusses only the secondary aspects of this sacrifice?

Says the *Emunas Itecha*, it is known that due to the increase of darkness in our exile, our *avodas* Hashem (worship of God) has become weakened to a point where many of us don't even fulfill commandments that we should. This is in addition to the fact that most *mitzvos* do not even apply today on account of the destruction of the Temple. And on top of that, the few *mitzvos* that we do get around to performing are not done with a high level of quality. One certainly cannot compare our service of God today with that of previous generations.

On the other hand, our minuscule and diminished service of God in this generation is much more beloved and cherished by God than the *avodas* Hashem of yesteryear. It is because of the fact that we are so weak and so distant, that extending any efforts in the service of God is considered to be a big deal in Hashem's eyes. Perhaps we can share an example to illustrate this idea.

Imagine an Olympic swimming competition. The referee shoots his gun into the air and all the athletes plunge into the swimming pool. They start out with such a force, coasting across the pool like dolphins. However, we're going to change the rules just a bit. Instead of the traditional 200-400 meter race, we are going to take a two-hour coffee break, allowing them to keep swimming while we drink. How would the swimmers look after two hours of constant swimming? What would happen if we decided to return the next day? Those healthy athletes would look pathetic. We'd be shocked if they were even treading water.

This is analogous to the history of the Jews. At Sinai, God said "Go," and in previous generations, our people went about the service of God with vim and vigor. Many years have passed since then, and the fact that we do anything in the service of God is impressive to Hashem. We should have drowned a long time ago and yet here we are, still treading water.

By the mere fact that the Jewish people have held on tenaciously serving God, we bring something to Hashem that our grandparents could never have brought, even though we don't perform the *mitzvos* with the same strength as in previous times.

In today's day and age, we are living in such darkness that people are very confused. After the occurrences of recent history, we have a lot of questions that remain, by and large, unanswered. We have suffered, and we live in a very broken world; but in spite of all that, we serve Hashem anyway. God says that is simply amazing. And therefore, our diminished service today finds the most favor in Hashem's eyes.

This is why the Torah waits for *Parshas Tzav* to teach us that the burnt offering is the highest, even though only the secondary aspects of the *korban* are being discussed. This is to teach us that our service of Hashem today, while of secondary value, is nevertheless the highest - *hee ha'olah*. What we think is the lowest, is in reality the highest. We may not be praying with as much *kavanah* (intent) as in previous generations, but the fact that we pray at all is a demonstration of Herculean strength.

We might add that this could be the reason that sometimes *Parshas Tzav* falls out on *Shabbos HaGadol* - because as a team, they convey to us the following message. *Parshas Tzav* deals with the secondary aspects of *avodas*

Hashem, so although we think it's the "lowest," *Shabbos HaGadol* comes along and says to us: on the contrary it is the most *gadol* - it is the biggest and the highest.

So, instead of beating ourselves up for not doing enough, we can make a list of three things we are doing correctly. Keep that list with us and look at it periodically throughout the day. Then we will start feeling good about who we are and what we do.

May we all be blessed during these dark and difficult times with the awareness of how high and holy we really are and just how important and beloved every *mitzvah* of ours is to Hashem. We are giving him the greatest *nachas*. May we merit to see the coming of *Moshiach* who will build the *Beis HaMikdash* and re-institute the offerings and other Temple-bound *mitzvos*, and put an end to Jewish suffering.

Tzav - Shabbos HaGadol

Big Talk

It is true that a reckless cab driver may get his passengers to pray, but a Rabbi can get his constituents to be cleansed from all sin.

This is the last Shabbos before *Pesach*, and is known as *Shabbos HaGadol* (the Big, or Great, Sabbath). In the *Sefer Ta'amei HaMinhagim* (*Inyanei Pesach* no. 473), the author cites the *Bnei Yissaschar* who offers a reason as to why it is customary for the Rabbi to give a special talk on *Shabbos HaGadol*. On the Shabbos before the Exodus from Egypt, Moshe delivered a lecture to the Jewish people, detailing the laws of Passover. Thus, we do the same. Furthermore, the *Bnei Yissaschar* says, when the wise ones of the community sit and expound, God atones for the sins of the Jewish nation. This also explains why the Rabbi customarily delivers a speech on the Shabbos before *Yom Kippur* (known as *Shabbos Shuva or Shabbos Teshuvah*).

The *Eliyahu Rabbah* writes in the name of the *Bach* that, recently, it has become widely accepted for the Rabbi to speak on Aggadic passages rather than on the Passover laws. He suggests that since there are many books on the laws of *Pesach*, which are widely accessible, even the less-learned are able to obtain answers to their queries in this way. Therefore, the Rabbi has the option of speaking on other matters besides *hilchos Pesach*.

Based on this idea, we could suggest that it is worthy for the Rabbi to expound on the *haggadah* on *Shabbos HaGadol*. As the *Rema* (*Orach Chaim* Ch. 430) says: it is the custom at *Minchah* time on *Shabbos HaGadol* to recite the *haggadah*, from the paragraph "*Avadim Hayinu*" until "*Lechaper al kol avonoseinu*." It is not for naught that we conclude with this section because, as we mentioned, the Rabbi's discourse on *Shabbos HaGadol* atones for our transgressions.

So this Shabbos, let's try to attend the Rabbi's lecture. If this is not an option for us, let's pull out a Passover *haggadah* and learn more about its content. Besides being inspired, we will also be equipped with additional information to share at the *Seder* table.

May we be blessed to be enlightened with the deeper meaning of the Torah and acquire forgiveness for any mistakes that we have made in the past. May we, thus, deserve to experience a complete redemption this Nissan (see *Rosh HaShanah* 17a).

Tzav - Shabbos HaGadol

The Time Machine

Time travel has always been something that has tantalized the mind; but what if the future was brought to the present, instead of us being transported to the future?

This Shabbos is called *Shabbos HaGadol.* Our Sages provide many reasons for this specific name. What is the significance of *Shabbos HaGadol* and why is it greater than any other Shabbos? (For two different approaches, see *Tur* in *Orach Chaim*, 430:1 and *Beis Yosef* there.)

Here is a new perspective on this topic. We are told (*Shemos* 12:40) that the Israelites dwelled in Egypt for 430 years. This seems to contradict what the Sages derive from *Bereishis* (42:2), where Yaakov instructed his sons to go down to Egypt, *redu shamah*, in order to obtain provisions, since there was a famine in Canaan. The Midrash (*Bereishis Rabbah* 91:2) points out that Yaakov deviated from the normative way of instructing another to leave. Usually, when commanding others to go somewhere, one would use the root word *lech*. An example of this is found in *Bereishis* (12:1) where God commands Avraham to leave his birthplace, "*Lech lecha* - Go for yourself."

Why did Yaakov tell his sons to "go down" (*redu*), when he could have said simply "go" (*lechu*, i.e. *lech* in the plural)? What was he alluding to with this specific choice of words?

An obvious answer to this question is that Egypt is located south of Israel. Naturally, then, he would instruct them to "go down." Another suggestion is that *redu* alludes to the spiritual descent they would experience traveling from Canaan to Egypt.

The Midrash, however, proposes that *redu* hints at something entirely different. By using the word *redu*, Yaakov was hinting to his sons that they (the Israelites) would stay in Egypt for a total of 210 years, the numerical value of the word *"redu"* (*reish, daled, vav*).

How can we understand this Midrash in light of the verse in *Shemos* (12:40)? Were the Israelites in Egypt for 210 years, as the Midrash suggests based on the verse in *Bereishis*, or 430 years, as the Torah states in *Shemos*?

One can reconcile this apparent contradiction with the assistance of the following idea from the *Nezer HaKodesh* (*Parshas Vayechi*).

Every moment in time has its own *mazal,* or constellation, appointed over it. The way the world runs down here is dependent upon the *mazal* which dominates at that specific instant. Sometimes, however, in urgent and critical circumstances, God will switch around the constellations (*mazalos*) in order to bring about a positive change for the benefit of the people. This phenomenon of moving around the constellations is described in the first blessing before the *Shema* which we recite in the evening prayer, "And He [God] changes the times, and arranges the stars in their constellations in the firmament according to His Will."

The *Nezer HaKodesh* explains: after 210 years in Egypt, the *mazal* governing that time was one of strict justice. In order to redeem the people from the harsh and cruel Egyptian bondage, an *"eis ratzon* - time of mercy" was necessary. God looked into the future, as it were, and saw that at 430 years the constellation was more favorable. He thus took this futuristic time period and planted it into that present point in time (of 210 years). (This can be likened to the frames of a film, where a frame from a latter portion of the film is "cut" from its original place and "pasted" into an earlier section.)

Thus, when Yaakov hinted to his sons that the Egyptian exile would last 210 years, he was, in fact, completely accurate. Based on the *Nezer HaKodesh*, the verse in *Shemos* does not oppose this information either. When it states that the Israelites were in Egypt for 430 years, it was referring to the constellation that governed over the 430th year, which God moved to a point earlier in history. Therefore, Yaakov's words and the Torah's statements are not in contradiction, but in fact enhance one another. Hence, in the words of the Sages, "*Eilu v'eilu divrei Elokim chaim* - These and those are the words of the Living God" (*Eruvin* 13b).

The *Divrei Yoel* (*Parshas Tzav*) adds to this idea. He proposes that God performed this switch of constellations on the Shabbos before *Pesach*. As we know, Shabbos has the power to positively impact the rest of the week (see *Ohr HaChaim* on *Bereishis* 2:3). Therefore, in order to extend the *eis ratzon* over a long period of time, and in order to allow the Israelites to leave Egypt, God exchanged the *mazalos* on the Shabbos day prior to the Exodus. In this way, the time period which followed Shabbos would be a propitious time for redemption. This is why the Shabbos before *Pesach* is referred to as *Shabbos HaGadol* (the Great Shabbos), because God performed for us a great and wondrous miracle by changing the times for our benefit.

This concept is alluded to in the *Shulchan Aruch*, as the *Emunas Itecha* explains. The *Shulchan Aruch* states that the Shabbos before *Pesach* is called *Shabbos HaGadol* because of the great miracle that occurred, but it does not specify what miracle actually happened. The *Emunas Itecha* points out that the topic of *Shabbos HaGadol* is discussed in the *Shulchan Aruch* in the 430th chapter. The location of the topic in the *Shulchan Aruch* is, in itself, an answer to the query regarding what miracle occurred on the Shabbos prior to *Pesach*! It is precisely God's movement of the 430th time period to the actual year of the Exodus (the 210th year) which allowed for our redemption - and that is the miracle we acknowledge and commemorate on *Shabbos HaGadol*.

Based on this idea, we learn about the tremendous potential of a regular Shabbos, but even more so, of *Shabbos HaGadol*. Our tradition teaches that time travels in a spiral (and not a straight line). Therefore, each year, in every generation, we relive the energy and potential contained in that time. Every *Shabbos HaGadol* we have the opportunity to benefit from the change of constellation from justice to mercy. Each *Shabbos HaGadol* is an auspicious time for creating constructive and positive change in our lives.

We could suggest further that this concept holds true according to two opinions in the Talmud (*Shabbos* 156a) regarding the effect of the *mazalos* on the Jewish people. Rav and Rabbi Yochanan maintain that the Jewish nation is above the constellations (*ein mazal l'Yisrael*) and that we are not controlled or affected by changes in the *mazalos*. Based on their perspective, we can always improve ourselves because we are constantly in control of our mood, feelings, behavior, etc. Rabbi Chanina, on the other hand, holds that the constellations do affect us (*yesh mazal l'Yisrael*) and, thus, our thoughts and actions are somewhat dependent on them.

Based on the ideas we have discussed, however, we see that *Shabbos HaGadol* is the exception to Rabbi Chanina's rule, since it is a time when we are freed from any negative effect of the constellations. On *Shabbos HaGadol* we experience, once again, an *eis ratzon* and, thus, have the opportunity and capability to redeem ourselves from our own personal bondage. For example, if we tend to become angered easily, we may habitually attribute it to the *mazal* under which we were born. However, as we have learned, *Shabbos HaGadol* is a unique and auspicious time of the year for successful positive change: to transform any negative traits or weaknesses and improve our *avodas Hashem*.

One method of causing God to make a positive change in our current times would be to become proactive, and make a change in our "times," i.e. busy schedules. If we come to *shul* just five minutes earlier, or start to learn Torah just a few minutes earlier, then Hashem will reciprocate and usher in times of compassion earlier than they were supposed to happen.

May we - holy superstars - be blessed with *mazal* and miracles, and a Shabbos that is truly *gadol*, as we take great strides to change for the better. May we, thus, deserve that the appointed time of *Moshiach's* arrival be moved to the present, so that we will be able to celebrate *Pesach* with the real *Pesach* sacrifice at the site of our Holy Temple, never to leave again.

Tzav - Shabbos HaGadol

Follow Me

Wouldn't it be great to have a life coach with us at all times, helping us get through the various difficult situations that arise. Well, in Judaism we always have a life coach with us helping us do the right thing.

It is common that on this Shabbos called *Shabbos HaGadol*, the Great Sabbath, our focus turns towards the upcoming holiday, Passover (see *Shulchan Aruch, Orach Chaim*, Ch. 430:1). We will follow this tradition.

At the onset of the *Pesach Seder*, some have the custom for the children to say or sing to their parents the fifteen "signs" or stages which map out what will be performed on this most momentous evening.

This song is made up of the following words: "*Kadesh, Urchatz, Karpas, Yachatz, Maggid, Rachtzah, Motzi-Matzah, Marror, Korech, Shulchan Orech, Tzafon, Barech, Hallel, Nirtzah.*"

The *Yesod V'shoresh Ha'avodah* (gate 9, chap. 6) says about this section, "*simana milsa hee* - signs have meaning." (See *Krisus*, chap. 1, *Shloshim V'shesh*, pg. 6a, the opinion of *Abaye*.) He goes on to say that there are many wondrous secrets contained in this song.

It is not only the children who are supposed to say the fifteen stages at the beginning of the *Seder*, but each and every person should say the "sign" that is connected to that stage right before we perform it.

For example, right before reciting the *Kiddush*, we should say the word "*Kadesh.*" Right before washing our hands we should say the word "*Urchatz.*" Right before eating the vegetable dipped into salt water we should say the word "*Karpas,*" and so on.

All of this information begs us to ask some questions. (After all, questions are in the spirit of this holiday!)

1) Why did the Men of the Great Assembly (the authors of the *Haggadah*) arrange it so that there are specifically fifteen stages to the *Haggadah*, no more, no less?

2) Why do the children have the custom of singing this song to their parents?

3) Why should we all say each stage immediately prior to fulfilling it?

The *Bnei Yissaschar* (*Chodesh Sivan*, *Ma'amar* 2, number 4) points out that God Himself chooses to observe His own commandments. A proof of this is the Talmud which says that God dons *tefillin*. (See *Berachos*, Ch.1, *Mei'eimasai*, pg.6a, the opinion of *Rav Avin* the son of *Rav Ada* in the name of *Rav Yitzchak*.)

This sounds puzzling at first, for most of the commandments are physical, but God is not (see the *Rambam's* Thirteen Tenets of Faith, Tenet number 3). How, then, can God keep the commandments?

One approach to understanding this is that every commandment has a *tzad haniglah* (revealed side) and a *tzad hanistar* (hidden side). Perhaps we could use a metaphor to explain this.

Take a look at a coin. Let's choose a quarter. On one side it's heads, and on the other side it's tails. Imagine that - it's one coin and yet there are two totally different pictures on the sides!

So it is with the Torah. There are two sides to every commandment, revealed and hidden. They are two totally different pictures. While keeping them in this world, one must be physical; nevertheless, to keep them in Heaven, one must be spiritual. It is on that spiritual level that God "keeps" the commandments, so to speak.

Another support to the idea that God fulfills the commandments is found in the text of the blessing that we recite prior to doing a *mitzvah* (commandment). The words are, *"Asher kideshanu b'mitzvosav v'tzivanu...* - that we have become sanctified with His commandments and You commanded us..."

The word *b'mitzvosav* (His commandments) does not only mean that these commandments came from God, but it also means that they are His commandments as well, for God Himself to fulfill.

The *Yerushalmi* (Jerusalem Talmud, *Rosh HaShanah*, Ch. 1 *halachah* 3, based on *Vayikra* 22:9) adds that God performs the *mitzvos* in Heaven before we do them down here on Earth.

The *Tiferes Shlomo* (*Parshas Vayeira*, the opening word "*HaMechaseh*") explains the benefit of God doing the *mitzvos* before we do. He says that this breaks the ice and paves the way for us to be able to do the *mitzvah*.

Moreover, when God does the *mitzvah* first, it creates spiritual energy above that we can tap into and receive below when we do that very same *mitzvah*. By doing so, we also benefit from all the thoughts and intentions that God puts into the *mitzvah*.

Parenthetically, this explains why it is better to do a *mitzvah* when we are commanded to do so, as opposed to doing a *mitzvah* optionally. (*Kiddushin*, Ch. 1, *Ha-isha Niknis*, 31a, the opinion of *Rav Yoseph* in the name of *Rebbi Chaninah*) This is because when we are commanded in a *mitzvah*, God performs it as well, before we do it. Then, when we do the *mitzvah*, we benefit by tapping into the spiritual energy that God already created above.

However, when a person does a *mitzvah* optionally, God does not perform that *mitzvah* up in Heaven first, and therefore the person below does not benefit from God's spiritual energy, because there was no such energy created by God. (see *Tosafos*, *Kiddushin*, pg. 31a, the opening word "*Gadol*" for an alternative explanation.)

This elucidates why, prior to fulfilling *mitzvos*, we say a preparatory prayer which states that with this *mitzvah* we are going to join the first two letters of God's Name (*yud hey*), to the last two letters of His Name (*vav hey*).

The understanding is based on what God said after the nation Amalek attacked the Jews in the desert. The verse says that God placed His hand, so to speak, on the *Kes* (Throne) of *Kah* (God - spelled *yud hey*) and swore to wage an eternal battle against Amalek (*Shemos* 17:16).

Rashi there, citing a *Midrash Tanchumah* at the end of *Parshas Ki Seitzei*, points out that the words *Kes* and *Kah* are really "half-words." The full words would have been *Kisei* (Throne) and *Havaya* (God's full Name). The reason that the Torah expresses itself with half-words is to teach us that as long as Amalek is around, God's Throne and Name are not complete, as it were.

The *Yismach Moshe* (*Parshas Beshalach*, the opening words "*Od peirush*") adds to this, based on the *Tikunei Zohar* (preface, pg. 9b), that the Name *Havaya* (spelled *yud, hey, vav, hey*) is found in the acronym of the words "*yismechu hashamayim v'sagel ha'aretz* - the Heavens will be glad and the Earth will rejoice" (*Tehillim* 96:11).

In Heaven, God's greatness is always apparent; therefore, there is always a reason to be happy. However, on Earth there is only reason to rejoice during times of redemption. But when we are experiencing exile there is little reason to rejoice, because God's greatness is concealed.

That is why God's Throne and Name are incomplete as long as Amalek is allowed to exist. Amalek, with their philosophy that everything is merely a coincidence, causes there to be Divine concealment.

This is why the second half of God's Name (*vav hey*) is missing as long as Amalek lives. The *vav* and *hey* stand for "*v'sagel ha'aretz* - the Earth will rejoice." Since Amalek generates exile and denies God's existence, there is little reason to rejoice on Earth, thus the letters *vav hey* (the Earth will rejoice) disappear.

Says the *Shvilei Pinchas* that according to all of this, whenever God fulfills a *mitzvah* in Heaven, it creates a situation of "*yismechu hashamayim* - the Heavens will be glad," for there is happiness at the great light that is created when God does a *mitzvah*.

The only way we can taste that light on Earth is if we go on to do that *mitzvah* also. Then we bring that light down and we can safely say, "*v'sagel ha'aretz* - that the Earth rejoices" as well. Now the Name of God is complete.

That is why we say that preparatory prayer (to join the *yud hey* with the *vav hey*) prior to performing *mitzvos*. This is a declaration that we are completing God's Name on Earth through fulfilling this *mitzvah*.

The *Shvilei Pinchas* goes on to explain that this is why the Men of the Great Assembly instituted the recitation of the *Kadesh Urchatz* song at the onset of the *Seder*.

The rituals of the *Seder* are so deep that we could not possibly contemplate all the lofty thoughts that go into them. Therefore, before we begin, we ask God to have a *Seder* above. This will break the ice and create a spiritual light with all the possible intentions contained within it. The *Kadesh Urchatz* song is that request.

Then, when we conduct the *Seder* below, we can draw upon that light, taste it, and be credited with having all those thoughts.

However, the children are the ones that sing this song to their parents. This serves as a reminder to the adults that just as our children are asking us about the meaning of all the stages of the *Seder*, we too, ask our Parent in Heaven to do all the stages of the *Seder*, so that we can benefit from them and their meaning as well.

That is why, when we get to each stage of the *Seder*, we all say the appropriate word beforehand. This is the adults' chance to ask God to perform that stage above so that we can experience it below.

This also explains why there are specifically fifteen stages to the *Seder*, no more and no less. This is because the number fifteen is the numerical value of the first two letters of God's Name (*yud hey*). The recitation of the "signs" is our way of asking God to do these *mitzvos* above; when God actually does them, He creates a situation of "*yismechu hashamayim* - the Heavens will be glad (*yud hey*)."

Only afterwards, when we go on to do those very *mitzvos,* do we bring that light down to us on Earth, completing the last half of God's Name (*vav hey - v'sagel ha'aretz*), which gives us reason to rejoice on Earth.

When I saw this piece of Torah, it made me think of how fitting it is for the thrust and theme of Passover's energy. In Egypt, the Jews worshiped idols and fell to the forty-ninth level of impurity. They did not deserve to be redeemed.

However, God did us a favor and lifted us to great heights, to the point that the simplest of Jews were able to point to God at the revelation that took place during the Splitting of the Sea (*Mechiltah Shemos* 15:2).

When God lifts us to great heights, it is called "*isarusa d'le'aylah* - the awakening comes from Above." This is a deeper reason as to why we eat *matzah* on Passover. *Matzah* does nothing to participate in making itself into *matzah*. The bakers take full credit for that, because from the time the water hits the flour, the *matzah* does not have a chance to breathe. Within eighteen minutes, we turn it into *matzah*.

This is unlike bread which is left alone at one stage of its making, in order to allow it to rise on its own. So, when we eat *matzah*, we are being reminded that at this time of year, we are likened to the *matzah*. Just as the *matzah* did not participate in making itself into *matzah*, so too, we did not participate in making ourselves holy and worthy of redemption.

Perhaps we could add that although the Jews did perform certain *mitzvos*, such as circumcision (*Shemos* 12:50) and the *korban Pesach* (*Shemos* 12:28), and they also had certain merits such as preserving their Jewish names, clothing, and language (*Vayikra Rabba, Emor,* 32:5), they had still fallen to the forty-ninth level of impurity. Their involvement in idolatry was so pronounced that prior to the Splitting of the Sea, the angels complained about God's intention to save the Jews and destroy the Egyptians. The angels argued that both the Jews and the Egyptians should be smashed! (See *Yalkut Shimoni, Beshalach, remez* 234.) Therefore, when you weigh the redemption against their merits, it seems unbalanced.

This is especially true in light of the numerous miracles that transpired (the Ten Plagues, the Clouds of Glory, the Pillar of Fire, and the parting of the water). One can hardly claim that the Jews deserved all of that just on account of a few good deeds that they did.

All Jewish transgressors have some *mitzvos* (like a pomegranate is filled with seeds; see *Reish Lakish, Eiruvin*, chap. 2, *Osin Pasin*, pg. 19a, based on Son. 6:7), but that does not necessarily make them deserving of one open miracle after another. Therefore, the Jewish people's participation in the redemption with the few *mitzvos* that they performed are nowhere near in proportion to the type of salvation that they received. This is why the *Arizal* compares the Jews to *matzah*. Just as *matzah* doesn't really have a part in its formation as *matzah*, so the Jews hardly did anything to merit such a miraculous redemption.

Just as the bakers take full credit for making the holy *matzah*, so does God take all the credit for making us holy at this time of year: *isarusa d'le'aylah*.

We focus on this at the *Seder* when we ask God to perform all the stages of the *Seder* above, breaking the ice, so that we can then do them below. The entire night of Passover, when we recite the *Kadesh Urchatz,* we are being reminded that the whole holiday is about *isarusa d'le'aylah.*

I was thinking that perhaps this serves as another reason why the Shabbos before Passover is called *Shabbos HaGadol* (The Great Sabbath). The first description we attribute to God every single day in the first blessing of the *Amidah* (Silent Prayer) is: *HaGadol* (Great).

Therefore, at this time of year, the Shabbos right before Passover is called *Shabbos HaGadol,* meaning to say that the "*Gadol*" One, God, is performing the "Shabbos" above, enabling us to keep it below.

In this way, the Shabbos prior to Passover prepares us for what's ahead for us on Passover itself. The truth of the matter is that *isarusa d'le'aylah* happens all year long; however, we stress this concept especially at this time of year.

This message of Passover is so comforting. How blessed we are to have such a caring Parent in Heaven who helps us achieve our goals on a daily basis. We are not alone! God is holding our hand every step of the way, just as a parent grasps the hand of his child.

So, let us say those preparatory prayers prior to fulfilling the *mitzvos* to remind us of this teaching.

With this thought in mind, may we all be blessed with the awareness that God is with us at all times, helping us emerge out of the *Mitzrayims* that we sometimes go through in the journeys of our lives, and may we merit to experience revealed goodness!

Shemini

Channel Three

Thoughts eventually become words; and words often lead to actions.

The beginning of this week's portion deals with offerings that were brought by Aharon and the Jewish people. There were two *eigels* (calves) that were to be presented, one for Aharon and one for the Jewish people (*Vayikra* 9:2-3). *Rashi* comments that the purpose of these *eigels* was to atone for the sin of the Golden *Eigel* (*Vayikra* 9:2).

However, the verses teach us that there was a difference between them. The *eigel* that Aharon brought was a *Chatas* (sin offering), whereas the *eigel* that the Jewish people brought was an *Olah* (burnt offering). This seems to be a touch problematic. If both animals were meant to atone for the same sin, then why were they different types of offerings?

The *Kli Yakar* explains that Aharon's participation in the sin of the Golden Calf was only in action. After all, the Calf was created because of his action. However, in the realm of thought, Aharon did not sin at all. Aharon never believed in the Calf as a god; rather, he acted for the sake of Heaven - in order to stall for time, so that Moshe would descend the mountain and put a stop to the panic and confusion that the Jews were experiencing at that time.

By contrast, the Jews sinned with their thoughts. They actually believed, in their minds and in their hearts, that there was power to the "Calf." This clarifies the difference between the two *eigels* that were offered.

A *Chatas* atones for sins committed in action, whereas an *Olah* atones for sins committed in thought. Therefore, Aharon, who sinned in action, needed only to bring a *Chatas*, whereas the Jews, who sinned in thought, had to bring an *Olah*.

It is interesting to note that later on in this portion we are commanded with the laws of keeping *kosher* (*Vayikra* 11:1-31). This subject matter is introduced with verses that say, "And God spoke to Moses and to Aharon saying to them, *leimor aleihem*, 'speak to the Children of Israel and tell them that these are the animals from which they may eat'" (*Vayikra* 11:1-2). The two words *leimor aleihem* seem superfluous.

The Torah could have just said "And God spoke to Moses and to Aharon, 'speak to the Children of Israel and tell them...'" (*Vayikra* 11:1-2), without the words *leimor aleihem*. Why were these two extra words necessary?

Reb Levi Yitzchak of Berditchev in his *Kedushas Levi* points out that when Moshe was a baby, God orchestrated that he would be nursed by his own mother and not by any Egyptian nursemaids. Moshe was destined to speak with God Himself. It would not have been fitting for Moshe's mouth to speak with God if that very mouth was spiritually polluted by Egyptian milk (*Shemos* 2:7; *Sotah*, Ch. 1, *Hamekaneh,* pg. 12b).

Similarly, it is forbidden for the Jewish people to eat from non-*kosher* animals. This is because, in the future, God is going to speak with every single Jew as it says, "And it will come to pass afterwards, that I will pour out My Spirit upon all flesh; and your sons and your daughters will prophesy" (*Yoel* 3:1).

This explains what those extra two words come to teach us. They serve as an introduction to the laws of keeping *kosher*. Before being told what we may and may not eat, we are being informed of one benefit with regard to keeping the laws of *kashrus*.

The benefit is that we will merit a direct audience with God Himself in which we will be able to converse with Him "mouth to mouth." (*Bamidbar* 12:8) This guarantee is contained within those two words.

Leimor aleihem means "I [God] will speak with them [the Jewish people]."

God is sending us a message. Since He will be speaking with the Jewish people directly in the future, it is therefore unbecoming and inappropriate for them to partake of spiritually-polluted food.

Not only must we keep our mouths clean by checking what goes into them, but we must also keep them clean by watching what comes out of them. This refers to abstaining from speaking about others in a derogatory fashion and from using filthy words in our speech.

What is interesting here is that when you put the two aforementioned lessons together, we find that this portion is instructing us to purify our thoughts, speech, and actions. These three faculties actually work as a team.

What we choose to think about can become the topic of our conversations. What we choose to speak about can influence us to take action. This is why it is important to think holy thoughts, speak about sacred topics, and engage in righteous activities.

When we do, we become a complete and whole person, because all three frequencies that we operate on have become sanctified.

Once a day, let us consciously think one holy thought in order to purify that faculty. Then, let us consciously say one holy word to sanctify our speech. And finally, let us consciously do one holy act in order to spiritually strengthen our physical movements. Although we entertain many holy thoughts, words and activities throughout the day, we suggest choosing one of them with the specific intent to fix the frequency in which we are functioning.

May we all be blessed to further purify our thoughts, speech, and actions so that we will be forgiven for any mistakes, and thus merit holding a private audience with our Parent in Heaven, obtaining Divine closeness.

Shemini

Drunk on God

It is a fact. We all experience moments of sadness, and even depression. The question is: where do we turn in order to reach a state of happiness again?

In this week's portion, *Shemini*, we read about the incident involving Aharon's sons, which ultimately led to their deaths. As the verses relate (*Vayikra* 10:1-2), "The sons of Aharon, Nadav and Avihu, each took his fire pan, and they put fire in them and placed incense upon it; and they brought before Hashem an alien fire that He had not commanded them. A fire came forth from before Hashem and consumed them, and they died before Hashem."

The commentators provide a variety of reasons explaining why Nadav and Avihu deserved the punishment of death (see *Rashi* ad loc. and *Yalkut Shimoni* on *Parshas Shemini* no. 524). One of the commentaries explains that Aharon's sons died because they entered the Holy of Holies in an intoxicated state. This explanation fits within the context of the *parshah* because the account of Nadav and Avihu's demise is juxtaposed with God's command to Aharon (*Vayikra* 10:9) saying, "Do not drink intoxicating wine, you and your sons with you, when you come to the Tent of Meeting, that you not die…"

The Midrash (*Vayikra Rabbah* 12:3) connects this verse (*Vayikra* 10:9) to *Tehillim* 19:9, which says, "The orders of Hashem are upright, gladdening the heart."

An obvious question arises: what is the connection between these two verses? In what way does the prohibition of drinking alcohol in the

Sanctuary relate to the joyous effect of God's commandments?

Rabbi Simchah Bunim of P'shischa offers a beautiful insight which answers this question. He begins by citing the Talmud (*Shabbos* 30b) that says: "The Divine presence does not rest on a person who is depressed." Furthermore, we are told that the *Kohen* is obligated to offer sacrifices with *hisromemus ru'ach*, an uplifted spirit.

Based on this information, we may ask: why, then, does the Torah forbid *Kohanim* to drink wine in the Sanctuary? We learn that wine "gladdens the heart of man" (*Tehillim* 104:15). That being the case, the consumption of intoxicating beverages should only **enhance** the priests' service in the Temple since it causes *hisromemus ha'ru'ach*!

Rav Simchah Bunim lays down a fundamental point which answers the aforementioned questions and leaves us with a powerful message: When the *Kohen* performs the *Avodah* in the *Kodesh* (Holy) or *Kodesh HaKedoshim* (Holy of Holies), he should be aware of the *chedvah*, joy, that stems from the *Avodah*. In other words, the only source of joy should be the Divine service itself.

This fits in beautifully with the conclusion of the Talmud (Shabbos 30b) cited earlier. The Talmud begins: "The Divine presence does not rest on a person who is depressed," and ends, "[but rests only] amongst [those involved in] the *simchah*, joy, of a *mitzvah*," implying that the *Shechinah* does not rest on people whose spirit is elevated due to other, external stimuli.

Now we can appreciate the connection between the verse in this week's portion, God's command against drinking wine in the Tent of Meeting, and King David's statement (*Tehillim* 19:9) that God's commandments gladden the heart. The precise reason as to why the *Kohen* is prohibited from drinking intoxicating beverages in the Sanctuary is that Hashem expects the *Kohen* to derive joy and happiness from the *Avodah* itself!

Based on this idea, we could suggest that Aharon's sons perished not so much because they were intoxicated, but rather because they turned to intoxicating beverages - external sources - to induce a state of *simchah*, instead of achieving true joy through the Divine service itself.

This insight can also provide us with a deeper understanding of the incident involving Noach's intoxication after the flood. We read in *Bereishis* (9:20), "**Vayachel** Noach ish ha'adamah vayita karem... - Noah, the man of the Earth, **began**; and he planted a vineyard." Verse 21 continues: "He drank of the wine and became drunk, and he uncovered himself within his tent."

Rashi (citing *Bereishis Rabbah* 36:3) comments: although the root of the word *vayachel* means "began," it can also be translated "profaned" (from the word *chullin,* meaning "mundane" or "profane"). Thus, *Rashi* explains, Noach debased himself by planting a vineyard; he should have sown *netiya acheres,* a different plant, instead. (Noach's degraded spiritual level is indicated in the description "*ish ha'adamah* - a man of the ground").

However, we may ask: what was wrong with planting a vineyard? After all, the world had just been destroyed, and as it says in *Tehillim*, "wine gladdens the heart of man." Perhaps Noach's motivation was simply to bring happiness into the world.

According to Rav Simchah Bunim's perspective, we could suggest that although Noach may have had sincere intentions when planting the vineyard, he was still deserving of criticism because he turned to external influences in order to experience joy. Earlier in the text (8:20), we read that, immediately after the Flood, Noach built an altar and offered sacrifices to God. We could suggest that through this *avodah* exclusively, Noach should have been able to derive true *simchah*. However, we see that he turned to intoxicating beverages to attain a state of joy.

We could suggest that on some level, Noach did not fully appreciate the *kedushah* (holiness) of the sacrifices that he offered, and consequently failed to derive complete *simchah* from the *avodah*. This idea is hinted at in *Rashi's* language: *Rashi* comments that Noach should have planted *netiya acheres*, a different plant, instead of the vineyard, but he does not specify which type of plant this should have been. We could propose that Noach had the opportunity to plant seeds of joy within himself, through the *avodah* itself!

In the same way that Nadav and Avihu were punished for depending on external sources to experience joy, Noach's intoxication also resulted in negative consequences. (See *Bereishis* 9:22 and *Rashi*, citing *Bereishis Rabbah* 36:7.)

We can apply the principle shared by Rav Simchah Bunim to our own lives. If we truly understand the beauty and holiness of God's Torah and commandments, and derive true happiness and joy from our *avodas* Hashem, then we will, *B'ezras Hashem*, deserve that God's presence dwell amongst us.

May we be blessed to appreciate the Torah and *mitzvos* so that our joy in life stems totally from them, constantly propelling us forward in our service of, and connection to, God.

Shemini

Overachievers

Striving for perfection is a beautiful ambition in life. But, since no one can ever reach true perfection in this world, we must always be aware that we can constantly improve ourselves, never being complacent with our previous accomplishments.

This week's Torah portion, *Shemini*, contains the dramatic story of Nadav and Avihu, two of Aharon's sons, who bring a foreign offering to God. This is so unacceptable, that a fire consumes them on the spot, and they die (*Vayikra* 10:1-2). The Midrash (*Yalkut Shimoni* 524) suggests seven reasons that Aharon's sons might have deserved death:

1) Nadav and Avihu were impatient for Moshe and Aharon to die so that they could take over leadership of the Jewish people.

2) They made Jewish legal decisions in the presence of Moshe, their Rabbi - a sign of disrespect.

3) They entered the holy area while intoxicated.

4) They entered the holy area without first washing their hands and feet.

5) They entered the holy area without wearing the priestly garments.

6) They did not get married.

7) They did not try to have children.

Although these reasons seem entirely unrelated, we could suggest that all seven of them stem from one fundamental fault. Nadav and Avihu were great people, and they were aware of their high spiritual level. Yet they felt they had already reached the pinnacle of their achievement, and therefore had no need to strive for further growth and self-improvement. This misjudgment was the root of all seven possible reasons for their death:

1)   Nadav and Avihu felt they had reached completion and perfection, so it was fitting for them to take over leadership of the Jewish people.

2)   They felt they had achieved the epitome of Torah knowledge, so they made Jewish legal decisions in front of their Rabbi.

3)   Since they assumed they had reached their maximum potential, they felt they could relax; so they entered the holy area while intoxicated.

4)   Since they felt they had reached the height of purity, they no longer needed water to become purified; so they entered the holy area without first washing their hands and feet.

5)   Since they felt they had achieved perfection, they no longer needed the atonement provided by the priestly garments (*Arachin* 16a chap.3, *Yesh b'arachin*, page 16); so they entered the holy area without wearing them.

6)   They assumed that, since they had perfected themselves, God could speak with them at any time - as He did with Moshe, who separated from his wife, Tzipporah, due to this consideration (*Bamidbar* 12:7-8); so they did not get married.

7)   Since they did not get married, they were halachically forbidden from having children outside of marriage.

Now that we see the common source of the seven reasons, let us examine another detail of the story.

The Torah tells us (*Vayikra* 10:2) that a fire consumed Nadav and Avihu after they brought their foreign offering. According to the *Yalkut Shimoni* (524), this fire came from the Holy of Holies. Why is it significant to know the source of the fire?

The Holy of Holies contained only one vessel, the Holy Ark. Unlike the other Temple vessels, the dimensions of the Ark were all fractions - 2.5 by 1.5 by 1.5 cubits (*Shemos* 25:10). According to the commentator *Kli Yakar*, the fractional measurements of the Ark teach us that we should always feel lacking in regard to the wisdom we have acquired. Each of the Ark's dimensions teaches us a different "dimension" of this lesson.

The height of the Ark shows us that we lack depth of knowledge; the length shows us that we lack breadth of knowledge; and the width shows us that we lack the ability to grasp concepts.

In Hebrew, the word *middos* means both "measurements" and "character traits." This is why the fire that consumed Nadav and Avihu came from the Holy of Holies; the resting place of the Ark. The Ark, with its fractional measurements (*middos*) teaches us that we, too, are fractional - lacking in Torah knowledge, and imperfect in our refinement of character (*middos*).

Nadav and Avihu thought that they had reached completion. The origin of the fire that consumed them showed that they still had work to do.

If this lesson was relevant to such great people as Nadav and Avihu, it is all the more relevant to us. Although we should take pleasure in our positive achievements, we should never take pride. We should not feel so satisfied with our accomplishments that we lose our yearning to stretch and grow further.

May we continually desire to push beyond our current level, and in the merit of this attitude, may we soon deserve to see the return of our centerpiece, the Ark, with the building of the Third Temple.

Shemini

I Get No Respect

Being a *mentch* means to treat other people with respect.

In this week's portion, *Shemini*, there is a discussion about three special offerings that were brought on the first day of *Nissan*. The first offering is called *korban Shemini*, which was an inaugurational sacrifice on Moshe's eighth day of building, taking apart and rebuilding the Sanctuary. The second offering is called *korban Nachshon*, which was the first offering brought by the first tribal leader (*Nachshon ben Aminadov* of *Shevet Yehudah*), and which began the inauguration of the Altar. The third offering was the *Rosh Chodesh* sacrifice, as it was the first day of *Nissan*.

Although Aharon, the High Priest, and his two sons (Elazar and Isamar) were mourners on account of the deaths of Aharon's two other sons, Nadav and Avihu, Moshe expected Aharon and his two living sons to eat from all three sacrifices, as is the law. Generally an *onen* (one in the first stage of mourning) is not required, and is even forbidden, to perform *mitzvos*. Aharon and his two sons only ate from the first two sacrifices, *Shemini* and *Nachshon*, but did not eat the third offering, *Rosh Chodesh*. When Moshe heard about this, he became angry with them and asked Elazar and Isamar why they disobeyed the law.

Aharon defended their position by making a distinction between the two types of offerings that were brought on that day. The first two, *Shemini* and *Nachshon*, were one-time offerings, never to be duplicated again. So, for those two offerings, an exception can be made wherein an *onen* can partake of its flesh. However, with regard to the third offering, *Rosh Chodesh*, which is brought every month, one need not be lenient with the laws of an *onen*, for there will be another opportunity in the future for the *Kohanim* to partake of that sacrifice's flesh. When Moshe heard this response, he was pleased (see *Shemini* 10:12-20 and *Rashi* there).

One might wonder why Moshe only questioned Aharon's sons and not Aharon himself. Besides which, if Moshe questioned Elazar and Isamar, why was it Aharon who came to their defense? Why couldn't they speak for themselves? Moreover, why didn't Moshe himself know about this distinction between one-time offerings and continual sacrifices? For a man of Moshe's stature, a differentiation of this nature would seem elementary. Here is a new approach that will, *b'ezras Hashem,* resolve these difficulties.

Aharon's two sons, Nadav and Avihu, were killed, and there are a variety of approaches as to the cause of their death. We will focus on one of them: the opinion of Rebbi Eliezer who says that they (Nadav and Avihu) decided a matter of Jewish law in front of their *Rebbe*, Moshe. For this disrespect, they were deserving of the death penalty (see *Rashi Shemini* 10:2 and *Eruvin* 63a).

Moshe, who wanted this lack of respect to be fixed and repaired, addressed the remaining two sons of Aharon, although he was well-aware of the answer to the question he was about to ask. Moshe, who obviously knows the difference between a one-time offering and a continual one, lambasted Elazar and Isamar as to why they did not partake of the *Rosh Chodesh* sacrifice. This was in order to see whether or not Elazar and Isamar had the proper respect for their *Rebbe*. Would they jump at the opportunity to show their master up, even though they would have been correct in their distinction?

When Moshe saw that it was Aharon who, in God's eyes was on equal par with Moshe, answered the question - meaning that Elazar and Isamar were silent, and took the heat out of respect for their *Rebbe* - Moshe was pleased. This approach can be dubbed a "master plan" or a "set-up" by Moshe, which addresses all the difficulties we raised above:

1) Moshe really did know the difference. Moshe's "anger" was part of the show he put on in order to see whether or not the remaining sons of Aharon learned the lesson of respect.

2) This is why Moshe questioned only Aharon's two sons who needed to be tested.

3) Elazar and Isamar's silence was the way in which they passed their test, and only Aharon was given allowance to speak with Moshe in that way.

The lesson we learn from this is the importance of respecting our Sages, which extends to our elders and our parents, and which ultimately teaches us to respect Hashem.

In the past we have stressed the importance of parents educating their children, and this week we stress the importance of children respecting their elders. Parents need to teach their children about respecting their elders. Rav Sheinberg, *zt"l*, used to say that, from the time our children are young, they should be trained to stand up completely for a mother and father when they walk into a room. May we all be blessed to educate our children properly and may we deserve to have children who respect and appreciate the previous generation.

Tazria - Metzora

Call a Spade a Spade

Identifying something as evil may be equally important as transforming bad into good. If this sounds contradictory, then please read on.

Often, the portions of *Tazria* and *Metzora* are read as a double portion. There is a connection between the ideas at the end of last week's portion, *Shemini*, and the beginning of *Parshas Tazria*. The end of *Shemini* details which animals are kosher and which are not, and the beginning of *Tazria* discusses ideas of childbirth.

The *Ramban* explains this juxtaposition as follows: the Torah in *Shemini* shares laws of impure animals and insects in order to teach us that if parents eat things that are not *kosher*, it will cause them to have children that are born with blemishes and a stuffed-up heart. Additionally, the second portion of the week, *Metzora*, adds the ideas of how to purify these blemishes.

Let's share a viewpoint of the *Leshem. Parshas Shemini* (10:10) commands us to make a distinction between holy and mundane. If all the blemishes in this week's portion stem from eating things that are not kosher, then with regard to the non-kosher foods, the *Leshem* makes the following comments.

The *Leshem Sh'vo V'achlama* (vol. 1 pg. 54b) says on that verse that there is an absolute Torah prohibition to think, to say, or to call something holy that the Torah does not call holy. Furthermore, there is a prohibition to call something holy that the Torah calls impure. This is not just forbidden, but it is considered close to idolatry, as seen in the verse (*Vayikra* 10:10): "*l'havdil bein kodesh u'bein hachol* - make a distinction between holy and mundane," and (11:47): "make a distinction between impure and pure."

Yechezkel (22:26) states that certain *Kohanim* were lambasted for not making this distinction. (Other sources to this idea include the *Zohar* in *Parshas Pikudei* pg. 227, at the end of first side, and the *Zohar Parshas Behar* pg. 110, at end of first side.)

The *Leshem* emphasizes the forbidden nature of attaching any amount of holiness to anything that is either impure or mundane. Even if a person does this without intending to worship idolatry, it inherently contains a smattering of idolatry.

The obvious question one can raise is as follows: isn't the existence of evil dependant on the ultimate Source of good? If God is not keeping something alive, it does not exist. If the dark side is dependant on the good side, there must be a spark of holiness within the impure.

The *Leshem* explains, based on the *Ari* (in *Sha'ar HaMelachim*), that when it comes to *kabbalistic* spheres of holiness, the spark of life which comes from God is found within them. However, the spark of life is not found within forces of evil because the spark of holiness does not become interwoven with mundane or impure. The spark of life stands above or next to the pockets of darkness, and the glow illuminates these pockets of darkness, but there is no holiness within them.

For example, when the sun is in the sky, it shines upon a person, but the light of the sun does not enter into the person's body. Just like there is no sun inside of the person's body, similarly there is not a spark of holiness in the darkness. Rather the light shines on the outside of the pocket of darkness. Therefore, one should never attribute holiness to something the Torah says is impure.

Although we try to transform negativity into positivism and elevate it, it is equally important to identify the elements in the world that are currently evil, and protect ourselves from them. If one day those pockets of darkness turn around and become good, that's fine. However, in the meantime, we must keep our distance from substances that can be harmful and damaging.

Can we pinpoint any such evil in our lives? If so, let's steer far away from it.

May we all be blessed with the ability to be honest, and discern between that which is good and that which is evil; and at the same time, may we be blessed to elevate everything and everyone we come into contact with, making it purposeful, meaningful, eternal, and therefore also spiritual.

Tazria

It's Like Candy from a Baby

We have all heard of the saying "talk is cheap." However, not only do our phone bills beg to differ with this position, but the Torah also disagrees vehemently with it.

This week, we read the portion of *Tazria* which discusses the spiritual skin disease, *tzara'as*. Usually, *Parshas Tazria* and the next portion, *Metzora*, are read as combined portions, on one Shabbos.

One might wonder why we need two portions in the Torah dedicated to the topic of *tzara'as*. Why not consolidate both portions so that the entire subject matter is contained in one *parshah*?

Furthermore, we read in the beginning of *Parshas Tazria* about childbirth and the days of impurity that ensue (see *Vayikra* 12:2-5). How does this topic relate to the theme of *tzara'as*?

There are many causes of *tzara'as*. One of them is *lashon hara*, derogatory speech (see *Vayikra Rabbah* 17:3.) The *Emunas Itecha* points out that even though *tzara'as* does not exist nowadays, its impurity remains inside of us. Moreover, just as the *metzora* (afflicted person) was expelled from Jerusalem, so too, a person in our times who speaks disparagingly about others, is sent away from the Holy City. How can we understand this?

We could either interpret the statement literally (i.e. that the person is actually rejected from Jerusalem), or we can understand it symbolically, as the *Emunas Itecha* explains.

There are three things that carry the essence of Jerusalem:

1) *Tefillah* - We see an association between prayer and Jerusalem in

Yeshaya (56:7), where the Temple in Jerusalem is referred to as God's "house of prayer."

2) Torah - The connection between Torah and Jerusalem is based on *Yeshaya* (2:3), where the prophet says: "For from Zion will the Torah come forth, and the word of Hashem from Jerusalem."

3) Shabbos - Jerusalem is the most sacred with regard to the dimension of place. Similarly, Shabbos has this status in the dimension of time. This similarity between Shabbos and the Temple is hinted at in the Shabbos *Shemoneh Esrei* and *Kiddush*, when we bless God for sanctifying the Shabbos day - "*mekadesh HaShabbos.*" If we change the vowels of the first word, *mekadesh,* we can pronounce it *Mikdash,* meaning Sanctuary. Thus, Shabbos is the Sanctuary of Time and is subsequently connected to Jerusalem, the most sacred city, where the *Mikdash* is located.

If someone speaks *lashon hara*, he is "thrown out of Jerusalem." In other words, based on the symbolisms discussed above, this person will encounter difficulties in the following areas:

1) Focusing on his *tefillah* (due to the foreign thoughts that will fill his head);

2) Feeling the sweetness of Torah; and

3) Experiencing the pleasantness of Shabbos.

These three aspects of Jerusalem - Torah, *tefillah* and Shabbos - can be viewed as our *Gan Eden* (Paradise) on Earth. When we misuse our mouths, our *Gan Eden* is negatively affected; similar to what occurred in the original Garden of Eden. In *Bereishis* (3:24), after Adam and Chava had been banished from the Garden following the sin, God stationed a *cherev mis'hapeches* (a revolving sword) to prevent them from entering the Garden and eating from the Tree of Life. If we speak *lashon hara*, we create evil angels that wave a revolving sword, so to speak, preventing us from concentrating on our *tefillah* and experiencing the sweetness of Shabbos and Torah.

Through *teshuvah* (repentance), however, we can rectify our ways, and thus taste the beauty of these three Divine gifts once again. If we truly regret our negative speech, and make amends, then the *nega* (affliction of *tzara'as*) will be transformed into *oneg* (pleasantness). (This idea is alluded to in the word *nega* which reads *oneg* if the letters are switched around - i.e. *nun, gimmel, ayin* to *ayin, nun, gimmel*.)

How, though, can we bring a real and permanent end to *lashon hara*? As much as we try to prevent ourselves speaking negatively about others, and implement different strategies to control our speech, the effects are often not so long-lasting.

We could suggest an approach which "nips the problem in the bud." Instead of focusing on *shmiras ha'peh* (controlling our mouths), let us be more careful about *shmiras ha'einayim* (controlling our eyes).

If we train ourselves to view others in a positive light, and see only their inner beauty, rather than being judgmental and focusing on their shortcomings, then automatically we will not speak disparagingly about others - because we will never have anything negative to say in the first place! The underlying cause of negative speech is "negative vision." In order to cure the "disease" of *lashon hara*, we should tend to the cause rather than alleviate the symptoms.

With this idea in mind, we can answer our second question.

The portions of *Tazria* and *Metzora* (which discuss primarily the different types of *tzara'as* and the laws pertaining to the afflicted person) open with the subject of childbirth because we can learn from the way we react to babies how to prevent *lashon hara*.

Often, we see people around us (e.g. on the bus) with very serious (sometimes even frowned) expressions on their faces. However, as soon as a mother appears carrying her baby, everyone suddenly brightens up as they turn to gaze at the cute, little infant and comment on the baby's pure innocence and wholesome beauty.

Just as we view little babies as holy and blameless human beings with no deficiencies or faults, so we should see only the good and beauty in every single person, regardless of their age, background, and so on.

This is the reason why the laws of childbirth appear before the topic of *tzara'as*. Once we change our perspective, and view and react to other people in the way we respond to babies, then we will succeed in uprooting negative speech.

We could suggest that the names of the two portions - *Tazria* and *Metzora* - provide another allusion to this concept. The word *Tazria* is translated literally, "you shall plant." The word *Metzora* (spelled *mem, tzadik, reish, ayin*), with different vowels, can be read "*motzi ra*," meaning, "extracting the evil." (This idea is a spoof of the Talmud in *Eruchin* 15b where the *Metzora/Motzi Ra* connection is discussed in relation to *motzi shem ra* - a specific type of slander. We are interpreting the phrase *motzi ra* differently, as discussed above).

When we implant in ourselves a fresh and positive outlook, and perceive adults in the same way that we look toward babies and children, then we will be able to completely remove ourselves from evil gossip. This, therefore, answers our first question. The topic of *tzara'as* is divided into two portions because the names of these specific portions teach us this fundamental lesson.

Finally, we find another hint to this idea in the *haftarah* reading of *Parshas Tazria*, (taken from the *Melachim* 4:42-5:19), which recounts the story of Geichazi (the attendant of the prophet Elisha) who contracted *tzara'as*.

The name "Geichazi," when divided into two separate words, alludes to the common cause of *tzara'as*.

The Hebrew word "*gei*" means "valley"; and "*chazi*" in Aramaic means "see."

When we view other people the way we look at valleys, i.e. when we look down at others, and focus on their weaknesses and deficiencies, then we will end up like a *metzora*, God forbid, losing out on the sweetness of Torah and Shabbos, and lacking in our *tefillah*.

Let us imbibe ourselves with the message of this week's portion (and the following portion) to see only the good in other people and appreciate their values and virtues.

So the next time you get annoyed with somebody: stop, close your eyes, and imagine them when they were just innocent infants. Then, open your eyes and realize that the bitter looking person next to you may have been jaded by harsh circumstances in life. Then offer up a prayer to God for that person to get back in touch once again with the pure child within.

May we be blessed with holy eyes and do complete *teshuvah* by seeing the beauty in others, as we do with babies, so that we usher in the Messianic era, which will heal us from all sicknesses - a time when we will serve God in "paradise Yerushalayim," in the holy Temple, with delightful Torah and *tefillah* on a *Yom Shekulo Shabbos*.

Tazria - Metzora

Big Things Come in Small Packages

On the one hand, we are told "be humble"; on the other hand we are told to have self-confidence. Although this may seem contradictory, it's really not. Before a performance, the performer needs self-confidence, but after his success he needs humility. Let us explore how to strike that balance.

The thematic ideas that take us through these two portions are the discussions of *tzaraas* (spiritual leprosy), the *metzora* (the person smitten with this spiritual disease), and the offering he must bring in order to become purified again.

One of the causes of *tzaraas* is the sin of *lashon hara* (evil speech about other people) (see *Eruchin*, chap. 3, *Yesh B'Eruchin*, pg. 16a, the opinion of Rabbi Yochanan). This is a fairly well-known concept.

However, the underlying cause of people speaking *lashon hara* is a topic for discussion. One character flaw that is responsible for *lashon hara* is arrogance.

This is because if a person would recognize his own shortcomings, he would not have the audacity to speak about others in a derogatory fashion. This flaw of haughtiness is hinted to in the offering a *metzora* must bring for his purification.

Amongst the ingredients of a *metzora's* offering are cedar wood and hyssop (*Vayikra* 14:4). A cedar tree is one of the tallest trees, representing conceitedness; whereas a hyssop is a very low bush, representing humility. These components of a *metzorah's* offering are meant to teach him a lesson.

That is, if he was as arrogant as a cedar tree, then he must lower himself like the hyssop (*Bamidbar Rabbah, Parshas Chukas*, 19:3). As a matter of fact, humility is at the root and foundation of Judaism and the entire Torah. Let us explore this now.

God chose the Jewish people to be His and to receive the Torah on account of their humbleness. The verse that supports this says, "Not because you were more in number than any other people did God desire you and choose you, for you were the fewest of all peoples" (*Devarim* 7:7).

It sounds as if God chose us because we were the fewest in number. It may seem a little strange to be chosen just because of being few in numbers. What does the population count have to do with being special? If another nation's populace would dip below the Jewish people's consensus, would that grant favor to that other nation over the Jews?

The Talmud (*Chullin*, chap. 6, *Kisuy Hadam,* pg. 89a) explains the meaning behind this verse, and says that it means that no matter how much greatness God bestows upon the Jewish nation, they make themselves small. It is the Jewish people's humility that makes them special; so much so, that God chose them because of it.

Not only were the Jews chosen to receive the Torah due to their humility, but the person chosen to deliver the Torah to them was picked because of his humility. That person was Moshe, as the verse says, "And the man, Moshe was very humble, more than any man upon the face of the Earth" (*Bamidbar* 12:3).

Moreover, the place chosen to deliver the Torah was selected on account of its humble nature. That mountain was Mount Sinai, as it says, "The Holy One, Blessed Be He, left all mountains and hills, and rested His Divine presence on Mount Sinai, because of its small size." (*Sotah*, chap. 1, *HaMikaneh*, pg. 5a, the opinion of *Rebbi Yoseph*)

The *Shvilei Pinchas* says that this approach will answer a famous question. The Talmud says that God held Mount Sinai suspended over the Jewish people's heads and gave them an ultimatum.

Basically, God said to them that if they accept the Torah, fine; then He will put the little mountain back down beside them. But if not, God said he would turn that place into the largest Jewish cemetery ever seen at that time, by dropping the mountain on top of them and thereby crushing them (*Shabbos*, chap. 9, *Amar Rebbi Akiva*, pg. 88a, the opinion of *Rebbi Avdimi Bar Chamah Bar Chasah*, based on *Shemos* 19:17).

The Jews must have said, "You know, You drive a hard bargain! Okay, we'll take it… You know what, we'll even take two!"

Many question this passage. Why was it necessary for God to force the Jews to accept the Torah, if they already said, "*na'aseh v'nishma* - we will do and we will obey" (*Shemos* 24:7)? (See the Tosafists, *Kufuh*, on this Gemara.)

The *Shvilei Pinchas* offers a beautiful approach to answer this question. He says that God did not have to force them to accept the Torah because they already agreed to it on their own. However, God did have to force them to accept the Torah with "humility."

The Jews were prepared to learn Torah and fulfill its commandments; however, they never promised to go about it with humility. So that is what God had to encourage them to do.

God held Mount Sinai over them, as if pointing to it, and said to them that if they accept the Torah in a way that lives up to the "Sinai expectation" (namely humility), then fine; but if not, they will bury themselves alive in all sorts of sin that arrogance leads to.

Humility should not be thought of as having tension with self-confidence. As long as we realize that our talents come from God and that He is helping us along the way, we can and should have self-confidence that we can achieve. It's when we forget about God and start to credit ourselves, that we begin to fill our chests with unhealthy pride, which ultimately brings our downfall.

Part of being humble means to see our own shortcomings. It means to remain teachable. Then we are not so judgmental of others, because who knows how we would have behaved given their challenges.

Humility is an attitude shift which will help us see others in a more positive light. This breeds camaraderie, which leads to the building of the *Beis HaMikdash*.

There are a few thoughts that we could ponder daily that may help encourage our humility. Here is a short list:

1) Think about how much we don't know.

2) Think about how susceptible we are to illness.

3) Think about the fact that we are going to die one day.

4) Think about how we have to move our bowels.

Thoughts like these are not meant to make us sad, but rather to put us in our places; to recognize our vulnerabilities, so that we don't stumble in arrogance.

May we all be blessed with the wisdom to see God's greatness and our own limitations, thereby bringing other people into a more favorable light, which will terminate *lashon hara* and bring about peace between all Jews.

Metzora

Men at Work… Together

Working on a project can prove to be highly beneficial. It keeps us busy, keeps us out of trouble, enables us to make a positive dent in the world, and even gives us an opportunity to get paid for it. However, you simply cannot compare a personal project to a project that is tackled as a team.

In this week's portion, *Metzora* (14:34), God says to Moshe and Aharon: "When you come into the land of Canaan, which I give to you for a possession, and I will put the plague of *tzara'as* in a house of the land of your possession.. ."

Rashi cites the *Toras Kohanim* (14:75), who says that the plague of *tzara'as* on the walls of the houses was good news for the Jewish people. The Amorites - who had inhabited these homes during the forty years that the Jews were in the desert - had hidden treasures of gold within the walls, fearing that the Jews would attack, inhabit the land and gain access to their riches. Little did they know that God would inflict the walls with *tzara'as*, forcing the Jewish owners to destroy the walls in order to remove the infected stones, and in doing so, discover all their treasures.

The implication of the *Toras Kohanim* is that *tzara'as* is a positive and favorable sign for the person whose home is afflicted. How can we understand this in light of the fact that *tzara'as* serves as a warning sign for the individual to repent for his misdeeds?

The Midrash explains (*Vayikra Rabbah* 17:4) that God, the Master of Mercy, "does not inflict a person first on his body" (where it hurts most). Rather, He first inflicts his home, in order to awaken the transgressor to repent. If the individual fails to heed the lesson, God then causes the plague to hit "a little closer to home" - his garments - to try to arouse remorse for his misconduct. If he does not pay attention to this warning sign, too, then He will cause *tzara'as* to plague his body.

With this Midrash in mind, we can ask an additional question. Why does the Torah mention first the affliction of *tzara'as* on the body (which is the last to be affected) and end with the affliction of the home (which is the first that is plagued). Should it not discuss them in reverse order, the sequence in which the affliction occurs?

We find an answer to this question earlier in the Midrash where it cites *Shemos* (2:23). Moshe, in God's name, warns Pharaoh about the (final) plague of the firstborn even before any of the plagues had begun! When it comes to forewarning us, God informs us of the most severe punishment first, to offer us a chance to repent. However, when it comes to implementing the punishment, it is done in a gradual, gentle manner.

We can infer from this Midrash that the plague of tzara'as on the home is not such good news because it serves as a form of punishment which could, in fact, be the first in a series of retributions, if the person is not moved to repent right away.

How, then, can we reconcile this Midrash with the seemingly contradictory proposition of the *Toras Kohanim*, which maintains that *tzara'as* was a positive sign?

We will be able to resolve these paradoxical positions in light of the following teaching.

There is a halachah regarding *tzara'as* that if the plague affects a wall which is shared by two tenants, then both households must participate in the effort to remove the infected wall, and in contributing to the cost of building a new one. Even if only one side of the wall is affected, both neighbors must, nevertheless, share in both the destructive work and payment for rebuilding. (See *Toras Kohanim, Metzora* 14:40, on *"V'chiltzu es ha'avanim* - and they shall remove the stones.")

This law seems unfair. Why is the innocent person, whose side of the wall is unaffected, required to participate in rectifying the situation? The *Emunas Itecha* describes the following scenario as a basis to answering our aforementioned question.

Imagine there are two neighbors - 1one is a *tzaddik* (righteous person), and the other, a *rasha* (wicked person). The nature of the *rasha* is to hate the *tzaddik* because he is a constant reminder as to the type of person he (the *rasha*) could be, and, indeed, should be. The feeling of guilt causes the *rasha* to hate the *tzaddik* and to speak disparagingly of him to others. This phenomenon is described by the *Rambam* (in *Hilchos Tumas Tzara'as* 16:10), who says that when the wicked convene, they first speak about issues of no significance or purpose, and then they speak about *tzaddikim* in disgraceful and disparaging ways.

The *rasha's* actions obviously cause the *tzaddik* to hate him, as the verse in *Mishlei* (27:19) indicates: "As water reflects a face back to a face, so one's heart is reflected back to him by another." In other words, whatever we provide in a relationship is what we receive in return. (For a more detailed analysis, see *Tosefos* in *Pesachim* 113b on the word *"Shera'ah."*)

The more the *rasha* speaks negatively about the *tzaddik*, the more the *tzaddik* retains feelings of animosity toward the *rasha*. And so, the cycle continues.

This is the point where *tzara'as* enters the picture. God inflicts *tzara'as* onto the side of the wall that belongs to the guilty party - i.e. the *rasha* - in order to motivate him to mend his ways. However, the *tzaddik* must also help remove the wall and participate in constructing a new one. (This *halachah* is reminiscent of the *mitzvah* to help with the loading of our enemies' animals; see *Shemos* 23:5 - *Azov ta'azov imo.*) In the process of destroying the infected wall, the *tzaddik* will come across treasures on his side.

Now we can understand how *tzara'as* is both a good sign (as the *Toras Kohanim* implies) and a negative indication (as the Midrash implies).

In the scenario depicted by the *Emunas Itecha*, the *tzaddik's* side of the wall is unaffected, and he even discovers treasures on his side of the wall whose worth amounts to far more than the expenses of building the new wall. Therefore, the plague of *tzara'as* is, in fact, beneficial for him! For the *rasha*, however, the *tzara'as* is a punishment from God for his transgressions. The plague affects only his side of the wall and he does not obtain any treasures in the process.

In the end, though, we see how the *tzara'as* is beneficial for both parties - for an entirely different reason. The *Emunas Itecha* explains that when the *rasha* and *tzaddik* work together toward a common goal, the joint participation helps to break the cycle of animosity. When two opposing parties work together to help one another, the hostility between them begins to dissipate. We see this concept in *Shemos* (23:5), where *Onkelos* comments on the *mitzvah* to help the load of one's enemies' animals: "Let go of what is in your heart."

When the *rasha* sees the *tzaddik* helping him, he starts to think differently about him, and even feels embarrassed about the negative things he said concerning him. Eventually, the *rasha* will come to repent and transform himself into a *tzaddik*.

Thus, we can appreciate the wisdom behind the *halachah*. Both tenants must partake in dealing with the infected wall because of the potential inherent in the situation, i.e. building their relationship by eliminating ill feelings and increasing admiration and respect toward the other.

This idea fits in well with the message of *Parshas Tazria*. What is it that changes the *rasha's* behavior and causes him to stop speaking disparagingly about the *tzaddik*?

As the *rasha* and *tzaddik* share in the common project of dismantling the wall and rebuilding it, an opportunity is provided for the *rasha* to change his outlook and view the *tzaddik* for the better. When his impression of the *tzaddik* is transformed, and he stops viewing him with a negative and critical eye, then his thoughts, speech and behavior are affected and transformed for the good as well. He no longer has anything negative to say about the *tzaddik* because he sees him only in a positive light.

This approach carries with it one of the most powerful secrets of *kiruv*. If people who are antagonistic to religion can be turned around by the kindness they receive from a religious person, how much more so can people who are not anti-religious be affected by the kindness extended to them by a religious person. Most irreligious people today are good people who were just never fortunate to have received a solid Torah education.

Let's choose one irreligious person that we know and go out of our way to bestow kindness on him or her. Not only will we have done the *mitzvah* of *chessed*, but we will have given them a positive impression of religious Judaism. You never know what seeds will be planted and what could develop from them.

May we be blessed with success in fostering a favorable outlook toward our neighbors and breaking all unnecessary animosity. Moreover, may the whole world be plagued with a contagious love in which each person views the other in a healthy and positive light, thus healing the entire world from all sicknesses. In turn, may we merit returning to *Eretz Yisrael* and liberate the homes that are occupied by those committed to our annihilation, and subsequently witness with our own eyes the return of God to Zion.

Acharei - Kedoshim

Take It Easy

The way we behave with permitted things is the true test of a man. It also determines how we act when it comes to prohibited areas.

This week, we read the portions of *Acharei Mos* and *Kedoshim* together. Why are these two portions usually combined?

Furthermore, in *Parshas Acharei Mos* (*Vayikra* 18:3), Hashem instructs the Jewish people not to behave like the Egyptians, whose culture we absorbed for many years, or the Canaanites, who inhabit the Land of Israel. What is the nature of this command? If the point is to steer us away from immoral behavior, the Torah explicitly tells us that shortly thereafter (*Vayikra* 18:6-30). What is meant then, by the instruction not to act like the Egyptian or Canaanite nations?

Moreover, at the beginning of *Parshas Kedoshim*, the Torah states, "Be holy" (*Vayikra* 19:2). *Rashi* interprets this statement to mean that we must separate ourselves from immorality. The *Ramban*, however, disputes this interpretation, since our Sages (in *Toras Kohanim*) explain the statement "Be holy," as "Be separate." From where did *Rashi* derive that we must separate ourselves specifically from immorality?

The *Tiferes Shmuel* (vol. 1) takes issue with a different aspect of *Rashi's* comment, and wonders: can someone who disengages from immorality really be called "holy"? Imagine the first eulogizer at a funeral beginning to speak about the deceased, and saying, "This man was truly holy. Not once did he engage in adultery, incest, or bestiality!" Committing these sins is wickedness; refraining from them seems to be merely maintaining the status quo. How can *Rashi* understand the statement "Be holy" as a command to stay away from obvious misdeeds?

The *Slonimer Rebbe* begins to address our second question by explaining what it means to act like an Egyptian. In his view, the Torah is not telling us to avoid performing prohibited actions; rather, it is teaching us how to engage in permitted physical activities. Even in the realm of permissible behavior, we must not overindulge or seek out passion for passion's sake, as the Egyptians did. Instead, we must act like Jews, striving to perform every action in a healthy, balanced way, with the ultimate goal being to fulfill Hashem's will.

The *Ramban* expresses a similar idea regarding the Sages' interpretation of "Be holy" as "Be separate." The Torah permits pleasurable physical activities - eating kosher meat, drinking kosher wine, intimacy between husband and wife - yet someone who is driven by lustful passions might overindulge in these activities while thinking that he is still within the bounds of Torah law. Such a person is called a glutton (see *Mishlei* 23:20); the *Ramban* calls him "a disgusting person with the Torah's permission."

Thus, after *Parshas Acharei Mos* lists all the specific prohibitions regarding immorality, *Parshas Kedoshim* takes us to the next level and says, "Be holy." We must separate ourselves from overindulging in permissible activities, curbing our appetites in order to maintain dignity and holiness.

Based on this idea, the *Tiferes Shmuel* answers our fourth question: how *Rashi* can imply that we are called "holy" merely by staying away from immorality. The Talmud states, "Sanctify yourself with that which is permitted to you" (*Yevamos* 20a).

Another passage (*Avodah Zarah* 17a) elaborates on this idea, in which a *nazir* (one who has voluntarily decided to abstain from wine) is advised not to take a shortcut through a vineyard, but rather to walk all the way around it. Strictly speaking, a *nazir* may pass through a vineyard - he is merely prohibited from partaking of the grapes. But since walking through a vineyard would put him in such close proximity to the prohibition, a "fence" is necessary to protect him from possible temptation. (See *Avos* 1:1, which states, "Make a fence for the Torah.")

The same logic is at play in this week's double Torah portion. *Parshas Acharei Mos* details the immoral behavior that is actually prohibited, while *Parshas Kedoshim* teaches us to be holy in permitted areas, so that we never even approach the prohibitions. If we accustom ourselves to avoid overindulgence in that which is permissible, we surely will not engage in prohibited behavior.

According to the *Tiferes Shmuel*, this is the answer to our third question: what *Rashi* means when he interprets "Be holy" as "Be separate from immorality." The words "be separate" indicate that we should curb our appetites even in permitted areas. Then, after restating our Sages' words, *Rashi* explains the reasoning behind them: "from immorality." The *Tiferes Shmuel* understands the word "from" to mean "because of." Due to the prohibitions against immoral behavior, we must make a fence around them to ensure that we stay far away from any wrongdoing.

Based on this view, there is no contradiction between *Rashi* and the *Ramban*; both are emphasizing the importance of maintaining holiness even in permissible activities. Furthermore, we can now understand why *Rashi*'s language seemed to differ from that of our Sages. In fact, he uses the same expression (be separate), but then adds a reason afterwards.

The connection between the two Torah portions is now obvious. In *Parshas Acharei Mos*, we are commanded not to act like the Egyptians - not to overindulge in permissible behavior. In *Parshas Kedoshim*, we are told, "Be holy," which means the same thing.

One exercise in curbing our appetites could be to leave over a small piece of food from our meal even though we are not yet completely full. By breaking our natural tendency to finish off a last piece of cake, we become holier.

May we be blessed to escape from the "Egypt" within us, little by little each day, by engaging in permissible behavior in a healthy, balanced way.

Acharei - Kedoshim

Do You Love Me, Do I Love You?

There is a secret contained behind *Parshas Kedoshim*. To find out what it is, please read on.

This week we read the double portion of *Acharei Mos* and *Kedoshim*. In *Kedoshim*, there is a sentence which is arguably one of the most famous verses in the Torah: "*V'ahavta l'rayacha ka'mocha* - love your friend as yourself" (*Vayikra* 19:18). *Rashi* on this verse cites *Toras Kohanim* (19:45) quoting Rebbi Akiva as saying that this is the greatest principle in Torah.

To understand this position, we can see the *sefer Tzidkas HaTzaddik* (198) which states that "Someone who loves the Torah, [then] the Torah will love that person." As it says in *Mishlei:* "Does not wisdom call; I love those that love me" (8:1 & 17). Once the Torah loves the person back, the Torah will share her secrets with that person. Just like when two close friends meet for coffee, they share secrets; so too, when one loves Torah and becomes close to Torah, the Torah will similarly share its secrets. The reciprocal love between the Jewish people and a single individual is the same. When a single individual loves the Jewish people, the Jewish people love that person.

Avos (1:12) states that Aharon loved the Jewish people. It was because Aharon loved his people so much, that when he passed on, all the Jewish people cried for 30 days (*Bamidbar* 20:29). *Rashi* states that when the verse says "all Jewish people," this includes not just men, but women too, because Aharon pursued peace - encouraging love between arguing people, husband and wife, etc. He loved them, so they loved him in return.

The *Zohar* says in *Shir HaShirim* (74:4), that just like there are 600,000 Jewish souls, so too there are 600,000 letters in the Torah. We see this in the acronym created by our national name, *Yisrael* (spelled *yud, sin, reish, aleph, lamed*), which expands to: "*Yesh shishim ribui osiyos l'Torah* - there are 600,000 letters to the Torah." This shows us that every Jewish soul contains the Torah secrets from the letter to which it is connected.

This is one reason that it says that Aharon carried the names of the Jewish tribes on the breastplate of the priestly garments (*Shemos* 28:29). Why does it stress this point? A Jewish name expresses the essence of the Jewish soul, and because Aharon loved each Jew, he merited knowing each soul's essence.

The Torah secrets contained in the Jewish soul are different than those secrets contained in the Torah. This is why information became known to Aharon based on the letters of the name that lit up on his breastplate. Every soul had a message for Aharon because he was their "best friend." He loved them and they loved him in return.

Adding to the approach of the *Tzidkas HaTzaddik*, we could suggest that the verse "*V'ahavta l'rayacha ka'mocha*" represents the love of Jewish people for each other, a love for every individual Jew. Once we have this inclusive type of love for every Jew, their souls will share their information with us.

This is hinted to in *Kedoshim*. There are sixty-four verses in *Parshas Kedoshim*. Sixty-four equals the numerical value of the letters *samech* and *daled*, which spell "*sod*," meaning secret. This alludes to the fact that if we follow this main principle of loving all Jews, we will become privy to the *sodos* (secrets) contained in all Jewish souls.

This is perhaps why these portions are read every year during *Sefiras HaOmer*. As we mourn the deaths of Rebbi Akiva's students, due to their lack of respect for each other (see *Yevamos* 62b), we are meant to correct, fix and repair their shortcomings by trying to cultivate respect, appreciation and even love for each other.

May we all be blessed to love every Jew, and connect with the letters of Torah and with the souls of *Yisrael*. And thus become filled with secrets and new ideas so that we deserve one day to have Aharon, the High Priest, officiate on our behalf once again.

Kedoshim

Ya Gotta Love It

Genuine, sincere care for others is what is going to make a difference in other people's lives.

In this week's portion, *Kedoshim* (19:18), we are commanded: "*V'ahavta l'rayacha ka'mocha* - You shall love your fellow as yourself."

The *Iturei Torah* (citing *Bi'urei Chazon Ish* on *Rambam's Hilchos De'os*) points out that the definition of *rayacha* (your fellow), extends also to Jewish transgressors. We find this concept in the Talmud (*Sanhedrin* 52b) where it states that even someone deserving of the death penalty (*chayav misah*) should be dealt with honorably.

For instance, if it is ruled that the transgressor die by *skilah* (stoning), the law states that he may not be thrown to the ground from too low a height, so as to prevent his suffering a slow and painful death. He should also not be thrown from too far above the ground, because although he would die instantaneously, it would be undignified since his body would suffer mutilation. The Talmud says that this law is derived from the *mitzvah* of "*V'ahavta l'rayacha ka'mocha,*" and thus provides support to the notion that the command to love others applies also to the sinners of Israel, and even to those who are *chayav misah*.

Furthermore, the *Rambam* in *Hilchos De'os* teaches that there is a *mitzvah* to hate *reshaim* (wicked people), but that this law is only applicable if the *reshaim* fail to heed the rebuke (*tochachah*) that was given to them. Rabbi Elazar ben Azariah questioned whether there was anyone in his generation who knew how to give *tochachah* in the correct manner (see *Eruchin* 16b). If this was the case at his time, around 2000 years ago, how much more so does this statement apply in our generation? It is unlikely that anyone today knows how to reprimand others in the right way. This is what makes giving *tochachah* very challenging today.

Based on this understanding, we are not permitted to hate *reshaim* even if they don't listen to the rebuke they are given, since *tochachah* nowadays is not valid (because there is hardly anybody qualified to reproof others properly.) Moreover, combining what we learned from the Talmud with this *Rambam*, we can conclude that the *mitzvah* of "*V'ahavta l'rayacha ka'mocha*" applies to *reshaim* as well, since they are considered to be at the stage prior to receiving *tochachah*.

May those of us who are in the position to reprimand others (e.g. as parents, teachers, etc.) be blessed to do so with tremendous sensitivity, coming only from a place of love, concern and warmth, and by no means from a place of anger or frustration. May we also make real efforts to stop judging others, and instead engender in ourselves genuine feelings of love for every Jew, realizing that, unfortunately, some people have never been shown the correct way to behave.

Moreover, let us remember to act toward ourselves using the same guidelines - by not being too hard on ourselves. Instead of becoming sad, depressed or paralyzed by our emotions, God forbid, we should always strive to move forward.

By acting with due care and concern toward ourselves and others, we will, with God's help, succeed in fixing the mistakes of Rebbi Akiva's students who lacked respect for one another (see *Yevamos* 62b), and who consequently all died in a plague - the tragedy which we mourn during *Sefiras HaOmer*.

Finally, once we learn to sincerely value others, we will be able to fulfill another command mentioned at the beginning of this week's portion (19:2), "*Kedoshim Tih'yu!* - Be Holy!" The fact that this command is juxtaposed with the words, "God spoke to all the congregation of the Children of

Israel," hints to us that by loving and respecting all Jews we will attain a state of authentic holiness.

May we be blessed to replace baseless hatred (which caused the destruction of the Second Temple) with unconditional love, so that we merit witnessing the building of the Third and final Temple, a time when true, lasting peace and tranquility will fill the entire Earth.

Acharei Mos - Kedoshim

One Step Back, Two Steps Forward

When it comes to concern for others, the question is: Are we willing to "take a hit" for the next guy?

This week's portion contains one of the most famous verses in the entire Torah: "You must love your friend like yourself" (*Vayikra* 19:18). Love is a huge topic today. The media is obsessed with it. Everybody craves it. People scramble to obtain it, and wonder how to maintain it.

This week, let us explore another perspective on this commandment and discover a practical lesson on how a Jew should lead his or her life.

The Talmud relates a story about a certain gentile who came before the great Sage Shammai and said to him, "Convert me, on the condition that you teach me the entire Torah while I stand on one foot." The Talmud reports that Shammai chased him away with an *amas habinyan* (a metal bar from a construction site).

The gentile was persistent and went to the other great Sage Hillel with the same request. The Talmud says that Hillel succeeded in converting him by telling him, "That which you hate, to your friend do not do; this is the entire Torah; the rest of the Torah is commentary: go and learn" (*Shabbos*, Ch. 2, *Bameh madlikin*, pg. 31a).

It seems a bit strange for the gentile to make such an unusual request of being taught the entire Torah while "standing on one foot." Was he auditioning to be in a circus where he had to perform a balancing act?

The *Maggid of Mezritch* explains where the gentile was coming from. He says that the gentile wanted to convert on condition that he would not have a life of ups and downs.

The gentile wanted to remain on the same spiritual level constantly. The gentile was willing to give up great highs just so that he would not have to experience deep lows. We can see that this was what the gentile meant by the choice of words that he used.

The gentile said that he wanted to convert on condition that the entire Torah could be taught to him while "standing on one foot." The *Maggid* explains that the intent behind the words "one foot" is that the gentile wanted to go through life like an angel.

Angels are described as having only one leg or one foot (see *Yechezkel* 1:6). The deeper meaning behind a spiritual angel having only "one leg" comes to teach us that angels stand in one place. In other words, they do not grow spiritually, nor do they sink. They are created by God on a certain spiritual level and they stay on that level for the rest of their existence.

The potential convert asked for the same type of life. He wanted to become Jewish, reach whatever elevated spiritual level he could achieve with his conversion, and then coast on that level for the rest of his life. He was prepared to forfeit higher transcendent levels and the benefits they offer, just so that he would not have to go through the difficult, low periods of life.

Shammai told him that his request was simply impossible to grant. Shammai explained that the lows of life are for a purpose. That purpose is to build us and make us even stronger than before. Without going through the challenging times, we would never be able to actualize our true potential. Shammai said to him that we are not angels. We do not have only one leg; we have two. This shows us that we are constantly moving; sometimes we go up and sometimes we fall down.

Shammai's words did chase the gentile away, because he was not ready to hear what Shammai had to say. The gentile wanted to accept God on his own terms, not on God's.

It would be very much out of character for Shammai to have chased away this gentile with a metal bar. After all, this is the same Shammai who says we should greet everybody with a pleasant countenance (*Avos*, Ch. 1, *Moshe kibel*, Mishnah 15). Did Shammai initially greet this person with a smile and then, in the next moment, proceed to chase him away with a swinging crowbar? This does not seem plausible.

Actually, the Talmud never said that Shammai chased him away with a metal bar. There are no vowels in the Talmud. We thought that the word used in the Talmud was *b'amas habinyan.* When pronounced this way, it does indeed mean with a metal bar.

However, the four Hebrew letters of "*b'amas*" (*beis, aleph, mem, saf*) are actually read as "*b'emes,*" meaning "with the truth." In other words, Shammai chased him away by telling him the truth, that the life of a Jew must have its ups and its downs.

The reason for this is so that we become even stronger by building ourselves as we go through the challenging times. This, too, is written explicitly in the Talmud's story. Right after it says that Shammai chased him away with the *emes,* it says *ha'binyan,* to build.

Shammai said that the *emes* is that we need the lows in order to truly build (*binyan*) our characters. Shammai told him that there can be no appreciation of light without darkness. This is the way Jewish life is. Every low brings us to an even higher place eventually. Therefore, Shammai said that he could not grant this person his request.

The gentile, who still wanted to be Jewish, but on his own terms, tried his luck by going to Hillel with the exact same request. Hillel agreed with Shammai; however, Hillel was able to explain it to this person in such a way that he was able to digest it.

Hillel asked this man how he thought he came so far. Becoming Jewish is no small or easy thing. Hillel inquired if the man knew what had motivated him to take this huge step - to want to be under the wings of the Divine presence. The gentile could not explain his drive and determination.

Hillel then said to him that he wanted to share a secret with him. Hillel said to him that even *tzaddikim* (very righteous people) experience downs. These lows serve a purpose: so that the *tzaddik's* soul can connect with other people who are already in a very low place.

This can either happen automatically, once the tzaddik's soul is in the same ballpark as others, or it can happen emotionally, because maybe the tzaddik will be more inclined to have dealings with people in lower spiritual places, that he otherwise would not have encountered.

Either way, once the *tzaddik* connects with these people who have drifted far away, they will benefit from this connection. This is because the *tzaddik* will not settle for remaining on a low spiritual level. Rather, he will fight to climb the spiritual ladder of success.

When he does, he will not only reach incredible heights himself, but he will also lift the other souls that he connected to. Hillel told this person that he, the gentile himself, was a product of some *tzaddik's* low, who subsequently worked at elevating himself. Hillel explained that this is where the gentile's motivation for increased spirituality came from.

Now we can dissect Hillel's words. Hillel said, "That which you hate...", meaning, the very thing you hate, which is having to go through lows in life; you should realize that you yourself are benefiting by standing here to convert due to somebody else's low and subsequent high.

Therefore, Hillel said, "Do not treat your friend that way"; meaning, do not deprive your friend of the same thing by refusing to experience lows yourself. After all, it says in the Torah that we should love others like ourselves.

When the gentile heard this, he was touched personally and accepted the responsibilities of Judaism, which include both the ups and the downs.

The *Lekach V'halibuv* says that this teaching of the *Maggid of Mezritch* should serve as incredible encouragement to each and every one of us. Just knowing that all the things that prevent us from serving God and the difficulties that get us down are for the purpose of reaching even higher, will help us make it through those low times.

Not only will we get stronger in the process, but when we start to climb out of the rut, we will help others who are struggling as well. This is extremely comforting to anybody who is going through times of darkness and concealment.

We can now accept our "downs" with happiness, in the knowledge that these moments serve a greater purpose. This is the vision of life we need to convert to: a lifetime of being willing to help others even at our own expense; because then, we will realize that we become stronger in the process.

May we all be blessed with the commitment to step down in order to help others. May we be comforted in the low periods of our lives with the knowledge that it will lead to raising other people and to building our own characters even stronger.

Emor - Sefiras HaOmer

Big Baby

R emember, if it's not sweet, it's not Torah.

It is very apropos that *Parshas Emor* is read at this time of year. This is because we are in the middle of counting the *Omer*, and the source in the Torah for this *mitzvah* is found in *Parshas Emor* (*Vayikra* 23:15-16).

The *Aron Eidus* reveals an overall objective that we are trying to achieve at this time of year. He says that we are involved in the process of sweetening any harshness found in our lives.

We can see this hinted to in the *Omer* offering. On the one hand, the stalks of barley used in this offering must be cut. The act of cutting is a harsh one. On the other hand, the cut barley is immediately brought to a *Kohen*, because a *Kohen* represents softness and kindness, as it says about the *Kohen*, "Your *Tummim* and Your *Urim* (Breastplate) for Your man of kindness" (*Devarim* 33:8).

In fact, when each letter in the Hebrew word "*Kohen*" (*chaf, hey, nun*) is spelled out (*chaf, phey; hey, yud; nun, vav, nun*), it has the numerical value of 221, the exact numerical value as the word *erech* (patience). This teaches us that a *Kohen* is meant to be the personification of patience and sweetness.

By bringing the cut barley (strictness) to a *Kohen* (sweetness), the intention is for the *Kohen* to superimpose the energy of gentleness into sharpness. During the rest of the *Omer* we are meant to continue this process of imbuing pleasantness into any ruggedness found in our lives.

This is why the barley offering flour is sifted specifically thirteen times (*Mishnah, Menachos*, Ch. 6, Rebbi Yishmael, pg. 66a). These thirteen siftings point to the thirteen attributes of God's mercy (*Shemos* 34:6-7).

All of this prepares us to receive the Torah on the holiday of Shavuos, when we get a chance to taste the hidden light which illuminates the world on that day.

This is why Shavuos is the only holiday in the Torah which is not given a specific date on the calendar when it should be celebrated. It just says that after counting fifty days, it will be Shavuos (*Vayikra* 23:16).

This is because the holiness of the other holidays is dependent on time, meaning, that when it comes to a certain date on the Jewish calendar, that holiday's light begins to flow from above, and we are sanctified with the holiness of that day.

However, Shavuos is not dependent on time, but rather on the preparation that we put into it during the *Omer* counting. To the extent that we try to become kinder and sweeter during the *Omer* counting, to that degree are we going to be able to receive and benefit from the light of Shavuos.

The way to sweeten strict justice is to return the harshness to its original source. For example, strong wine represents harshness because it damages people by making them drunk and confused. However, as long as the wine is still in its first source, meaning, inside of the grape, it does not have the power to intoxicate, even if many grapes are consumed.

This is why we count each day leading up to Shavuos by referring back to the first day, when the *Omer* offering was brought (e.g. "Today is the eighteenth day of the *Omer*"). This is because the *Omer* offering is the first, and the source, of all the days that follow. So, if our task during the days that we count is to sweeten harshness, then we must always go back to the source.

We also find this unique way of counting elsewhere. When the *Kohen Gadol* (High Priest) counts the blood sprinkling of the bullock and goat on *Yom*

Kippur to achieve atonement, he says, "One, one and two, one and three, etc." By each count, he also recalls the first sprinkle in order to connect all that follows to the beginning, so that everything gets sweetened.

This is why the word *reishis* (first) is used by the newly cut barley of the *Omer* offering (*Vayikra* 23:10). It comes to teach us that if we want the harshness (represented by the cutting) to be sweetened, we must connect it back to its beginning.

To me, this idea of softening the roughness by going back to the original source means the following. Sometimes, we may find a bit of an edge in our personalities. Sometimes we may wish that we could be a little more easygoing and socially pleasant. We may ask ourselves how we can overcome this sharpness. Well, here's one thought.

Before those moments of aggravation and toughness hit us, let's stop and imagine ourselves when we were little babies. At that time, we were not harsh. Rather, we were cute and soft. We were creatures who brought countless smiles to so many people. This is what it means to go back to the source.

Naturally speaking, we were born pure and innocent. The bitterness was learned along the way. Fortunately, we still retain our original beauty within us. After all, we are all just a bunch of grown babies. We have never lost that innocence which is our essence.

If only once a day we would stop, close our eyes, and connect with that child on the inside, we could slowly take that uncomfortable edge off of our characters.

May we all be blessed this *Omer* to get back to the basics of who we really are, transforming jaggedness into smoothness, and making our lives all that more enjoyable.

Emor

Take It with a Grain of Salt

Eating a meal can be filled with as much spiritual nutrition as physical nourishment.

In this week's portion, *Emor*, the *lechem hapanim* (Show-breads on the Table of the Sanctuary) are discussed (*Vayikra* 24:5-9). There were twelve loaves in all, which were eaten by the *Kohanim* every Shabbos.

Today, with the absence of the *Beis HaMikdash*, its vessels and its offerings, the two loaves of *challah* (bread) on the *Shabbos* table remind us of the *lechem hapanim*. There are two ways in which this hint is visible.

First of all, we are enjoined to lift the *challos* with both of our hands. This means that ten fingers touch the two *challos*, equaling twelve altogether, hinting at the twelve *lechem hapanim*.

Secondly, our *challos* are traditionally baked in an oval shape. This makes the *challos* appear to be in the shape of the Hebrew letter *vav*. Two such *challos* mean that we have two *vavs*. The letter *vav*, numerically six, multiplied by two is twelve, once again hinting at the twelve *lechem hapanim*.

Speaking of *challah* at a Jewish table, we all know that we are supposed to have salt on our tables as well. There are three reasons for this.

In *Vayikra* (2:13), it says, "And every meal offering you must season with salt; you may not discontinue the covenant of salt of your God from upon your meal offering; on your every offering, offer salt."

In the *Me'am Lo'ez*, the reasons for this are explained.

1) On the second day of Creation, God divided between the lower waters

and the upper waters (see *Rashi* on *Bereishis* 1:6). The lower waters cried because they too wanted to be close to God. (This may be why the oceans are so salty - namely, from the tears that the lower waters shed!)

God guaranteed the lower waters that they would indeed be close to Him, because on every offering, salt would be brought as well. Salt is a derivative of sea water, and as such, the lower waters would go up to Hashem through the offering.

Now, the Talmud (*Chagigah*, Ch. 3, *Chomer BaKodesh*, pg. 27a), cites *Rabbi Yochanan* and *Reish Lakish* who say that when we had a Temple, the Altar atoned for us. Today, in the absence of the Temple, a person's table atones.

So, just like there was salt on the offerings of the Altar, so too is there salt on our tables, which substitute for the Altar. This reminds us that our tables are mini-Altars, and that our food is in place of the offerings, and that we are likened to the *Kohanim* (see *Shemos* 19:6).

2) Another reason for having salt on the table is to remind us to share words of Torah at our meals. The salt reminds us that just like it is impossible for the world to exist without salt (or without water from which salt comes), so too, it is impossible for the world to exist without Torah (see *Avos* 3:4).

When words of Torah are shared at the table, then the angel appointed over our tables takes those words, forms them into the shape of a table, and presents it to God. This is in accordance with what it says, "And he said to Me, this is the table that is before God" (*Yechezkel* 41:22).

3) A third reason to have salt on the table is to remind us to have compassion on the poor. This is because Lot's wife was cheap with the salt, and did not want to give their guests salt when Lot asked for it.

Lot's wife said, "Fine, you want salt, I'll get you salt." She went around to their neighbors and asked to borrow salt so that Lot could give it to his guests in order to make their food tastier.

Since it was against the constitution of Sedom to have guests, and violation of this law carried with it the penalty of death, Lot's wife was endangering her husband's life. This is why she was later punished by turning into a pillar of salt (see *Bereishis* 19:26; and *Bereishis Rabbah* 49:5; *Yalkut Shimoni, Vayeira, remez* 85).

My son, Reb Menachem Shlomo, suggested that these three reasons are hinted to in the Hebrew word for salt, *melach*. This word is spelled with three letters: *mem, lamed,* and *ches*, which form the acronym for *mizbe'ach* (Altar), *limud HaTorah* (Torah study), and *chessed*, (kindness). Therefore, salt is supposed to remind us of these three things.

Dipping the bread into the salt three times is a further way of remembering the messages of salt. First, it helps us realize that our eating should be for the right reasons - thus turning that activity into a holy offering to God. Second, it reminds us to share words of Torah. And third, to act with kindness to the poor, or to everybody for that matter.

As an exercise, let's try to think of these three thoughts when we dip the *challah* into the salt three times, and in so doing remind ourselves to fulfill what they represent.

May we all be blessed to learn Torah at our tables in a way that will bring us to act kindly with others, and thus deserve to witness the coming of our Messiah, the building of the *Beis HaMikdash*, and the re-institution of the *lechem hapanim*.

Emor - Sefiras HaOmer

The "Jew-eled" Letter

Once we realize just how precious we are, we would never allow ourselves to stoop to activities that are beneath our dignity.

In this week's portion, *Emor*, we read about the man who blasphemed God. The Torah says (*Vayikra* 24:10): "The son of an Israelite woman went out - and he was the son of an Egyptian man - among the Children of Israel; they fought in the camp, the son of the Israelite woman and an Israelite man."

Rashi, citing *Toras Kohanim*, asks: From where did the son of the Israelite woman go out?

The *Masnisah* maintains that he had come out liable from the courthouse of Moshe. This man, whose father was Egyptian, pitched his tent by the encampment of *Shevet Dan* (the tribe of Dan). When asked what he was doing there, he responded that he is a Danite from his mother's side. *Shevet Dan* pointed out to him that one's tribe is decided based on the father and not the mother, as we see (*Bamidbar* 2:2) where God instructs *Bnei Yisrael* to encamp "according to the insignias of their father's household." Therefore, he was told, "Since your father was Egyptian, you do not belong to any tribe of Israel." The case was brought to Moshe's courthouse and the son of the Egyptian man came out liable. He became angry at the verdict, and subsequently cursed God (see *Vayikra* 24:11).

An obvious question arises from the explanation of the *Masnisah*. Why did the tribe of Dan refuse the man permission to pitch his tent by their camp? At that point in time, the Israelites were traveling in the desert so there was certainly no shortage of space; plus, there is the fact that it would have been a temporary arrangement since the Jews were constantly on the move. So, why wasn't this lone man permitted to encamp among the Israelites?

The *Emunas Itecha* answers this question based on a well-known concept that the 600,000 letters in the Torah correspond to the 600,000 primary souls of the Jewish people (see, for example, *Megaleh Amukos* on *Parshas Vayikra*, based on the *Zohar*). The Jewish nation as a whole, it follows, comprises a complete Torah scroll (*Sefer Torah*). This idea is alluded to in *Yeshaya* (54:13), where the prophet says, "*V'chol banayich limudei Hashem* - All your children are students of God." This phrase can be interpreted differently: "*Vechol banayich* - All your children"; "*limudei Hashem* - are the learning item of God," i.e. the Torah! The Jewish people are the Torah!

The *Emunas Itecha* points out that when *Bnei Yisrael* camped at Sinai, they were not placed randomly around the mountain; rather, each person was situated in a specific location, arranged in order of his letter's appearance in the Torah. In other words, a spiritually-sensitive person with a bird's eye view of the encampment at Sinai would have perceived the Jewish nation as a *Sefer Torah*, since every Jew, who corresponded to a particular letter in the Torah, was placed according to his letter's position in the Torah.

Just as this was the case at Sinai, so it was in the desert. Each member of every tribe - who represented a particular letter in the Torah - was situated accordingly, so that, collectively, the Jews appeared as a Torah scroll. This is why *Shevet Dan* could not allow the son of the Egyptian man to encamp by their side. This man wanted to place himself in the exact spot where one of the Jewish Danites was supposed to camp. Had *Shevet Dan* consented to his request, the corresponding Torah letter of the Jewish Danite would have been absent, thus ruining the encampment of the nation as a whole. This would also have invalidated the Jewish people in the same way that a Torah scroll is deemed invalid if only one letter is missing.

Once we begin contemplating the implications of this idea for ourselves as individuals - that each and every one of us corresponds to a letter in the

Torah - we realize the tremendous responsibility that lies on our shoulders. Just as we are careful to inspect a Torah scroll for any anomalies, so must we constantly check ourselves by evaluating our actions, speech and thoughts, to ensure that we - Torah letters - are not "out of place." Moreover, even if we find that we are on the right path, let us aspire to even greater levels of creating enhanced Torah scrolls, so that when God reads His Torah, as it were, He will derive much pleasure from the polished letters found within.

Moreover, once we understand that every Jew correlates with a specific letter in the Torah, then we will learn to respect everyone, regardless of his or her external appearance. Armed with this heightened awareness, we will view every Jew as if he were a holy letter of the Torah - his very absence would render the entire Jewish nation invalid! It is by imbuing this awareness within ourselves that we will come to truly value and respect every single person.

This message, which stems from *Parshas Emor*, coincides very appropriately with the counting of the *Omer* (*Sefiras HaOmer*). At this time, we mourn the death of Rebbi Akiva's students who perished on account of the insufficient respect shown toward one another (*Yevamos* 62b). Thus, *Parshas Emor* brings to our attention a crucial message to help rectify the cause of this tragic event in our history.

So, before leaving the house each morning, stop at the front door and say to yourself, "I am a holy letter of God's *Sefer Torah*." This reminder will help us keep the letter (ourselves) whole, pure and clean even though we may be exposed to the spiritual pollution found in the streets.

May we be blessed to polish our own letters and appreciate the holiness in others, respecting every person completely, so that this *Sefiras HaOmer* will serve as the catalyst for Hashem, our King, to assemble the Jewish people, performing *Hakhel* on us at the end of the *Shemittah* year, when He will read from His *Sefer Torah* - that is, the Jewish nation.

Emor - Lag BaOmer

Sifting

One of the greatest gifts that can be used to advance us towards perfection is mastering the art of sifting. This means, to take only the good from each person or situation, and leave the bad behind.

Being that *Parshas Emor* often falls out around *Lag BaOmer*, (the thirty-third day of the *Omer* - counting between *Pesach* and Shavuos), we have taken the liberty of discussing the holiday at hand, and not focusing directly on this week's portion, *Emor*.

The story of *Lag BaOmer* is found in the Talmud (*Shabbos*, the second chapter, *Bameh Madlikin*). There is a simple way to remember on which page of the Talmud this story is found: page 33b. How apropos to find *Lag BaOmer*, the thirty-third day, on page thirty-three!

The story basically goes like this. Three sages sat together talking about the accomplishments of the Romans, who were in power at that time. Rabbi Yehudah praised them, pointing out how they built marketplaces, bathhouses, and bridges. Rabbi Yosi did not comment.

However, Rabbi Shimon Bar Yochai criticized the Romans by claiming that they only built up society for their own interests. For example, they built marketplaces in order to promote prostitution; they built bathhouses in order to beautify their bodies; and they built bridges just in order to tax the people.

A Jewish man by the name of Yehudah ben Geirim was present during this conversation. Yehudah ben Geirim shared this information with fellow students and with his parents, and eventually, word leaked out to the Roman authorities.

The Romans said that Rabbi Yehudah, who praised them, should be promoted; Rabbi Yosi, who kept quiet, should be exiled; and Rabbi Shimon, who disgraced them, should be put to death.

To save his life, Rabbi Shimon ran away and hid in a cave. His son, Rabbi Elazar, went with him. They spent twelve years in the cave, involved constantly in Torah study and prayer.

Eventually, when the Caesar died and the death decree was abolished, they came out of the cave. When they were found to be too intolerant with people who took time away from Torah study in order to make a livelihood, God sent them back into the cave for another year. When Rabbi Shimon finally emerged from the cave, he saw Yehudah ben Geirim (whose negligence caused Rabbi Shimon to be locked up in a kind of prison for so long). Rabbi Shimon cast his eyes upon him and turned him into a pile of bones.

We have to wonder why Rabbi Shimon was so harsh with Yehudah ben Geirim. After all, Yehudah ben Geirim was a scholar himself. In fact, he was one of Rabbi Shimon's students (*Tosafos, Shabbos*, 33b, *Huchi garis Rabbeinu Tam,* citing *Moed Katan*, chap. 1, *Mashkin Beis Hashlachin,* pg. 9a).

As such, it would be safe to assume that Yehudah ben Geirim felt horrible when the nature of their conversation leaked out to the local authorities because he caused his *Rebbe* such anguish.

Besides, didn't Rabbi Shimon believe the accepted Jewish philosophy that states, "This too is for the best" (*Ta'anis*, chap. 3, *Seder Ta'anios Eilu*, pg. 21a)? After all, Rabbi Shimon's experience in the cave certainly helped him reach the exalted spiritual level for which he is so famous (see the poem *Bar Yochai,* second stanza).

So the question stands: why did Rabbi Shimon treat Yehudah ben Geirim so harshly? On the contrary, Rabbi Shimon should have thanked him.

There are deep *Kabbalistic* dimensions going on here behind the scenes that will shed light on the inner mechanics that transpired historically. Mystical sources reveal that Rabbi Shimon Bar Yochai was a *gilgul* (reincarnation) of Moshe Rabbeinu, whereas Yehudah ben Geirim was a *gilgul* of the Egyptian that Moshe killed (*Shemos* 2:12).

Just as Moshe killed the Egyptian, history repeated itself and Rabbi Shimon Bar Yochai killed Yehudah ben Geirim. We can see clear hints that Rabbi Shimon was a *gilgul* of Moshe.

First of all, just like Moshe wrote the "Five Books" of the Torah, so did Rabbi Shimon write five chapters to his work "*Sifra D'tzniusah*," so that they would correspond to the Five Books of Moses. Moshe and Rabbi Shimon also led parallel lives.

Moshe had to flee from Pharaoh (*Shemos* 2:15), and Rabbi Shimon had to flee from the Caesar. After Moshe fled from Pharaoh he reached a spiritual level of completion at the Burning Bush (*Shemos* 3:2). Similarly, after running away from the Caesar, Rabbi Shimon obtained a spiritual level of completion in the cave.

Moshe had to run from Pharaoh because certain people misused their speech and snitched on Moshe to the Egyptian authorities, saying that Moshe had slain an Egyptian (*Shemos* 2:14-15, *Shemos Rabbah* 1:31). Similarly, Rabbi Shimon had to run from the Caesar because somebody was not careful with his speech, which led to the Roman authorities' becoming aware that Rabbi Shimon had criticized them.

(See *Seder HaDoros, Cheilek Tannaim* and *Amoraim*, #10, *Eirech Yehudah ben Geirim*, citing the *Navlos Chochmah*, chap. 4, pg. 154b; And see Arizal in *Likutei Shas* on *Maseches Shabbos*.)

The *Arizal* (in *Sha'ar HaPesukim, Parshas Bereishis, Drush Daled*, and in *Parshas Shemos*, the opening words "*Vayehi ba'yamim*") traces Moshe's and the Egyptian's ancestry further back. He says that Moshe was a *gilgul* of

Hevel (Abel), and that the Egyptian was a *gilgul* of Kayin (Cain).

Since Kayin murdered Hevel (*Bereishis* 4:8), God orchestrated that Moshe, alias Hevel, would kill the Egyptian, alias Kayin. Nobody walks! What comes around, goes around.

In fact, when Moshe (Hevel) saw the Egyptian, he realized that the Egyptian's soul was that of Kayin, his brother. He saw that his brother's soul was so damaged that it was not able to enter Paradise. Therefore, Moshe had to kill the Egyptian as a form of retribution, so that Kayin's soul could be fixed and enter Heaven.

Generations later, Rabbi Shimon (alias Moshe, alias Hevel) saw that Yehudah ben Geirim (alias the Egyptian, alias Kayin) was not completely fixed. Rabbi Shimon tried first to mend his soul through Torah study.

However, when Yehudah ben Geirim caused such a terrible chain of events to occur, culminating in Rabbi Shimon having to flee for his life, cooped up in a prison-like cave for thirteen years, he realized that the spiritual filth of the Egyptian and of Kayin still clung to this soul.

The only way to finally mend the situation was to kill Yehudah ben Geirim. These two killings did not come from a place of anger or revenge, but rather from compassion. It was to ensure Kayin's soul's eternal rest.

Rabbi Shimon was not being too harsh with Yehudah ben Geirim. Rabbi Shimon also believed in the tenet of Jewish philosophy that states that everything is for the best. Nevertheless, Rabbi Shimon did what he had to do for Yehudah ben Geirim's own good.

This is why they (Moshe and Rabbi Shimon) used the Name of God, and not a sword, to kill him. When the Name of God is used, it connects the soul to the side of sanctity and repairs it. (See *Shemos* 2:13-14 and *Shemos Rabbah* 1:30. Also see *Megaleh Amukos Va'eschanan* 195 citing *Arizal* in *Sefer HaKavanos* and in *Pri Etz Chaim, Sha'ar Krias HaTorah*, chap. 5. Also see *Zohar, Parshas Balak*, pg. 194b.)

We learn an important lesson from this whole story. We are beginning to understand the power of Rabbi Shimon Bar Yochai and his teachings. To boil it down to one word, Rabbi Shimon Bar Yochai's wisdom is all about "sifting" - meaning, to sift out the negative aspects of life; so much so, that we are only left with the positive points.

Just like Rabbi Shimon sifted out the filthy components of Kayin's soul, so do Rabbi Shimon's teachings help us remove any negative aspects of our personalities. Just as Rabbi Shimon worked on Kayin's soul until there was only good left, so his teachings also do that for our souls.

This is actually one of the foundations upon which *Chassidus* was built (see *Me'iras Einayim*, preface to the *Ba'al Shem Tov Al HaTorah*, paragraph #59).

Back in Paradise, Adam and Eve originally lived under the energy of the Tree of Life, which is completely good. Once they chose to partake of the Tree of Knowledge, they altered the picture. Now all of mankind would dwell under its shade, which is a mixture of good and evil.

This means that the world we know is never perfect; rather, it is always a mixed bag of good and evil. The job of every one of us is to sift out the bad, and collect the good, to the point that there is no bad left. Then, we will find ourselves living under the energy of the Tree of Life once again. Then we will be coming full circle.

Rabbi Shimon's teachings help us achieve this goal. These lessons can be found in the *Zohar*. Often, people shy away from this type of study. They quote the *Rema* in the *Shulchan Aruch* (*Yorah Deah, Hilchos Talmud Torah*, 246:4) that says that a person must fill his stomach with *Shas* and *Poskim* (the entire Talmud with its Halachic authorities) before entering the study of *Kabbalah*.

They also cite the *Shach* there (*Se'if Katan* 6) that adds another criterion of being at least forty years old. This is based on a statement by Rebbi Yehudah Ben Teimah that says that a forty-year-old attains the level of *binah*, understanding. (See *Avos*, Ch. 5, *Ba'asarah Ma'amaros*, Mishnah 21.)

However, in *Sefer HaHakdamos* (*Hakdamah L'Talmud Eser Sefiros*, paragraph 30) he explains that all those conditions for the study of *Kabbalah* only apply for the material that needs to be transmitted by a Kabbalist orally, which reveals what is found between the lines.

However, anything already in print, and accessible to all, is permitted to be learned even by the layman. Even in the simplistic understanding of the *Zohar* one can find the way to lead life as a dedicated Jew, no matter where one finds oneself.

Rabbi Shimon's teachings will guide us in how to focus on each other's good points, learn from them, and cultivate them into our own systems. This is the cause of the joyous celebrations on *Lag BaOmer*, the day that the *Zohar* was completed.

May we, who are mostly *gilgulim* today, commit ourselves to be students of Rabbi Shimon Bar Yochai and Moshe Rabbeinu, by learning their teachings. Thus, we will merit reaching our ultimate fixing, by sifting out any negative aspects of our personalities, in order that we will be left with a world that is completely good.

Behar - Bechukosai

Rock the Bottom

Once we realize that holiness can permeate into the lowest of things, even dirt, then we will never feel too far from connecting with God.

The portions of *Behar* and *Bechukosai* are often combined as a double *parshah*. The portion begins (25:1) with the words "and God spoke to Moshe at Mt. Sinai saying…" In the second verse, it says, "Speak to the Jewish people and say to them: When you come into the land that I give to you, the land will keep a Sabbath to God."

Rashi (25:1) asks one of the most famous questions in the entire *Chumash*, "What is the matter of the Sabbatical year doing near Mt. Sinai?" (Meaning, why did the Torah have to stress that God taught Moshe the *mitzvah* of the Sabbatical year at Mt. Sinai?) *Rashi* continues to ask, weren't all the commandments given to Moshe at Mt. Sinai? In other words, why was it necessary for the Torah to state the obvious?

Rashi's first approach is known. Let's turn to *Rashi's* second interpretation. He says that we do not find *Shemittah* (Sabbatical year) repeated when the Jews were in the plains of Moav in the book of *Devarim;* meaning that other commandments were repeated when the Jews were in the plains of Moav, because in their repetition, more details of all those laws were added.

The following question arises: if the *mitzvah* of *Shemittah* was not repeated in *Devarim*, from where are we to learn all of the added details? *Rashi* says that this comes to teach us that all of the principles and details regarding *Shemittah* were taught at Sinai and therefore, there was no need to repeat this *mitzvah* in the book of *Devarim*. Moreover, once the *mitzvah* of *Shemittah* has been singled out, it serves as an example for all the other commandments. In other words, just as *Shemittah* was given in its entirety at Sinai, so it was with every other commandment, i.e. God taught them to Moshe entirely at Sinai. It's just that other commandments were repeated in the plains of Moav.

The way this *Rashi* concludes begs the obvious question: if indeed other commandments were taught in their entirety to Moshe at Sinai, why is there a need to repeat them in the book of *Devarim*? Besides this difficulty, another question could be asked. What we have just gleaned from *Rashi's* words is that one of the only *mitzvos* that was not repeated in *Devarim* was the *mitzvah* of *Shemittah*. So the question is: Why was it specifically the *mitzvah* of *Shemittah* that was left out? Apparently, one could argue just the opposite.

The Jews were standing in the plains of Moav, just about to enter the Promised Land. If there is one type of *mitzvah* that we would think needs to be repeated, it would be the Sabbatical year *mitzvah* because this *mitzvah* is dependant on the Land of Israel, and the Jews will need to implement this *mitzvah* immediately. So, when you think about it, that would be one of the only *mitzvos* necessary to repeat in *Devarim* as a way of refreshing their memories and preparing them to do this *mitzvah* as soon as they enter the Land.

Let us begin by mentioning that there are four basic elements. They are (in descending order): fire, wind, water, and earth (see *Rambam Yesodei Ha'Torah* 4:1). The *Arizal* says that these four elements correspond to the four letters in God's Tetragammaton name: *yud, hey, vav, hey*. This means that fire corresponds to the *yud*, wind to the first *hey*, water to the *vav*, and earth to the last *hey*.

The *Emunas Itecha* points out that the element of earth is the lowest of the four, and yet, we find a verse in this week's portion that says "When you come into the Land, the Land will keep a Sabbath to God" (*Behar* 25:2).

This verse is teaching us that the sanctity of Shabbos (which is one of the greatest types of holiness that we have) descends and is infused into the earth itself, the lowest of the elements. In other words, the highest of the high is being infused into the lowest of the low, to the point where the sanctity of Shabbos is present in the earth itself.

This will help us understand why other commandments were repeated in *Devarim,* and why it is specifically the *mitzvah* of *Shemittah* that is not repeated. It is because of another teaching from the *Arizal* who says the following. We all know that there are five books of Moses. He says that the last four books of the five correspond to the four letters in God's Tetragammaton name. This means that *Sefer Shemos* is connected to *yud*; the book of *Vayikra* corresponds to the first *hey*; the book of *Bamidbar* corresponds to the *vav*; and the book of *Devarim* is connected to the last *hey*. The book of *Bereishis*, however, is connected to the tip of the *yud*.

Right now, let's focus on the book of *Devarim*. According to the *Arizal* this book corresponds to the last *hey*, the last letter of this name of Hashem. We mentioned a moment ago that the last *hey* is also connected to the element of earth.

When we put all these ideas together, it goes like this - If *Devarim* is connected to the last *hey,* and the last *hey* is connected to earth, this means that *Devarim* is connected to the Earth. And this is why there was a need to repeat all the other commandments in the book of *Devarim*: in order to teach us that the sanctity of all the commandments can even reach "*Devarim*-ness," or Earth-ness, meaning that the sanctity of all the commandments can even reach the lowest of places.

However, the *mitzvah* of *Shemittah* does not have to be repeated in the book of *Devarim* in order to teach this very lesson because the essence of *mitzvas Shemittah* already shows this to us. The composition of *Shemittah* dictates that the highest *kedushah* (holiness) of Shabbos permeates even the lowest of levels.

We, too, can demonstrate that holiness permeates even the lowest level, earth, by doing a *mitzvah* with the Earth. Kicking a rock - which might cause somebody to trip - to the side, where it won't bother anybody, is a *mitzvah* done with the Earth. This brings *kedushah* to the lowest of places.

This teaches us that just like the greatest holiness resides in the lowest of elements, so it is that the greatest of holiness lives within even those who have fallen to the lowest of places. Our souls, which are Divine sparks, are still pure within even those who have drifted to the furthest of places. The only problem is that sometimes we lose sight of this, and then we think that we are so far, when in fact, we are really so close.

When we appreciate this holy spark in others, it will enable us to treat everybody with utmost respect. This will begin the process of bringing the *Moshiach,* when we will witness the Third Temple come down from a fire above to the Earth below, and then we will live in a *Yom Shekulo Shabbos;* or should I say, a *Yom Shekulo Shemittah.*

Bechukosai

Unshackling

Every one of us can climb the spiritual ladder of success. All we need to know is the secret to getting there.

Unfortunately, there are so many tragedies in our broken world. People suffer from so many different kinds of challenges. Many of them are listed in this week's portion, *Bechukosai* (*Vayikra* 26:16-42).

However, there is hope. God promises us, "*Va'eshbor motos ulchem* - And I will break the bars of your yoke" (*Vayikra* 26:13).

The word *ulchem* (your yoke) is spelled with the letter *vav* missing. The *Agra D'Kallah*, cited in the *Lekach VeHalibuv*, explains why. It is because the remaining letters - *ayin, lamed, chaf, mem* - are an acronym for "*ayin, lev, klei [ha]ma'aseh* - the eye, the heart, and the limbs through which we take action." These are key limbs of our bodies. If misused, they can bring us to very low places. (See *Yerushalmi Berachos*, Ch. 1, law 5.)

Being pulled down to low places is also hinted to in the word before *ulchem* in our verse, which is *motos* (bars), and is also spelled with two *vav's* missing.

The missing *vav's* hint at the idea of "missing" or "losing," referring to one who falls to the lowest of places, and misses out on the true meaning of life. *Motos* (bars) can even be translated as "falling down" because it is related to the word *hismotetus*.

When these two words (*motos ulchem*) are put together, they refer, on a deeper level, to a person who falls to low places by misusing their *ayin, lev,* and *klei hama'aseh.*

However, God guarantees us, "*Va'eshbor motos ulchem* - I will break the yoke of misusing the eyes, heart, and other limbs," the parts which can bring us to very low places. God promises to break the vicious cycle of sin. However, there is one condition we must fulfill in order to deserve this guarantee.

The condition is to accept upon ourselves the yoke of Heaven. This means to accept the fact that God is our Sovereign. We must pledge allegiance to God, consenting to the idea that God is our Boss. As such, we commit ourselves to obeying His command.

When we place the yoke of God on ourselves, then we will be relieved of the other yoke (*ulchem*) which pulls us down.

Accepting the yoke of Heaven is the basic idea behind the recitation of the *Shema Yisrael* (Hear O' Israel) every single day. As a matter of fact, when you take the numerical value of "*Va'eshbor motos ulchem*," it equals 1,118. This is the same numerical value as the verse, "*Shema Yisrael Hashem Elokeinu Hashem Echad* - Hear O' Israel, the Lord our God, the Lord is One."

This numerical equivalency teaches us that we will benefit from God's breaking the yokes that pull us down, but only in the merit of living up to the "*Shema Yisrael* expectation," which is to accept God's authority upon ourselves.

However, what does it mean to accept the yoke of God? Here is one good example. Each and every one of us is made up of two components: the body and the soul. Sometimes there is tension between the two. When we prioritize the needs of the soul over the needs of the body, then we are accepting God's authority.

Let us be clear. We must take care of our bodies. It is forbidden to harm our bodies. That is why we may not smoke, drink alcohol excessively, or take illegal drugs. It is extremely important to eat healthy and exercise.

However, catering to the needs of the soul is even more important, for it determines our eternity. So, when the body tugs at us to go in one direction, and the soul yanks us in the other, we must be vigilant and choose the way of the soul - the meaningful activity over the temporary lustful pleasure.

We have to ask ourselves: what are our values? Are we going to live a soul-based life or a body-based life? The choice is ours.

But, what gives us the power to lead a life where the soul is foremost, as opposed to an existence where the body is in charge? One answer is: to be involved in the study of Torah. Torah study is one of the greatest vehicles that gives us the strength to overcome temptation. Through Torah study we can climb the spiritual mountain of success.

Speaking of mountains, often, the portions of *Behar* (mountain) and *Bechukosai* are read together as a double portion. Perhaps we could suggest one reason for this.

Behar (by a mountain) represents one who wants to climb the spiritual mountain of success (see *Tehillim* 24:3). One may ask, "How can I ascend such a high peak?" The answer can be found in the next portion, *Bechukosai*, which begins, "If you will walk in My statutes" (*Vayikra* 26:2).

Rashi cites a *Toras Kohanim* which explains that this refers to toiling in the study of Torah. A solid Torah education is the key to spiritual success and to Jewish continuity. Moreover, Torah study is even hinted to in the portion of *Behar* itself.

Behar is "by a mountain." But which specific mountain is it referring to? The answer is Mount Sinai (*Vayikra* 25:1), the mountain upon which God chose to give the Torah. This, too, points at Torah study as the crucial component necessary for spiritual growth.

It is so comforting to know that there is a practical way of developing ourselves within our reach, and that is through Torah study. Through the study of Torah we can channel our bodies to serve our souls, and thereby sanctify the body itself. We can then break the yoke of misconduct and instead obtain great spiritual achievements.

May we all be blessed to commit ourselves to Torah study, which will break the yoke of slavery (to desire), and transform our physical bodies into spiritual entities. Then we will be able to enjoy both this world and the next.

Bechukosai - Lag BaOmer - Sefiras HaOmer

Whaddaya Gonna Do About It?

With all of our Torah learning, the only thing that matters is using that knowledge in order to become a *mentch*.

This week's portion begins with those famous words, "If you will follow My decrees and observe My commandments and do them... [then blessings will come]" (*Vayikra* 26:3). *Rashi* (citing *Toras Kohanim* 26:2) on that spot brings down the well-known comment that the meaning behind the words, "If you will follow My decrees" is that we are being commanded to toil in the study of Torah.

There is another Midrash related to this verse which will add an additional dimension to the aforementioned *mitzvah*. Rabbi Yochanan, in the Midrash, said that if a person learns Torah with no intention of carrying it out, then it would have been better for him not to have been born into this world (*Vayikra Rabbah* 35:7).

Upon reading this piece, one begins to wonder at the connection between this type of person and the specific way he is cursed. What does a lack of intention to carry out Torah lessons have to do with not being born into this world?

The Modjitzer Rebbe shares an approach to explain this Midrash based on a different Talmudic passage. The Talmud (*Niddah*, chap. 3, *HaMapeles Chatichah*, pg. 30b, *Rebbi Samlai*) teaches that before a child is born, an angel teaches him the entire Torah while he is still in his mother's womb. Once the child enters the air space of this world, the angel touches him on his mouth and causes him to forget all the Torah that he had been taught.

This passage has perplexed many scholars. Why is it necessary for the child to forget all that Torah knowledge? Wouldn't it be great to have that type of head start before learning Torah in this world? Imagine how much more we would be able to accomplish.

The Modjitzer Rebbe answers that the Torah learned by the child inside his mother's womb is a Torah that cannot come to fruition. As long as the child lives inside of his mother, he can never put the Torah learning into practice. There are no opportunities to do *mitzvos* inside the embryonic sack.

Therefore, the study of Torah there is without intention to act. This is why the child is made to forget all that Torah. It is in order to show us that Torah study without the intention to fulfill what is learned is not called authentic Torah study, and therefore, it is not worth much.

However, once the child is born, we say to him, "Now start learning all over again," because now he is in a world in which the study can be put into action. There are so many opportunities to achieve in this world. This world is a virtual "candy store" of possibilities to do *mitzvos*.

Based on this, the Modjitzer Rebbe answers why it would have been better not to have been born if one never intends on carrying out his Torah learning. It is because this type of learning already took place when the person was in his mother's womb. Therefore, nothing improved when this person was born. He is, in effect, still learning Torah without carrying it out. For that price, he could have remained in his mother's womb.

Now the opening verse of our portion takes on a whole new meaning. It is true that we must "follow God's decrees" by toiling in Torah study. However, the verse goes on to say, "and observe My commandments and do them." The intention here is that it is not enough to learn Torah, but we must study with the commitment to actually fulfill and carry out what the Torah tells us to do.

It is not random that this message is being conveyed to us on the heels of *Lag BaOmer*. On *Lag BaOmer*, Rebbi Shimon Bar Yochai (*Rashb"i*) revealed the hidden teachings of the Torah contained in the *Zohar*. What do all the *Kabbalistic* teachings boil down to? The answer to that secret is as follows.

The *Bnei Yissaschar* (*Iyar*, #3) says that the reason that the *Rashb"i* gave permission to his faithful scribe, Rebbi Aba, to write down the *Zohar* specifically on *Lag BaOmer*, is because there are forty-nine days in the *Omer*. The number forty-nine is the numerical equivalent of the Hebrew words "*lev tov*" (good heart).

The whole point of *Sefiras* (counting) *HaOmer* is to polish our souls with good character traits to the point that they shine like "sapphire" (which also comes from the word *sefirah* when the vowels are changed to spell "sappir," or "sapphire"). All character traits stem from the heart. A bad heart will prevent us from becoming truly refined, whereas a good heart is at the root of all good qualities. This is why a good heart was considered to be the greatest path for a person to choose in his journey towards God (*Avos*, Ch. 2, *Rebbi Omer*, *Mishnah* 9).

Therefore, *Lag BaOmer* was chosen by the *Rashb"i* to be the day that the Torah's secrets should be revealed, because *Lag BaOmer* falls out after thirty-two (*lev* = heart) days. *Lag BaOmer* is also the first day of the seventeen (*tov* = good) days. Since *Lag BaOmer* falls out smack in the middle of *lev* and *tov*, the *Rashb"i* taught us that all the teachings of the *Kabbalah*, which were publicized on that day, were meant to iron out the wrinkles of the heart so that we truly obtain an authentic *lev tov*.

It is only a kind-hearted person who winds up doing for others. This is the connection between *Lag BaOmer* and *Parshas Bechukosai*. The *parshah* teaches us to learn with the intention of doing, and *Lag BaOmer* tells us how to become that type of giving person. The teachings of the *Rashb"i*, that were written down on *Lag BaOmer*, have the power to transform a person's heart into something of beauty.

Maybe over this weekend we could adopt an easy exercise which will help us in further cultivating good hearts. Every day, before learning Torah, say the following prayer (which I found in some Talmudic volumes), which is only one sentence long.

It reads, "Behold, I want to learn in order that the study will bring me to action, and to upright character traits, and to knowledge of Torah, for the sake of the unification of the Holy One Blessed Be He and His Divine presence."

In this way, before we learn, we are making ourselves aware of the purpose of our learning, which is to be endowed with the knowledge of how to improve our character traits, and that will lead us, in turn, to actually do for others as much as we can.

So, this *Lag BaOmer*, may we all be blessed to learn the teachings of the *Rashb"i*, and put that knowledge to good use by mustering up the strength to polish our hearts and personalities, and actually do for others. This will fix the upper worlds and bring eternal peace to Earth.

Behar - Bechukosai

No Pain, No Gain

Perhaps one of the most bitter pills to swallow is the teaching which states, "This too is for the best." How can we live by this adage in the face of pain, suffering, and tragedy?

This week we read the double portion of *Behar-Bechukosai*. Before we begin discussing these portions, and due to the sensitive nature of the material we will address, let me offer a disclaimer: in no way are the ideas presented here intended to belittle the challenges we all struggle with in life. I am fully aware of my own weaknesses and shortcomings in this area and do not claim to have all the answers (or any of them). Essentially, then, I am sending this message to myself, and you are all invited to peek in.

Parshas Bechukosai, the second portion we read this week, contains a series of blessings and curses. Surprisingly, only eleven verses are dedicated to blessings (*Vayikra* 26:3-13), while a full thirty-six verses are dedicated to curses (*Vayikra* 26:14-46). The contrast is striking. Why are there so many more curses than blessings? It almost seems as though Someone is out to get us!

Furthermore, King David writes, "Your staff and Your rod have comforted me" (*Tehillim* 23:4). It seems strange that King David would use this imagery to depict comfort, since staffs and rods are instruments of pain. If King David wanted to use soothing symbolisms, why didn't he write something like, "Pillows and cushions have comforted me?"

The *Chofetz Chaim* cites the Talmud (*Brachos* 5a), in which Rava (in the name of *R' Schora*, in the name of *R' Huna*) explains that Hashem smites His desired ones with pains and difficulties, as the verse says, "The one whom Hashem desires is smitten with illness" (*Yeshaya* 53:10). We also find support for this idea in the verses, "Hashem chastises the one He loves, like a parent who desires the child" (*Mishlei* 3:12); and "Fortunate is the one whom God afflicts with pains and sufferings" (*Tehillim* 94:10).

Based on these verses, we can understand why King David used staffs and rods as examples of comfort. Staffs and rods are instruments of pain - and this is precisely the idea that King David found so comforting! The pain itself is a sign that Hashem loves him. But how is this so? Let us explore this idea with a concrete example.

Imagine walking down the street, and a few yards ahead, a group of children are playing ball. At a certain point, the ball is kicked in the gutter, and a five-year-old boy runs out to retrieve it. He is so focused on the ball that he doesn't look for oncoming traffic, and he dashes into the street directly in front of a car. The driver notices the boy at the last second. He slams on the brakes, and the car comes to a screeching halt, missing the boy by an inch.

Your reaction to this scene, as a pedestrian, would most likely be to hold your breath in horror; and then, when you see that the boy is unharmed, to continue on your way, perhaps shaking your head about the impulsiveness of children. If the boy's mother were witnessing the scene, on the other hand, she would react differently. Initially, she would also hold her breath in horror - but when she would see that her son is unharmed, she would run over to him, drag him off the street, and spank him soundly, all the while yelling that he should never, ever, **ever** do that again.

What's the difference between the pedestrian and the boy's mother? It's simple. The pedestrian doesn't care about the boy as much as his mother does. She loves him so much that she will temporarily inflict pain on him in order to teach him a lesson.

Let us quickly explore five additional points that support the idea that pain indicates Hashem's love for us:

1) The *Ramchal* (*Mesillas Yesharim* 1) states that challenges and difficulties remind us of the transience of this world. When, due to our pain, we realize that life is really about the next world, we can realign our values and live in accordance with what is lasting and true.

2) Rabbi Shimshon Refael Hirsch explains that pain strengthens our moral fiber and molds us. Going through difficult experiences helps us to be sensitive to others' pain and helps us to appreciate the good in our lives. Pain is, therefore, a gift from the One who loves us (as the saying goes: "No pain, no gain"); and crises and problems can be seen as opportunities for growth.

3) Our pain can cause us to cry out to Hashem; thus, we are afforded the opportunity to develop a relationship with our Creator. This is not the same as prayer by rote; it is a much deeper level. Calling out from the depths of our hearts, and initiating a conversation with Hashem in our own language, is a powerful way to build a relationship with Him.

4) The *Rambam* (*Hilchos Ta'aniyos* 1:3) teaches that tragedies strike in order for us to repent and return to Hashem.

5) Pain cleanses us from any sins we may have done in the past.

Of course, despite all the benefits of pain, we must never ask for challenges in this area. But when troubles come on their own, then ironically, our very suffering should bring us happiness and joy. The tractate devoted to the laws of mourning is called "*Maseches Smachos* - Tractate of Happiness" (found at the end of *Avodah Zarah*). On a simple level, we can understand this as meaning that a mourner is not permitted to attend festivities and celebrations. On a deeper level, however, the title indicates that mourning is actually a happy occasion.

This explains why *Parshas Bechukosai* contains more curses than blessings. The curses themselves are a sign that Hashem loves us and wants us to receive all the benefits that come from the difficulties. As the Midrash (*Devarim Rabbah* 1:4) points out, Bilaam ultimately blesses the Jewish people, while Moshe ultimately curses the nation. Why would God orchestrate that our archenemy gives us a blessing and our devoted leader gives us a curse?

God taught us that, deep down, Bilaam doesn't want us to benefit from all the positive opportunities that come with pain. He simply wants to compliment us, to reassure us that everything is okay, so that we will not have the chance to grow beyond our current level. Moshe, on the other hand, who loves us and really cares, doesn't let us off the hook. He chastises us harshly in order to make sure we become the best that we can be.

Hashem loves us even more than Moshe Rabbeinu. Because of this, the curses in *Parshas Bechukosai* are even harsher than the curses that Moshe gives in the Book of *Devarim* (see *Rashi* on *Vayikra* 26:19 in contrast to *Devarim* 28:23). We see this in the most tragic month of the Jewish calendar, which is the month in which both Temples were destroyed and numerous other National tragedies occurred. This month is called "*Av*," which is the Hebrew word for "father." The calamities of *Av* teach us that our Creator loves us deeply, as a parent loves a child. If Hashem didn't care abut us, He wouldn't bother to send us the opportunities of pain.

We can each choose whether or not to implement these ideas in our own lives. If we do, it may help us cope, change our attitudes and better manage our own challenges. We must remember, however, never to lecture other people with this material when they are going through a period of suffering. When others are in pain, our job is simply to be there for them, cry with them, feel their pain, and do whatever we can to provide comfort.

Cultivating this philosophy into our systems can be very difficult. There is one way of improving our attitude in the face of challenges. When something frustrating happens, i.e. getting caught in traffic and missing an appointment, or losing a wallet with a hundred dollars in it, let us make up our minds to say the words, "This too is for the best" (*Ta'anis* 21a, *Nachum Ish Gamzu*), even if we don't feel like it, and even if we may be angry. Then, as time goes on, and we settle down a little bit, we should keep repeating this mantra. Eventually, this will help us to actually live by the standard of *emunah* and *bitachon*. This will also help us react more positively to other aggravating issues that come our way.

May we all be blessed with the strength to face challenges and difficulties with a healthy frame of mind, so that we stretch ourselves to the maximum, and become as close as possible to Hashem, who is loving us every moment. May we thus merit returning to the Promised Land and living a life of Torah, singing with complete happiness, so that when we continue our journey on the other side, all our mistakes will be wiped away.

Sefer Bamidbar

Bamidbar - Shavuos

Souls and Love Letters

There are two types of knowledge; one is acquired by reading books, whereas the other stems from experience with other people. Both types have their merits. A wise man will try to master both.

This week, in addition to beginning a new *parshah*, we also begin a new *sefer*. The portion of *Bamidbar* begins *Sefer Bamidbar*. In this portion, a lot of counting of the Jewish people is going on. As a matter of fact, it says (1:19), "*Ka'asher tzivah Hashem es Moshe vayifkedeim bamidbar Sinai* - as Hashem commanded Moshe, so did he count them in the wilderness of Sinai."

Apparently the ordering of this verse should be the other way around. In other words, first it should have said, "and he counted them in the wilderness of Sinai" and only afterwards should it say, "as Hashem commanded Moshe," because this is the way the Torah speaks regarding all other cases. In other instances, the Torah first tells us what the person did and only afterwards the verse says it was a commandment from God. For example, "And Noach built the Ark just as God commanded him to do" (*Noach* 6:22). So if that is the case, why does the Torah share with us this *mitzvah* of counting the people with the phrases out of order?

The Berditchever Rebbe in his *Kedushas Levi* says: We all know that God gave the Torah to the Jewish people; however, we should be aware of the fact that the souls of the Jewish people comprise the body of Torah. This is explained in the *Zohar* in *Shir HaShirim* (74:4), which says that just as there are 600,000 letters in a Torah scroll, so too, are there 600,000 primary Jewish souls. This is hinted at by our national name *Yisrael*, spelled *yud, shin, reish, aleph, lamed*; which create the acronym for "*Yesh shishim ribui osios laTorah* - there are 600,000 letters in the Torah." If these Torah letters are hinted at in the name of the Jewish nation, it shows that every person in the Jewish nation is connected to a different letter in the Torah.

This is the meaning of the above-mentioned statement that the Jewish people comprise the body of the Torah. Just as we have a Torah scroll that we read from, God also has a Torah scroll that He reads from, so to speak, and that "scroll" is the Jewish people themselves. Therefore, when Moshe counted the Jewish people, what he was doing, on a deeper level, was learning the specific aspect of Torah that is contained within each of those Jewish souls.

The following idea will enhance the depth of the Berdichever Rebbe's words. The portions from a few weeks ago, *Acharei-Mos* and *Kedoshim*, contain an idea that when a person falls in love with the Torah, then the Torah falls in love with that person. That leads the Torah to share her deepest secrets with that person, just like two best friends getting together and sharing their innermost secrets. Similarly, when a person falls in love with the Jewish people, the Jewish people fall in love with that person. Then the Jewish souls begin to share their Torah secrets with that person, because each Jewish soul contains a different portion of its secrets.

There are two different types of Torah secrets:

1) Secrets that stem from the letters.

2) Secrets that stem from the souls.

Once upon a "*parshah*" we mentioned that Aharon and Rebbi Akiva were "people *tzaddikim*," who fell in love with every Jewish soul, and in turn the Jewish souls revealed to them their Torah secrets. Moshe and Ben Azai, however, were "Torah tzaddikim," who fell in love with the Torah that subsequently caused the Torah to fall in love with them, and thus share her deepest secrets with them.

We mentioned that this explained the story in *Menachos* (29b) where Moshe goes up to receive the Torah and finds Hashem drawing lines and crowns on top of the letters. Moshe asks, "What is their purpose?" And Hashem responds, "Many generations from now, Rebbi Akiva will extrapolate piles and piles of Jewish laws from those crowns." Hashem grants Moshe's request to see Rebbi Akiva and his students in action, and enters into their heavenly academy. After taking his seat in the back of the room, Moshe does not understand the give and take between the teacher and his students. Moshe began to feel bad until, in response to one of the student's questions, Rebbi Akiva replied, "That bit of information is a law that was given to Moshe at Sinai." When Moshe heard this, he felt better.

Moshe first felt badly because he thought something was wrong with him. Why couldn't he understand the Torah's discourse? Only after Rebbi Akiva answered his student in such a way, did Moshe understand what was going on. Moshe realized that his type of Torah understanding stemmed from the letters of the Torah, whereas Rebbi Akiva's Torah understanding stemmed from the souls of the Jewish people. And these two understandings are two completely different frequencies. So Moshe, who represents the "Letters Understanding," stepped into an academy that had a completely different school of thought, stemming from the souls of the Jewish people. That was why Moshe was not familiar with it.

The reverse is also true, because the moment Rebbi Akiva had to quote a Torah idea that stemmed from the letters, and one of the students stopped him on that point, Rebbi Akiva waved the white flag and surrendered, saying, "I don't know, it is a law that was given to Moshe at Sinai." Since Rebbi Akiva represented the understanding that stemmed from the souls of the Jewish people, he didn't understand the Torah secrets stemming from the letters. In as much as Moshe couldn't understand Rebbi Akiva, Rebbi Akiva couldn't understand Moshe either. Moshe felt better when he realized there was nothing wrong with him, per se; it was just that they represented two different approaches.

Now we can get back to the words of the *Kedushas Levi*, which explains why the verse with which we began is apparently out of order. The first half of the verse says that Hashem commanded Moshe. The Berditchever Rebbe explains what exactly it was that God commanded Moshe. He says that Hashem told Moshe that it was time for him to master all of the Torah's secrets - not just those rooted in the letters, but also those rooted in the Jewish souls.

This commandment appears in this week's portion, and takes place after the story with Moshe Rabbeinu and Rebbi Akiva. When Moshe came down from the mountain, he had only mastered the Torah secrets that stemmed from the letters. Now, in the first half of the verse, Hashem commands Moshe to become the master of both parts of Torah understanding. This is why the second half of the verse continues to say, "and so Moshe counted them in the wilderness of Sinai." This was God's way of getting Moshe to become the master of the other set of the Torah's secrets as well.

Hashem commanded Moshe to count every Jewish soul. When Moshe comes into contact with every *Yiddishe neshamah* (Jewish soul), he'll fall in love with it, and in turn, they will fall in love with him. Then they will share their Torah secrets with Moshe as well. This is why the verse is arranged the way it is - precisely to teach us this approach.

May we all be blessed to love the Torah and the Jews, and grow deeper and higher, and become privy to empowering, motivating, and inspirational Torah ideas. Then, next week on Shavuos, when we all say "*Na'aseh v'nishma*" again, we will accept upon ourselves the entirety of Torah, which includes both schools of thought and both approaches.

Perhaps the word *na'aseh* (to do) represents the approach of loving the people to the point that we actually get up and do good things for others; whereas, the word *nishma* (we will listen) refers to the second approach, signifying a love for Torah whereupon we open ourselves up and listen to what the Torah is trying to tell us.

One way to become an active member of both types of Torah would be to learn regularly from a *sefer* that discusses ways of improving in *mitzvos bein adam lachavero*. Then we can carry out what we have learned by doing *chessed*. By learning from the *sefer*, we are tapping into the letters. By doing the *chessed*, we are tapping into the Jewish souls. We will develop a greater love for them, and they will reciprocate, and love us back.

Shavuos

Compartmentalize

There is a time and place for everything. This proverb indicates that everything must have its place. After all, when our stuff is organized, we can think more clearly and accomplish much more.

The portion of *Bamidbar* coincides every single year with the Shabbos preceding Shavuos. Based on the teaching that the Shabbos prior to a holiday prepares us for that holiday, there is a lesson to be gleaned this weekend which will get us ready for Shavuos.

One of the practical keys to success in our Torah study is to be organized. When our belongings are in order, we can think clearly as well.

This, said Rav Aharon Kotler, *zt"l*, is one reason why the portion of *Bamidbar* falls out on the Shabbos preceding Shavuos. It is because in *Bamidbar* we discuss the Jews' encampment around the Sanctuary (*Bamidbar* 2:2-32).

The Jews were situated in a very orderly formation. Everybody had their place. Therefore, it is very fitting to read about this right before receiving the Torah on Shavuos. First, *Bamidbar* teaches us about order. Then we can go into Shavuos to receive the Torah, and excel in it by categorizing the concepts in an orderly fashion.

The idea of categorizing could explain one reason why *Megillas Rus* is read on Shavuos (*Maseches Sofrim* 14:8). In order to understand this, let us share some more information about the reading of *Rus*.

Ultimately, we want to read a section from every aspect of Tanach on Shavuos. With *Krias HaTorah* (*Shemos* chapters 19-21), we will have read from Torah. With the *haftarah* (*Yechezkel* chap. 1), we will have read from the *Neviim* (Prophets). With *Megillas Rus*, we will have read from the *Kesuvim* (Writings). (See *Bava Basra*, chap. 1, *HaShutfin*, pg. 14b; *Otzar HaMinhagim*.)

On the day that we receive the Torah, we want a taste of each component of that Torah. However, we could add another reason for touching upon each section of Tanach on Shavuos.

It is in order that we understand which commandments come from the Torah, which ones come from the Prophets, and which ones come from the Writings. Jewish Law is sometimes decided upon based on its source.

Whether we go with a stringent or lenient view may depend on whether it is a Biblical law or a law instituted by the Prophets. This shows us the importance of categorizing things in their proper places. This requires organizational skills. Similarly, it is paramount to know what comes from the Oral Tradition. This serves as yet another reason for reading *Megillas Rus* on Shavuos (*Zichron Devarim* and the *Chiddushei HaRim*).

The entire ruling regarding the permissibility of Boaz marrying Rus is dependent on the Oral Tradition. Although it says in the Torah that one may not marry the people from Ammon and Moav (*Devarim* 23:4), Boaz was allowed to marry Rus (who came from Moav) because the Oral Tradition teaches that this restriction applies only to the Moabite men, but not to their women (*Yevamos*, chap. 7, *Almanah L'Kohen Gadol*, pg. 69a).

Once again we see the importance of categorizing the laws properly, which makes it possible to apply them appropriately. This can be achieved only if we make sense of the commandments by placing them in their proper places.

A great Rabbi once came to see how his son was doing in *yeshivah* (academy). The Rabbi did not go to see how his son was behaving in the study hall; rather, the Rabbi went to his son's dormitory room. When the

Rabbi saw that his son's bed was made and that his shoes were arranged neatly underneath it, he said that he was certain that his son was growing properly in his Torah studies as well.

This is a practical way to prepare ourselves for Shavuos. Being a little bit more neat and organized, in a balanced way, is something we can implement because it is within our reach.

So let's try to be a bit more organized with our belongings by straightening up and having a place for everything, as this will help us be organized in our Torah learning as well.

May we all be blessed to add a little bit more structure to our lives, and thus grow even more in our Torah studies, so that we can fulfill God's Will properly.

Bamidbar - Shavuos

The Torah Center

A successful relationship is when each party takes himself out of the center, and focuses on the other.

Although we begin the *Sefer Bamidbar* this week, we will, take some time now to focus on the upcoming holiday of Shavuos.

The Talmud (*Shabbos* 88a, in name of *R' Simoi*) states that when the Jewish people received the Torah and said "*naaseh*" - "we will do" before "*nishma*" - "we will hear" (*Shemos* 24:7), sixty myriad ministering angels approached every Jew and tied two spiritual crowns to his head - one for *naaseh* and one for *nishma*.

The *Nesivos Shalom* notes the greatness of saying *naaseh* before *nishma*. When the Jewish people stated their unconditional desire to do the will of God (*naaseh*) even before hearing or understanding it (*nishma*), they reached the level of *hisbatlus* (self-nullification). In other words, they took themselves out of the center and focused exclusively on Hashem's Will, regardless of their own feelings or desires. They were prepared to do whatever Hashem commanded, simply because He commanded them.

Self-nullification is not the final goal, however. *Hisbatlus* leads to a higher level: *d'veikus* (clinging and attaching oneself to Hashem). We see an example of this in the verse where Moshe tells the Jewish people, "I am standing between Hashem and you" (*Devarim* 5:5). The simple meaning of this verse is that Moshe is the intermediary between God and the people. On a deeper level, however, the *Ba'al Shem Tov* explains this verse to mean that the primary barrier standing between us and Hashem is the "I" - the very concept of an independent self. We cannot develop a close relationship with our Creator if our ego is in the way.

The final step in the process that begins with *hisbatlus* and continues with *d'veikus,* is the acquisition of *nitzchiyus* (eternity). When we are attached to Hashem, the source of eternity, we assume the same status. This is why the Jewish people are the eternal people. Our statement of *"na'aseh v'nishma"* demonstrated our unconditional commitment to fulfilling the will of God and indicated that Hashem's desires were more important to us than our own. This level of *hisbatlus* led us to a profound attachment to Hashem (*d'veikus*), which in turn gave us the key to eternity.

On the night of Shavuos, when the energy of *Matan Torah* enters the world once again, every Jew should strive to tap into this idea. At some point during the night, try saying out loud to yourself, *"na'aseh v'nishma,"* and visualize connecting to the source of life and eternity.

May we be blessed to listen to the will of Hashem, and fulfill it unconditionally, by taking ourselves out of the center and instead focusing on Him. In this way, may we become inseparable from the Source of good, and thus live forever.

Shavuos

Want a Light?

Although our goal is the final product, we are aware that there are necessary steps that we must take before enjoying the benefits of what we want to produce. Without the preparation, there will be no final product. However, investment without profit is also worth very little.

Since the holiday of Shavuos is approaching, we will focus on this festival instead of the portion of *Bamidbar* in this piece.

The Slonimer Rebbe (vol. 2, *ma'amar* 3 on Shavuos, citing the *Yesod HaAvodah*) quotes a verse in *Mishlei* (6:23), "*Ki ner mitzvah v'Torah ohr* - For a commandment is a lamp, and Torah is light," and comments that this *pasuk*, which compares a *mitzvah* to a candle, and the Torah to light, hints at the two elements which are vital for the path to holiness:

1) *Ohr* - light

2) *Kli* - a vessel

He explains: if there is a vessel but no light, then the primary ingredient is lacking. However, the reverse scenario is also problematic, as there can be no light without the appropriate vessel to contain it. This concept can be illustrated by the following: if a person wishes to make a bonfire, he needs sticks as well as a flame. If he has a pile of sticks (the *kli*) but lacks the flame (the *ohr*), then the main component is absent. However, the sticks are also essential, because it is impossible to create and maintain the fire without them.

The sticks in this allegory correspond to the *keilim* (vessels), which represent the *mitzvos*. The fire, corresponding to the *ohr* (light), represents the Torah.

Now we can explain the verse in *Mishlei* from a new perspective:

> "*Ki ner mitzvah v'Torah ohr*"

The Torah is the *ohr* - the light or flame of Hashem - while the practical *mitzvos*, represented by the candle, are the vessels that contain the light of Torah. Both the Torah and *mitzvos* are crucial in the service of God. If we perform the commandments but do not study the Torah, then we are missing the fundamental point! If, in the opposite case, we study the Torah but fail to execute God's commandments, we will be incapable of receiving and preserving the light of Torah due to the absence of vessels.

This concept clarifies why the Jewish people at Sinai proclaimed first that they will do God's Will, before hearing or understanding (*na'aseh v'nishma*), when it would seem more logical to hear Hashem's word before pledging to implement it.

The Slonimer Rebbe explains that with the word *na'aseh* (which means "we will make" as well as "we will do"), *Bnei Yisrael* declared that they would prepare a *kli* by carrying out the *mitzvos* - in order to be able to *nishma*, understand and appreciate the Torah, the light of Hashem. The commandments serve as a means to receive and retain the light of Torah.

This idea enables us to answer a common question concerning the name of the holiday. The Torah refers to this festival as Shavuos (see *Devarim* 16:10). The root of this word is *shevuah*. Although one definition of this word is "week," an alternative translation is "an oath" reflecting *Bnei Yisrael's* vow to accept the Torah. Why is the holiday referred to as "Shavuos" in the plural if only one oath was taken?

Based on the Slonimer Rebbe's insight, we could suggest that on Shavuos we made two oaths: one to accept the *ohr*, the light of Torah, and the other to perform the *mitzvos*, which are the *keilim*.

The Slonimer Rebbe continues: this explains why at the time that the Jewish people declared *"na'aseh v'nishma,"* 600,000 angels descended and tied two spiritual crowns onto every individual Jew (Rabbi Simoi in *Gemara Shabbos* 88a). *Bnei Yisrael* received one crown for *na'aseh* - for preparing the *keilim* by accepting the *mitzvos*; and the other crown for *nishma* - for acquiring the Divine light by accepting the Torah.

We could suggest that even the shape of a crown hints at this idea, since a crown bears resemblance to a vessel. Thus, we received a crown in the shape of a *kli* for accepting the *mitzvos*, which are the *keilim*! The crown we received for accepting the Torah was to teach us that the light of Torah can be acquired and maintained only if it is contained in the *kli* - i.e. through the performance of *mitzvos*.

The Berdichever Rebbe, in his monumental *Kedushas Levi* (under the section *Shavuos*), highlights the importance of the *kli*. He warns: When we feel inspired and are spiritually aroused with an intense love for God, we must involve ourselves in the performance of a *mitzvah* immediately, in order to ensure that the spark of inspiration is contained and concretized appropriately. If we do not involve ourselves in a *mitzvah*, we risk losing the flash of inspiration as quickly as it came. Thus, the *mitzvos* function as *keilim* to actualize and preserve the light of the Divine.

This year we should take out a moment on Shavuos and say the words *"na'aseh v'nishma,"* with the understanding that we are accepting upon ourselves the responsibility of doing *mitzvos* and studying Torah.

Here is a practical application of this idea. We could accept upon ourselves on Shavuos to learn five more minutes of Torah a day (maybe right before going to sleep). However, right before the Torah session, let us also accept upon ourselves a *mitzvah*. For example, give a coin or two to *tzeddakah*. That will create the *kli*. Then sit down to learn. That will create the flame of light. Together the warm glow of *mitzvos* and Torah will permeate ourselves and our homes.

May we be blessed with holy vessels so that we can receive the Torah, flaring up our candles with the greatest light. May we hear and do the will of God with all of the commandments, and subsequently live to see the day when we will once again wear our spiritual crowns atop our bodies, which will have become the holiest of *keilim*.

Naso

Every Jew Counts

Imagine how differently we would treat each other if we were able to see the other person's greatness and uniqueness. Think about how we would act towards people if we actually got a chance to see their souls. This vision is accessible to each and every one of us, as we are about to see.

This week's portion, *Naso*, shares a commonality with last week's portion, *Bamidbar*. In both portions, the Jewish people are counted (*Bamidbar* 1:2, 4:22). The question is often asked, "Why were the Jews counted in the Torah so many times?"

Each tribe of Israel had it's own flag, emblem, color, and even it's own stone on the Breastplate of Justice (*Bamidbar Rabba* 2:7). This comes to teach us that each tribe had their own function and mission to carry out.

For example, some tribes were more involved with the military, while other tribes were busier with finances, and yet other tribes were meant to be dedicated to the study of Torah or to the service in the Temple.

These different approaches in serving Hashem do not just apply to us on the tribal level, but they also relate to us on an individual level.

Each and every person has a purpose and a mission to carry out in this world. Each human being is unique, with special qualities that only he can utilize for the service of God. Every single soul can impact this world and humanity in a specific way that nobody else can mimic.

This is why the Torah counts every single Jew: It is to teach us that every single Jew counts! Without each Jewish person's participation in service of God, we would all be incomplete. This lesson is especially relevant at this time of year.

Often *Parshas Naso* follows Shavuos, which represents the Jewish people receiving the Torah. The Torah that we accepted contains 600,000 letters (*Zohar Chadash, Shir Hashirim*, 74:4).

Those 600,000 letters correspond to the 600,000 primary, or root, Jewish souls. This is hinted to in our national Jewish name, *Yisrael*, spelled with five Hebrew letters: *yud, shin, reish, aleph*, and *lamed*.

These five letters create an acronym for the following five Hebrew words: "*Yesh shishim ribui osios laTorah* - There are 600,000 letters to the Torah." If this idea is coded into our national name, it comes to teach us that every single *Yisrael*, Jew, is connected to a different letter and that every single Torah letter represents a different Jew (*Megaleh Amukos, Va'eschanan*, #186).

This concept begs us to treat every single Jew with the same respect with which we treat each and every letter. Just as we hold every single letter in reverence and try to delve into its message, so too, must we have that same attitude towards every single Jew.

We should try to learn from each and every person's positive points. They are lessons of life. No two letters are the same. Even two letter "*yuds*" are different. Although they look alike, since they are found in different contexts, they carry different messages.

Just like no two "*yuds*" are alike, similarly, no two "*Yids*" (Jews) are alike. They may be identical twins, but each one still has an individual message that he or she brings to the table. No two people are the same. Each one is special, carrying a distinct lesson to be learned.

This is part of accepting the Torah. It is not just accepting our Torah that we received at Sinai, but accepting God's Torah as well. If our Torah contains 600,000 letters, then God's Torah also contains the same amount of letters, because God's "Torah" is the Jewish people themselves (*Emunas Itecha*).

After all, the 600,000 Jewish souls are linked to the 600,000 letters. As such, each Jewish soul is like a Torah letter, making up God's Torah Scroll. To accept the Torah completely means to accept both Torahs, ours and God's.

When we see the beauty in every person, as much as we see it in each letter, then we can be assured that we have truly accepted the Torah in totality.

May we holy letters be blessed to lead a healthy life in which we learn from everybody with which we come into contact by focusing on their positive aspects. Thus, may we deserve to witness the day when God will proclaim throughout the world, "Who is like My Nation Israel… My beautiful *Sefer Torah!*"

Naso

Ask Not What...

"Ask not what your country can do for you; ask what you can do for your country." For some of us, these words still ring nostalgic in our ears. If only we would ask this question regarding our spouses, we would live much happier and fulfilled lives.

In the portion of *Naso*, it discusses giving *terumah* to a *Kohen*, priest (*Naso* 5:10). The next topic in the portion discusses the scenario of a *Sotah*, a wife that is suspect of being unfaithful (*Naso* 5:12). *Rashi*, on the spot, cites a Talmud (*Berachos* 63a), which explains the juxtaposition between these two adjacent topics. He says that it teaches us that if a person does not go to the priest to bring him his gifts, then God guarantees that he will have to go to the priest with his wife who is suspected of adultery, so the priest can conduct a specific ceremony for her. It almost sounds like the Talmud is saying that if you don't go to the priest for good reasons, then you will be forced to go to the priest for unfortunate reasons.

We could still ask, "What is the deeper relationship between not giving the tithe and the topic of a *Sotah*?" In other words, on a deeper level, why does one cause the other to happen? The *Emunas Itecha* explains that every married couple should have firmly planted in their minds the goal of marriage; and that goal is to be a giver to one's special other. In other words, a spouse should not be thinking, "What's in it for me?" Rather they should be thinking, "How can I help my other?" When they both succeed in keeping this fundamental law, then there will be peace and harmony between them. However, if each one selfishly thinks of him or her self, it will create an atmosphere that is antithetical to peace and harmony.

This idea will help us understand the answer to the aforementioned question. When a person does not give the priestly gifts to the *Kohen*, he demonstrates that his personality is not about giving, but rather about keeping everything for himself. With this insight into his constitution, one can safely assume that this is the way he behaves within his own home. He is constantly thinking about himself, selfishly, without a care as to helping his wife selflessly. Obviously, that environment is not conducive to peace and harmony, and his wife will begin to seek greener pastures for the love that she so much craves.

In view of this lesson, let us change our mindset from: "What can my spouse do for me?" to "What can I do for my spouse?" Asking ourselves this question daily will make a world of difference in the types of lives we experience in our homes. Additionally, it doesn't hurt to leave a love note for each other occasionally.

May we all be blessed to become givers, and thus live to see the day when Hashem (the Husband) is reunited with the Jewish people (the Wife) in the coming of *Moshiach*.

Naso

Blessings That Stand the Test of Time

What is the most important day in our lives? When we answer this question correctly, we will be able to truly appreciate the blessings in our lives.

Every day during the morning service, the *Birkas Kohanim* (Priestly blessings) are said. In *Eretz Yisrael,* the *Kohanim* themselves bless the people, whereas outside the land of Israel, according to *Minhag Ashkenaz,* the one leading the repetition of the *Amidah* (silent prayer) recites the blessings, except for the three festivals and high holidays when the *Kohanim* bless the people themselves.

The source for these blessings is found in this week's Torah portion, *Naso.* There are three verses in all. They are:

1) "May Hashem bless you and safeguard you" (*Bamidbar* 6:24).

2) "May Hashem illuminate His countenance for you and be gracious to you" (*Bamidbar* 6:25).

3) "May Hashem lift His countenance to you and establish peace for you" (*Bamidbar* 6:26).

When the one leading the service recites these blessings, he follows the text of the liturgy which says, "Bless us with the *meshuleshes* (three-fold) blessing." The reason for the word *meshuleshes* seems obvious. After all, there are three verses for the three blessings.

However, on a deeper level, we can understand the word *meshuleshes* differently. This is based on the Name of God which is used in these blessings. That Name of God is known as the "*Shem Havayah* - The Tetragrammaton

Name, spelled *yud, hey, vav, hey*."

Every time we mention the *Shem Havayah,* we are supposed to think about the implication of that Name. The meaning of this Name is that God *Hayah* (was), *Hoveh* (is), *V'yiheyeh* (and will be) (See *Shulchan Aruch, Orach Chaim,* chap. 5).

The *Shevilei Pinchas* explains that when the *Shem Havayah* is used to bless us, the understanding is that the blessings should be truly good for us through and through, spanning all the dimensions of time - past, present and future.

This means to say that when God blesses us, He looks to our past, and even to a previous life, to see whether this particular gift was truly a blessing or not. Take wealth for example. For some people wealth is good (see *Mishlei* 10:22), while for others it is not (see *Koheles* 5:12). Hashem examines our behavior with that wealth in the past.

God also looks to see how we behave currently with our money. And finally God looks to the future as well to see how we will behave.

Rabbeinu Bachyah says that this idea is hinted to in the *Birkas Kohanim* itself. He points out that in the first blessing, there are fifteen Hebrew letters; whereas, in the second blessing there are twenty; and finally, the third blessing has twenty-five letters.

These numbers are not arbitrary. The number fifteen (in the first blessing), is equivalent to the numerical value of God's Name, *Yah,* spelled *yud, hey.* This Name of God is neither in past nor future tense. This means that its referring to the present tense.

The number twenty (in the second blessing) is the same numerical value of the word *Hayah,* "was" (spelled *hey, yud, hey*), referring to the past.

The number twenty-five (in the third blessing) has the same numerical value as the word *Yehi*, "will be" (spelled *yud, hey, yud*), referring to the future.

This comes to teach us that when God blesses us, He takes into consideration our past, present and future to ensure that the blessing is complete, with no negative side effects or destructive outcomes. This is a deeper reason for calling it a *meshuleshes* blessing. Not only does it denote a three-verse blessing, but it also implies a blessing that spans the three dimensions of time: past, present and future.

Rabbeinu Bachyah gives one reason to explain why the present tense is mentioned first (and not the past tense, as it should have been in chronological order). It is to show that, from Hashem's perspective, everything is happening in the present.

Rebbi Nachman of Breslov offers an additional reason as to why the present tense is mentioned first. He explains by first asking a question, "What is the most important day in your life?" Some would say the day of birth, while others would suggest the wedding day, and yet others would argue the day of death.

While these are all great answers, Rebbi Nachman begs to differ. He says that the most important day in your life is today! This is why the present tense is mentioned first.

We could suggest that the second most important time period in a person's life is his past. This is because we learn from our past mistakes and successes as to what works and what does not.

The next most important time period in a person's life is his future. Because only when we presently (today) take our past experiences (of yesterday) and apply them to the future (tomorrow) will we achieve the desired results. Thus, the correct order is present, past, future.

A support for this order is found in our liturgy. For example, every morning during *Pesukei D'zimrah*, in the *Yehi Chevod* paragraph, we say, "God reigns, God has reigned, God will reign for all eternity." This *pasuk* is gleaned from three separate verses (see *Tehillim* 10:16, *Tehillim* 93:1, and *Shemos* 15:18).

The order mentions present first, past second, and future third. One reason for this is to confirm the order of importance.

We all know that God treats us in the way we treat others, so if we want God to bless our lives, we have to try to bring blessing into other people's lives. So during *Birkas Kohanim* let us think of how we can bring blessing into somebody else's life and then do it.

May we all discover how to take advantage of our present, learning from the past and building for the future, so that God blesses us all with a *berachah meshuleshes* spanning all of time.

Naso

God Bless You

When somebody sneezes, we all jump to wish him "God bless you." But we don't have to wait for somebody to sneeze in order to bless him. How sweet it is when we constantly bless each other.

This week's portion, *Naso*, contains the famous "*Birkas Kohanim,*" Priestly Blessings (*Bamidbar* 6:24-26), which are divided into three parts, as follows:

Verse 24: "*Y'varechecha Hashem v'yishmerecha* - May Hashem bless you and safeguard you."

Verse 25: "*Ya'er Hashem panav eilecha vi'chuneka* - May Hashem illuminate His countenance for you and be gracious to you."

Verse 26: "*Yisa Hashem panav eilecha v'yasem lecha shalom* - May Hashem lift His countenance to you and establish peace for you."

The commentaries offer an array of approaches to explain these verses and the lessons contained within them. We will, *B'ezras Hashem*, propose another interpretation, focusing on each *pasuk* separately.

VERSE 24
"*Y'varechecha Hashem v'yishmerecha* - May Hashem bless you and safeguard you."

We could suggest that the three words in this verse correspond to the three Patriarchs, indicating that Hashem will bless us in their merit.

1) "*Y'varechecha*" (He will bless you), corresponds to Avraham Avinu since we find (*Bereishis* 12:2) that God blesses Avraham saying,

"*VaAvarcha mevarechecha* - I will bless those who bless you." Thus, Hashem blesses us in Avraham's merit.

2) "Hashem" correlates with Yitzchak Avinu because Yitzchak was willing to give up his life for God at the *Akeida* - the ultimate expression of *mesiras nefesh*, self-sacrifice. Thus, Hashem blesses us with His presence on account of Yitzchak.

3) "*V'yishmerecha*" (He will safeguard you), corresponds to Yaakov Avinu since Hashem says to Yaakov (*Bereishis* 28:15), "*U'shemarticha bechol asher teileich* - I will guard you wherever you go." So, God provides us with protection in the merit of Yaakov.

VERSE 25

"*Ya'er Hashem panav eilecha vi'chuneka* - May Hashem illuminate His countenance for you and be gracious to you."

This section of *Birkas Kohanim* relates specifically to success in Torah.

Firstly, the word *Ya'er* (He will illuminate), reminds us of the blessing that precedes the *Shema* where we request of God, "*V'ha'er Eineinu B'torasecha* - Enlighten our eyes with Your Torah."

Secondly, this verse (*Vayikra* 6:25) consists of five words which, we could suggest, correspond to the Five Books of Moses:

1) "*Ya'er*" (He will illuminate) correlates with *Sefer Bereishis* since *Bereishis* deals with the creation of the world, and specifically, the formation of light - one of the principal creations. According to the *Kabbalah*, all that existed prior to the world's creation was a supernal, endless light. One of the mystical purposes of Creation was for Hashem to share this light with humanity.

2) "*Hashem*" corresponds to *Sefer Shemos* because God's presence is overtly recognized in the stories recounted in this *sefer* - from the

miracles that He performed in Egypt to the Exodus, crossing of the Sea, revelation at Sinai, etc. Furthermore, the word *Shemos* means "names," alluding to the various Names of Hashem which represent the different ways in which He manifests Himself in this world. For example, Hashem revealed Himself at the parting of the Sea as a mighty warrior; while at Sinai, He was like an old man, full of mercy (See *Rashi* on *Shemos* 20:2, citing the *Mechilta*).

3) "*Panav*" (His face) is associated with *Sefer Vayikra*. *Vayikra* describes the sacrifices that the Jews were obligated to bring for their transgressions. Since the performance of a sin creates spiritual barriers between the offender and God, the sacrifices - which ultimately atone for the person's wrongdoings - help to eliminate the spiritual obstructions. Then, the individual can reestablish his connection with Hashem and experience, once again, a direct relationship with God, i.e. a relationship that is *panim el panim* (face to face).

An example of such a relationship to which we can aspire is found in *Shemos* (33:11) where Hashem speaks to Moshe *panim el panim*. It is also interesting to note that the *keruvim* (cherubs) were fashioned and placed on the Ark of the Sanctuary "with their faces toward one another" (see *Shemos* 25:20), symbolizing God's relationship with the Jewish people. When God was angry with *Bnei Yisrael*, the faces would turn away from one another.

The association between offering sacrifices and getting close to God is highlighted by the *Ramban* (*Vayikra* 1:9), who comments that the root of the word *Korban* (sacrifice) is *Kerav* (spelled *kuf, reish, beis*) which means "to approach" or "draw near." The sacrifices described in *Vayikra* enable us to do *teshuvah* and grow closer to God.

4) "*Eilecha*" (for you) corresponds to *Sefer Bamidbar*, which relates incidents of the Jews' rebellious behavior and the subsequent reprimands

from God. These punishments, however, allowed *Bnei Yisrael* to do teshuvah and develop their relationship with God. Thus, *Bamidbar* represents Israel's return *Eilecha*, to You, i.e. God (See *Eichah* 5:21 where the word *Eilecha* is employed in connection with *teshuvah*: "*Hashiveinu Hashem Eilecha v'nashuvah…* - Bring us back to you, Hashem, and we shall return…").

5) "*Vi'chuneka*" correlates with *Sefer Devarim,* where Moshe reminisces about *Bnei Yisrael*'s journeys and experiences. Moshe's recollection of all of the travels, events and challenges that faced the Jewish people demonstrates his love and God's love for the Nation, as *Rashi* (*Bamidbar* 33:1), citing the *Midrash Tanchumah,* explains.

"[The recalling of the journeys of *Bnei Yisrael*] can be compared to a king who took his ill son to a distant place in order to cure him. On their return, his father began to count all of the journeys, and related to his son the events that occurred in all of the different places. He pointed out where they slept, where they were cold, where his son felt unwell, and so on."

Similarly, the King (God) recalls the journeys with His son (the Israelites) because He loves the Nation. The word *chen*, favor, which is the root of *vi'chuneka*, is therefore associated with the book of *Devarim*, where Moshe recalls *Bnei Yisrael's* travels because they are favored by God and His servant, Moshe.

This idea could explain why *Sefer Devarim* mentions the blessings that were imparted to the Twelve Tribes. The commentators explain that Moshe blessed each of the tribes in order to complete the task of Yaakov Avinu who blessed his sons before he died (see *Ohr Hachaim Hakadosh, Devarim* 33:1). Since God favors His people in *Sefer Devarim*, it is fitting that the continuation of the blessings is included here.

Finally, since *Sefer Vayikra* corresponds to our drawing close to God through the offering of sacrifices, and *Sefer Bamidbar* represents our returning to God through overcoming trials and challenges, it is appropriate that the final book of the Torah is associated with *Bnei Yisrael* reaping the reward of all their efforts and growth by finding favor in God's eyes and receiving blessings.

VERSE 26

"*Yisa Hashem panav eilecha v'yasem lecha shalom* - May Hashem lift His countenance to you and establish peace for you."

Rashi interprets "*Yisa Hashem panav eilecha*" as "May He suppress His anger [against the Jewish people]." In what way does God hold back His anger? How is this achieved?

On *Seder* night we beseech God, "*Shefoch chamascha el hagoyim asher lo yeda'ucha* - Pour out Your wrath on the nations who do not know You*" (*Tehillim* 79:6). In other words, we ask Hashem to kindle His anger against the nations who, because they do not recognize God, are committed to the Jews' annihilation. So, in this section of the Priestly Blessing, where we ask God to "lift His countenance" to us by restraining His anger, we are, in effect, requesting that He protect us from our adversaries.

We find another hint to this idea in the number of words contained in Verse 26. The Nation of Israel is compared to a lamb amongst seventy wolves - the seventy nations of the world. The final part of the Priestly Blessing (Verse 26) contains seven words, representing the seventy nations. (In *gematria katan* - a numerical system where all the zeros are dropped - the number seventy is represented by the number seven.) It is appropriate, then, that the *berachah* concludes by blessing us with peace. We will achieve peace between ourselves and the other nations once we attain and maintain harmony between ourselves and God.

We all want blessings in our lives. One practical way to increase well-being would be to bless at least one person with these verses on Friday night. The custom is to bless our children with these words. In a case where there are no children, bless a relative or friend who is present at the table. In a situation where one is alone, one may lift their hands and send this blessing to anybody one chooses, whenever they may be. In this way, we will also be blessed, because God always blesses those that bless others.

May we be blessed in the merit of our forefathers with success in Torah and a life of tranquility, as is alluded to in the Priestly Blessings, which, ultimately, include all possible blessings.

Beha'alosecha

Just One Mitzvah

At times, tending to all of our responsibilities may overwhelm us - there is so much to do. When we start to feel that way, we should remind ourselves that all we need to do is take the first step and focus on one item. Eventually the rest will follow.

In this week's portion, *Beha'alosecha*, we read the following well-known verses (*Bamidbar* 10:35-36).

"*Vayehi binso'a HaAron vayomer Moshe, kuma Hashem veyafutzu oy'vecha veyanusu mesanecha mipanecha. U'venucho yomar shuvah Hashem rivevos alfei Yisrael* - And it came to pass, when the Ark set forward, that Moshe said, 'Rise up, Lord, and let your enemies be scattered; and let those who hate you flee before you.' And when it rested, he said, 'Return, O Lord, to the myriad thousands of Israel.'"

We find in the Torah scroll that one reversed letter *nun* is inserted immediately preceding Verse 35, and that another follows Verse 36, effectively sandwiching the aforementioned *pesukim* between two, large, backward letter *nuns*.

Rebbe comments (in Shabbos 115b-116a) that these two verses are to be considered a *sefer* (book) within themselves. He brings support for this from Rabbi Shmuel bar Nachmeini who says in the name of Rabbi Yonasan: we learn from *Mishlei* (9:1) that the Torah is composed of seven books, as it says, "*Chatzvah amudeha shivah* - she has hewn out her seven pillars." The seven "pillars," i.e. books of the Written Law, are divided as follows:

1)   *Bereishis*

2)   *Shemos*

3)   *Vayikra*

4)   *Bamidbar* Ch.1, v.1 to Ch.10, v.34

5)   *Bamidbar* Ch.10, vs.35-36 (our two verses)

6)   *Bamidbar* Ch.10, v.37 to the end of that book

7)   *Devarim*

Why did God choose to cordon off Verses 35 and 36 with two letter *nuns*, as opposed to using any other letter? Furthermore, why are the *nuns* written in reverse?

The *Vilna Gaon* (in *Peninim MiShulchan HaGra*, citing the *Matzevet Moshe*) answers these questions, and simultaneously leaves us with a powerful and important message.

The numerical value of the letter *nun* is fifty, representing the fifty levels of *tumah*, impurity, and the fifty levels of *taharah*, purity. Thus, these *pesukim*, which are separated by the letter *nun* teach us that each *sefer*, however small it may be, can raise a person from the depths of impurity; and he may, ultimately, reach the highest level of purity. We could suggest, based on the *Vilna Gaon's* teaching, that the letters are written in reverse to hint to us that we can go back, i.e. return to our original state of pure innocence prior to committing the erroneous actions.

Thus, the *Vilna Gaon* is imparting to us a crucial lesson. Each and every item in the Torah can ultimately bring us to acquire the entire Torah. Sometimes, we become overwhelmed with the vastness of Torah and *mitzvos* to the point that we feel defeated before we have even begun! One possible remedy to this problem, and, indeed, one of the keys to spiritual success, is to concentrate on fulfilling just one *mitzvah* - but this one *mitzvah* must be performed with all of its details and nuances, stringencies and enhancements. In this way we will eventually merit to perform ALL of the commandments.

A basis for this idea is found in the Talmud (*Kiddushin* 39b, Ch.1, *Mishnah* 10) where it says that anyone who performs one *mitzvah* will be rewarded [by Heaven] with goodness, extension of days and inheritance of the Land. Although this guarantee seems to refer to the physical world, Rabbeinu Ovadiah of Bartenura claims that the Talmud is speaking about reward in the World to Come. The *Arizal* says on this Mishnah (in his preface to *Sefer Shàarei HaMitzvos*, Gate 5): Each person should take upon himself one *mitzvah*, and devote ALL of his energy to accomplishing this one commandment.

It is vital to mention at this point that focusing on fulfilling one *mitzvah* does not preclude our obligation to perform all of the other commandments. Similarly, we should not use this approach as an excuse to carry out only one of the commandments! Rather, this specific technique is intended as a tool to help us execute ALL of the *mitzvos* and to acquire the entire Torah.

We can illustrate this idea by comparing the *mitzvos* to the body. As we know, there are 248 limbs and 365 sinews, representing the number of positive and negative commandments, respectively. If a person pulls on someone else's limb, all the other limbs will follow. Just as the organs and limbs of the body are interconnected, so too, are the *mitzvos*. If we concentrate on doing one *mitzvah*, all the other commandments will ensue - as it says in *Avos* 4:2, "*Mitzvah goreres mitzvah* - one *mitzvah* leads to another."

May I take this opportunity to suggest to stop for one moment, close your eyes and think of your favorite *mitzvah* - one commandment that you enjoy doing the most or that you connect with the most - and adopt this *mitzvah* as your "pet mitzvah," i.e. the commandment that you intend to fulfill completely, with all of its details, and perform it with extra care and devotion.

May we be blessed to learn one *sefer*, focus just on one letter, or do only one *mitzvah* - in its entirety - so that we reach the fulfillment of all the *mitzvos* and the fiftieth level of purity.

Beha'alosecha

All Aboard

Why do we live in the places that we do? Why do we often work in locations that are far from our residences? Why do we have urges to vacation in specific spots? The answer to these questions may be deeper than we think.

Let us, once again, focus on two verses from our *parshah* that, perhaps, stand out more than any others: "And it came to pass, when the Ark traveled, that Moshe said, 'Rise up, O Lord, and scatter Your enemies and make flee those that hate You from before You'" (*Bamidbar* 10:35). The next verse goes on to say (10:36), "And when it rested, he said, 'Return, O Lord, to the myriad thousands of Israel.'"

The reason why these two verses stand apart and above all the others is due to the Talmudic passage in *Shabbos* (pages 115b-116a), where the Talmud discusses the reason that these two verses are set apart in a Torah scroll with two upside-down and backwards letter *nuns*. Rebbi says, "It is because these two verses are really considered to be a book unto itself," which is in accordance with the opinion of Rabbi Shmuel bar Nachman, in the name of Rabbi Yonason, who points out that the verse (*Mishlei* 9:1) says, "She has carved out her seven pillars," which is a reference to the seven books in the Torah. According to these opinions there are not just five books of Moses, but rather there are seven.

The way we get to the number seven is as follows: *Bereishis* is the first, *Shemos* is the second, *Vayikra* is the third. But when you get to the book of *Bamidbar*, the first third of the book is from the beginning until the first upside-down and backward *nun*, which is a book unto itself. Then in the second third you get the two verses between the two upside-down and backward *nuns* as its own book. And the final third is from the second upside-down and backward *nun* until the end of the *sefer*, which is also its own book. After we divide the book of *Bamidbar* into three separate books, the total is six books. Then there's *Devarim*, the seventh book.

This information begs the question: how could just two verses be considered a book unto itself? What is the importance of these two verses which give them equal standing to the rest of Moshe's books? The *Ohr HaChaim HaKadosh* in *Parshas Behar* (*Vayikra* 25:39), shares with us the *Kabbalistic* idea that says that there are sparks of holiness that fill our world. Even the furthest and lowest of places contain holy sparks.

One approach is that these holy sparks originate from the first sin of Adam and Chavah, in which their lofty souls "fell," and thus shattered like a broken vase. Another possibility is that they stemmed from Creation itself, when the vessels broke because they could not handle the light. Alternatively, they stemmed from previous worlds that God created and subsequently destroyed (*Zohar*, vol. 1; p. 25), and the good, redeeming qualities of those previous worlds are the leftovers that have been planted into our world. Wherever these sparks come from, they are waiting and yearning to be fixed; and the way to repair them is by going to those places, and engaging there in the study of Torah, prayer, and *mitzvos*.

As a matter of fact, according to the *Kabbalah*, the whole point of exile to begin with is to fix those dispersed sparks. This is the deeper meaning of a passage found in *Pesachim* (87b), which states that "the Jewish people went into exile only in order to gather converts." One cannot learn from this Talmudic passage a literal translation, which is to convert the nations of the world, because the Talmud elsewhere states that we are not supposed to proselytize (*Yevamos* 47b). So "gathering converts" really refers to gathering the sparks and "converting" them from the side of darkness to the side of holiness.

When we serve God in all these different places, these sparks are naturally extracted from the places they currently are; then, they are drawn to us and become part of our souls. Ultimately, we are expected to bring all these lost sparks back to the Holy Land. If the Jewish people would never have sinned, and thereby would never have experienced the Temples' destructions and gone into the exile, then the Jewish people would have merited a very powerful force that would have attracted all the holy sparks throughout the world to *Eretz Yisrael*, our headquarters.

Since, unfortunately, we did stumble in sin, and our Temples were destroyed, our spiritual powers have been weakened, and therefore, we need to go to far-flung places in order to retrieve those holy sparks. When the Jews complete this mission and gather every last spark, then God will bring us all back to *Eretz Yisrael* with the coming of *Moshiach*.

This approach explains the deeper reason for the Jews' spending specifically forty years wandering in the desert. It was in order to gather all the holy sparks found in those places. For example, in this week's portion, it mentions how the Jews would stay in some places just for a month and in others for a few years, and yet in others for just a couple of days (chapter 9:19-23). The *Kabbalistic* reason for this discrepancy is that it depended on how many sparks were found in that place. In some places there were more sparks, which required the Jews to spend a longer allotment of time there to extract them; while in other places there were just a handful of sparks, and a day or two sufficed. So when you add it all up, it took the Jews forty years to extract all the holy sparks that were in the desert.

Based on the *Emunas Itecha*, this approach of the *Ohr HaChaim HaKadosh* addresses our aforementioned question. The importance of these two verses, to the extent that they are considered to be a book unto themselves, is that they teach us what our job is in our travels and, especially, in our exile. These two verses talk about the Ark moving and the Ark resting, in other words, they discuss when the Ark is en route.

Just like the Ark and the Torah remain holy not just when they are stationary, but even when they are traveling; so too, do we need to maintain our levels of spirituality, dedication and devotion to the service of God even when we go on a journey. When we accomplish this, we gather the sparks of holiness. This is the purpose of all travels; this is the purpose of exile as well. The lesson is that wherever we go, we are part of a process in *avodas* Hashem of gathering sparks. This concept is so paramount that it deserved to be a book unto itself.

The *Emunas Itecha* quips, saying that in today's day and age, at this time of year, we seem to have a *minhag* (custom) that during the summer months we begin to travel from place to place. So many of our brothers and sisters are going up to the mountains, the bungalows, or camps, and we think that the reason for these excursions is for R&R (rest and relaxation).

However, the *Ba'al Shem Tov* teaches us that the real reason for our vacations is in order to go to those places and gather those sparks. We don't just gather any sparks; rather, each person's soul is connected to a certain amount of sparks, and only that person can redeem them. And the sparks are waiting there to be elevated with that Jew's Torah study, prayer, and *mitzvah* performance in those places. So the reason that different people go to different places for their vacations is because, deep down, their souls are gravitating to their unique set of sparks.

The message here is that we have to be aware of what the *Yerushalmi* says (*Berachos* 4:4), that "All roads are presumed to be dangerous." This is true, not just physically, but (as we know) spiritually as well; and therefore, we need to be careful when we go on vacation. We must ensure that it is done in the framework of Torah and the spirit of *halachah*, which means we have to prepare for our trips, not just by packing our suitcases, but by setting up fences to safeguard ourselves from falling into a rut where we can become lax in our observance. On the contrary, let us imbue our vacations with holiness by viewing them as fulfilling a Divine mission, which is to gather our sparks of holiness.

May we all be blessed to travel through the journey of life with pride, purity, and sanctity, collecting all the holy sparks, especially at this time of year, so that one day, soon, we will all be gathered into *Eretz Yisrael* once again, where we will reminisce about the successful excursions of our life.

Beha'alosecha

Getting Down to Basics

Sometimes we wonder what the fundamentals of Judaism are. We are about to encounter them right now.

Amongst many topics, this week's portion discusses a number of sins committed by the Jewish people during their stay in the desert. As a matter of fact, a high percentage of *Sefer Bamidbar* is devoted to retelling a whole array of crimes of which the Jews were guilty.

Being that the Torah does not share stories just for the purpose of factual information, we must ponder the eternal relevance these stories carry for us.

Moreover, when analyzing the various offenses, they do not seem so terrible. Yet, the punishment that came down on them was fast and furious. The penalties were so harsh that the people of that generation eventually lost their portion in the World to Come (*Sanhedrin*, chap. 11, *Cheilek*, pg. 110a, the opinion of *Rebbi Akiva*).

It is hard to conceive that they would have been punished so severely for just performing some misdemeanors; and yet, that is precisely what happened. Let's take a look at some of the examples.

The first sin was done by the *misonenim*, complainers. The people complained about how weary they became due to all the *schlepping* around in the desert. God was so angry at them that a fire came out of Heaven and devoured untold numbers of Jewish people (*Bamidbar* 11:1).

This is difficult to understand. What was so bad? We all complain from time to time. Have you ever observed somebody in the rear view mirror of your car during a traffic jam? Have you ever seen somebody miss his flight? It's human to become agitated and whine. Why was the punishment so harsh?

The second sin was committed by the *misavim*, lusters. Instead of being content with the *manna*, they wanted to eat meat (*Bamidbar* 11-33). God was so mad at them that He gave them the meat, from which they subsequently died. While they were chewing, with meat between their teeth, they perished.

Again, we are disturbed. What was so bad? What's wrong with saying to your spouse, "You know what honey, let's go out to eat tonight at this new *fleishig* restaurant." You mean to tell me that if I want to have a barbeque, I deserve to die in a plague? All they wanted was a hamburger. Was that so bad? The punishment does not seem to fit the crime.

One approach in unraveling this mystery is found in the teachings of the Slonimer Rebbe in his monumental *Nesivos Shalom*. He says that a huge lesson can be gleaned from these stories.

We all know that there are 613 *mitzvos* (commandments) in the Torah (*Makkos*, chap. 3, *Eilu hein halokin,* pgs. 23b-24a, the opinion of *Rebbi Samlai* expounding on *Devarim* 33:5). However, we should ask ourselves, "What is the purpose of it all? In the big picture, what does God want from us with all of these *mitzvos*?"

The Slonimer Rebbe says that the point of it all is to achieve *d'veikus*, closeness, to God (see *Devarim* 10:20). In other words, God wants to be close to us. It's all about relationships. Therefore, do not look at the 613 as *mitzvos*; rather, view them as *eitzos*, pieces of advice. God gave us 613 pieces of advice on how to achieve *d'veikus*. The 613 are different methods and channels through which we can get close to God. The 248 positive *mitzvos* bring us close to God, whereas the 365 negative *mitzvos* prevent us from drifting far from God.

It would reason that anything which creates the most distance between us and God would be deemed the worst possible sin, because it is diametrically opposed to the whole thrust of Torah, which is to achieve *d'veikus*.

The Slonimer Rebbe teaches that when you boil it down, there are two areas upon which Judaism is built. They are *emunah* (faith), and *kedushah* (holiness). When we live by them, we become the closest we can possibly be to God. When we lack them, we drift the furthest we can from God.

Emunah means to live with God in every facet of life. It means that we realize that God is with us constantly. It means that we understand that God is in control, and everything that happens is for a purpose, and that purpose is good. A lack of *emunah* means that God is not a part of our lives. As such, people who lack *emunah* grow further apart from God.

Kedushah means to lead a holy life. Since God describes Himself as being "Holy" (*Vayikra* 19:2), the only way we can get close to Him is to be holy ourselves. To be unholy is antithetical to holiness. When a person behaves in an unholy manner, it creates a huge gap between him and God.

This explains the problem with the *misonenim*. By complaining, they demonstrated a lack of *emunah*. They did not believe that the long journey was orchestrated by God and that it was for the best. They did not live by the motto "All that the Merciful One does is for the best" (*Berachos*, chap. 9, *Haroeh*, pg. 60b, the opinion of *Rebbi Akiva*).

Although there is no punishment in our earthly courts for complaining or for lacking *emunah*, in the heavenly court, however, it is considered to be a huge sin because it creates the most distance between the person and God. No longer do we necessarily judge the severity of a sin by its punishment, but by how much distance from God it creates.

Since the people lacked *emunah*, they were already lost from God. This is why a fire came out and consumed untold numbers. The fire did not originate below, but in the Heavens above - it was sent by the Tribunal on High.

The punishment did fit the crime. The people caused the greatest possible distance between themselves and God through their lack of *emunah*, thereby living antithetically from a true Torah lifestyle. Ruination of this fundamental component of Judaism caused an extremely severe consequence.

The *misavim* were guilty of ruining the other fundamental Jewish building block. God told us time and again to be holy (*Shemos* 19:6; 22:30) in order to be able to cling to Him. However, the verse says that the *misavim* "*hisavu ta'avah*" (*Bamidbar* 11:4). How does one translate those two words?

Traditionally, translators say that since the word is repeated twice, it is meant to stress the point. Therefore, the translation would be "They surely had a lusting."

However, the *Pri Ha'Aretz* offers an alternative translation. He says that *hisavu ta'avah* is to be read as follows, *hisavu* - they desired. But, do you know what they desired? Well, keep reading. They wanted *ta'avah* - lustful passions.

In other words, these people loved lustful passions. They loved the whole process. They loved the tug at their hearts for the passion. They loved pursuing it. They loved obtaining it. They loved experiencing it. They loved everything about it.

However, they felt frustrated because they could not get their passions going, on account of the *Manna* that they were eating. Being that the *Manna* was angelic food (*Tehillim* 78:25), it removed the inclination for evil.

However, there is one activity that can trigger lustful passions, and that is, eating. When a person eats for the wrong reasons, it can lead to an entire host of lustful passions in other areas as well. This is why they said, "We want meat." They wanted a good steak so that they could jumpstart the process of lusting.

Indeed, that is precisely what happened. When it says that Moshe heard them crying family by family, it meant that they were crying about family matters (*Bamidbar* 11:1, *Shabbos*, chap. 19, *Rebbi Eliezer D'Milah*, pg. 130a, the opinion of *Rabban Shimon Ben Gamliel*). In other words, they also wanted to have illicit relations. The first, fleshy, lustful passion for meat spilled over into another lustful passion for immorality.

Obviously, the pursuit of lustful passions is leading an unholy life, which is contrary to Torah values. Their overindulgence created partitions and barriers between them and God.

Their severing of the Divine umbilical cord, that was intended to keep them close to God, was considered so severe, that they died of a plague whilst engaging in those very passions. Once again, the punishment did fit the crime.

This is why the Torah chooses to share these stories with us. It is in order to teach us that there is a whole category of sins that are most severe, even though their Earthly punishments are not explicitly mentioned in the Torah.

There is also incredible encouragement that we can glean from all of this. Based on the fact that the side of good is by far more powerful than the side of evil (*Sanhedrin*, chap. 11, *Cheilek*. pg. 100b), imagine how close we become to God with every little bit of *emunah* and *kedushah* we create.

Perhaps we could suggest a practical exercise to help us improve in these two areas. Regarding *emunah*, when something aggravating happens (i.e. sitting in traffic, waiting on line forever at the post office, losing a wallet, breaking something precious, stubbing a toe, breaking a finger, etc.), just say the words, "Whatever God does is for the best," even if we are angry and even if we don't feel like saying it. Then, keep on saying it. Eventually, when we start to calm down, the words will begin to make their impression on our hearts. Then if something else upsetting happens, we will slowly learn to accept God's decisions more easily.

Regarding *kedushah*, many of us see things, watch things, hear things, say things, and dress in things that are not necessarily holy. These things can happen a thousand times a day. What if we were to decide to cut down just once a day? We could still transgress 999 times that day, but, we are already on the road to recovery. This is not to say that we should stop there; rather, it is a suggestion to begin there.

One small step in the right direction brings us so close to God. God knows that this is difficult for us. God understands that we are human. All God wants is for us to try our best. When we do, we draw so close to God.

May we be blessed to keep all 613 commandments, but more importantly, to listen to their advice, fortifying ourselves with the foundations of Judaism, *emunah* and *kedushah*, so that we constantly experience closeness to God.

Beha'alosecha

"Meat-ing" of Minds

There may be times that we don't understand how the Torah could say such a thing. We may question the position of our Sages. One piece of advice we could all keep in mind is to not be quick to pass critical judgment. The Written Law and Oral Tradition are very deep, and we can only hope and pray to eventually understand them.

In this week's *parshah*, *Beha'alosecha*, we find one of the most perplexing passages in the Torah. The Jewish people in the desert are suddenly overwhelmed by a craving for meat (*Bamidbar* 11:4). Hashem is angered by the people's desire, but nevertheless promises to provide an abundance of meat for them - an entire month's worth, "Until it comes out of your noses" (*Bamidbar* 11:20).

At this point, Moshe Rabbeinu asks Hashem a series of seemingly outrageous questions: "I am living amidst 600,000 people who are traveling by foot, and You say You will supply a month's worth of meat for them? Can enough sheep and cattle be slaughtered for them? Would all the fish in the sea be enough for them?" God responds to Moshe's questions, "Is My Hand short? Now you will see whether I am good for My word or not" (*Bamidbar* 11:21-23).

It is difficult to understand how Moshe Rabbeinu, who had the closest possible relationship with the Divine, could have explicitly doubted Hashem's ability to provide. If Hashem created the entire world from nothing, why should it be difficult for Him to provide sufficient meat for the Jewish people? Although many commentators grapple with this issue, we will present the opinion of the *Da'as Zekeinim* (*Bamidbar* 11:23).

The generation of Jews in the desert had a unique law that prohibited the slaughter of meat solely for personal consumption. Therefore, a person who wanted to eat meat was obligated to bring an offering to the Sanctuary. He would slaughter a sacrificial animal, place a portion of the meat on the Altar, and give a portion to the priests. Only the remaining third of the meat belonged to the owner who had brought the offering.

The priests were required to finish their portion of meat before dawn of the following day. Any meat that was left over at daybreak became invalid and had to be burned - an act that, ideally, was to be avoided. Therefore, the priests made every effort to consume the meat within the appointed time.

Based on these laws, the *Da'as Zekeinim* explains Moshe Rabbeinu's words in the following way. Hashem said that He would provide the people with a month's worth of meat in one day. Moshe is certain that Hashem can fulfill His word - but imagine hundreds of thousands of people suddenly converging at once on the Sanctuary with their sacrificial animals! There were only three priests (Aharon and his two sons) to serve the entire Jewish people! How would it be possible for them to eat such a vast quantity of sacrificial meat before dawn?

According the *Da'as Zekeinim*, Moshe Rabbeinu's question, "Can You provide enough fish for them?" (*Bamidbar* 11:22) is to be read as a statement. Moshe Rabbeinu was implying, "If You had promised to provide fish for them, they would be able to eat whatever they wanted, since we don't bring sacrifices from fish. But because You said, 'I will provide meat for them,' they will need to bring a sacrifice! How can You expect Aharon and his sons to eat so much meat within the allotted time?"

Hashem responded, "Is My Hand short?" When Hashem said He would provide meat, He meant quail - a type of bird from which no sacrifice is brought. Therefore, the people would have no need to bring a sacrifice, thus circumventing any possibility of leftover meat.

Fowl is considered to have the *halachic* status of meat, but the origins of this categorization are debatable. Was this law derived directly from the Torah, or did it result from a later decision of the Rabbinic Council? From this passage we see that when Hashem said "meat," He was referring to quail. According to the opinion of the *Da'as Zekeinim*, we could, therefore, suggest that fowl's status as meat is given directly by the Torah (This is the view held by *Tosefos*; see *Chullin* 104b).

However, the *Rambam* (*Hilchos Mamrim* 2:9) disagrees, claiming that anyone who believes that the Torah considers fowl to be meat is transgressing the prohibition of adding to the Torah. (For further analysis, see also *Yorah Deah* 87:3 and *Shach* 4). It is not surprising that the opinions of the *Da'as Zekeinim* and *Tosefos* are the same. It is a classic example of a group conforming to its own opinion - since the *Da'as Zekeinim* are also Tosafists (their proper title is "*Da'as Zekeinim Mi'Ba'alei HaTosefos*")!

One lesson we can learn from this approach is not to be so quick to pass critical judgment about what our Sages say and do. Often, we do not understand what they mean or where they are coming from. In general, it is a good practice not to judge people unfavorably, but with righteous Sages all the more so. So the next time we see or hear something that makes us jump to conclusions, let's take a moment and try to interpret his words or actions favorably.

As we sit down to eat meat at our Shabbos meals, may we also merit to sink our teeth into some meaty *divrei Torah*, and in this way have a full and complete Shabbos experience.

Shelach

For Your Eyes, Holy

Y̶ou know, sometimes it's all a matter of perspective. With a positive outlook on things, the situation in which we find ourselves may not be all that bad.

In this week's portion, *Shelach*, the main story revolves around Moshe sending the spies to scout the land of Israel. Among the long list of instructions, Moshe tells the spies to investigate if there are any trees in the land (*Bamidbar* 13:20). The Talmud in *Bava Basra* (15a) cites the opinion of *Rava*, who says that Iyov (Job) lived during the time that Moshe sent the spies to check out the land. He says we learn this from two verses that share a similar word. In the book of *Iyov* (1:1), it says, "There was a man in the land of *Utz* and Job was his name." And in this week's portion Moshe instructs the spies to see if there is an *eitz*, tree, in the land (*Bamidbar* 13:20). These two words in Hebrew (*Utz* and *eitz*) share the same letters, an *ayin* and *tzadi*. Together, these two verses teach us that Iyov lived during the time that Moshe sent the spies.

The Talmud adds that Moshe told the spies to see if a certain man lived in Israel. This person's years were as many as the years of a tree, and his merit protected the land's inhabitants, as a tree protects those that are under it. That person was Iyov. From this Talmud it is obvious that Iyov was a righteous man.

The *Emunas Itech*a points out that Iyov's righteousness was due to his vigilance in guarding his eyes from gazing upon the wrong things. There is a verse in the book of *Iyov* to support this idea where it says "I forged a covenant for my eyes, and I would not gaze upon a maiden" (*Iyov* 31:1). Protecting one's eyes from gazing at the wrong things is the primary way to safeguard ourselves in sanctity and purity. We are even told about this precaution at the end of this week's portion when it says, "And do not go astray after your own heart and after your own eyes" (*Bamidbar* 15:39).

Rashi on the spot cites the *Tanchuma* (15) that points out that the Hebrew word for "going astray - *sasuru*," is similar to a word found earlier in this portion, *misur* (*Bamidbar* 13:25), which means "from spying out." These two words come together to teach us that the heart and the eyes are the spies of the body; they are the agents which bring a person to sin. The eye sees, the heart desires, and then the body carries out the deed. We see from here that everything starts with the eyes.

We could suggest that *shemiras einayim*, guarding the eyes is not only looking away from immorality, but it even includes the idea of not focusing on evil in general. Therefore, when Moshe instructed the spies to see if there were trees in the land, he really meant that the spies should investigate whether or not Iyov lived there.

This is because Moshe wanted the spies to look Iyov up, and thereby, come into contact with a person who was a master of *shemiras einayim*. This was in order that the spies should take a lesson from him to safeguard their own eyes from focusing on any negative aspects of *Eretz Yisrael*. Unfortunately, the majority of spies did not heed Moshe's warning, and their eyes beheld the negative aspects of the land. Consequently, their hearts desired to remain in the desert, and that led their bodies to carry out the deed through derogatory speech.

It should be noted that the *Zohar* (vol. 1, pg. 59b) points out that one who is careful in the areas of sanctity and purity is called a *tzaddik*. With this piece of information, the *Emunas Itecha* pulls all this together with a beautiful conclusion that sheds light on Moshe's choice of words.

Moshe tells the spies, "See if there is an *eitz*." Moshe didn't just mean trees; he specifically had in mind Iyov, the righteous one. And Iyov was called a "righteous one" because he guarded his eyes, as indicated in Moshe's choice of the word *eitz,* spelled *ayin tzadi.* The letter *ayin* isn't just a letter; it is also the Hebrew word for "eye." The letter *tzadi* is not just a letter either, it is also the Hebrew word for "a righteous person - a *tzaddik*" (in some circles the letter *tzadi* is actually called the letter *tzaddik*). This comes to teach us that one who closes his or her *ayin* (eye) from seeing evil is automatically called a *tzaddik* (a righteous person).

Perhaps, we could suggest an exercise to remind us to look with clear vision and not with filth-seeking eyes. Every morning when we get up, let's wash the dirt off our glasses or contacts, and decide at that moment that today we do not want to see any filth or negativity in others. (For those of us who do not wear glasses or contacts, we can think these thoughts as we wash our eyes.)

May we all be blessed to become real *tzaddikim* by safeguarding our eyes from evil, which will subsequently guard our hearts and protect our bodies from sin. Then, we will deserve to be planted like trees in *Eretz Yisrael.*

Shelach

Cluster Buster

Each stage of life brings with it different experiences and different challenges. If we could identify which stage of life we are going through at this very moment, we would be better equipped for dealing with the circumstances that present themselves to us.

In this week's portion, *Shelach* (13:23) we read about the spies: "They came to *Nachal Eshkol* (Cluster Valley) and cut down from there a branch with a cluster of grapes, and they carried it between two people upon poles. [They also took] some pomegranates and figs."

The next verse says: "The place was called *Nachal Eshkol* (Cluster Valley) because of the cluster of grapes the Children of Israel cut down from there."

An obvious question arises: if the place was named on account of the incident that occurred there (i.e. cutting the grapes), then how can the Torah refer to the location by name already in verse 23, before the event even happened? The *Vilna Gaon* (in *Peninim MiShulchan HaGra*, *Kol Dodi*) relays some information which will enable us to answer this question.

Whenever a word in the Torah is written in its complete form, i.e. with a letter *vav*, it denotes plurality. Conversely, when a word is written in an incomplete form, without a letter *vav*, it implies singularity. This principle is referred to in *Sukkah* (ironically on page *vav* (six), side two) where the Talmud cites the various opinions concerning the required number of walls in a *sukkah*.

The Talmud relates the dispute between the Rabbis and Rabbi Shimon regarding whether the transmitted, written form of a word in the Torah has primacy over the pronounced form or vice versa. The Rabbis maintained that the written form has primacy over the articulated form, while Rabbi

Shimon held the opposite. To illustrate the Rabbis' opinion, we will take a closer look at the Talmud which focuses on three instances where the word *baSukkos* is written in the Torah.

The Torah says (*Vayikra* 23:42-43), "*BaSukkos teishvu shivas yamim kol ha'ezrach b'Yisrael yeishvu baSukkos. Lema'an yeid'u doroseichem ki baSukkos hoshavti es Bnei Yisrael* - In *Sukkos* you shall dwell for seven days; every native in Israel shall dwell in *Sukkos*. In order that your generations will know that I caused the Children of Israel to dwell in *Sukkos*."

If we look at this text as it is written in the Torah we will notice that the first two mentions of the word *baSukkos* are written without a *vav*, whereas the third appearance is in its complete form, **with** a *vav*.

The Rabbis, who maintain that the written form has primacy, interpret the deficient spellings (where the word *baSukkos* lacks a *vav*) as denoting the singular form, thus alluding to one wall, while the complete form of the word *baSukkos* (with a *vav*) denotes plurality, implying **two** walls, since the minimum of plurality is two.

Thus, the Sages derived from here that a *sukkah* requires four walls; two singular forms (= two walls), and one plural form (= two walls), totaling **four** walls in all (see the Talmud inside for the final ruling.)

Based on this information, we can answer the original question concerning how the Torah could refer to the place *Eshkol* by name, before relating the event that brought about this specific name.

In Verse 23, the Torah says that the Israelites reached the valley of *Eshkol*. There, the word *Eshkol* is written without a *vav*, indicating singularity, i.e. that it was called this name for **one** reason. The *Vilna Gaon* says that this place was previously named *Eshkol* after one of Avraham's three friends who was also called *Eshkol* (see *Bereishis* 14:24.) It is interesting to note that the personality *Eshkol*, mentioned in *Bereishis*, is also spelled without a *vav*.

Once the spies cut the grapes in *Nachal Eshkol*, as verse 24 reports, the name of the place was changed to *Eshkol* spelled with a letter *vav* (indicating plurality) because now there was an **additional** reason for this specific name.

We could suggest that Avraham's three friends - *Aner, Eshkol* and *Mamrei* - represent the three stages of a person's life.

(1) *Aner* correlates with the phase of childhood, the stage of the *katan,* minor, since the word *Aner* (spelled *ayin, nun, reish*) contains the same letters as *na'ar* which means "lad" or "youth." Young people are often involved in what is termed *na'arishkeit* - meaningless, silly activities.

(2) *Eshkol* corresponds to adulthood, hinted at in the word *eshkol* (spelled *aleph, shin, kaf, vav, lamed*) which, when the letters are unscrambled, can be read *"kulo eish* - full of fire." This phase of life marks the time when we are confronted with the challenges of our fiery passions and lustful drives.

(3) Finally, *Mamrei* represents the *zaken,* the older person, whose life is filled with *moreh Hashem,* the awe of God. *Mamrei* (spelled *mem, mem, reish, aleph*) can also be read *memorah* - meaning "from awe." A *zaken,* a person faced with death, realizes the significance of life, and is therefore filled with a great awe for Hashem.

Based on this information, we can analyze and explain Moshe's advice to the spies. In *Bamidbar* (13:18) Moshe says: *"U're'isem es haaretz mah hee* - And see the land what it is." The *mesorah,* tradition, notifies us that the word *u're'isem* appears in the Scripture three times: once here in *Bamidbar* (13:18); once in *Shemos* (1:15); and once in *Bamidbar* (15:39).

(1) In the first instance (*Shemos* 1:15), Pharaoh commands the midwives to kill the baby boys, saying, *"U're'isen al ha'ovanayim...* - and see upon the birth-stool..."

(2) The second appearance is in *Bamidbar* (13:18) where Moshe says to the spies, "See the land."

(3) Thirdly, in *Bamidbar* (15:39), the word is used in reference to *tzitzis*: "*U're'isem oso* - and you shall see it…"

What is the connection between these three seemingly unrelated sources? The *Likutei Basar Likutei* (cited in *Torah LeDa'as* vol.1) says that these three occurrences of *u're'isem* allude to three pieces of advice (*Avos* 3:1) that help us fight our evil inclination.

"*Akaviah ben Mahalalel* said: consider three things, and you will not fall into the hands of transgression. Know from where you came, to where you are going, and before whom you are to give an account and reckoning. From where you came - from a putrid drop; to where you are going - to a place of dust, worm and maggot; and before whom you are to give an account and reckoning - before the King of Kings, the Holy One, praised be He."

The *Likutei* explains that the three instances that the word *u're'isem* appears in the Written Law correspond, in order of appearance, to the three pieces of advice in the Oral Law, as follows:

(1) *Shemos* (1:15): "See upon the birth-stool" correlates with "Know from where you came," because both relate to a person's birth or creation.

(2) *Bamidbar* (13:18): "See the land" corresponds to "[Know] to where you are going," because both refer to the earth or land.

(3) *Bamidbar* (15:39): "See it [*Tzitzis*]" corresponds to "[Know] to whom you will give an account," because "*U'reisem oso*" can mean both "See it" (the *Tzitzis*), as well as "See **Him**" (God), hinting at the final piece of advice that refers specifically to Hashem.

We could suggest that these three pieces of advice from Rabbi Akaviah apply to the three distinct phases of our lives:

1) "Know from where you came" is applicable primarily to the *naʿar*. Children cannot comprehend the concept of mortality, but they can understand the idea that they "came from Mommy." This can be used to help guide the child on the right path.

2) "Know to where you are going" is appropriate advice for the adult who is *kulo eish*, since the awareness of mortality helps the individual ward off his inappropriate desires and control his drives.

3) "Know before whom you are to give an account and reckoning" applies principally to the *zaken* whose mind needs to turn to thoughts of eternity. The *zaken*, who may be weary from a life's worth of struggling, needs to be encouraged to continue, and is therefore reminded of the purpose of life and that his mission is not yet complete as long as he is in this world.

We could propose that when Moshe said the word *u're'isem* to the spies, he actually divided the twelve spies into three groups and offered different counsel to each of the groups;

1) Moshe reckoned that ten out of the twelve spies were at the stage of *naʿarus*, youth, and therefore gave them the advice that relates to the first *u're'isem* - "Know from where you came."

2) To Calev, Moshe gave counsel that relates to the second *u're'isem*, i.e. "Know to where you are going" because he gauged that Calev was at the stage of *kulo eish*. We find a hint to this in *Rashi* (*Bamidbar* 13:22) who cites the Talmud (*Sotah* 34b) that says on the words, "He came to Chevron"; "Calev separated himself to pray at the graves of the forefathers." Seemingly, Calev understood the importance of being aware of his mortality. Perhaps his decision to go to the graves was inspired by Moshe's advice.

3) Moshe addressed the final spy, Yehoshua, with the message of the third *u're'isem*; "Know before whom you will give an account and reckoning," since he assessed that Yehoshua was at the stage of the *zaken. Rashi (Bamidbar* 13:16), cites the Talmud (*Sotah* 34b) that says that Moshe added a *yud* to Yehoshua's name so that *Hoshea* became *Yehoshua,* blessing him with the words "*Kah yoshiacha* - May God save you." Yehoshua was given the Mishnah's third piece of advice, which enabled him to carry within him a constant awareness of God, a feeling that he is always "before God."

We find that Moshe's advice to Calev and Yehoshua was successful, but that it failed for the rest of the spies. We could suggest that Moshe's counsel to the ten spies was inappropriate, which is why it failed to guard them against the Evil Inclination. Moshe thought that the ten spies were at the stage of *na'arus*; but ostensibly, this was a misjudgment.

We find support for this idea in *Bamidbar* (13:2) where Hashem apparently criticizes Moshe as he instructs him, "Send **anashim**" (men); and (13:3), "All of them (the spies) are **anashim.**" The word *anashim* implies *gedolim,* adults. Thus, Hashem was emphasizing to Moshe that all of the spies were at the stage of adulthood - in the phase of *eshkol* or *kulo eish* - and, therefore, required the Mishnah's **second** piece of advice: "Know to where you are going." Adults are motivated more by looking to the future than by reminding themselves of their pasts.

We should take a moment to think about what stage of life we are currently in and act accordingly, by keeping in mind the appropriate knowledge that will motivate us to stay on the correct path.

May we be blessed to live through all our lives' stages with the clarity to see ahead, so that we may prevent any lustful passions, or *na'arishkeit*, from leading us astray. May we subsequently live to a ripe old age, filled with the *mora*, awe, of Hashem.

Shelach

Mastering the Art of Synthesis

Spirituality is not only found in Torah study or in prayer; it can also be found in every seemingly mundane activity in which we engage.

After spying out the Land of Israel, the majority of the spies gave an evil report about the Land (*Bamidbar* 13:28) with the intention of dissuading the people from entering it. Why would such righteous people not want the Jews to live in the Land of Israel? (See *Rashi Bamidbar* 13:3).

The Belzer Rebbe (cited in the *Shvilei Pinchas*) quotes the *Kadmonim* (earlier Sages) who say that the majority of spies wanted to remain in the desert in order to continue receiving the *manna*.

Manna is food that angels eat (*Tehillim* 78:25; *Yoma*, chap. 8, *Yom Hakippurim*, the opinion of Rebbi Akiva). As such, it is very conducive to spirituality. The majority of spies maintained that it is impossible to study Torah and serve God properly without a daily dose of *manna*.

Most of the spies also wanted to remain in the desert because deserts lend themselves to spirituality, since there are no distractions there. You cannot "go to town" in a desert. In the wilderness, the only thing to occupy a person's time, preventing him from going crazy from boredom, is engaging in Torah study and spiritual pursuits.

The *manna* and the desert, combined, created the perfect environment for spiritual growth. Not only did they lend themselves to spirituality, but there were no preparations necessary for *manna* eating. It was served to them on a silver platter, ready to go.

However, the spies realized that all that would change upon entering the Land. They knew that the *manna* would stop falling, and instead they would have to eat regular food. They also understood that there would be many distractions in Israel that would pull them away from serving God 24/7.

For example, once in Israel the Jews would have to work the fields and vineyards in order to provide food - a very time-consuming endeavor. Besides, Israel is described as a land "flowing with milk and honey" (*Bamidbar* 13:27). This means that Israel is a very physical place that flows, and even overflows with possibilities to enjoy physical pleasures. Even Cocoa-Puffs are available at the local *makolets* (grocery stores) in Israel!

Whatever physical pleasure one seeks, it can be obtained in Israel. Everything is at our fingertips. This can be very tempting and distracting. How much time would there be left for spiritual endeavors? This is why the majority of the spies preferred to remain in the desert, a spiritual cocoon, rather than enter a Land that posed a spiritual danger.

For people that are interested in spirituality, this does not seem to be a bad idea. It is even tempting to follow their advice. The spies were righteous and they were concerned about spirituality. All they wanted was to continue living a holy life. What was wrong with their philosophy?

The *Kadmonim* say that this is precisely where the majority of the spies were mistaken. God basically said to these spies that He had already created creatures that live in a spiritual cocoon and serve Him without distractions. Those creatures are the angels. For an angel, it is fine to function on that level.

However, God's vision for mankind was altogether different. God wanted man to be very much involved in the physical domain. He should utilize it, channel it, direct it, and transform it into something meaningful, purposeful, and eternal, i.e. spiritual.

We can see this is man's intended mission by the manner in which he was created. Man is made up of two components. When discussing the human condition, everything will boil down to one of these two aspects.

The two parts of man are a body and a soul (*Bereishis* 2:7). Everything about man can be traced back to one of these two ingredients. Whatever issues man has to face, whether psychological, emotional, medical, etc., they either stem from the body or stem from the soul.

These two components are diametrically opposed to each other. The body comes from the lowest world of materialism, whereas the soul stems from the highest world of holiness. When God brought these two extreme opposites together, He was teaching us what He intended man to accomplish during his tenure on Earth. Namely, to take all the raw materials with which the body comes into contact, and elevate them to a higher spiritual purpose. God's Will is that man, who comes from both worlds, should lead a healthy, balanced life by constantly joining these two distant universes together. This is called synthesis.

Precisely because the Land of Israel is such a physical place, God wanted us to enter it, engage in it, and elevate it to a higher goal, which is to serve Him.

The majority of spies, however, wanted to live the life of an angel. That was a gross mistake for human beings because it goes against the will of God. It derails us from the track God intended for us.

We are blessed with so many opportunities to serve God. We are surrounded with materials that can be harnessed and directed towards God.

Wouldn't it be great to whisper to ourselves even just once a day right before engaging in a physical activity, "I am going to... in order to have the strength to serve God properly, and be in a happier frame of mind so that I can better help others."

This one exercise a day will help us live the healthy, balanced life that God has prepared for us.

May we all be blessed with the wisdom to harness this materialistic world for our ultimate future of spiritual bliss.

Shelach

It Tastes Divine

Facing our fears and dealing with them is what truly demonstrates the greatness of man.

It is unanimous that the highlight of this week's portion, *Shelach*, is the story of the spies. Therefore, it is possible that less attention is directed to a topic found later on in the *parshah*.

Let us begin with the overshadowed subject matter first, and see how it possibly ties into the main thrust of the portion.

We are told that when we enter the Land of Israel and eat the bread of the Land, we are to first set aside a portion of the kneading dough for God (see *Bamidbar* 15:17-21). This *mitzvah* (commandment) is referred to as "taking *challah*."

We already see that eating is supposed to be for a higher purpose. One approach as to what eating is all about, on a deeper level, is based on a teaching in the *Kabbalah*.

This world is filled with *nitzotzos shel kedushah*, sparks of holiness. These sparks originate from Hashem. We were sent to this world to carry out a mission. That mission is to extract those sparks and make them a part of our souls. When we do so, we become spiritually stronger.

Much focus has been directed to the sparks found within items that we either crave, lust after, or desire. According to the *Avodas Yisrael*, Hashem is the One who imbued us with a drive that motivates us to eat, just so that we are directed to food. It is then that we are expected to engage in the activity of eating for the right reasons, and thereby extract the sparks hidden within the food or beverage.

The *Ba'al Shem Tov* supports this idea with a verse that says, "Hungry as well as thirsty, their soul was enwrapped in them" (*Tehillim* 107:5). The *Ba'al Shem Tov's* interpretation of this verse is as follows. When a person gets hungry and thirsty, it is in order to extract the soul, or spark, that is enwrapped in that food. This could be why people often say after biting into a good piece of seven layer cake, "This simply tastes Divine." Subconsciously, we all know that there are holy sparks in the food. Not only that, but the taste of the food also comes from those sparks.

The Slonimer Rebbe, explains in his *Nesivos Shalom*, that there are two areas in life for which most of us have a passion. One is eating, and the other is relations. Both of these areas are hinted to in the loaf of bread mentioned in our *parshah*.

On a simple level, bread represents eating in general, because bread is considered to be the primary food and staple of life.

On another level, bread hints at relations. This is seen in a verse where Potifar (Pharaoh's chief butcher) says to Yosef that although Yosef is appointed over his entire household, there is one exception, and that is, "The bread that he eats" (*Bereishis* 39:6). *Rashi* on the spot cites the *Bereishis Rabbah* (86:6) that says that this really refers to Potifar's wife, but the Torah is expressing it in a decent manner.

Many holy sparks are contained within these two areas of life. Therefore, it is of paramount importance that we involve ourselves in these activities with a good measure of holiness. Then, we can successfully extract those sparks, become spiritually stronger, and accomplish the mission for which we were originally sent here.

We could suggest that this is one idea behind the two loaves of bread that accompany every Shabbos meal (see *Shabbos*, chap. 16, *Kol Kisvei*, pg. 117b;

and *Shulchan Aruch, Orach Chaim* chap. 274:1, the laws of breaking bread on Shabbos). Since we are told to engage in physicality on Shabbos to an even greater degree, the two loaves remind us to channel these two areas of life to God.

When we do so, it is considered as if we brought the offering called *shtei halechem* (the two loaves of bread) to God on our Altar, which is our table.

We could suggest, that this implied lesson on the subject of *challah* found later in our portion, actually sheds light on what was happening, behind the scenes, in the story of the spies earlier in our portion.

The spies brought back to the desert huge fruits from *Eretz Yisrael*. Specifically mentioned are the grapes, pomegranates and figs (*Bamidbar* 13:23). The spies claimed that those fruits represent the physical overabundance that the Land of Israel has to offer. The spies argued that it would be unwise to bring the Jews into the Land because they would be materialistically overwhelmed and would pursue their lustful passions. This is especially true in light of the fact that, until now, the Jews were living in a spiritual bubble, surrounded by Clouds of Glory, and eating *manna*, spiritual angel food.

This is what the spies meant when they said, "*Eretz ocheles yoshveha* - a land that consumes its inhabitants" (*Bamidbar* 13:32). A deeper translation could be "One who inhabits this land becomes an **eater,**" implying they would do so for the wrong reasons. This would surely undermine the national goal of elevating everything and each person spiritually.

The spies also said that the people living there are *anshei middos,* huge people (*Bamidbar* 13:32). With this, they implied that the reason for their size is that they eat so much. Certainly, the Jews would also fall prey to the same bad habit.

The spies also hinted at the other lustful passion, immorality. The three fruits that were chosen by the spies were the grapes, pomegranates, and figs (*anavim, rimonim* and *te'einim*). The acronym of these three words are the letters *ayin, reish, taf*. When these three letters are put together, they spell the word *eres*, bed. (Although *eres* is generally spelled with the letter *sin*, phonetically the letter *taf* [or *saf*] suffices.) (See *Rashi, Vayikra* 19:16).

With this, they hinted at the immorality performed on a bed. Incidentally, the *eres* is also hinted to in the *mitzvah* of *challah*, because it says to take the "*reishis arisoseichem* - the first of the kneading dough" (*Bamidbar* 15:20). The word *arisoseichem* (dough), is related to the word *eres*, (bed). This is found in the verse, "*Arso eres barzel* - his bed was an iron bed" (*Devarim* 3:11).

When the Jews heard that ten out of the twelve spies suggested that they remain in the desert because it is much more conducive to a life focused on spirituality, they began to cry (*Bamidbar* 14:1). They cried because they wanted the life of lustful passions that Israel had to offer. However, since the majority of spies ruled it better to remain in the desert, they understood that this would be the verdict.

In other words, the majority of spies were right about how they sized up the Jews. Why, then, were those ten spies punished? Because Hashem wanted the type of leader who would show the Jews how to use physicality in a healthy, balanced way. God has no need for a leader who runs away from a challenge. Hashem wanted those leaders to enter the land and teach the people how to deal with the challenges. This, after all, is the secret to true growth.

Since the spies fell short of their responsibilities as leaders, and failed their mission, they were put to death by God.

In order to try to live up to God's vision for us, we could attempt to get a stronger hold on how and why we eat. During one of our daily meals, stop and think of the Hebrew word *ma'achal*, food, spelled *mem, aleph, chaf, lamed*. The numerical value of this word is ninety-one, which has the same numerical value as two names of God *Adu-Noi* (*aleph*, *daled*, *nun*, *yud* = sixty-five) and *Havaya* (*yud*, *hey*, *vav*, *hey* = twenty-six). This will remind us to eat for a higher purpose. (See *Tzetel Katan* by the *Rebbe Reb Elimelech of Lizensk* paragraph 15). Then we can become like angels, which also hinted to by the word "*ma'achal*," whose letters, when rearranged, spell the word *malach*, angel.

May we be blessed to be drawn to the various temptations of this world, and engage in them with utmost sanctity in order to extract their intrinsic holiness. We will, thereby, become spiritually stronger, and thus deserve to enter the Land, live there, overcome any challenge, and merit to witness the building of the *Beis HaMikdash* and reinstitution of the *Korban Shtei HaLechem*.

Korach

Might Makes Right

It is not so rare to find that just a slight deviation from the intended way can upset the whole system and wreak havoc.

One of the motivating factors that stirred Korach to rebel against Moshe and Aharon was that Korach foresaw that one of his own descendants would be Shmuel HaNavi (the prophet Samuel). Since Shmuel's status equaled that of Moshe and Aharon (*Tehillim* 99:6, *Berachos*, chap. 5, *Ein Omdin*, the opinion of *Rabbi Yochanan*), Korach reasoned that this indicated that he himself was the righteous one. This gave Korach the confidence to rebel against the established authority (*Tanchumah* #5).

This Midrash begs us to ask how Korach could have come to such a conclusion. There are many personalities who were righteous and yet their ancestors left much to be desired. For example, Avraham came from Terach, who spent the majority of his life as an idolater. Rachel and Leah came from Lavan, who was a trickster and a gangster.

The same pattern could apply to Shmuel and Korach. Shmuel was a righteous person, but that does not necessarily mean that Korach was righteous. How, then, did Korach conclude that he must have been the righteous one, based solely on the fact that Shmuel would descend from him?

The *Arizal* says that, *Kabbalistically* speaking, Aharon was reincarnated into Shmuel (*Sha'ar Hagilgulim*, preface, #33). Based on this, the *Megaleh Amukos* (*Vaeschanan* 33) explains that Korach did not only see that Shmuel would come from his loins; he also saw that Shmuel was a reincarnation of Aharon.

Since Shmuel was a *Levi* (see *Radak, Shmuel I*, 1:1), Korach asked himself, how could it be that a *Kohen* could wind up as a Levite. Of the three classes of Jews, a *Kohen* is the highest, Levites are second, and Israelites are third. We have a rule of thumb that states "We always ascend in matters of holiness and we do not descend" (*Megillah*, chap. 1, *Megillah Nikreis*, pg.9b).

Korach concluded that if Aharon would become a Levite it must be an indication that he was being demoted because he never deserved to be the High Priest to begin with.

Moreover, Korach thought himself to be greater than Aharon because Korach, as a Levite, never participated in the Sin of the Golden Calf. On the other hand, not only did Aharon participate in that sin, he orchestrated it. Korach thought that this served as another reason that it was necessary for Aharon to become a Levite. This would be part of Aharon's *tikkun*, fixing. Aharon would need to spend time inside a Levite, who never sinned with the Golden Calf, so that the Levites' positive energy would rub off on him (*Shvilei Pinchas* citing the *Divrei Emes*, "*B'Medrash lamnatzeiach al shoshanim livnei Korach*").

Because of all this, Korach argued that a Jew of the highest class should not be a *Kohen Gadol*. Rather, a Levite should be in first place (maybe he would be called the *Levi HaGadol*), whereas the *Kohen* should be in second place. Korach did not want to be a *Kohen*, he was already a Levite. Instead, Korach wanted to switch the order around so that Korach would be the gold medalist, as it were, and Aharon would be the silver medalist.

By wanting to set this in motion, Korach threatened the existence of the world. This is because a *Kohen* comes from the right side of God (so to speak) which is the side of *chessed* (kindness), whereas a Levite comes from the left side of God (so to speak) which is the side of *din* (strict justice) (*Zohar, Korach*, pg. 176a).

It is imperative for the left to be subservient to the right, and for the Levite to be humbled before the *Kohen*, so that *din* is secondary to *chessed*, which must remain primary. Only in a world dominated by *chessed* can we exist. In a world of *din*, there is no tolerance for sin; punishment for misconduct is fast and harsh. It would not take long for the human race to disappear altogether in a world governed by *din* (see *Rashi, Bereishis* 1:1 citing *Bereishis Rabbah* 12:15).

Since Korach wanted to reverse the order, he endangered the world. This is why Korach had to be stopped. Korach was taken out before he could do any further damage.

Besides, Korach was mistaken about the reason that Aharon, the *Kohen*, was reincarnated into Shmuel the Levite. This was not a demotion. On the contrary, it was to assist Shmuel in protecting the *Kohen* status of Eli, who was the High Priest in Shmuel's generation (*Shvilei Pinchas*).

Shmuel did descend from Korach. As such, there was a real concern that Shmuel would follow in the mistaken footsteps of his great grandfather Korach, and try to place the *Levite/din* above the *Kohen/chessed*. To ensure that Shmuel not commit a repeat performance of Korach his ancestor, Aharon entered into Shmuel to help him appreciate the high position of the *Kohen*. It worked, and Shmuel was dedicated to preserving the holiness of the *Kohen* and his essence of *chessed*.

There is a Jewish practice that we perform many times daily which supports this idea that *chessed* must prevail over *din*. That practice is *netillas yadayim* (ritually washing our hands).

It is important that the left hand first pour the water over the right hand. This demonstrates that the left hand is the servant and the right hand is the master, which means that *din* is subordinate to *chessed*. *Chesed*, obviously, is most important (*Reikanti, Levush, Eikev*, 199a).

I would like to suggest an exercise that we can implement every single day that will enhance kindness in the world. We wash our hands ritually so frequently; in the morning, after the bathroom, or prior to a meal with bread. Let us think about the deeper meaning behind those washings even just once a day.

When we remember that we wash in this way in order to place the emphasis on *chessed*, then let's go out there and do a *chessed* for somebody that we would not have done otherwise. This will continue to build into the world the *chessed* that we so desperately need for our existence.

Additionally, living a life far from *din* means not to judge people harshly. Rather, we should view others through the lenses of *chessed*.

May we all be blessed to place the emphasis on *chessed* which will transform this world of ours from a harsh place into a sweet paradise, with Moshe, Aharon, and Shmuel at the helm of the Third and final *Beis HaMikdash*.

Korach

Parallel Universes

In today's day and age of scientific and technological advancement, who hasn't heard of parallel universes and multiple dimensions? It has taken science thousands of years to begin realizing that which has always been found within the Torah.

The rebellion against Moshe and Aharon in this week's portion, *Korach*, is nothing less than intriguing. Korach was not only wise (*Rashi Bamidbar* 16:7, citing *Tanchuma* #5), but he is even considered to have been righteous. This comes from a teaching by the *Arizal*, who says that there is a hint to this in the Torah.

In *Tehillim* (92:13) it says, "*Tzaddik katamar yifrach* - The righteous man flourishes like the palm tree." When you look at the last Hebrew letter of each of these words (*kuf, reish, ches*) they spell the name "Korach."

This comes to teach us that Korach was a *tzaddik*, a righteous person. Additionally, since Korach's name appears at the end of each word, it further indicates that at the **end** of days, Korach's righteousness will become realized.

In light of all this, it becomes increasingly difficult to understand how and why Korach would lead such a mutiny against one of the greatest people that ever lived, Moshe Rabbeinu.

Furthermore, the Talmud says something which is simply shocking. Rabbi Shmuel Bar Nachmeni said in the name of Rabbi Yonasan, that Korach suspected Moshe of committing the sin of adultery with a married woman (see *Sanhedrin*, chap. 11, *Cheilek*, pg. 110a). Again, this begs us to ponder how anybody could have suspected one of the greatest of all people of committing one of the lowest crimes?

An idea found in the teachings of the *Ba'al Shem Tov* offers a new way of looking at this entire story. The *Ba'al Shem Tov* says that Korach suspected that Moshe had all the character flaws that Bilaam had. Moreover, Korach suspected that Moshe was guilty of all the sins that Bilaam transgressed.

Now, get ready for what the *Ba'al Shem Tov* says next. I hope you're sitting down. Okay, here it goes: The *Besh"t* (*Ba'al Shem Tov*) says that Korach wasn't far from the truth! I know that this is highly controversial and makes the blood boil, but let us allow the *Besh"t* to explain himself.

The *Besh"t* reveals to us that Moshe and Bilaam shared the same spark (or soul, if I may). It's just that Bilaam came from the dark side of the soul, whereas Moshe came from its light side.

In other words, Bilaam was Moshe's opposite on a parallel universe. However, these two universes coexisted on the same planet. Perhaps it could be put this way. Bilaam was Moshe's spiritual twin brother. It's just that Bilaam was diametrically opposed to Moshe. As great as Moshe was, that's how evil Bilaam was. Moshe was the greatest of the Jewish prophets (*Devarim* 34:10), whereas Bilaam was the greatest prophet the nations ever had (*Sifri* 34:10). Hashem does this with all *tzaddikim* in order to maintain balance in this world.

Based on all this, we could suggest that when Korach looked at Moshe, he looked into his soul in order to determine what type of leader he was. Korach gazed so deeply into Moshe, that Korach saw through to the other side of Moshe's soul, the dark side - the Bilaam on the other end.

This led Korach to think that the person standing in front of him was not Moshe at all; rather, it was Bilaam. Korach thought that Bilaam was an imposter and a spy from the dark side, who had penetrated the Jewish people's fortress of security, and assumed the highest position of authority in order to mislead the Jews, and turn them away from God.

It's no wonder that Korach suspected "Moshe" of committing adultery. It wasn't Moshe after all. Rather, it was Bilaam - or so Korach thought.

Now we can understand how a righteous Korach could lead a rebellion against Moshe. In Korach's mind, he wasn't fighting Moshe at all; rather, he was trying to tear down Bilaam. Korach knew that this would not be a popular thing to do; and worse yet, it could even be dangerous. Nevertheless, he was willing to sacrifice himself in order to save the Jewish people from following a wicked man down the path of destruction.

However, Korach's eyes misled him, and he did not see clearly (see *Rashi*, *Bamidbar* 16:7, citing *Tanchuma* #5). This was a mistake of mega proportions. If Korach was able to mistake Moshe for Bilaam, it could only be a result of one thing. Namely, it is a sign that there was corruption in Korach's own personality. If Korach saw such crookedness in the world's greatest *tzaddik*, it could only have been a reflection of his own shortcomings.

There must have been something rotten in Korach's own soul that was not yet ironed out. As a result, Korach superimposed this negativity on Moshe. In time, however, when Korach fixes the wrinkles of his heart, he will be recognized as a true *tzaddik*. After all, he was willing to give up his life for the cause. This has always been a trait of the righteous.

In conclusion, we must realize that every single one of us has a spiritual identical twin on a parallel universe that coexists on this planet. If we want to be the righteous twin, then we should get working on it right away with self-sacrifice, causing our opposite to be the wicked one.

If we don't, then our opposite may be working on being the righteous one, causing us to become the wicked one. Ideally, however, if both counterparts work on being righteous simultaneously, then we can succeed in crushing wickedness completely.

May we all be blessed to purge ourselves of our inner demons by refining our characters, siding with Moshe and holiness, and thus merit that Hashem will send us a true leader who will fix this world with all of its universes, doing away with death forever (see *Yeshaya* 25:8).

Korach

Good Shabbos, Tzaddik

What has been the secret to the Jewish people's survival? Within the next few paragraphs we will discover an interesting perspective on the matter.

In this week's portion, *Korach*, we read about the dispute that occurred between Korach and Moshe. The Midrash (*Tanchuma, Os* 5) describes Korach as a wise man, implying that his debate with Moshe was deeper than may be perceived from a simple reading of the text. We may ask: What precisely were Korach and Moshe arguing about?

In order to fully appreciate an approach that addresses this matter, I ask my dear readers to pose the following question at the Shabbos table this week, and to discuss amongst yourselves the reasons for your responses: What has been more beneficial for the Jewish people - Shabbos or a *tzaddik*?

Inevitably, both are necessary; however, the question is: which is more crucial for our Nation's survival? I am certain that this subject matter will trigger much involved discussion, and may evoke surprising suggestions.

It seems that an argument could be presented for both sides of the debate, because both Shabbos and a *tzaddik* have unique advantages. For instance, we could have access to a *tzaddik* every single day, whereas Shabbos occurs only once a week. On the other hand, there are potential drawbacks to a *tzaddik*. There is a risk that he will become proud and arrogant. There is also a danger that the *tzaddik*'s followers will become extreme and worship him like an idol. Shabbos, however, holds none of these hazards because it is neither an object nor a person and can therefore never become proud, nor risk being worshipped as a deity.

We could suggest that Korach and Moshe were disputing this matter - whether Shabbos or a *tzaddik* has prime significance. Korach maintained that a *tzaddik* has primary importance. Moreover, he viewed himself as being the most righteous person of his time. (It is possible that Korach **was** greater than Moshe in Torah because we see that he asks questions which Moshe, apparently, cannot answer.) Moshe, however, held that Shabbos has superiority over a *tzaddik*. This fits in well with the idea that Moshe's spiritual essence was Shabbos; his primary concern was upholding the sanctity of Shabbos. We will see an allusion to this momentarily.

In the meantime, from the Torah's report that Moshe was victorious in the debate with Korach, we could propose that Moshe won the argument; because Shabbos, which he regarded as more important than a *tzaddik*, presents less severe potential pitfalls. We mentioned earlier that a possible drawback of a *tzaddik* is that he risks becoming haughty and that he may even be worshiped like an idol.

The Talmud (*Sukkah* 52a) teaches us that only once the evil inclination is slaughtered at the time of the *Moshiach*, will a *tzaddik* no longer be at risk of becoming proud. Furthermore, a *tzaddik*'s followers will be free of the *yetzer hara,* which may cause them to go too far and worship the *tzaddik* as an idol. However, until then - as long as the *yetzer hara* exists - these dangers remain, particularly when a *tzaddik* attempts to promote himself as the pious person of the generation, just as Korach tried to do.

These ideas about Moshe preferring Shabbos and Korach preferring the *tzaddik* are alluded to in *Tehillim* (92:1). The Psalm begins, "*Mizmor shir l'yom HaShabbos* - a song with musical accompaniment for the Shabbos day." The initial letters of these four opening words (*mem, shin, lamed, hey*) can be unscrambled to spell the word *l'Moshe* (to Moshe) hinting at Moshe's connection to Shabbos.

Later in the Psalm it says, "*Tzaddik katamar yifrach* - The righteous one flourishes like the palm." In this case, the final letters of these three words (*kuf, reish, ches*) form the name "Korach," alluding to Korach's association with a *tzaddik*.

It is not for naught that Moshe's name appears in connection with Shabbos, and that the acronym is formed from the initial letters of the words that appear at the beginning of the Psalm. From the very **beginning** of time, Shabbos was deemed far greater than a *tzaddik*.

It is also not coincidental that Korach's name is found in association with a *tzaddik,* and that the hint is found in the final letters of the words, which appear towards the **end** of the Psalm. Only at the **end** of days, when the evil inclination is finally destroyed, will the *tzaddik* come to the forefront and receive his deserved recognition and appreciation - on an equal stature with Shabbos.

The *Arizal* (*Likutei Torah, Tehillim* 92:13) says that the hint to Korach's name in the final letters of the words "*Tzaddik katamar yifrach*" teaches us that at the end of days Korach will emerge as a *tzaddik*. Therefore, Korach's argument was **not** incorrect, but its timing was inappropriate. Moshe attempted to explain this to Korach, but unfortunately, Korach did not have the patience to listen and was consequently punished.

Perhaps it would be advisable to strengthen our appreciation of our *tzaddikim* and of Shabbos. One way to do this would be to share stories about our *tzaddikim* at the Shabbos table. The story of a *gadol* coupled with the ambience of Shabbos would create memories to last a lifetime.

May we be blessed to cling to, but not idolize, our holy *tzaddikim* - who are free of pride - every day of the week. More importantly (for the time being), may we live Shabbos to its full extent so that one day, we will witness the complete blossoming of the *tzaddik*.

Korach

Sing Along With Me

Sometimes something so good happens to us that we burst forth with song, and other times it is our singing that can lead us to incredible things. Either way, song can transport us from where we are to where we want to be.

This week's portion discusses Korach's fate together with his followers. The Earth opened its mouth and swallowed them alive after they led a rebellion against Moshe and Aharon. When this happened, the Torah states, "And all of Israel that were round about them - *nasu l'kolam* - fled at their cries because they said, 'lest the Earth swallow us' (16:34)." In this sentence, the Torah is trying to tell us how the surrounding people ran away from the Earth's mouth, which made noise when it opened.

If that's the case, then the Torah's choice of words, grammatically speaking, does not seem to concur with what the Torah is trying to say. The Torah should have said something like *nasu mipachad kolam*, which means "they fled from the fear of the cries," implying that the people ran **away** from the destruction. However, the Torah instead uses the words *nasu l'kolam*, which literally translates as "they ran **to** the cries [or to the noise]." Why would the Torah use an expression which implies the opposite of what is intended?

Furthermore, if we jump to the portion of *Pinchas*, it says there, "And the sons of Korach did not die" (26:11). The Talmud in *Sanhedrin* (110a) explains how this occurred. The Talmud says that a place (or a ledge) was set apart for them in Purgatory, and they sat on it and began to sing a song to God. This passage raises another question. It is understandable for the Talmud to supply us with details about how Korach's sons were saved since there is a verse that says explicitly that Korach's sons did not die. So the Talmud is merely telling us how this happened specifically. However, from where do the Sages know that Korach's sons began to sing a song? Where is the Scriptural verse supporting that idea?

The *Emunas Itecha* says that it is obvious that Korach's sons were saved because they repented before falling completely into Purgatory. And it is because of this that the Talmud knew that Korach's sons must have sung a song. This is precisely what transpired when the first person repented.

The Midrash tells us (*Bereishis Rabbah* 22:13), that Adam HaRishon met with his son Kayin, after Kayin murdered his brother Hevel. Adam asked Kayin, "What was the heavenly verdict regarding your crime?" Kayin responded by saying that "I repented and we came to a compromise" (in other words, Kayin wasn't immediately killed for his sin of murder). When Adam heard this, he began to hit himself on his face and said, "Such is the power of *teshuvah* (repentance) and I never knew." So immediately Adam got up to repent and said, "*Mizmor shir l'yom haShabbos* - a psalm, a song, for the Shabbos day" (*Tehillim* 92:1).

From this Midrash we see that Adam's *teshuvah* was with song; and just like the first person's repentance was amidst singing, so too, the Talmud teaches us that the sons of Korach repented by singing. In other words, singing is part and parcel of *teshuvah*.

Perhaps we could suggest that song adds a whole new dimension to repentance. It is the singing that defines whether our *teshuvah* is coming from a place of fear or from a place of love. (See *Yoma* 86b for the difference between *teshuvah* from fear as opposed to *teshuvah* from love, in that when it stems from fear, it can transform intentional sins into accidental ones; whereas, when it stems from love, it transforms the sins into merits.) And this will answer the first question as well. The Torah chose to express itself with the words *nasu l'kolam* to teach us that the Jews did not run away from the Earth's open mouth. On the contrary, they ran toward the Earth's opening, because from within that hole, Korach's sons were in the process of their *teshuvah* and their voices were heard singing.

Let's not forget that Korach's sons were Levites who were blessed with the beauty of song. When the Jews heard the pleasant singing of repentance that came from Korach's sons, they were aroused to repent for their sin of following Korach in the depths of their hearts. And so, the Jews ran toward the voices of pleasant repentance that brought them all back to the faith that Moshe and his Torah are true (see *Bava Basra* 74a). The people no longer believed in Korach, who had planted seeds of doubt into their minds about Moshe's authenticity. So the people ran to the source of *teshuvah*, and yet, were not afraid of falling into the hole because they knew the concept, mentioned in *Avos* 4:13, that *teshuvah* serves as a shield against tragedies and retribution.

Every Shabbos serves as a time of repentance for mistakes committed throughout the previous week, repentance is even hinted to in the root of the word Shabbos, which is *shav*, repent. So, let us "repent" or "return" to God on Shabbos through song at the Shabbos table. Choose a couple of favorite songs with moving melodies to be sung at each meal, and transform the Shabbos meal into an everlasting experience.

May we all be blessed to be empowered with the gift of *teshuvah* so that we deserve the coming of *Moshiach*, who will rebuild our Temple where the Levites will sing the most beautiful of songs. And then, every day will be like Shabbos.

Chukas

Up For Grabs

Let us explore the greatest weapon of the Jewish people - the one that can rid us of all our enemies.

In this week's portion, *Chukas*, the first topic is that of the red heifer (*parah adumah*). Rabbeinu Bachya (19:1-3) cites the *Midrash Psikta D'rav Kahana*, # 9, that says that these verses about the red heifer can be divided in such a way that they represent the five kingdoms: Egyptian, Babylonian, Midian (Persian), Greek, and Roman (see there all the details and verses that support this parallel).

However, the heifer seems to have the most in common with the Roman exile. This is based on a teaching from the *Hafla'ah* in his *Panim Yafos*, where he says that the red heifer is called a *parah **adumah***, which hints at Esav, the progenitor of Rome, who is called Edom, red (see *Bereishis* 25:30 and 36:1). This shows a strong correlation between the red heifer and Esav, the father of the **red** people.

To understand this connection, the *Zohar* (Volume 2, page 78b) says that the months of *Nissan, Iyar*, and *Sivan* were given over to Yaakov's authority; however, the months of *Tammuz, Av*, and *Elul* were given into the authority of Esav. Then, Yaakov grabbed the month of *Elul* away from Esav.

Although it may seem that Yaakov did a terrible thing, by grabbing away from Esav what should belong to him, the *Emunas Itecha* shares with us a "reality check" by pointing out that, in fact, everything belongs to Yaakov and nothing belongs to Esav, as all of Creation was only for the Jewish people (see *Rashi* in *Bereishis* 1:1 and *Yirmiyah* 2:3). On the contrary, the fact that Esav has authority over *Tammuz, Av*, and *Elul*, is an indication that

Esav grabbed those months away from Yaakov first. By Yaakov grabbing the month of *Elul*, he is simply taking back what is rightfully his.

The meaning behind Esav having authority over certain months of the year is to say that, at those times, opportunities for spiritual growth have been robbed from the Jewish people to a certain degree. It follows, on the other hand, that those months which fall under the auspices of Yaakov contain even greater opportunities for spiritual growth. Not only has Esav grabbed opportunities of spiritual growth away from Yaakov, but throughout the ages, the descendants of Esav have grabbed opportunities of spiritual growth away from Yaakov's descendants.

Just like Yaakov began the process of taking back what is rightfully his, it is incumbent upon us, the descendants of Yaakov, to finish the job and take back what is rightfully ours. When we do so, we will transform the months of *Tammuz* and *Av* from months of destruction (see *Yoma* 9b) into months of redemption.

The way to achieve all of this is hinted to in the ceremony with the *parah adumah* - which, as we said earlier, hints at Esav who is Edom. We are told in this *parshah* to destroy the *parah adumah*. This takes on an added dimension of meaning in that it refers to nullifying the powers of Edom. The way to achieve this is through fire, meaning through the study of Torah, which is called a fiery law (see *Devarim* 33:2).

Yaakov represents the pillar of Torah study. So, just like Yaakov used Torah to begin reclaiming that which was his, we too must use the same tool of Torah study to reclaim our rights. This is why the portion of *Chukas* is read at the beginning of *Tammuz* - to remind us that we have just entered into Esav's territory and are under the claws of Esav. The way to combat the forces of evil is by strengthening ourselves in the study of Torah.

Let us try, over the next two months (*Tammuz* and *Av*) to take up upon ourselves five extra minutes of Torah study a day. Seek to make it exciting, and study something that interests you. Study with a partner or go to a class that motivates you. In this way, we will be able to ignite the Torah burning in our hearts.

May we all be blessed to gird ourselves with the most powerful weapon we have in our arsenal, Torah study, and wipe out the Esavs in this world who seek to destroy us, so that we can reclaim what is rightfully ours and transform the months of *Tammuz* and *Av* into times of happiness and joy.

Chukas

The Needs of the Many Outweigh the Needs of the Few

Perhaps one of the greatest demonstrations of sincere care and love for another person is to give to that person even though we lose out in the process. In other words, the willingness to "take a hit" for others is the epitome of selflessness.

The first topic that is discussed in this week's portion, *Chukas*, is the *parah adumah* - the red heifer. The Torah introduces the subject (19:2) with the words, "*Zos chukas HaTorah* - This is the statute of the Torah." A statute is a type of command for which no reason is provided. The verses go on to describe how the *Kohen* prepared the ashes of the cow for the purification process, and then lists the situations which required spiritual purification, for example, contact with a corpse (see 19:11-22). Although the impure person was purified by the *parah adumah*, some of those involved in the preparation of the concoction became impure (see 19:7-8 and 19:10).

An obvious and frequently asked question arises: How can the same thing purify an impure person, and simultaneously contaminate one who is pure? If the impure individual is purified through the *parah adumah*, does it not logically follow that the pure person should become even **more** pure than he was before? How can we understand this dichotomy?

The complexity of this law is highlighted in the Talmud (*Niddah* 9a), where it expounds on King Solomon's words, "*Amarti echkemah v'hi rechokah mimeni* - I said I will be wise, yet it is beyond me" (*Koheles* 7:23). King Solomon, the wisest of all men, delved into the depths of the *parah adumah*, but was unable to fully comprehend its inner mechanisms. Despite this, we still thirst for an explanation.

Rashi (*Bamidbar* 19:22 in the name of *Rabbi Moshe HaDarshan* and the *Midrash Tanchuma, Os* 8) connects the *parah adumah* with the *Eigel HaZahav*, the Golden Calf. We can appreciate their deep relationship based on the following insight.

Although the incident of the Golden Calf is perceived as the Jews' greatest crime, the Talmud (*Avodah Zarah* 4b) provides a completely different perspective. Rabbi Yehoshua ben Levi says that the Jewish people committed this sin to provide an opening for future penitents.

Rashi explains that the Israelites in the desert were at a lofty spiritual level and were in complete control of their inclinations. They had no desire to transgress even slightly - never mind commit a great offense like worshipping an *Eigel*! What actually occurred is that Hashem removed the Jews' free will, allowing their evil inclination to triumph and causing them to sin. God engineered this situation intentionally to allow any transgressors in the future to look back at this incident and realize that *teshuvah* is always possible. (One could question this Gemara by asking why the Jews were punished for the Golden Calf if they were forced into it. As explained above (See *Ki Sisa, Parshas Para*, "Holy Cow"), there are at least two possible answers. One is that they enjoyed the sin while it was happening. The punishment was for the enjoyment and not for the sin itself. A second approach will be mentioned momentarily.)

In the meantime, *Rashi* goes on to say that, similarly, should there be a sinner in the future who thinks that God is so disgusted with him that He will not excuse him, we say to that person, "Go and learn the episode of the Golden Calf." God pardoned the Jews for the grave offense of the *Eigel*, made even more offensive after the people had witnessed numerous miracles in the desert. It follows, then, that any transgression **we** commit can never be as severe as theirs, since we have never experienced God's overt presence as they did. Therefore, through the *Eigel*, we recognize that *teshuvah* is always possible.

Although the incident of the Golden Calf was orchestrated to help later generations, we know that some of those involved in the *Eigel*, perished (see *Shemos* 32:28 and 32:35.) We see from here that there are often times when the few are expected to sacrifice themselves for the benefit of the many, even if they lose out in the process. (When we talk about "losing out" we are referring to loss in this world. Of course, anyone who gives of himself for the benefit of others will be rewarded in the World to Come.)

Based on this idea, we can answer our original question concerning the antithetical nature of the *parah adumah*. Just as some of the priests, who prepared the *parah adumah* for the Jewish people, lost out by becoming impure themselves, so must we, as individuals, be prepared to sacrifice **our** needs for the sake of the community, even if we experience a loss in the process. Although there is no logical explanation for the law of the red heifer, we could suggest that God created this contradictory law deliberately, in order for us to learn this specific lesson - to forgo our individual needs for the benefit of the many.

This explains the connection between the *Eigel HaZahav* and the *parah adumah* as they share a common message. By the Golden Calf, one generation gave of themselves - and even died - for the benefit of future generations. Similarly, by the red heifer we find that one *Kohen* assists the community even though he incurs a loss. Therefore, both represent the concept of the few sacrificing for the many; of the individual devoting himself to the community, even at his own expense.

Now we can understand why the *parah adumah* is introduced with the phrase, "*Zos chukas haTorah* - This is the statute of the Torah," when it would seemingly have been more logical to specify, "*Zos chukas haParah* - This is the statute of the heifer." Based on the ideas we have discussed, we can appreciate that the lesson which we learn from the *parah adumah* - sacrificing our needs for the benefit of the whole - does not apply only to the law of the red heifer. Rather, it is a universal Torah law. God expects each and every one of us to imbibe this message, and to apply it to **all** aspects of Torah, and to our day-to-day lives.

There are a few areas in which we can live up to this teaching. For example, we could give up some of our sleep time in order to help our spouse with whatever chores need to be done. Additionally, we could give up time that we reserved for our own recreation in order to spend quality time with our children. Not only will we embody this lesson, but the benefits we reap will be priceless.

May we be blessed with the strength to give of ourselves for the greater good, whether in Torah or *mitzvos* - even if it kills us... so that we live to see the day when we will be purified by the red heifer, ushering in the Messianic era, with all the good that follows.

Chukas

Between a Rock and a Hard Place

Every leader finds himself in precarious situations. After all, you can't please all of the people, all of the time. Inevitably, the masses will be disappointed and accuse the leadership of being incompetent, but where does the real blame lie?

One of the topics in this week's portion is the story about Miriam's death (*Bamidbar* 20:1), which caused the waters to stop flowing from the rock (*Ta'anis*, chap. 1, *Meyaimasai*, pg. 9a, the opinion of *Rebbi Yosi* in the name of *Rebbi Yehudah*) and led the people to become thirsty. God commanded Moshe to speak to the rock so it would give out its waters once again. Instead, Moshe hit the rock. As a result of that mistake, Moshe was denied entrance to the Land of Israel (*Bamidbar* 20:7-13).

There are numerous questions that surround this episode. One of them is, "How could such a spiritual giant like Moshe disobey a direct Divine Order?"

There are many approaches addressing this issue; however, according to the *Shvilei Pinchas*, the explanation is as follows. Moshe served as an appointed messenger who officiated on behalf of the congregation. As such, Moshe's success largely depended on the spiritual level of the people he was representing.

There are a number of sources which support this notion. For example, the Talmud says that if a person makes a mistake in his prayers, it is a bad sign for that individual. However, if the one appointed to lead the service makes a mistake in his prayers, it is not a bad sign for that person, rather it is a bad sign for the people that he represents (Mishnah, *Berachos*, chap. 5, *Ein*

Omdin, Mishnah 5, pg. 34b).

Therefore, even though Moshe had reached spiritual excellence, his lack of success in this mission had nothing to do with him; but rather, it was a reflection of the lack in the people he was representing. It was the people's low spiritual status that caused Moshe to hit the rock. (See *Tikkunei Zohar, Tikkun* 21, pg. 44a that complements this line of thinking.)

Part of the problem with the people was that they grew impatient with Moshe and Aharon, who were searching for the specific rock that God had commanded them to speak to. That specific rock was known as Miriam's Well. That was the rock from which water flowed until Miriam passed away.

The people were thirsty and irritated. So, they complained that God could do anything. God could bring water from any rock He so desires. Therefore, they wanted to know why it was necessary to waste time searching for a particular rock.

This is where the people were mistaken. They lacked faith in God. They did not believe fully that God has reasons for doing things in a precise way. They also did not completely trust their spiritual leaders. They could not understand why Moshe and Aharon were taking so long.

Having faith in God and in the *tzaddikim* (righteous ones) means following what they say, even if there does not seem to be a logical reason for what they are doing. This is the lesson of the first topic of our portion, the *parah adumah* (red heifer), which is called a *chok*, a commandment that we do not understand (*Bamidbar* 19:2).

Since the people did not follow God and Moshe implicitly, things did not go smoothly for Moshe, which was a poor reflection on the people. Had the people chosen to be on a higher spiritual level, then their leaders would have been lifted even higher and would therefore have been able to perform more efficiently.

Moshe was like a tool in the hands of the people. It was the people's job to keep Moshe sharp. Moshe's accuracy depended on the spiritual level of those that he represented.

This is a very important lesson for us to learn, especially in today's day and age. Occasionally, people are disappointed with some of our leadership. They do not understand why more is not being done about a certain situation.

I do not know the answers to these questions (or to any questions, for that matter). However, perhaps we could suggest at least a partial answer.

Maybe we, the people, are to blame. Maybe we do not deserve to experience complete success through our leaders.

Maybe a mistake made by a leader is a reflection of a lacking in people he represents. Maybe it has nothing to do with the leader. Maybe it is our fault.

We cannot just sit back and engage in finger-pointing, by blaming the *tzaddikim* for our problems. Maybe we need to turn inward and examine our own personalities for flaws that bring our spiritual giants down.

Perhaps we could suggest two areas of self-improvement. Even those who believe in God sometimes forget just how involved God is in our everyday lives. Even those who believe that everything is for the best, tend to lose sight of it from time to time. Even those who know that God has a reason for everything can grow frustrated when they do not understand what's happening or not happening.

Therefore, all we need to do is remind ourselves about God's participation in our lives. We need to retell ourselves that God loves us unconditionally; therefore, everything that happens is actually for the best. Everything has a reason behind it.

This would require study, maybe once a day or even just once a week.

Practically speaking, let's take out a book on faith and trust in God, and read a little bit in order to remind ourselves of these truths.

A second suggestion is to take out some books about our *gedolim* in order to appreciate who they were. We need to get a glimpse of a world that is way out of our league. In this way, we can focus more on what we need to improve in ourselves. Maybe then, we will start to see better results.

May we all be blessed to strengthen ourselves in faith in God and in our spiritual giants, and thus deserve to benefit from proper leadership.

Chukas

Long Lasting

Living with wisdom means to envision the effect and repercussions of today's actions on tomorrow.

Let us examine the end of the *parshah*, which discusses the generally overlooked topic of Og, king of Bashan.

The Torah tells us that Og and his entire nation went out to battle the Jewish people (*Bamidbar* 21:33), whereupon Hashem reassures Moshe, "Do not fear him, for I have delivered him into your hands" (*Bamidbar* 21:34). Surely the physical and military might of Og was no match for Hashem's protection. Why then, would Moshe be so afraid of Og?

The *Da'as Zekeinim* (on 21:34) and *Sifsei Chachamim* (80) explain that Moshe was afraid of the merit that Og had acquired by helping Avraham during the war of the four kings and the five kings. Og informed Avraham that the four kings had been victorious and that they had captured his nephew, Lot (*Bereishis* 14:13, *Midrash Tanchuma* 25). This information enabled Avraham to enter the battle and rescue Lot.

According to the Midrash (*Beresihis Rabbah* 42:8), Og had evil motives for providing this information; he hoped that Avraham would be slain in battle and that he, Og, could then take Sarah as a wife. Despite Og's wicked intentions, his action was good. Moshe thought that the merit of Og's good deed would grant him Divine protection. This is why he was afraid.

Moshe's fear was not unfounded. The Talmud (*Sanhendrin* 105b, *Horiyos* 10b the opinions of *Rabbi Yehudah* in the name of *Rav*) teaches that, because of the forty-two offerings that the wicked King Balak brought to Hashem, Balak merited to have Rus as one of his descendants. Balak's motives were far from virtuous; he brought the offerings in an attempt to "sway" Hashem to his side so he could annihilate the entire Jewish people! Nevertheless, although Balak's intentions were evil, his deeds, in and of themselves, i.e. bringing offerings to Hashem, were positive. In this merit, he was rewarded by having Rus as a descendant.

We see that the power of positive actions, even when marred by evil intentions, lasts for generations. However, we can also learn a deeper lesson from these examples. Not only do positive deeds have powerful ramifications for the future, but so do negative deeds, as well.

In the Midrash (*Bereishis Rabbah* 42:8, *Bamidbar Rabbah* 19:32), Hashem tells Og, "Since you walked to tell Avraham that Lot had been captured, I promise to give you longevity. [In other words, since you walked to do an act of kindness, you will walk the Earth for a long time]. But because you had evil intentions [hoping for Avraham's demise], I promise that you will see hundreds and thousands of Avraham's descendants, and that your downfall will be at their hands."

One lesson we can take from the story of Og is that our behavior, be it positive or negative, always has consequences. We must develop the habit of asking ourselves, "What will the future ramifications be of my actions, speech and thoughts? How might this deed, comment or thought manifest itself later? Will it help or hurt me?" Imagining the future repercussions of our behavior is one of the most effective tools in deciding how to act in the moment.

May we be blessed with the ability to see the future, in order to appreciate the outcome of our deeds, speech and thoughts. In this merit, may we also see the future of Jewish history unfold with the coming *Moshiach*, the ingathering of the exiles, peace on Earth, and the building of our holy Temple.

Balak

The Opposite Express

Our upbringing has taught us that in order to truly enjoy something, it has to be in moderation. After all, too much of anything is not good. But, are there ever instances where extreme actions need to be taken?

This week's *parshah Balak*, contains many interconnected ideas which combine to form a fundamental point. I will attempt, with the help of God, to extract one small thought from the *parshah* which, I hope, will adequately convey an important message.

Bilaam says to Balak (*Bamidbar* 23:3), "*V'eilcha, ulai yika're Hashem likrasi... vayeilech* **shefi** - and I will go; perhaps the Lord will come to meet me...and he went [**shefi**]."

Onkelos translates *shefi* as "alone." The *Chasam Sofer*, in his monumental work, *Toras Moshe*, offers an alternative, creative definition of this word. He maintains that the letters that spell *shefi* (*shin, pey, yud*) are an acronym for three Hebrew words: *shemanam* (their oil); *pitam* (their bread); and *yeinam* (their wine).

What is the significance of these three items? The Talmud (*Shabbos* 17b, citing *Rabbi Acha* the son of *Rabbi Ada*, in the name of *Rabbi Yitzchak*) says that the Sages instituted a ruling that we must avoid eating the bread and oil of the gentiles, to prevent us from partaking also of wine in their company and risking assimilation.

We learn from *Rashi* (*Bamidbar* 24:14 based on *Sanhedrin* 106a) that Bilaam advised Balak to promote harlotry amongst the Jewish people - a type of misconduct that Hashem loathes - so that God's anger would be kindled against the Jews, culminating in their destruction.

This, says the *Chasam Sofer*, is what Bilaam was pondering as he went, *shefi*. He was devising a plan to engage the Jews in *shemanam* (their oil) and *pitam* (their bread), so that ultimately they will involve themselves in promiscuous activity due to indulging in *yeinam* (their wine). Consequently, he hoped, God would despise the Jews and annihilate them.

Although this insight into the *parshah* may seem minute, we can derive an extremely crucial message from it. Sometimes, we find ourselves in the clutches of a spiritually decadent evil. In response, we must run to the opposite extreme in pursuit of goodness - Torah and *mitzvos* - to save ourselves from spiritual regression.

Bilaam's evil strategy epitomizes the tactics of the dangerous forces which surround us in this world - both externally, by the nations; and internally, by our *yetzer hara*. Our wise and holy Sages recognized the extent of these risks and, therefore, cautioned us to establish boundaries which prevent us from falling into their traps and wandering off the Torah path.

As I impart this message, I cannot help but hear the echoes of some people's voices as they claim: "Aren't the Sages going too far? Why are they so fanatical? After all, what's wrong with eating a piece of their bread or drinking a sip of their wine?"

It is essential to reaffirm repeatedly the pure wisdom of our Sages. *Chazal* understood exactly the extent of the danger which our involvement in gentile society presents. They were also aware of the workings of the *yetzer hara*, and that the very things which we perceive as "fanatical" on the part of the Sages are, in fact, the safety nets that protect us from the very traps that the perpetrators set to ensnare us.

We learn from Bilaam that evil knows no boundaries, and that our enemies will do whatever it takes to corrupt us and bring us down into the deep, dismal depths of darkness and oblivion. In order to counteract these forces, we must involve ourselves in Godly pursuits - in the study of Torah and performance of *mitzvos* - to elevate us, and transport ourselves onto a wonderful path of light and lucidity. Moreover, as the Sages advise, we sometimes need to become "kosher radicals" to keep us on the right track.

This concept is highlighted by the *Rambam* in *Peirush HaMishnayos* as he comments on the instruction, "You shall be exceedingly humble" (*Avos* 4:4). He says that sometimes a person must go to an extreme in order to finally reach a beautiful and harmonious balance.

Each and every one of us has his own unique challenges which necessitate taking excessive measures from time to time, in specific areas, on our journey to spiritual wholesomeness. The *yetzer hara* is extremely powerful, and we must assert absolute control over it, whatever it takes.

One practical application could be that in the moment that we are tempted to transgress, then at that very instant, we should run to do the opposite. For example, if one is being pulled to do something immoral, then at that moment run to the opposite extreme and engage in a *mitzvah* of holiness. This will surely guard us from the evil with which we were tempted.

May we be blessed with healthy fanaticism, leading to complete dedication to Torah and *mitzvos*. May we have the strength and clarity to do the total opposite of what our *yetzer hara* desires so that we deserve *Moshiach's* arrival, the destruction of all evil, and the building of the final Temple.

Balak

Hi Ho, Hi Ho, It's Off to Shul We Go

When our minds and hearts are soaked in purity, we will forever be connected to the Holy One.

In this week's portion, *Balak*, the King of Moav (whose name was Balak) hires a prophet from Aram, called Bilaam, to destroy the Jewish people with his curses. However, God transformed all of his curses into blessings. The Talmud says (*Sanhedrin* 105b citing the opinion of *Rabbi Yochanan*) that since the curses were turned into blessings, one can study the blessings and work backwards to discover how Bilaam really intended to curse the Jewish people.

For example, when it says (24:5), "How goodly are your tents, O Jacob, and your dwelling places, O Israel," the inference is that Bilaam wanted to curse the Jewish people so that they would no longer have synagogues in which to pray or study halls in which to engage in Torah study. The Talmud goes on to say that all these curses that were transformed into blessings only remained blessings temporarily. Eventually they all reverted back to curses except for one blessing, which remained a blessing forever.

That eternal blessing was that the Jews would always have synagogues and study halls. Proof that only one curse turned into a permanent blessing stems from a verse (*Devarim* 23:6) where it says, "And God, your Lord, turned for you the curse into a blessing because the Lord, your God, loves you." Since the verse mentions "curse" in the singular, we derive that only one curse remained a blessing, whereas all the other curses that were turned into blessings eventually became curses again.

This passage raises a few questions. First of all, the verse in *Devarim* says that God transformed the curse into a blessing because He loves us. If He loves us so much, why didn't He transform all the curses into permanent blessings? Secondly, what is unique about synagogues and study halls that this was the only blessing that remained permanently?

The Slonimer Rebbe points out that the nature of a blessing is a connection with God, because at the time a Jew is connected to God, blessing comes to that person. The essence of a curse, however, is that a Jew is severed or distanced from God; because when a Jew drifts away from God, all sorts of curses can affect him. With this foundation, the Slonimer explains that Bilaam's goal was to sever the Jewish people's relationship with God because then, all sorts of curses could infiltrate. We have to realize, however, that attaching oneself to God completely means having an intellectual connection as well as an emotional one.

This is hinted to in the *mitzvah* of *tefillin*, where the box on the arm is opposite the heart (the emotional aspect), and the box on the head is opposite the brain (the intellectual aspect). The straps which tie the *tefillin* to the body represent the connection to God. Therefore, this *mitzvah* teaches us that the way to connect to God completely is through the mind and the heart, intellectually and emotionally.

Since Bilaam's objective was to sever the ties that we have with the Divine, he thought up two ways of accomplishing his goal.

1) Bilaam advised Balak to cause the Jews to stumble in idolatry (25:3), which ruins the mind and creates all sorts of anti-Torah philosophies.

2) Bilaam convinced Balak to cause the Jews to stumble in immorality with the Moabite daughters (25:1), inviting the ruination of the heart, by filling it with lustful passions.

By attacking these two parts, mind and heart, Bilaam hoped to cause the

Jews to be disconnected from Hashem and, thereby, create a situation where curses could settle in. The remedies for these two sins are:

1) Torah study, which purifies the mind.

2) Prayer, which purifies the heart (see *Ta'anis* 2a and *Eichah* 2:19).

Both Torah study and prayer reconnect the mind and heart to God. This will help us understand the uniqueness of the permanent blessing regarding synagogues and study halls remaining with the Jewish people until the end of time. Synagogues are places designated for prayer, which is the process of purifying the heart; and study halls are places designated for learning Torah, which is the process of purifying the mind.

We could suggest that the boxes of *tefillin*, which are in the shape of cubes, represent the two buildings, synagogues and study halls, which are also generally in the shape of cubes. The *tefillin* on the arm, opposite the heart, correspond to the synagogue; whereas, the *tefillin* on the head, opposite the brain, correspond to the study hall.

Bilaam wanted to curse the Jews to lose their synagogues and study halls so that they would not be connected to God. This disconnection would have opened the door to all sorts of curses, which would have led to the Jewish people's annihilation, God forbid. This is something that God would not allow to happen. And that's why this blessing, specifically, was singled out to remain with us permanently, so that we would always be connected to Hashem and, thereby, become the eternal people.

This also helps us understand the extent to which God loves us. By turning this one curse into a permanent blessing, God ensured the survival of the Jewish people and protected them from all the curses of the world. This blessing is not limited to a specific area; rather, it carries global implications.

Not only would it be a good idea to spend a little time each day in a synagogue and a study hall, but when we step foot into those places we should make a declaration. Upon entering a synagogue we should say, "I am now going to pray in the synagogue in order to purify my heart and thereby connect to God emotionally." Upon entering a study hall we should say, "I am now going to study Torah to purify my mind and thereby connect to God intellectually."

May we all be blessed to focus on directing our minds and hearts to God through learning Torah and through *tefillah*, so that we can transform these Three Weeks from the lowest of times to the highest. May our efforts in this regard make us deserving the coming of *Moshiach*, who will build the best tent and dwelling place we have ever seen, at a time in which we will be completely connected to God, and accordingly, all forms of curse will be removed from the universe.

Balak

Who Gives a Care?

Enthusiasm is contagious. Once we are excited about doing something, there is almost nothing that can stop us. When this passion is channeled into Torah and *mitzvos*, we can really go places.

After Balak hired Bilaam to annihilate the Jewish people by cursing them, one of Bilaam's prophesies says, "*Oy mi yichyeh misumo Kel* - Alas, who will live after the appointed one of God?" (*Bamidbar* 24:23).

The *Arizal* (*Sha'ar Hagilgulim*) reveals that what Bilaam was actually bemoaning was the birth of Shmuel. This is hinted to in the last two words of this verse, *misumo Kel*. When these two words are put together, they spell "*MiShmuel.*" In other words, Bilaam was grumbling about the birth of the appointed one of God, who was Shmuel. We have to ask ourselves why Shmuel's birth bothered Bilaam so much.

Well, a little bit earlier on, Bilaam also laments the destruction of Amalek (see *Bamidbar* 24:20 with *Rashi* there). The following questions arise: Why would Bilaam care about Amalek's obliteration? Is there some connection between Bilaam's fear of Shmuel's birth and Bilaam's trepidation as to Amalek's downfall?

The Zohar (*Rayah Mihemnah*, *Ki Seitzei*, pg. 281b) teaches us that the root of Bilaam's and Balak's souls stem from Amalek. This means to say that Bilaam and Balak drew their impure power from the negative energy and spiritual pollution of Amalek.

The connection that links Bilaam and Balak to Amalek is coded into their names. The last two letters of Bilaam's name (*ayin, mem*) joined with the last two letters of Balak's name (*lamed, kuf*) spell "Amalek." This shows us that

Bilaam and Balak were outgrowths of Amalek, and they joined together, like two pieces of a puzzle, in order to draw from the filthy cesspool of Amalek for the purpose of destroying the Jewish people.

However, Shmuel anointed Shaul as the first King of Israel (*Shmuel I*, 10:1) and then commanded him to eradicate Amalek (*Shmuel I*, 15:2-3). Shaul did not carry out his mission completely and left Agag, the king of Amalek, alive (*Shmuel I*, 15:9). Shmuel himself severed Agag (*Shmuel I*, 15:33) and later anointed King David, who is the progenitor of the *Moshiach* (Messiah) and who will conclude the annihilation of Amalek (*Smag. Lo Sa'aseh* 226).

We now see a connection between Shmuel and Amalek. Shmuel began the process of Amalek's eventual downfall. This explains why Bilaam bewailed Shmuel's birth. It is because Shmuel would cause the destruction of Amalek. Amalek's annihilation also pained Bilaam because he realized that his own strength stemmed from Amalek. Therefore, if Amalek is abolished, then that would mean that Bilaam would be wiped out for eternity as well. This is why Bilaam cried, "Who can survive *misumo Kel*," from the appointed one of God, who is Shmuel. Shmuel's appointment would seal the end of Bilaam's fate.

Today, although we may not know exactly who descends from Amalek, his infectious poison may still run through our blood stream. Many negative traits have been connected to Amalek. One of the more obvious ones is indifference.

Amalek spreads an attitude by which our approach to Torah and *mitzvos* is icy cold. This means to say that, perhaps, sometimes we lack enthusiasm, excitement, and motivation in our *avodas Hashem* (service to God).

This trademark of indifference is found amongst the ranks of Amalek. The verse says about Amalek that they *karcha*, met us, on the way (*Devarim* 25:18). One definition of *karcha* comes from its root word *kar*, which means "cold."

This indicates that Amalek says: "It's okay to do the *mitzvos*, just don't do them with passion." They want all feeling to be left out of our service to God, and thus we won't give a care. Without inspiration, we certainly won't connect with God, and we may eventually stop practicing altogether. But until *Moshiach* comes to cleanse the world of Amalek's spiritual filth, we can pave the way by eradicating the Amalek within us.

Here are some practical suggestions for how we can muster up some eagerness in our *mitzvah* performance. Study is always a good idea. The more we study about a *mitzvah*, the more interested we become in that *mitzvah*.

Besides that, there are two actual exercises that we can implement that can be very beneficial:

1) Choose one *mitzvah* a day that we actually run to do. By deciding to get a little out of breath to do a *mitzvah*, it will impress upon us the importance of that *mitzvah*.

2) Choose just one *berachah* (blessing) a day, or just one sentence of the liturgy a day, and decide to say it slowly out loud. This can be done in the privacy of our homes. Saying it out loud can generate strong feelings for that prayer, which means that the prayer will have a much greater impact on us.

These are methods that can create a sense of caring and warmth. Sharing that warmth with other people is a very beautiful thing.

May we all be blessed to become more impassioned with our *avodas* Hashem, and thereby, burn out the Amalek within us, so that we deserve to witness the coming of *Moshiach*, who will completely destroy the Bilaams and Balaks of the world.

Balak

Soar Like an Eagle

Like "karma," we tend to attract the type of energy we put out into the world. This can have enormous ramifications.

The verse tells us that there will never rise up again a prophet amongst Israel like Moshe, whom Hashem knew face-to-face (*Devarim* 34:10). The *Sifri* infers from the words "amongst Israel" that, although the Jewish people will never again have a comparable prophet to Moshe, the gentile nations will. This prophet is Bilaam.

In order to understand the difference between Moshe and Bilaam, the *Torah Temimah* (26, on *Devarim* 34:10) cites R' Chaim of Volozhin, who states that Moshe and Bilaam can be compared to an eagle and a bat, respectively. Both animals recognize the difference between day and night, yet they come from opposing perspectives. The eagle loves sunlight, but its vision is not effective in the darkness. The bat, on the other hand, thrives in darkness but it's afraid of the light of day. When the sun rises, the eagle knows it is time to awaken and become active, while the bat knows it is time to hide away in a dark cave. When the sun sets, the eagle knows it time to rest, while the bat knows it is time to get up and begin its activity.

The difference between the eagle and the bat, in terms of their relationship to daylight, is exactly comparable to the difference between Moshe and Bilaam in terms of their knowledge of Hashem (see *Bamidbar* 24:16). During the times that Hashem wanted to shower the world with light and blessing, Moshe's prophetic abilities were aroused. Since Moshe was sensitive to the sweetness of Divine blessing, he became active at the times that this blessing was heightened.

Bilaam also recognized this aspect of Hashem, however, he was repelled by the sweetness. Instead, Bilaam's prophetic abilities were aroused during the times that Hashem expressed wrath and anger. Bilaam was attracted to bitterness and darkness, and he thrived when these qualities prevailed. To sum it up, although both Moshe and Bilaam had prophetic knowledge of the Divine, Moshe was attracted to the side of light, while Bilaam was attracted to the side of darkness.

We could call this the "Law of Attraction," which dictates that sweetness is drawn to sweetness, and bitterness is drawn to bitterness. On a practical level, this means that we have the power to mold ourselves into either sweet or bitter people. If we think bitter thoughts, speak in bitter terms, and act in bitter ways, we will develop into bitter people. We will be attracted to bitterness, and bitterness will be attracted to us. However, if we practice thinking sweet thoughts, speaking sweet words, and doing sweet deeds, we will be drawn to the sweetness in life, and sweetness will be drawn to us.

May we be blessed with sweetness in all of our mannerisms, so that we will soar like an eagle and be attracted only to sweet people, places, and things. May we, thus, merit to usher in the sweetest and gentlest of eras - the returning of our holy prophets, who will bring down the word of Hashem with the softest of prophesies and the clearest of visions.

Pinchas

Cut It Short

Medically speaking, if a person discovers a growth or tumor in his body, the best way to treat it would be to cut it out, if possible. Similarly, if we find an impurity within our system, it is best to cut it out.

This week's portion picks up from where we left off in last week's portion, where Pinchas eliminated both Zimri and Cozbi, who were engaged in an act of immorality. So happy was Hashem with this move that He said, "Therefore, tell him that I have given him My covenant of peace." Yonason ben Uziel on that verse mentions that God said, "I swear, tell him in My name that I decree that I will make him a living angel and he will live forever to bring news of the redemption at the end of days."

The *Yalkut Shimoni* (#771) tells us into which angel Pinchas was transformed. Pinchas became Eliyahu the Prophet, who was later promoted to become the angel who oversees circumcision. This is hinted to in the verse in the portion of *Pinchas* (25:12) which says, "I have given to him my covenant of peace." In Hebrew, "my covenant of peace" is *brisi shalom*. The word *bris* hints to us that Pinchas became the person who would oversee the *bris* (circumcision).

One must wonder why Pinchas was given the promotion specifically at this time. What is the connection between eliminating Zimri and being promoted to Eliyahu the Prophet, who later became the angel that oversees circumcision? There is another striking aspect to these words, *brisi shalom*. The Talmud (*Kiddushin* 66b) cites the opinion of Rav Nachman who says that the letter *vav* in the word *shalom* should be written as a cut-off *vav*, or half a *vav*, with the bottom half of the *vav* missing and the upper half of the letter almost appearing as the letter *yud*.

Although many authorities question cutting a letter in half, as this would lose the correct shape of the letter (as Rebbi Akiva Eiger discusses in his response #75), many professional scribes have, nevertheless, written the letter *vav* as a half letter (see the *Ritva* there). This too is difficult: how could a letter be missing half of its shape and maintain its state of *kashrus*? And why was specifically this letter, of this word, in this context, chosen to be the cut-off letter?

The Midrash (*Shemos Rabbah* 40:3) says that when Adam HaRishon, the first person, was being formed and reached the stage of a *golem* (which means an unfinished man of clay) God showed him every righteous person that was destined to come from his loins. In fact, we all come from Adam HaRishon. Adam had an all-inclusive soul which contained all of our souls collectively. Additionally, each part of his grand soul corresponded to a different part of his body.

The Midrash goes on to specify that there are some people whose soul sparks are connected to Adam's head, and other people whose souls are connected to the hair on top of his head. There are some who are connected to his forehead, and some who are connected to his nose. While there are others connected to his mouth, and yet others connected to his ears. And there are still others who are connected to the place of his circumcision. The *Emunas Itecha* tells us that Zimri was connected to Adam's foreskin. But there was something else to which Zimri was connected.

In *Zohar Chadash* on *Shir HaShirim* (74:4) it says that there are 600,000 letters in the Torah scroll, which correspond to the 600,000 primary Jewish souls. This means to say that each of our souls is connected to a different letter in the Torah scroll. Once again, the *Emunas Itecha* tells us that Zimri's soul was connected to the cut-off letter *vav* of the word *shalom* that we mentioned before.

So, if Zimri is connected to the foreskin, and Zimri is also connected to the cut-off letter *vav*, it turns out that the letter *vav* is connected to the foreskin. Or at least some of the letter *vav* is connected to the foreskin, while the other part of the letter *vav* is connected to the *kodesh* (the holy place of circumcision). Since the letter *vav* is connected to circumcision, it teaches us that just as the letter *vav* often connects two ideas or two things, so does the *bris kodesh* connect us to Hashem.

All this explains to us how and why this letter *vav* is cut in half and yet still maintains its state of being a kosher letter. Because the part of the *vav* that has been cut off (the lower half) is the part connected to the foreskin and the removal of this lower half, which represents the foreskin, is by definition the perfection of the letter.

When God commanded Avraham to circumcise himself, He said, "Be perfect" (*Bereishis* 17:1). And so it is here with the removal of half of the *vav*; it is tantamount to removing the foreskin of circumcision, and therefore it is kosher and perfect. On the contrary, before circumcision is when a person is considered to have a defect.

So, when Pinchas killed Zimri, it was as if Pinchas circumcised the foreskin and fulfilled the *mitzvah* of circumcision, because Zimri was connected to the foreskin of Adam HaRishon. The hint to this in the verse itself is when it says *brisi shalom*, with the letter *vav* of *shalom* cut in half. This teaches us that when Pinchas killed Zimri, it was likened to removing the foreskin (hinted at by the letter *vav* being cut in half). And that is why **brisi** *shalom* hints at circumcision, *bris milah*.

This is why Pinchas was promoted to become Eliyahu the Prophet, who eventually became the angel to oversee circumcision specifically at that time. It is because Pinchas was involved in removing the foreskin (Zimri). It was as if Pinchas was involved in the *mitzvah* of circumcision; therefore, he merited becoming the angel that oversees circumcision until the end of time.

Throughout the journey of our lives, we can repeatedly fulfill the *mitzvah* of circumcision. Anytime we cut away some spiritual impurity, we are removing an obstacle that used to block us from becoming closer to God. An example of this could be to carve out something we watch, listen to, or speak about, which is not healthy for our souls. Every time we cut away just a little bit of this filth, we are advancing in the process of perfecting ourselves.

May we all be blessed to remove any negativity in our lives and, thereby, reveal the holiness, so that we merit to see Eliyahu the Prophet sent to us with the good tidings of *Moshiach's* arrival. Then the spirit of impurity will be completely removed from the Earth.

Pinchas

"J & R"

The Western traditional court system demands that all litigants tell, "The truth, the whole truth, and nothing but the truth." However, the Kotzker Rebbe demanded even more of his *chassidim*. He expected the "truth of the truth." This means to first be honest with oneself. Only then, can one trust the motivation behind one's actions.

The story of Pinchas already began in last week's portion, *Balak*. Basically, Zimri (the Prince of the tribe of Shimon) took Cozbi (a Midianite Princess) for immoral purposes. Pinchas put a stop to their lewdness, and thereby stopped a plague that had already taken many Jewish lives. This plague had begun to decimate the Jewish people on account of the prostitution in which they were involved with the daughters of Moav.

The Zohar (*Pinchas*, pg. 237a) says that in order for Pinchas to have accomplished the slaying of Zimri and Cozbi, putting a stop to the death plague, he had to draw upon the quality of Yitzchak, which was *gevurah*, strength. One hint to this idea is found in the numerical value of Yitzchak's name, which is 208 - the exact numerical value of Pinchas's name when spelled with a *yud*, as it is in this week's portion (see *Bamidbar* 25:11).

The *Zerah Kodesh* (cited in the *Shvilei Pinchas*) quotes the *Arizal* who adds that not only did Pinchas draw upon Yitzchak's power, but Pinchas was a reincarnation of Yitzchak. Moreover, Zimri was a reincarnation of Esav.

Esav was a tricky person. Esav attempted, and maybe even succeeded, in fooling his father Yitzchak, at least to some degree. This is evident from a verse that says that Esav "*Tzayid b'piv* - trapped him with his mouth" (*Bereishis* 25:28). The Midrash elaborates that Esav would ask his father how to tithe salt and straw, which didn't have to be tithed at all. In this way, he wanted to appear as an incredibly righteous person when in fact he behaved wickedly (*Bereishis Rabbah* 63:15).

Following in Esav's footsteps, Zimri continued to trick the Jewish people. Zimri claimed that taking Cozbi was a *mitzvah*. This is because Zimri knew that the spark of David was buried amongst the nations at that time. Zimri claimed that it was important to convert Cozbi so that the spark of King David would be born into the ranks of the Jewish people.

Zimri claimed that he was involved in the process of bringing about the *Moshiach* (*Imrei Yosef* at the end of *Parshas Balak*, cited in the *Shvilei Pinchas*). Zimri instructed the Jews to take non-Jewish women in order to extract the holy sparks found amongst the nations, and bring them over to the Jewish side.

Zimri's claim, however, was inaccurate. The spark of David was found amongst the Moabites, and not from Cozbi, who was a Midianite. Rus was a Moabite, and David was a descendant of Rus. Furthermore, David and the *Melech HaMoshiach* would have to come from the tribe of Yehudah, the progenitor of kings. How then, could Zimri, from the tribe of Shimon, produce the Davidic dynasty?

As far as the rest of the Jewish men are concerned, although they did take Moabite women, their actions were considered sinful because it was not done in order to convert them to be their wives and raise their children; rather, they were just interested in the act of prostitution.

At first, Zimri's claim appeared to be righteous. Deep down, however, Zimri wanted to trick the Jewish people to follow his lead and engage in immorality, which would bring the plague of death upon the Jews. Zimri's plot was effective as many Jews were misled. The plague was activated and the Jews were threatened to be completely wiped out.

Pinchas (alias Yitzchak) saw what Esav (alias Zimri) planned to do. Pinchas/ Yitzchak said, "That's enough! No more trickery!" Pinchas took action and finally put an end to Esav and his deception.

Esav's arch-angel is the famous *Samech Mem*. The power of the *Samech Mem* is to blind the Jewish people from seeing the truth. This is hinted to in the letters of his name, *samech mem*. When the vowels are changed around, those two letters spell the word *sumah*, blind (see the *Kli Yakar*, *Bereishis* 32:25). This describes the essence of the *Samech Mem*. How does he accomplish this?

The *Samech Mem* paints a sin to make it look like a *mitzvah*. He convinces us that negative behavior is actually necessary and good. That's when we start to hear statements like, "For the principal of the matter I...!" "It was a *mitzvah* what I did!" "What I said was a *mitzvah*!"

I like to term this "J&R" (justification & rationalization). We become convinced of our self-righteousness and fail to see the truth. The difference between sinning when we realize it is wrong, versus sinning when we think it's a *mitzvah*, is huge. If we don't realize we were wrong, we lose the possibility for *teshuvah*, repentance.

When we recognize that we have sinned, we begin to feel remorse. Then, we can apologize to God and promise to try to do better next time. This is the process of *teshuvah*. However, when we think that the sin is a *mitzvah*, we will never come to do *teshuvah* - because we don't do *teshuvah* on *mitzvos*.

It's not random that the *Samech Mem* is Esav's arch-angel. Both deal in trickery. Both try to appear righteous, when in reality, they are setting a trap to convince us that sinning is for the sake of Heaven.

How can we fortify ourselves against this shrewd tactic of the *Samech Mem*? Perhaps we could suggest an exercise. For example, before going to hang out with friends, let us sit down for 30 seconds and ask ourselves some questions: "Is God going to be proud of me now?" "If my parents could see me, would they be proud or disappointed?" "If my children could see me now, would I make them proud of me or embarrassed?" "If my Rabbi, friend, neighbor would become aware of my activities, would I be proud or ashamed?"

These questions tend to clarify whether we should embark on a certain activity or not. If, after asking these questions, we are still in doubt, then it is time to ask *da'as Torah* (a competent Rabbi) for advice. We can save ourselves much anguish by asking ourselves these serious questions before we enter the club of "J&R."

May we all be blessed to ask ourselves the right questions in order to see the truth and act accordingly.

Pinchas

Inside Out

Medically speaking, it is far more effective to treat the cause rather than the symptoms of an illness. This holds true for spiritual illnesses as well.

Parshas Pinchas often falls out right at the beginning of the Three Weeks of mourning over the destruction of our Temples. It is at this time of year that we are supposed to focus a little bit more on the collective pain that we have been experiencing ever since our Temples were obliterated. By feeling the suffering that we now endure, we are supposed to be motivated to pray for the final redemption, putting an end to all this aching.

There is a reason why Ezra the Scribe arranged the Torah portions in just such a way that *Parshas Pinchas* kicks off this time of year on the Jewish calendar. (See *Rebbi Shimon ben Elazar, Braisa Megillah,* chap. 4, *Bnei Ha'ir,* pg. 31b, where it discusses the reason why Ezra arranged that the curses in *sefer Vayikra* fall out before Shavuos and that the curses in *sefer Devarim* fall out prior to *Rosh HaShanah.* This shows us that the *parshios* of the Torah do not randomly coincide with different periods of time on the Jewish calendar. Rather, there is a connection between each *parshah* and the time of year it coincides with.) It is because the action of Pinchas set into motion a process that will lead to the salvation of our people from *galus,* exile.

God blessed Pinchas with the Covenant of Peace. Yonasan ben Uziel (*Bamidbar* 25:12) reveals to us that this Covenant of Peace means that God transformed Pinchas into Eliyahu the Prophet, who later became an angel. Eliyahu will bring us good news at the End of Days about the coming of the Messiah.

The *Yalkut Shimoni* (*Pinchas*, *Remez* 771) quotes Rebbi Shimon ben Lakish, who adds that eliminating evil from the world brings us peace and closeness to God. Just as Pinchas removed evil from the world and brought about peace, creating closeness with God, so will he merit repeating his salvation at the End of Days.

This is the connection between *Parshas Pinchas* and the Three Weeks. By mentioning Pinchas/Eliyahu at the onset of the Three Weeks, we remember his self-sacrifice in carrying out God's Will, which saved the Jewish people from destruction. We hope that the very recitation of this portion awakens Divine compassion and will lead God to fulfill His promise to bring about true peace on Earth.

It is not random that our *parshah* also discusses dividing up *Eretz Yisrael* among the various Tribes of Israel (*Bamidbar* 26:53-56). It is to encourage us to keep hoping for the time when the entire Land of Israel is liberated from the enemies of the Jewish people and returned to her eternal owners, *Am Yisrael.*

Additionally, it is not coincidental that our portion also talks about the daily offerings and the offerings brought on the various holidays (*Bamidbar* 28:2-39). This too urges us to anticipate the time when actual offerings will be brought on the Altar of our Temple.

It is very fitting to express such hope at this time of year, when we yearn for salvation from our exile and from the constant hatred and attacks perpetrated by those who wish to destroy us.

So, how can we defeat our enemies? How can we put an end to all this terror? There are many fine suggestions. We could study more Torah, pray with added concentration, and desist from *lashon hara* as much as possible.

However, perhaps we could propose a specific area on which to focus, which just may nip it in the bud. In order to destroy our enemies from without, we must first destroy our enemies from within. In order to extinguish the hatred from the outside, we must first uproot the hatred from the inside.

To be more specific, the enemy on the inside refers to the *yetzer hara*, evil inclination. The precise area of *yetzer hara* regarding which we need to be extremely cautious is that of harboring hatred in our hearts for others.

Who knows if the animosity that we experience from without is just a reflection of the animosity from within? If we could just get rid of the inner loathing, we might just be able to eradicate the outer hostility.

In times like this, everybody needs to do what they can in order to try to improve the situation. So, this Shabbos, let's sit around the Shabbos table and discuss the aforementioned idea with our family and friends.

Then, suggest the following exercise. Ask everyone to be silent for two minutes and think of somebody that rubs them the wrong way. During this period of silence, each person should try to think of three positive points that even these obnoxious people possess.

After the two minutes, let us tell our families and guests that the next time we see those upsetting people, we will try to think of their positive qualities. This will help breed tolerance, respect, and appreciation for them. Eventually, we may even start liking those people.

May we all be blessed to expunge any trace of disgust that we may harbor for others in our hearts, and replace those negative feelings with sincere appreciation for each other. Thus, may we deserve to witness the complete downfall and defeat of our enemies. Then, may we merit to see Eliyahu the Prophet come, bringing us the good news about our complete return to the entirety of *Eretz Yisrael*, where we will build the *Beis HaMikdash* and bring the Thanksgiving Offering to God.

Pinchas

Holy Hatred

Society today teaches acceptance and open-mindedness. While this philosophy resonates well with so many of us, should we really accept everything and everybody? What if they are dangerous? Should we be so open-minded to the point that our brains fall out?

In this week's *parshah*, the Jewish people are commanded to "Harass the Midiantes and smite them" (*Bamidbar* 25:17). The *Ohr HaChaim* questions the purpose of this command since the Jewish people are not told to wage war against the nation of Midian until next week's *parshah* (see *Bamidbar* 31:2). What does it mean to "harass" the Midianites?

According the *Tosefes Zohar* (3:305a), no time in history was more dangerous for the Jewish people than when Balak, the Moabite king, and Bilaam, the gentile prophet, joined forces to destroy us. The prophet Michah refers to this when he implores the Jews, "Remember, my people, what Balak advised and what Bilaam answered" (*Michah* 6:5).

The *Nesivos Shalom* explains that, as long as the Jewish people are connected to Hashem, no one can hurt them. Balak hired Bilaam to curse the Jewish people in the hope that this would bring about a separation between Hashem and us. However, his mission failed - as the Torah teaches, "Hashem transformed the curse into a blessing" (*Devarim* 23:6). When Balak saw that Bilaam's curses were unsuccessful in creating distance between the Jews and God, he decided to join forces with Bilaam in order to cause the Jews to commit acts of idolatry and immorality (see *Bamidbar* 24:14, *Sanhedrin* 106a). Balak hoped that these two crimes, which are the antithesis of sanctity and purity, would cause a division between the Jewish people and Hashem.

According to the *Ohr HaChaim*, the underlying message of the command to harass the Midianites is that Hashem wishes us to hate evil and its perpetrators. As King David says in *Tehillim* (139:21), "Those who hate You, Hashem, I hate, and I quarrel with those who rise up against You." Love is the glue that binds people together, whereas hatred is the wedge that pulls people apart. The command "Love your fellow as yourself" (*Vayikra* 19:18) - referring to people whom the Torah does not consider wicked - is counterbalanced by the command to harass the Midianites, a people who actively desire to harm others. Just as we are commanded to love, so are we commanded to hate.

The only way to distance ourselves from evil is to hate it with a passion and wage war against it. If we fail to master the art of holy hatred, and do not channel this trait in the service of Hashem, then we run two risks. Either our neutrality is a sign that we already harbor the evil within us, which is why it is so hard to hate it (who wants to hate a piece of themselves?), or our continued passivity could cause us to begin to accept the evil and allow it to dwell within us.

One way of ensuring that we maintain a healthy balance between loving good and hating evil is to speak up when we see an injustice. This could include a letter written to the powers that be, expressing our concerns, and thus conveying the message that we won't sit idly by while perpetrators of evil move about freely.

May we be blessed with holy hatred, healthily directed at appropriate targets, so that we completely disengage from evil. May this increase our closeness and attachment to Hashem, which will lead to the destruction of our enemies from within and without.

Matos - Masei -- The Three Weeks

R.E.S.P.E.C.T. What Does It Mean to Me?

One of the universally-accepted norms of society is respecting other human beings. The trick is to respect others regardless of how annoying, disappointing, or agitating they are to us.

In this week's double portion, *Matos-Masei* - which concludes *Sefer Bamidbar* - we read (32:1-18): "*U'mikneh rav hayah livnei Reuven v'livnei Gad...* - The children of Reuven and the children of Gad had a great multitude of cattle." The Torah describes how the Reuvenites and Gadites saw that the land of Ya'zer and Gil'ad was fit for rearing cattle, and then appealed to Moshe to allow them to settle there (in Trans-Jordan) rather than in the Land of Israel.

The commentaries point out that the tribes of Reuven and Gad had far loftier motives for wanting to take possession of Trans-Jordan than the mere materialistic incentive, which the text seems to purport.

Reb Simcha Bunim of Peshischa explains that, from the words *mikneh rav*, we learn that the children of Gad and Reuven made a "*kinyan*" (acquisition) on their "*Rav*," i.e. their master, Moshe. In other words, the children of Gad and Reuven were strongly attached to Moshe, to the extent that as soon as they heard that he would not be entering the Promised Land, they decided to remain with him rather than join the rest of the people entering *Eretz Yisrael*.

Moreover, Reb Simcha explains, since they fully appreciated how much Moshe longed to step into the Land of Israel, the two tribes reasoned that if they inherited Trans-Jordan, annexing it to Israel, then on some level it would obtain comparable sanctity to that of *Eretz Yisrael*. In this way - since Moshe was already in Trans-Jordan - he would realize his dream, and the tribes would, retroactively, be able to repay Moshe in some way for all he had done on their behalf. (See *Parshas Va'eschanan*, "*A Trans-Jordan Flight to Israel*," where this issue is discussed in detail.)

Although the tribes did not wish to enter Israel, the Torah informs us that they were fully prepared to fight alongside their brothers in the battles that would ensue in the Canaanite land.

In response to Gad and Reuven's request, however, Moshe Rabbeinu chastises them harshly. We will paraphrase some of these verses.

"Moshe said to the children (tribes) of Gad and Reuven, 'Shall your brothers go to war while you sit here? Why do you dishearten the Children of Israel from going over to the Land which God gave to them? This is exactly what your forefathers did when I sent them to scout the land - they disheartened the people, convincing them not go into the Land that God gave to them. And God was angry on that day, and He swore saying, 'These men that came up out of Egypt will not see the Land because they have not completely followed Me...' and He made them wander in the desert for forty years until all of that generation was consumed. And, behold, you have risen up in place of your forefathers, a brood of sinful men, to increase the anger of God on Israel because if you turn away from Him, He will leave them in the wilderness once again; and you will destroy this entire nation.'"

We see quite clearly that Moshe lambasted Gad and Reuven with extremely severe accusations! And yet, how did they respond?

"...We will go armed in front of the Children of Israel in battle until we have brought them to their place... and we will not return to our homes until every Jew has inherited his possession."

Perhaps we could make an observation on this dialogue. After being falsely accused by Moshe, the tribes' reaction did not contain even a trace of disrespect. I would imagine that if any of us were spoken to in such a way, we would go ballistic, particularly if the accusations came from a *Rav,* whom we would expect to refrain from being "*choshed bikesheirim,*" suspecting innocent people. Gad and Reuven, however, responded with utmost respect.

We could suggest, that by honoring Moshe, the tribes of Gad and Reuven were ultimately granted their request, consequently annexing Trans-Jordan to *Eretz Yisrael.* From here we derive a powerful lesson: once we learn to master the art of respecting one another, we will not only maintain the Land of Israel, but actually broaden its borders.

The inverse is also true. When we lack respect towards one another, the borders of Israel begin to shrink, something we have been unfortunate to witness in our times.

How appropriate is this lesson for the "*Bein Hametzarim*" (literally, within the straits) (see *Eichah* 1:3) and more commonly known as "the Three Weeks," as we mourn, once again, the destruction of the Temple.

The Talmud (*Yoma* 9b) states that the Second Temple was destroyed due to baseless and senseless hatred, which stemmed from a lack of respect. Once we fail to respect someone, how far are we from actually hating that person? This could explain why the portions of Matos and Masei always coincide with the Three Weeks: because these portions contain the antidote to our situation in exile: We must have sincere respect for our fellow man.

Let us resolve that the next time somebody insults us, instead of biting back, we will treat the person with respect, in speech and manner. In addition to the great reward we receive for behaving this way, we might be pleasantly surprised when that person may start to treat us with respect as well.

May we be blessed with an infusion of a deep sense of respect for all people by recognizing their innate God-like qualities, so that we may merit *Eretz Yisrael* with its expanded borders and the arrival of *Moshiach* by this *Av.*

Matos - Masei

Peace, Brother

When you boil it down, it all comes to peace. Let there be peace.

This week's double portion discusses the journeys of the Jewish people during their stay in the desert. From the time they were on their way out of Egypt until they reached the borders of the Promised Land, there were forty-two stations altogether in which the Jews encamped.

The verses do not repeat the stories that transpired in the places that are mentioned. Rather, a very brief phrase appears over and over again: "*Vayisu vayachanu* - and they journeyed and they encamped" (*Bamidbar* 33:5).

Even when we mention places where important events in Jewish history happened, we only mention the place, not the whole story again. For example, it mentions "the Wilderness of Sinai" (*Bamidbar* 33:15), but Scriptural verse does not get into the story about receiving the Torah which occurred there.

One reason for this is because the Torah relies upon the fact that we will remember the story on our own from *Parshas Yisro* in *Shemos*. This pattern begs us to ask a most difficult question.

There seems to be a lack of consistency when the verse mentions Mount Hor. In this week's portion, the Torah **does** repeat what happened there; the passing of Aharon (*Bamidbar* 33:37-39). This is strange, because it was just three weeks ago that we mentioned the story of Aharon's passing in *Parshas Chukas* (*Bamidbar* 20:23-29).

If the Torah did not repeat the story about receiving the Torah because we should be able to remember it on our own from *Parshas Yisro* (which is quite a distance from this week's portion), then the Torah could certainly omit the repetition of the story of Aharon's death. We should surely be able to remember it on our own from *Parshas Chukas* (which is much closer to this week's portion). Why, then, did God repeat the story of Aharon's death in our portion, *Masei*?

Furthermore, when Aharon's death is repeated in *Masei*, an interesting detail is added that was not mentioned back in *Chukas*: the date of Aharon's death. In *Masei*, we are informed that Aharon died on the first day of the fifth month (*Bamidbar* 33:38). Why wasn't this mentioned the first time around, in *Chukas*?

Additionally, Scriptural verse doesn't tell us the date of anybody else's passing. We are not informed about what date the Patriarchs or Matriarchs died. We are not even told what day Moshe Rabbeinu himself died. If we want those dates, we have to turn to the Oral Tradition.

The one exception to this is Aharon's death, the only such date given specifically in Scripture. Out of all the great personalities in the Torah, why is Aharon's date of death the only one mentioned?

The Talmud teaches us that when it says that Aharon died in the fifth month, it is referring to the month of *Av*. (See *Rosh HaShanah*, chap. 1, *Arba'ah roshei shanim*, pg. 2b, and see the Tosafists there, the opening words "*Bachodesh hachamishi*.") Since the verse says that Aharon died on the first day of the fifth month, it follows that Aharon died on *Rosh Chodesh Av*.

Rabbi Yehudah Aryeh Leib of Gur in his *Sfas Emes* (*Masei*, starting with the opening word "*Ksiv*") says that the reason God orchestrated Aharon's death in the month of *Av* is because both Temples were destroyed in the month of *Av*.

The reasons for their destruction were different. The First Temple was destroyed because the Jews sinned with idolatry, immorality, and murder. However, the Second Temple was destroyed because of baseless hatred between the people (*Yoma*, chap. 1, *Shivas Yamim,* pg. 9b). Today, we still feel the effects of the Second Temple's destruction, as we continue to suffer in exile. The cause behind all this agony is the hatred that we still harbor for each other.

Aharon was the antithesis of hatred. Aharon was a man who loved peace and pursued peace by making peace between warring parties and between husband and wife. Aharon loved people unconditionally and brought them close to Torah (See *Rashi Bamidbar* 20:29 and *Avos,* chap. 1, *Moshe Kibel,* Mishnah 12, the opinion of *Hillel*).

God caused Aharon to die on *Rosh Chodesh Av* so that, specifically during the month in which our Temple was destroyed due to hatred, we can begin to repair this particular flaw, by celebrating his *yahrtzeit* and reminding ourselves of what Aharon represented: love and peace.

Hashem wants us to be impacted by Aharon's ways. We should strive to become his disciples by improving ourselves in the area of love and peace, and purging ourselves of hatred. We will, thereby, fix the flaw of baseless hatred in our personalities and, thus, merit restoring the *Beis HaMikdash*.

The *Shvilei Pinchas* says that this is why the detail of Aharon's date of death is mentioned specifically in *Masei*, and not earlier on in *Parshas Chukas*. This is because, in most years, *Parshas Masei* is read either on the Shabbos right before *Rosh Chodesh Av* or on Shabbos *Rosh Chodesh Av* itself.

By reading about Aharon's death in *Parshas Masei*, the Torah is preparing us for *Rosh Chodesh Av*. The Torah wants us to be cognizant of Aharon's passing so that we shed a tear on *Rosh Chodesh Av*, not just to mourn the loss of a great person, but to mourn the lack of peace in our lives and in the world. Hopefully, we will decide to improve our relationships with others, so that we can fix the damage of hatred, and bring about the building of the third and final *Beis HaMikdash*.

This explains why God repeated the story of Aharon's death and did not rely on our memories from *Parshas Chukas*. God wanted to connect the story of Aharon's death to that date on the Jewish calendar (*Rosh Chodesh Av*) so that we can prepare ourselves accordingly.

This also clarifies why only Aharon's date of death is recorded in Scriptural verse. The story of Aharon's *yahrtzeit* is crucial in that it reminds us of what he represented; and when you get down to it, it all boils down to love and peace.

If we cannot reach perfection in the ways of love and peace, we should not be discouraged from trying to make some improvement in this area. Even a fraction of peace is still called peace. Any little advancement is precious and worth the effort.

How can we increase *shalom* and diminish *machlokes*, dispute? Here is one exercise. On *Rosh Chodesh Av* (and on every *Rosh Chodesh*) let us think about a person that we don't care for that much and write down three good things about that person.

Then we can keep that paper handy all day. We can put it in our wallets or change-purses so that we come across it often. By focusing on that person's positive points, we will generate positive feelings for that person. We will begin to appreciate the qualitative side of that person. This will lead us to deal with others in a more peaceful and loving way.

May we all be blessed, especially this month, to sorely miss Aharon and mourn our world that is filled with so much strife. May the pain hurt so much that we become motivated to do something about it, namely to pursue peace by becoming true disciples of Aharon. In that merit, may we deserve to witness the building of the third *Beis HaMikdash*. Then our *Av* (Father) will be so very proud of us.

Matos - Masei

Pearls in the Sand

Who would've thought that within the most bitter situation lies the sweetest of all things.

Often the portions of *Matos-Masei* are combined to make a double portion, which concludes the book of *Bamidbar*. A variety of topics are mentioned in this double header; we will focus on one of them.

In the second of the two portions, *Masei*, the Torah delineates the borders of *Eretz Yisrael*. For example, it says (34:3), "And it will be for you the southern side from the wilderness of *Tzin*, on the side of Edom, and it will be for you the southern border from the end of the Salt Sea to the East." The Salt Sea (known as *Yam HaMelach* or the Dead Sea) is the point at which Israel's borders begin. We also conclude the borders of Israel with the Salt Sea as it says, "The border shall descend to the Jordon and its edges will be the Salt Sea, this will be for you the land according to its borders all around" (34:12).

The question arises: why would the Torah specifically use the Salt Sea with which to begin and end its borders? Of all the places in Israel, the Salt Sea is a strange choice since it has a corrupt history. Before becoming the Salt Sea, that place used to be known as Sedom. Only after the upheaval of Sedom did that area turn into the Salt Sea (see *Bereishis* 19:25-26). The Salt Sea represents the first destruction that ever occurred in *Eretz Yisrael*.

The Great Flood, in the time of Noach, never reached *Eretz Yisrael* (see *Bereishis Rabbah* 33:6 citing the opinion of Rebbi Levi). After all, where would the dove have gotten the olive leaf if the entire world was destroyed? Rebbi Levi says that the dove got that olive leaf from *Eretz Yisrael*, which was not destroyed, and the olive leaf came specifically from the Mount of Olives. The destruction of the Tower of Babel also did not happen in Israel, but rather in Bavel (see *Bereishis* 11:9).

The *Emunas Itecha* (*Masei*, 34:2-3, based on *Rashi*, *Masei*, 34:3) says that ever since Sedom was turned into the Dead Sea, it has been a place used to symbolize destruction. When the Jewish people disobey God, then the Torah promises "Sulfur and salt burning the entire land like the upheaval of Sedom and Amora" (*Devarim* 29:22). So again, why would the Torah choose this decadent place as the marking of Israel's border from both ends? And why does the Torah honor this place by mentioning *Yam HaMelach* twice, whereas all the other places in Israel are only mentioned once in Scriptural verse? In other words, why would the Torah begin and end Israel's borders on such a bad note?

The *Emunas Itecha* points out that Sedom is referred to as "the Garden of Hashem" (*Bereishis* 13:10), because God is the ultimate Sovereign, and Sedom is His garden. This means that Sedom is a place of sovereignty. We see this with Lot, who chose to live in Sedom, and carried within him the Messianic spark.

We know this from the fact that Lot and his daughter had a male child called Moav (*Bereishis* 19:37). This boy grew up to be the father of a nation called the Moabites, from which Rus descended (see *Rus* 1:4). And King David was Rus's great-grandson (see *Rus* 4:22). The culmination of this Davidic dynasty is the Messiah. The Messiah is a king, and his sovereignty stems all the way back to the place of Sedom.

Since the Messianic spark was hidden in Sedom, it is actually apropos that this place, Sedom, should be used to delineate the borders of *Eretz Yisrael*. The *Moshiach*, whose roots began in Sedom, will gather the Jews back into the borders of *Eretz Yisrael*.

So, even though today Sedom appears to be a place of sulfur and salt, representing strict justice and destruction; in the future, that place will be transformed back into the garden of Hashem with its lush pastures. (We could suggest that today, as we witness the Dead Sea disappearing, we need not feel that this is a bad sign. On the contrary, this may very well indicate that its long-awaited process of returning to a beautiful garden of God has begun.)

That Sedom is going to return to its original beauty is hinted to by the very fact that Sedom is the starting point of Israel's borders, as well as its finish line. In order to show this on a map, one must draw a line all the way around *Eretz Yisrael* (going clockwise from the East, to the South, to the West, to the North, and then finishing back at the East), coming full-circle, which itself indicates that this salty place will one day be completely turned around to take its place again as Hashem's garden.

One lesson we learn from this is that even though the Salt Sea appears to be a bad place, this is only an external perspective. When we dig beyond the surface, however, we find the most precious of jewels contained in Sedom.

This should serve as a training ground for us to always search for the good points in others. We can do this even for people who misbehave, like the ancient Sodomites did. We should endeavor to search for the good points in every place, in every time, and in every circumstance. When we invest our efforts to this end, then God will reveal to us all the good that is buried, like a hidden treasure, in every person, place, and circumstance. This, by definition, will be the transformation from bitter to sweet, from dark to light, and from the lowest to the highest.

Here is a practical way to practice seeing the good in everyone. On Shabbos when you have a bowl of two items, like nuts and raisins, and you want the raisins but not the nuts, then take with your hand the "good" (raisins) from the "bad" (nuts). Have in mind that this lesson is meant to last throughout the week - to always take the good and leave the bad.

May we all be blessed during the Three Weeks to search for the good points in people, places, and times, and try to bring them out. That will turn these days of mourning into days of festivity, when we will merit the coming of our Messianic King, the son of David, who will return all the children to their borders of Hashem's garden, stretching from *Yam HaMelach* all the way to Sedom.

Matos - Masei

Welcome to the Hood

Our surroundings make a huge impact on us. We all carry the impressions that have been stamped on us by our environment.

This week's double portion, *Matos-Masei*, concludes the Book of *Bamidbar*. In *Parshas Masei*, the Jewish people are commanded to set up three cities of refuge in Trans-Jordan, and three in the Land of Israel (*Bamidbar* 35:14). These cities are intended as places to which accidental murderers can flee and be protected from vengeful family members of the deceased. The Talmud (*Makkos* 9b) notes that the cities seem to be disproportionately distributed. Why are the cities of refuge evenly split between Trans-Jordan and Israel when only two-and-a-half out of the twelve tribes live in Trans-Jordan?

Abaye answers that more murderers live in Gilad (a city in Trans-Jordan) and therefore, more cities of refuge are required there. However, the *Ramban* (*Bamidbar* 35:14) and the *Sifsei Chachamim* (no. 400) take issue with this answer. Since the cities of refuge are intended as safe havens for the perpetrators of **accidental** murders, why is it relevant that a greater number of intentional murderers live in Trans-Jordan (See *Tosafos* in *Makkos* 9b, *B'Gilad*, as well as *Maharsha*, *Ramban*, *Gan Raveh*, and *Divrei Chanoch* on *Bamidbar* 35:14, for alternative approaches to this question)?

We can understand *Abaye's* answer in the following light. The *Rambam* (*Hilchos De'os* 6:1) states that people are profoundly influenced by their surroundings. A place where there is a higher percentage of intentional murders creates an environment where people are less sensitive to each other. People who live in an environment of wanton killing will not be scrupulously careful to avoid causing injury to others accidentally.

Therefore, more intentional murders will lead to more accidental murders as well.

This idea will help us understand a later verse, which states, "If he kills another with an iron instrument, then he is a murderer and shall be put to death" (*Bamidbar* 35:16). Since the Torah is in the midst of discussing cities of refuge, which is about accidental murders, this verse seems out of place, because it discusses intentional murder. *Rashi* explains that unlike the preceding and following verses, this verse refers to a person who **intentionally** kills.

Why would Hashem have put a verse about premeditated murder in the midst of a whole passage about accidental deaths? According to our approach, there is nothing out of place about this verse. It is showing us that accidental murders occur in an environment where less care is taken in general - as in a city with a higher percentage of murderers.

One of the lessons we can take from these verses is the importance of wisely choosing where to live, who to befriend, and with whom to spend time. All of these factors have a powerful effect on our development. The opposite is true as well. We must strive to be the best people we can be, as we never know how our behavior is affecting others. We are not only products of our environment, but we have the power to shape it as well.

May we be blessed to live in the highest of places, spend time with the holiest of people, and merit to spread this greatness to others so that we can watch the world evolve into a virtual paradise.

Sefer Devarim

Devarim - Shabbos Chazon

Say What?

Did you ever say something to somebody that you later regretted? Did you ever wonder how you could have been so insensitive? Did you ever wish you could have taken back those words? Would you like to know how we can minimize those embarrassing moments? If the answer to all of these questions is yes, then please read on.

This week we commence not only a new *parshah*, but also a new *sefer*, both of which share the same name: *Devarim,* meaning "words."

In *Devarim* (1:1), we read: "*Eileh hadevarim asher diber Moshe el kol Yisrael* - These are the words that Moshe spoke to all of Israel."

What specifically did Moshe say to the Nation besides what is revealed in the text? The *Megaleh Amukos* answers this question by pointing out that the first word of the portion, "*eileh*" (spelled *aleph, lamed, hey*) is an acronym for the phrase "*avak lashon hara*" - literally, "dust of derogatory speech." The word *eileh* thus alludes to the words of warning Moshe gave to the Jewish people to refrain from disparaging speech. In particular, he warned them to abstain from any form of communication that carries even the slightest negative inference about another (hence the term **avak** *lashon hara*, implying even a **hint** of *lashon hara*.)

The People of Israel were specifically cautioned against this sin because, as we learn from the Talmud in *Bava Basra* (164b-165a), *avak lashon hara* is one of three transgressions that we commit on a constant basis. Rav Amram, in the name of Rav, lists the three sins as follows:

1) *Hirhurei aveirah* - improper thoughts

2) *Iyun tefillah* - depth of prayer (*Rashi* explains that this refers to a type of person who expects Hashem to answer his prayers and to reward him)

3) *Lashon hara* - derogatory speech

The Talmud clarifies that Rav Amram was referring to **avak** *lashon hara* - a more subtle form of negative talk. Although we may not overtly speak detrimentally about others, we commonly stumble when it comes to conversations which contain nuances of *lashon hara*, expressed either verbally or non-verbally (e.g. through facial expressions or body language.) In fact, Rabbi Yehudah says in name of Rav, that unlike thievery where most people falter, and unlike immorality where few of us fall, **everyone** is guilty in regard to *avak lashon hara*. This is why, as the verse (1:1) states, Moshe spoke to ALL of the people - *diber Moshe el **kol** yisrael* - because every individual within the Jewish Nation warranted this particular caution.

The *Ohr HaChaim*, citing the Talmud (*Yoma* 19b), offers an alternative approach to explain the opening words of this week's portion. Our Sages teach (*Devarim* 6:7), "*Vedibarta **bam*** - you shall speak **in them**." What exactly does the word *bam* refer to? *Rava* says that *bam*, in them, refers to words of Torah. Therefore, anyone who is involved in mundane, day-to-day conversation already transgresses this mitzvah.

The *Ohr HaChaim* connects this teaching to the opening verse of this week's portion. *Sefer Devarim* begins: "*Eileh hadevarim asher diber Moshe el kol yisrael.*" Which "*devarim*" did Moshe engage in with Israel? Based on *Rava's* opinion, the *Ohr HaChaim* suggests that Moshe spoke **only** words of Torah to the people - then, and throughout his entire life - thus fulfilling the command of "*vedibarta bam.*"

Even when Moshe expressed seemingly controversial statements and was criticized by God, we find that all his words were, nevertheless, warranted and in the framework of Torah. For examples, see the following.

(1) *Shemos* (4:13): "*Shelach na beyad tishlach* - send with whoever You send" - Although in the next verse God became angry with Moshe, *Rashi* comments that Moshe argued only out of concern for Aharon.

(2) *Shemos* (5:23): "*U'mei'az basi el Pharoh*…and from when I came to Pharoh it has turned worse for this nation" - Despite these seemingly harsh words, all were appropriate and came from a place of Torah (See *Ohr Hachaim Hakadosh, Shemos* 5:23).

(3) *Bamidbar* 20:10: "*Shimu na hamorim… Listen now O rebels.*" According to the *Ohr HaChaim*, Moshe had good reason to say this.

We can combine the explanations of the *Ohr HaChaim* and the *Megaleh Amukos* to derive a fundamental lesson. Moshe warned the people against *avak lashon hara* (as the *Megaleh Amukos* says) because Moshe exemplified one who was careful with his speech (as the *Ohr HaChaim* implies). Since Moshe perfected himself in this particular area, he was the most fitting individual to impart this crucial message to the people, as the saying goes: "*Keshot atzmecha techilah* - fix yourself first [and only then may you rebuke others]."

We find this idea hinted at in the *Abudraham*, who offers three distinct approaches regarding the opening words of the *Shema*. Every day we read *Shema Yisrael*, Hear O' Israel. To whom are we referring when we say these words?

There are three possibilities:

1) We, the Children of Israel, are speaking to ourselves.

2) We are talking to our fellow Jew, who is also Yisrael.

3) We are implying "*Yisrael Saba*," i.e. Yaakov Avinu.

These differing opinions can be connected in the following way:

Before attempting to correct others (opinion number two), we must first and foremost focus on **our own** spiritual growth and refinement (opinion number one). Only after these two stages, can we then turn to "*Yisrael Saba*" to offer *nachas* from all of his descendents (opinion number three).

As we re-commence *Sefer Devarim*, which focuses on rebuke, let us imbibe within ourselves this fundamental message. We should always inspect our behavior to ensure that we improve our own character traits before attempting to fix others. Moreover, we learn from this week's portion to exercise utmost care and sensitivity to avoid speaking in a critical manner about others, whether verbally or non-verbally, overtly or discreetly. Let us reflect on these messages over *Shabbos Chazon* - the Shabbos that precedes *Tisha B'Av* - so that we succeed in rectifying the baseless hatred which caused the destruction of the Temple (see *Yoma* 9b). We may accomplish this by refining ourselves and by loving each and every Jew unconditionally.

Practically speaking, the more we converse in words of Torah, the less time we have to speak *lashon hara*. Additionally, we should choose five minutes during the day (when we are aware) and keep a *taanis dibbur*, a fast of words. This not only reminds us to watch what we say, but it purifies the soul as well.

May we be blessed to successfully improve ourselves and to stand as shining examples for others to emulate, so that together we deserve the coming of *Moshiach* before this *Tisha B'Av*. Then we will merit to celebrate it the way it was intended, in *Eretz Yisrael*, as a day of feasting with the tastiest of meats and the sweetest of wines.

Devarim - Shabbos Chazon

The Brightest Darkness

I think it's pretty safe to assume that most of us have had some difficult and challenging times in our lives. We may have wondered why these things happen. We ask ourselves if there is, indeed, any light at the end of the tunnel. Well, the following paragraphs contain a ray of hope that lies right under our noses.

This week we don't just begin a new portion, we begin a new *sefer*, book, which shares the same name, *Devarim*. This *parshah* is always the portion that is read on the Shabbos right before *Tisha B'Av*. And this Shabbos is special in that it is called *Shabbos Chazon*, named after the *haftarah* read this week from the first chapter of *Yeshaya* which begins with the word *chazon*.

This week we moved from the period known as the Three Weeks into the more tragic time known as the Nine Days. This whole section on the Jewish calendar is known as the *Bein Hametzarim* (between the straights) (see *Eichah* 1:3), and it is the zenith of our days of darkness. As we know, both of our Temples were destroyed at this time of year (see *Yoma* 9b) and much Jewish tragedy is traced to this period of time.

The Slonimer Rebbe teaches us that not only can we reach the light after the darkness, but light is actually hidden within the darkness (See *Parshas Bereishis, "From the Bashes,"* where this issue is explained in more detail). In *Yeshaya* (45:7) it says, "Former of light and creater of darkness; maker of peace and creator of evil; I, the Lord, do all these things." This verse states that God creates evil.

Many philosophers and thinkers have questioned this statement by asking how evil could stem from the source of all good, which is God? The Slonimer Rebbe offers one explanation with an analogy of a seed planted into the ground. The seed rots almost to nothing, and it seems very bad because it represents death and destruction. Yet we all know that this very process is the beginning of growth, which is really a very good thing.

The same applies to what appears to be darkness and evil. They themselves give birth to what is known as light and good. Therefore, darkness and evil are intrinsically good. In other words, within the darkness there is light, and within the evil there is good. This is also related in the story of Creation, where darkness preceded light (see *Bereishis* 1:2-3).

One very crucial lesson that we learn from this is that when we go through difficult and dark times in our own personal lives, we must always be aware that from that very darkness the light will be cultivated. There is a beautiful verse that drives this message home as well, when it says, "If I ascend to Heaven, You are there; and if I make my bed in the lowest depths, behold, You are there" (*Tehillim* 139:8). Similarly it says in *Parshas Yisro* (20:18), "And Moshe drew near to the thick darkness where God was."

There are three levels of darkness:

1) *Choshech* - darkness.

2) *Annan* - cloud.

3) *Arafel* - thick darkness.

Each level is darker than the one that precedes it. Yet it says that Moshe went into the thick darkness, which is the worst, but that's where God was. This comes to teach us that we, too, can find God in the most difficult of times.

Although this may be a very difficult lesson to implement, there could be a concrete way to start developing ourselves in this area. When something bitter happens to us, let us get into the habit of saying "I am feeling hurt or low right now; however, I believe that there is light within this darkness, even though I don't know what it is. Therefore, thank you, Hashem, for the difficulties that I am going through." Even if we may not mean it when we say it, in due time we may start to feel differently and cultivate a more positive attitude.

May we be blessed that no matter where we've made our beds, we never lose hope because even when we go through the darkest of times and most challenging of situations, we realize that we can move forward. Moreover, may we be blessed to understand that the light of salvation is buried somewhere in those lowest of places.

Devarim - Tishah B'Av

Mirror, Mirror on the Wall

This week we are all preparing ourselves for *Tisha B'Av*, which is right around the corner. We would all love to celebrate *Tisha B'Av* with rejoicing and festivities, marking the rebuilding of our *Beis HaMikdash*. If this does not occur, then we have to observe *Tisha B'Av* this year as we have done in the past.

Actually, many of us have difficulty connecting to the *Beis HaMikdash*. Why should we want it? What's so great about having it? What's so bad about life without it?

The *Shevilei Pinchas* says that the whole purpose of having a *Beis HaMikdash* is so that the Divine presence will rest on Earth. Proof of this is found in the verse that says, "And they shall make a Sanctuary for Me, so that I may dwell among them" (*Shemos* 25:8). This concept can still seem abstract for many of us. What's the big deal about having the Divine presence rest on Earth?

Perhaps we could suggest that the implication of having the Divine presence reside on Earth is that we will then have a close relationship, once again, with our ultimate Parent, God. There is nothing more comforting than knowing and feeling the closeness and love, warmth and protection that we receive from a parent.

The opposite is also true. There is nothing more disturbing than the knowledge and feeling of distance, ambivalence, coldness, and being left alone from a parent. Yet this is precisely the situation that we are in when the Divine presence does not rest on Earth. This is why the Talmud says that from the day the Temple was destroyed, the world has to get by with only two letters from God's Name, the *yud hey* (see *Eruvin*, chap. 2, *Osin Pasin,* pg. 18b, the opinion of *Rebbi Yirmiyah Ben Elazar*). This means to say that the other two letters of God's Name, *vav hey*, are missing.

This passage seems like a riddle. What is the significance of the letters of God's Name? The *Yismach Moshe* (*Parshas Beshalach*, based on *Tikkunei Zohar*, preface, pg. 9b) says that there is a verse into which God's Name is coded. That verse is "*Yismechu hashamayim v'sagel ha'aretz* - The Heavens will be glad, and the Earth will rejoice" (*Tehillim* 96:11).

The acronym of this verse spells *yud, hey, vav, hey*, which is God's full name. The *yud hey* appear in the words "the Heavens will be glad," whereas the *vav hey* appear in the words "the Earth will rejoice."

However, there is a huge difference between the Heavens and the Earth. In the Heavens, they are always glad. Meaning, even during times of exile and concealment, the angels and souls of the righteous are still glad because they still see and feel that special closeness with God. The happiness in Heaven is a constant situation. Therefore, the *yud hey* (*yismechu hashamayim* - the Heavens are glad) is still functioning. They are always happy on account of the closeness to God that they always sense.

Unfortunately, this is not always the case with us down here on Earth. On Earth, only during times of redemption do we see and feel God's closeness. During exile we do not see God in our lives as much. We feel distant from Hashem. As a result, our happiness down here on Earth is dependent on the situation. Therefore, the *vav hey* (*v'sagel ha'aretz* - the Earth will rejoice) is absent when we do not have a Temple, and the closeness of the Divine presence. This is why the Talmud says that since the destruction of the Temple, we have to get by with just the *yud hey*. This is because the *vav hey* is no longer functioning.

Our prayers at this time of year should be focused on bringing the *vav hey* back. We should be asking for a time of *v'sagel ha'aretz*, when the Earth will rejoice upon experiencing that special closeness to God once again.

However, Moshe Rabbeinu throws his hands up in the air, as if to demonstrate surrender. Moshe says that he could never bring the *vav hey* back as long as there exists "contentiousness and quarreling" amongst the Jewish people (*Devarim* 1:12).

We still suffer today because of the baseless hatred we harbor in our hearts for each other (*Yoma*, chap. 1, *Shivas Yamim*, pg. 9b). In the final analysis, all this distance comes down to baseless hatred. The *tikkun* for this is baseless love. How do we increase love? Perhaps we could suggest that often the hatred we bear in our hearts for others is a reflection of the poor impression that we have of ourselves.

It is when we feel so low about ourselves that we cannot stand seeing others who seem to be doing much better. The only way we can live with ourselves is to tear the next guy down. So to nip it in the bud, once a day in the "Nine Days," we should pronounce the following statement to ourselves. "I am a human being; therefore I make mistakes. That's okay, as I am still a worthwhile and good person."

Then write down three positive qualities we find in ourselves. Carry that paper with us in a place that we will notice it periodically throughout the day. In this way we will have begun the process of healing ourselves. The better we feel about ourselves, the more inclined we will be to viewing other people in a positive light as well.

May we all be blessed to see God's holy letters within ourselves, and thus come to appreciate those Divine letters in others as well. This way, we will join the *vav hey* to the *yud hey,* and then Hashem will redeem us from exile, build the Temple, and bring The Divine presence back to Earth, so we will experience closeness with Him once again.

Devarim - Shabbos Chazon - Tishah B'Av

A Tale of Two Temples

Here we are again at the threshold of our national day of mourning. At times, it looks as though we are going to celebrate (if you can call it a celebration) *Tisha B'Av* the same way we have been for close to two thousand years. What could we do in order to change the manner in which we celebrate this holy day?

Well, this week's *parshah*, *Devarim*, is usually read on the Shabbos before *Tisha B'Av*, which is known as *Shabbos Chazon* because of the opening words of the *haftarah* that is read this Shabbos (*Yeshaya* 1:1). *Tisha B'Av* is the date on which both Temples were destroyed and numerous other calamities occurred throughout Jewish history.

The Maharal (*Netzach Yisrael*, Ch. 4, p. 21) states that the First Temple was built in the merit of the three Patriarchs, while the Second Temple was built in the merit of the congregation of Israel. Based on this idea, we can gain an insight into the Talmud's statement (*Yoma* 9b) that the First Temple was destroyed because the Jewish people engaged in the three cardinal sins: idolatry, immorality, and murder. Each of the three Patriarchs was particularly careful to guard himself in one of these areas. The *Maharal* correlates them as follows.

Avraham guarded himself against immorality. We find that Iyov also notes his righteousness in this area, saying: "I made a covenant with my eyes; why should I gaze upon a virgin?" (*Iyov* 31:1). The Talmud (*Rava in Bava Basra* 16a) comments that dirt should be thrown into Iyov's mouth for congratulating himself in this way. Although Iyov did not gaze at what did not belong to him, Avraham did not even gaze at his own wife! We can infer this from an incident when Avraham accidentally notices Sarah's reflection in the water, and comments, "Behold, now I know that you are a beautiful woman" (*Bereishis* 12:11). Thus, Avraham stayed extremely far away from immorality.

Yitzchak safeguarded himself against idolatry. The Torah (*Bereishis* 22:10) describes his willingness to be brought as a sacrifice on the altar, simply because it was God's Will. Yitzchak, who was prepared to give up his entire being to Hashem, personifies the antithesis of idolatry.

Yaakov guarded himself against murder. The *Maharal* cites the Talmud (*Taanis* 5b) that states, "Yaakov never died." Many commentators are perplexed by this statement, since the Torah itself describes Yaakov's death, embalming, eulogies, and burial. We could suggest that the *Maharal* interprets this statement to mean that Yaakov never brought death upon others. Yaakov was the direct opposite of his twin brother Esav, "the red one" (*Bereishis* 25:25). Esav's redness indicated his intrinsic nature, which was drawn towards murder and the spilling of blood. Yaakov's nature was the opposite (See *Bereishis* 49:3, *Yevamos* 76a, *Niddah* 13a and *Yeshaya* 57:5 for further support of the concept that Yaakov stayed far away from murder).

Since the First Temple was built in the merit of the Patriarchs, who guarded themselves against the three cardinal sins, we can understand that the First Temple was destroyed when the Jewish people transgressed in precisely these three areas. When the Jewish people strayed from the path of the Patriarchs, we destroyed their merits. In fact, the Talmud (*Shabbos* 55a) states that the merit of the Patriarchs was used up after the destruction of the First Temple.

As the *Maharal* noted, the Second Temple was built in the merit of the congregation of Israel - meaning the unity of the Jewish people. Through this, we can understand the Talmud's statement (*Yoma* 9b) that the Second Temple was destroyed because of baseless hatred. The breakdown of Jewish unity, resulting in interpersonal hatred, destroyed the foundation of the Second Temple.

We could suggest that the First Temple represented the *bein adam laMakom* relationship (our relationship with Hashem). In fact, the three cardinal sins can be seen as direct affronts to God. Idolatry obviously runs counter to Hashem's Will. Immorality, even between two consenting parties, creates impurity, which is the antithesis of Hashem's sanctity. Even murder, which would seem to be an interpersonal issue, is in fact a rebellion against Hashem, since the Torah teaches us that man was created in the image of God (*Bereishis* 1:27). Therefore, a person who commits murder is eliminating a manifestation of Godliness in the world. When the Jewish people engaged in these three crimes, our relationship with God deteriorated and as a result the Temple was destroyed.

The Second Temple represented the *bein adam lachaveiro* relationship (interpersonal relations). As we mentioned, the Second Temple was built in the merit of Jewish unity. When Jewish interpersonal relationships deteriorated, the Temple was destroyed.

In these days leading up to *Tisha B'Av*, we must seek to strengthen ourselves in both *bein adam laMakom* and *bein adam lachaveiro* relationships, increasing our commitment to serving Hashem, as well as our commitment to improving our interpersonal relations. Both elements are necessary in order to be a truly observant Jew. A person who keeps Shabbos according to every technicality of Jewish law, but cheats in business, is no better than one who is outstandingly generous and caring towards others, yet disregards Shabbos. Although each person demonstrates certain valuable qualities, neither exemplifies the goal of synthesis towards which we are striving. When we improve ourselves and perfect both relationships, we will fix the flaws of the First and Second Temples and bring about the building of the Third.

The Nine Days is the perfect time to kick it up a notch in both areas. With regard to *bein adam laMakom*, let's add an extra prayer besides the regular service. One apropos suggestion would be to recite a paragraph or two out of the *Tikkun Chatzos* which mourns the destruction of our Temple. Each day we can choose different paragraphs. With regard to *bein adam lachaveiro*, one could choose one person a day with whom to share a smile or a kindness.

May we be blessed to mend our relationships with Hashem and with other people so that we deserve to witness the End of Days and the building of the Third Temple. May we feel the full impact of the prophet's words, "The hearts of the fathers will return to the children" (*Malachi* 3:24) - perhaps hinting to the Patriarchs (fathers) and the congregation of Israel (children). May we achieve balance in our Divine service, and may the Patriarchs soon be reunited with their children.

Va'eschanan

A Trans-Jordan Flight to Israel

Many of us have not yet achieved our goals. For example, there are so many people who want to live in *Eretz Yisrael* today, but find it so hard to do so for a wide variety of reasons. If there is one thing we can learn from Moshe Rabbeinu, it is to never give up hope.

This week's portion, *Va'eschanan,* begins with Moshe stating, "And I besought the Lord at that time, saying… 'Please let me go over and see the good land'" (3:23-25). *Rashi* (3:24) cites the *Sifrei* (24) that says Moshe thought that the Divine decree forbidding his entry into the Promised Land had been nullified (also see *Rashi* in *Parshas Pinchas* 27:12 citing the *Sifrei*).

The *Parashas Derachim (derush* 8, citing the *Mahari)* explains the *Sifrei* as to why Moshe thought that the Heavenly decree had been nullified. It is because Moshe thought that Trans-Jordon had the status of Israel proper (see *Rashi* on *Devarim* 1:4), and Moshe made it into Trans-Jordon alive and was even buried there. So in Moshe's mind, the Heavenly decree had already partially been nullified, and Moshe thought that a vow that is partially nullified is in reality completely nullified according to Jewish law. Therefore, Moshe thought that since he was already allowed to enter into Trans-Jordon, which has the status of *Eretz Yisrael,* and witness the inheritance given to the tribes of Reuven, Gad, and half the tribe of Menashe, he reasoned that he would also be allowed to see the rest of Israel divided amongst the other tribes. This is why Moshe thought that he could pass over the Jordon River into *Eretz Yisrael.*

However, God responded to Moshe by telling him that Trans-Jordan has the status of *chutz la'aretz,* a place outside of Israel, and therefore, the Divine decree had not been nullified partially and it wouldn't be nullified at all. Thus, the original prohibition forbidding Moshe to enter the land remained intact.

The *Chidah*, in his book *Rosh David*, says that the status of Trans-Jordon regarding whether it is likened to *Eretz Yisrael* or *chutz la'aretz* is dependent on a Tannaic dispute. According to Rebbe Shimon Bar Yochai, Trans-Jordon is just like *Eretz Yisrael* proper; however, according to Rebbe Yehudah ben Beseira, Trans-Jordon has the status of any other country outside of *Eretz Yisrael*. Moshe maintained the law to be according to Rebbe Shimon Bar Yochai, whereas God decided the law to be according to Rebbe Yehudah ben Beseira.

The *Divrei Yoel* asks: since the various opinions of all the sages through the generations were revealed to Moshe at Sinai, how could the decision of Rebbe Yehudah ben Beseira have been hidden from Moshe? Also, how could Moshe be unaware that God ruled like Rebbe Yehudah ben Beseira? The *Gina D'Pilpali* shares with us a fascinating approach. He says that inside every single one of us is the DNA of all the descendants that will stem from us until the end of time. This is true not just physically, but spiritually as well. Most of us cannot detect this by looking at each other. However, righteous people, with their holy eyes, can actually see all the descendants that are destined to be born from a person.

For example, in the beginning of *Shemos* it says that Moshe came out of the palace and noticed an Egyptian beating up a Jew. The verse says that Moshe looked this way and that way "And he saw that there was no man," and consequently struck a fatal blow to the Egyptian. Then Moshe proceeded to bury the Egyptian in the sand (see *Parshas Shemos* 2:12). The simple reading of the story implies that when it says, "And he saw that there was no man," it means to say that Moshe realized that nobody was watching, and therefore felt safe in killing the Egyptian, since no one would be able to alert the authorities.

However, *Rashi* on the spot cites the Midrash found in the *Yalkut Shimoni*

(167) that has a different interpretation of the words "And he saw that there was no man." It means that Moshe saw that no kosher person would descend from this Egyptian, and this is why Moshe was justified in killing him. If even one decent person would have been destined to descend from him, Moshe would have found an alternative way of dealing with the Egyptian. We see from here how a righteous person has the capability, with his holy eyes, to see a person's future descendants that are all contained in the person's physical and spiritual DNA.

At Mt. Sinai, 600,000 Jews stood around the mountain; within them was the physical and spiritual DNA of all their descendants until the end of time. When Moshe went on high to receive the Torah, God handed him the Written Law. The oral teachings and traditions that would be taught by all the Sages of Israel until the end of time were also shown to Moshe, but in a different way. Hashem told Moshe, "Look at the people standing around the mountain. Use your holy eyes to see all their descendants that are contained within their physical and spiritual DNA. Through that you will be able to see every novel and creative approach any forthcoming Sage will ever utter." This is the method Hashem used to inform Moshe about all future Torah messages.

There is a fascinating Talmud (*Sanhedrin* 92b) which discusses a famous, miraculous event found in *Yechezkel* (Ch. 37). That chapter discusses the story of Yechezkel resurrecting a whole bunch of dead bodies. The Talmud says that the people Yechezkel resurrected made *aliyah* to *Eretz Yisrael*, married, and begot children. Then the Talmud tells us that Rebbe Yehudah ben Beseira stood on his feet and said, "I am a descendant of those that were resurrected, and this pair of *tefillin* was given to me by my father, passed down all the way from those people who were resurrected."

The Talmud asks who those people that Yechezkel resurrected were? Rav says they were the half of the tribe of Efraim, who made a miscalculation as to when the exodus was supposed to occur, and left Egypt before the appointed time; then, the people from Gat (the Philistines) came and completely wiped them out. [It's interesting to note, by the way, that the tribe of Efraim was divided in half. Half of them died and half of them lived. Just like Efraim's brother tribe, Menashe, where half lived in Trans-Jordan and half lived in Israel proper. Not only is that a correlation, but Efraim and Menashe are, to begin with, half-tribes of the father tribe called Yosef. In other words, the tribe of Yosef is split into two, Efraim and Menashe, and those two further are split, each one into two parts.]

From this episode we see that Rebbe Yehudah ben Beseira's ancestors did not stand at Sinai with the rest of their brothers and sisters because this half of the tribe of Efraim left Egypt before the official exodus and were killed. So if they weren't with the rest of the Jews at the time of the exodus, certainly they were not with the Jews at the time they received the Torah.

The *Gina D'Pilpali* says that according to this, Moshe did not see all the Torah understandings of the descendants of this half of the tribe of Efraim, since they were wiped out, and were not present at Sinai. When Moshe looked at the foot of the mountain he did not see them, and subsequently did not see their descendants that were contained in their physical and spiritual DNA.

Therefore, Moshe did not see the opinion of Rebbe Yehudah ben Beseira, who maintained that Trans-Jordon is as much *Eretz Yisrael* as New Jersey is. Moshe only knew of the opinion of Rebbe Shimon bar Yochai, that Trans-Jordon was like Israel. Since Moshe made it into Trans-Jordon alive, it could only mean one thing; that the Heavenly decree had been partially lifted, which really results in the nullification of the entire decree.

However, God informed Moshe that he made a mistake because he was unaware of the opinion of Rebbe Yehudah ben Beseira, who came from that half of the tribe of Efraim that was wiped out. Rebbe Yehudah ben Beseira maintained that Trans-Jordon is just like any other place outside the land of Israel. So, Moshe's success in entering Trans-Jordon did not indicate a partial lifting of the Divine decree, and there would not be any nullification of this Heavenly decree.

Regarding the tribes of Reuven and Gad who wanted Trans-Jordon as their inheritance, the Torah tells us that this was because they had *mikneh rav*, which means a great multitude of cattle. They wanted the Trans-Jordon because it had great pastures for their cattle (see *Bamidbar* 32:1 and the entire chapter for that matter). One could ask, how could these tribes give up their portion in the Holy Land just for some grass?

The *Sh'lah* tells us of a deeper approach, explaining that these tribes were so dedicated and loyal to their Rebbe Moshe that they refused to leave Moshe Rabbeinu behind. Not only could they not part with Moshe in life, but even in death they couldn't bear to distance themselves from him. So they were willing to forgo their portion in the Promised Land to stay connected with their Rebbe. Additionally, the children of Reuven and Gad knew that Moshe's greatest yearning was for permission to enter the land of Israel, and it was precisely that one desire that was denied to him.

Therefore, these tribes had a master plan to get Moshe into *Eretz Yisrael*. They would request their inheritance to be in Trans-Jordan. They reasoned that if God would acquiesce, Trans-Jordon would then be transformed from *chutz la'aretz* into *Eretz Yisrael* (Just as Moshe thought that Trans-Jordan was like *Eretz Yisrael* proper, so his faithful students thought the same way). And since Moshe made it into Trans-Jordon, once it would belong officially to these tribes, it would mean that Moshe did enter the Land of Israel, and that he was buried in *Eretz Yisrael*. This elucidation is hinted to by those very words: *mikneh rav*, which doesn't just mean a great multitude of cattle, it can also be translated as "they made a *kinyan* (an acquisition) on their *Rav*, or Rabbi."

We could suggest that even though God ruled against them, and Trans-Jordon does not have the status of *Eretz Yisrael*, this is only the law in today's day and age (according to Rebbe Yehudah ben Beseira). However, in the future the law will be according to Rebbe Shimon bar Yochai, and Trans-Jordon will be just like *Eretz Yisrael* proper.

We find this idea demonstrated in the dispute between Beis Shammai and Beis Hillel. For the most part today, the ruling is according to Beis Hillel because, in general, he is the more lenient opinion, the one that we can handle and cope with in today's day and age. However, in the future, the law will be decided according to Beis Shammai, which is generally the stricter approach, because in the future we will be equipped to handle this approach, which raises the bar (see *Tosfos Chadashim* on *Avos* 1:1 who cite the head of the court of Nickelsberg; also see *Edios*, chap. 4. "*Eilu Devarim*," which lists only twenty-three cases where Beis Shammai is lenient and Beis Hillel is stringent. In most other cases the opposite is true.).

In the same way, in the future, the law will be according to Rebbe Shimon bar Yochai because his is the stricter approach. We find an example of this in *Berachos* (35b), where Rebbe Shimon bar Yochai says that a person should make the study of Torah one's occupation and have faith that money will just come. In contrast, Rebbe Yishmael is of the opinion that a person needs to have a job in order to earn a living and one should study Torah the rest of the time. The Talmud says that many tried Rebbe Shimon bar Yochai's way, but failed. However, many tried Rebbe Yishmael's way and succeeded. It seems that the law has been decided like Rebbe Yishmael because, since time immemorial, most Jews have had jobs, and very few are able to dedicate their entire lives to the study of Torah.

We could suggest that this is the law only in today's day and age. Because we are living in a world of sin, and we all know that on account of the first sin, when Adam and Eve chose to eat from the forbidden fruit, God cursed us and said that from now on, "by the sweat of your brow you shall eat bread" (see *Bereishis* 3:17-19). From here we see the formula: sin causes curses, and curses cause work. However, in the future, when the world will be restored from sin, then curses will be lifted and there will no longer be a need to work for our food. As the Talmud in *Shabbos* (30b) points out, in the future, ready-made cakes will grow out of the ground. In the future we will certainly rule according to Rebbe Shimon bar Yochai, and Torah shall be our full-time occupation because we will then be able to handle such an exalted level.

Therefore, in the future, we will also rule according to Rebbe Shimon bar Yochai regarding Trans-Jordon, and it will indeed have the status of *Eretz Yisrael* proper. This ruling will be retroactive, meaning that retroactively Moshe did, after all, enter the land of *Eretz Yisrael* and was, indeed, buried in the Land of Israel.

From this whole approach we learn to never give up hope. Moshe never lost hope of obtaining *Eretz Yisrael* and in the end he got it. We could extend this lesson to mean that not only does bad lead to good, i.e. Trans-Jordon lead into *Eretz Yisrael,* but its more than that. The good is in the bad, meaning that *Eretz Yisrael* is already buried within Trans-Jordon, it just hasn't come to fruition yet. This could be why Trans-Jordon is called *eiver hayardein*. The Hebrew word *yardein* is made up of the words *yeireid nun*, which means "to go down to the fifty" (the letter *nun* is numerically fifty).

This teaches us that even when a person falls to the fiftieth level of impurity and hits rock bottom, there's only one way to go - and that is up! As we once mentioned, the Dead Sea, the lowest point on planet Earth, teaches us that when we get to the bottom, there is only one place to go from there and that is upward (see Matos-Masei, "Pearls in the Sand," pages 258-261). The lesson is the same from *eiver hayardein*. We have to maintain the hope that in the end, we will succeed in everything that we strive for.

So, every day, if we cannot say all of the thirteen tenets of our faith, let's at least say the twelfth one, which expresses our hope for the coming of *Moshiach*, and then, all the aforementioned dreams will be realized.

May we all be blessed to never lose hope even when we go through the lowest

Va'eschanan

Superman

Somebody once asked me: if you were God, what changes would you make? While we realize that we could never be God, we can, nevertheless, become quite "God-like." Let us explore one way that we can achieve that level.

In this week's portion, *Va'eschanan* (4:21-22), Moshe tells the Israelites, "Hashem became angry with me because of your deeds, and He swore that I would not cross the Jordan and not come to the good Land that Hashem, your God, gives you as a heritage. For I will die in this land; I am not crossing the Jordan - but you are crossing and you shall possess this good Land."

The *Meshech Chochmah* points out that these two *pesukim* - which deal with Moshe's impending death - are inserted between verses that detail Moshe's warning to the people to refrain from serving foreign gods.

The juxtaposition of verses often implies association of topic. In this case, the *Meshech Chochmah* explains that the Torah is indicating to us that Moshe's death occurred outside of *Eretz Yisrael* specifically to prevent the nation from performing *avodah zarah* (idol worship). Had Moshe died **in** Israel, the Jewish people would most certainly have treated his gravesite as a shrine, thus transgressing the prohibition of *avodah zarah*.

We see from the *Meshech Chochmah* that Moshe's greatness could have caused the people to mistakenly believe he was actually a god. The fact that this was possible just goes to show how great he really was. We could suggest that the potential to become so great exists even in our times and applies to each and every one of us.

In *Bereishis* (2:18), God says, "It is not good for man to be alone." *Rashi* (citing *Pirkei D'Rabbi Eliezer* Ch.12) comments that Adam required a counterpart in order to prevent the angels mistaking him for God. Since God was "alone" in the Heavens, and Adam was alone on Earth, the angels were in danger of perceiving Adam as a god.

This Midrash teaches us of Adam's greatness - he was so God-like that he became indistinguishable from the Divine! From here we can also derive a lesson for ourselves, since we are all descendants of Adam. Each of us has the capability to grow spiritually and improve ourselves to the point that **we** become indiscernible from God. How exactly can we reach this goal?

The answer to this question lies in this week's portion (4:4) where Moshe says to the people, "*V'atem hadeveikim baHashem Elokeichem chaim kulchem hayom* - But you who cling to Hashem, your God, you are all alive today."

The *Ohr HaChaim* explains the aforementioned verse based on a *Rambam* in *Yesodei HaTorah* (Ch. 6, law 3). The *Rambam* discusses the law which forbids the erasing of God's name. He elaborates: a prefix to Hashem's name (e.g. **la**-*Hashem*) may be erased, but a suffix (e.g. *Eloke*-**cha**) may not.

The *Ohr HaChaim* thus interprets the verse, "*V'atem hadeveikim baHashem* - You, *Bnei Yisrael*, cleave to God," in the following way.

What is the nature and intensity of our attachment to Hashem? This is indicated in the next word, *Elokeichem* (your God), which contains the suffix **chem** (**you** plural), referring to the people of Israel.

Bnei Yisrael are connected to Hashem just like the suffix *chem* is attached to the name of God, *Elokei*. In the same way that His name may not be erased, neither can the suffix **chem** (i.e. the people of Israel) ever be eradicated. Just as Hashem is eternal; so are we an everlasting nation - *chaim kulchem hayom*.

These words, which apply for all of eternity, conclude the *pasuk* by emphasizing the message of our national immortality; all of *Bnei Yisrael* (*kulchem*) are a living nation (*chaim*) every **day** for eternity (*hayom*). We, therefore, assume the God-like quality of immortality. So the way we become God-like is by attaching ourselves to God. How do we practically achieve this perpetual connection to God?

Once we learn to become the "suffix," by consistently placing Hashem's Will before our desires, then we will truly become attached to Him and attain eternal existence. If, on the other hand, we assume the role of the "prefix," and decide that our wishes are more important than God's commands, then we risk severing our connection with Him, causing self-destruction, Heaven forbid.

One practical application of this lesson is related to eating, which is so basic to our survival. Firstly, let us be careful to *daven* in the morning before eating, [unless a person is weak or sick, in which case he should eat first]. (See *Shulchan Aruch, Orach Chaim* 86:3, and Mishnah *Berurah* #22). Additionally, when one stays in *shul* until the very end of *davening*, instead of running home in order to eat earlier, we demonstrate that we place God as primary and ourselves as secondary. Becoming *tafel* to God means becoming one with Him.

May we be blessed with the will and the strength to place God as the priority in our lives. May we cleave to Him forever in a way that is indestructible, becoming impressions of the Divine to the point that the angels will have a hard time differentiating between us and Hashem.

Va'eschanan - Shabbos Nachamu

Getting Back Up Again

Practically speaking, most of us have fallen in some form or fashion. We ask ourselves if we'll ever be able to get back up again. Wouldn't it be great to know that there is always another chance?

This Shabbos is called *Shabbos Nachamu*, Sabbath of Comfort, on account of the *haftarah* read from *Yeshaya* (40:1) which begins with the words, "*Nachamu, nachamu ami* - Comfort them, comfort My people." *Shabbos Nachamu* is always read in conjunction with *Parshas Va'eschanan* (meaning, and I besought).

In which way is this *Shabbos* a form of comfort? Also, how is this comfort connected to *Parshas Va'eschanan*?

The Slonimer Rebbe, points out that the Three Weeks of mourning over our Temple's destruction, is the height of our darkest days. Yet, immediately after this period of time, we read from *Parshas Va'eschanan* which contains the Ten Commandments (5:6-18).

This juxtaposition comes to teach us that even after we fall to the darkest of places, we can, nevertheless, accept the Torah upon ourselves again for a fresh start. In other words, there is always a second chance. This is hinted at even further in the Ten Commandments, mentioned specifically in this *parshah*. They were written on a second set of Tablets, known as *Luchos Sh'niyos*. The second set of Tablets teach us that there is always a second chance.

This is our *nechamah* (comfort), and it's connection to *Parshas Va'eschanan*. It is comforting to know that there is always another chance.

The message here is, in fact, even more powerful. Even after drifting to the furthest of places, we can still ascend the highest of peaks. Not only can we return to Torah, but we can even obtain the zenith of Torah, which is the Ten Commandments.

This is why, specifically, *Parshas Va'eschanan* contains some of the most profound statements in the entire Torah. For example, the *Shema Yisrael -* Hear, O Israel (*Devarim* 6:4); the commandment to love God (*Devarim* 6:5); and the 613 *Mitzvos*, hinted to in the *Aseres HaDibros* (see *Makkos*, chap. 3, *Eilu hein halokin*, pgs. 23b-24a, based on *Devarim* 33:4; *Rav Sa'adia Gaon*). All this comes to teach us that although we may have sunk to the lowest of places on *Tisha B'Av*, we can still achieve the highest of ideals.

There is a lesson here, put very succinctly by the Admor of Kuvrin. He says that if a Jew transgresses a serious crime, and later feels inadequate to approach God in prayer, then that person has not even crossed the threshold of *chassidus* and has not begun to understand the ABC's of Judaism.

As God's children (see *Devarim* 14:1; *Kiddushin* chap. 1, *Ha'ishah Niknis*, pg. 36a; *Mishlei* 3:11), we need to be reminded that we are never banished from Him (see *Shmuel II* 14:14). This means that we can always return to Hashem in repentance.

There are some additional points that should be made. From the low and dark times, we come to appreciate the high and bright times, through the contrast. Additionally, we must remember that sometimes the light is hidden within the darkness. For example, only after a seed rots and dies, do we experience life and growth. Don't forget that *Moshiach* is destined to be born on *Tisha B'Av* itself (see *Pri Tzaddik*, by *Rabbi Tzaddok HaKohen MiLublin, Parshas Devarim* #13).

This serves as a powerful lesson for us. Not only can we continue after disappointments, but we can even grow from them and reach the epitome of heights.

May we all be blessed to be truly comforted with the knowledge that no matter what challenges we've gone through, we can still move forward and even excel, becoming better and stronger than ever before.

Va'eschanan - Shabbos Nachamu

Southern Comfort

Nobody likes it when things are done only half-baked. So let's see what it means to be a whole and complete Jew.

This week's *parshah*, *Va'eschanan*, is always read on the Shabbos following *Tisha B'Av* (known as *Shabbos Nachamu* after the opening words of the *haftarah* (*Yeshaya* 40:1). What is the connection between *Parshas Va'eschanan* and *Shabbos Nachamu*?

This *parshah* also includes the Ten Commandments and the *Shema*, two of the most powerful ideas in Judaism. Why are they found specifically in *Parshas Va'eschanan*?

On *Tisha B'Av* we are forbidden to study Torah, except for those sections dealing with destruction and tragedy (*Taanis* 30a, *Orach Chaim* 554:1). The Maggid of Koznitz (*Avodas Yisrael*) explains this restriction based on the verse, "It is a time to act for Hashem; they have voided Your Torah" (*Tehillim* 119:126). Hashem's Will overrides everything, even Torah study - so, at times, we must make Torah "void," because doing so fulfills Hashem's Will. This is the case on *Tisha B'Av*.

According to the Maggid of Koznitz, reading *Parshas Va'eschanan* immediately after *Tisha B'Av* gives us a fresh start. This will help us understand why the Ten Commandments and the *Shema* are both found in this week's *parshah*. Reading the Ten Commandments (*Devarim* 5:6-18) is a way to re-accept the Torah of which we have just been deprived, and reading the *Shema* reaffirms our commitment to fulfilling God's Will (since the letters of the word **Shema**, backwards, form the acronym for the phrase "**ol malchus shamayim** - the yoke of the kingdom of Heaven.")

We could suggest that these two concepts represent the two areas of service we mentioned in the past: *bein adam laMakom* (our relationship with Hashem) and *bein adam lachaveiro* (interpersonal relations). The *Shema*, which urges us to love God, could thus represent our relationship with Hashem. The Ten Commandments could be seen as representing the transition from one relationship to the other. The first Tablet continues to address *bein adam laMakom*, while the second Tablet is devoted exclusively to *mitzvos* regarding other people. These two areas of service are particularly important for us to strengthen at this time of year.

The *haftarah* for *Parshas Va'eschanan* begins with the words "*Nachamu, nachamu ami, yomar Elokeichem* - Comfort, comfort My people, says your God." The Midrash (*Yalkut Shimoni* 445 on *Yeshaya* 40:1) gives several explanations for the repetition of the word *nachamu*. Some of the reasons for the double language are that it refers to both the upper world and the lower world; the living and the dead; this world and the next world; and the Ten Tribes and the Two Tribes. The Midrash concludes with the idea that the double language of consolation (comfort, comfort) comes to parallel the double language of crying, "She weeps bitterly in the night, and her tear is on her cheek," that we read on *Tisha B'Av* (*Eichah* 1:2).

R' Baruch of Medzibozh offers another explanation as to when we will truly be comforted. He states that comfort (*nachamu*) will come only when Hashem will call us "My people" (*ami, yomar Elokeichem*) - an expression that indicates closeness and love. We could add to this idea that the letters of the word "*ami*" form the acronym for the phrase "*ezri mei'im Hashem* - my help is from Hashem" (*Tehillim* 121:2). This hints to the *bein adam laMakom* relationship; since we are Hashem's nation, we rely on Him for our help and support.

Yet the word "*ami*" can also indicate the *bein adam lachaveiro* relationship, since the root of the word is "*am*," nation. The nature of a nation is unity; this is what distinguishes a nation from a collection of individuals. The double language of *"nachamu, nachamu"* can thus refer both to our relationship with God and our relationships with others, providing a hint that our ultimate consolation will arrive when we are able to balance the two.

This idea clarifies the connection between *Parshas Va'eschanan* and *Shabbos Nachamu*. The word *va'eschanan* is an expression of prayer (see *Onkelos*). Our prayer, right after *Tisha B'Av*, is to be able to improve ourselves in both areas.

One resolution we can take upon ourselves, in order to remind us to improve in both areas, is to recite the Ten Commandments every morning (see *Shulchan Aruch, Orach Chaim* 1:5). With the Ten Commandments reminding us about the two types of *mitzvos*, we set the pace for a day filled with a balance between *mitzvos bein adam laMakom* and *mitzvos bein adam lachaveiro*.

May we be blessed to take these concepts to heart and learn to integrate both approaches in serving Hashem. We could, thereby, deserve the building of the Third combination Temple (built from the ruins of the first two) which will usher in eternal peace on Earth.

Eikev

Footsteps

Sometimes our responsibilities seem overwhelming. The trick is not to let such circumstances paralyze us. All we need to do is take the first step in the right direction.

This week's portion begins with the famous words "*V'hayah eikev tishme'un…* - And it will be when you listen… to these laws, then Hashem will bless you." (*Devarim* 7:12). The Hebrew word for "when" in this verse is *eikev*. This seems a bit strange since generally the translation for *eikev* is "heel." Why would the word *eikev* be used in this context when there are so many other words that would have been more accurate, such as *ya'an*, or *ka'asher*? (See the *Sifsei Chachamim, Os Aleph*.)

Rashi (citing the *Midrash Tanchumah*) says that the word *eikev* comes to teach us that if we listen to the commandments which one tramples upon with his "heels" (*ba'akeivav*), then all the blessings will come.

We could still ask, which *mitzvos* are those that a person tramples upon with his feet?

The *Aron Eidus* says that this refers to the *mitzvah* of walking to a *beis hamidrash*, the study hall. The actual walking to a study hall is a *mitzvah*, even if the person does not learn Torah when he gets there.

This is supported by the Mishnah that says that if a person goes to a study hall and does not do anything there, he still receives reward just for going there (*Avos*, chap. 5, *Ba'asarah Ma'amaros*, Mishnah 17). This is considered a *mitzvah* that a person tramples upon with his heel, because he is not doing anything other than taking steps with his heels.

One reason for this reward is that even though he, himself, may not have learned anything there, he will nevertheless overhear others who are learning there. Although he may not be on a high level of scholarship himself, he will be able to absorb Torah lessons through other people who are discussing Torah teachings there. And for this he is rewarded.

The *Aron Eidus* says that it is very important that we designate a *beis midrash* that we visit regularly in order to hear the *mishnayos* (the Oral Tradition) and words of *halachah* (Jewish law) that are being learned there. This is hinted to in our verse which said *tishme'un*, listen. The numerical value of this word is 866, the same numerical value as the words *mishnayos halachah*.

So, when we "*eikev*" to the *beis midrash*, we will "*tishme'un*" *mishnayos* and *halachah*. This all takes place in the study hall, which is considered to be a *Mikdash Me'at* (miniature Sanctuary). This is why the numerical value of *tishme'un* (866) also equals the numerical value of "*ve'assu li Mikdash* - make for me a Sanctuary" (*Shemos* 25:8), hinting at the *beis midrash*.

The *Aron Eidus* goes on to say that hearing words of Torah is beneficial even if one does not understand what the Torah students are discussing. As long as the words of Torah penetrate the person's ears, good things will come from it!

This is because it is impossible for Torah words not to have a positive effect on a person. The Midrash says that the light contained within the words of Torah automatically bring a person closer to the Source of All Good (God), even if the person does not understand them (see the *Pesichah* to *Eichah Rabbasi*).

Just by virtue of listening to Torah words, a person will feel spiritually awakened. Moreover, in the end, the words of Torah will illuminate the person's heart to understand their meaning.

This too is hinted at in our verse, "*Vehayah eikev tishme'un*." The word *eikev* represents "the end" because the "heel" is found at the "end" of a person's body. This teaches us that at the end, meaning "eventually", *tishme'un*, one will come to hear and understand those very words of Torah. (See *Ba'al HaTurim Bamidbar* 22:2.)

This is why the final letters of the three words *vehayah eikev tishme'un* spells *havein*, understand, further driving the point home that eventually one will understand those words of Torah just by listening to them.

We could add that there is another *mitzvah* that we "trample upon" and that is living in the Land of Israel. Walking four cubits in *Eretz Yisrael* is a *mitzvah* of such proportions that it atones for all our sins, and guarantees us entrance into *Olam Haba* (See *Kesubos*, chap. 13, *Shnei Dayanei,* pg. 111a, the opinion of *Rebbi Yirmiya Bar Aba* in the name of *Rabbi Yochanan*). We also know that the air of *Eretz Yisrael* makes one wise (*Bava Basra*, chap. 9, *Mi Shemeis,* pg. 158b, *Memra D'Rebbi Zaira*).

Our study halls in the Diaspora are considered *Eretz Yisrael's* embassies abroad. This is why dwelling in them grants longevity, as does living in the Land of Israel (see *Berachos*, chap. 1, *Mai'aimasai,* pg. 8a, based on *Devarim* 11:21...this week's *parshah*). For those of us who are as of yet unable to fulfill the positive Torah command of living in *Eretz Yisrael* (see *Ramban Bamidbar* 33:53), and find ourselves stuck amongst the nations temporarily, the urgency of attaching ourselves to the *beis midrash* is even more profound.

The *Aron Eidus* says that our verse goes on to address this matter when it says, "*Ushemartem va'asisem osam* - And keep and do them… the *mitzvos*." The word *ushemartem* does not only mean "keep them," but it also suggests "longing" or "yearning" for them.

We find evidence for this reasoning in the story where Yaakov heard about Yosef's dreams. The verse reports Yaakov's reaction to the dreams when it says, "*V'aviv shamar es hadavar* - And his father kept the matter in mind" (*Bereishis* 37:11). The word *shamar* is translated as "watched."

However, *Rashi* translates the word *shamar* as "*mamtin umetzapeh* - waited and hoped." This means that Yaakov was hoping, longing and yearning for the time that Yosef's dreams would come to fruition (see *Yishaya*. 26:2 and *Iyov* 14:16).

If the word "*shamar*" from Yaakov can be understood as yearning, then the word "*ushemartem*" in our portion can also be understood in the same way, because the root of "*ushemartem*" is "*shamar*" (see the *Ohr HaChaim HaKadosh, Parshas Ki Sisa, Shemos* 31:16, and how he applies this concept to the observance of the Shabbos).

This teaches us that a person must long, yearn, and hope for the day when he will have the ability to fulfill a *mitzvah* that he currently does not have the opportunity to achieve. If we want it badly enough then we will figure out a way to obtain it. As the saying goes, "When there's a will, there's a way." One could assume that the opposite is also true. If we say, "there's no way," then it demonstrates that "there's no will."

As long as we truly desire to do that *mitzvah*, we are credited as having already fulfilled it, even if the moment of actually performing it has not yet arrived (see Tractate *Kiddushin*, chap. 1, *Ha'ishah Niknis*, pg. 40a, the opinion of Rav Asi, based on *Malachi* 3:16).

The *Aron Eidus* adds that it is important to remember that God only asks us to try our best. He cites proof of this from another famous verse in our portion where it says, "*Mah Hashem Elokecha sho'el mei'imoch* - What does Hashem your God ask of you?"

The *Aron Eidus* questions the use of the word *sho'el* for "ask." A different, more common word for "ask" could easily have been used, such as *mevakesh*. He suggests that the difference between *sho'el* and *mevakesh* is that *sho'el* is used when asking for a small thing, whereas *mevakesh* is used when asking for a big thing.

The *Aron Eidus* goes on to explain that God is not trying to impose on us by making things difficult beyond our capabilities (see *Avodah Zarah*, chap. 1, *Lifnei Eideihen,* pg. 3a, the opinion of *Rebbi Yehoshua Ben Levi*).

All God *shoʾels,* asks, of us is to start doing *avodas* Hashem (service of God), even just a little bit. Once we begin, God will help us fulfill it completely, taking us to higher and higher spiritual places (see *Shir HaShirim Rabbah* 5:2, and Tractate *Yoma*, chap. 3, *Amar Lahem HaMemunah,* pg. 38b, the opinion of *Reish Lakish*).

Parenthetically, based on this distinction between *shoʾel* and *mevakesh,* I was thinking that this could explain the double expression of Achashveirosh to Esther when he says, "*Mah sheʾeilasech umah bakashasech* - What is your request and what is your petition?" (*Esther* 5:6). Achashveirosh was telling Esther that whether she was *shoʾel-ing* (requesting) for something small, or *bakasha-ing* (petitioning) for something big, it would be fulfilled. Afterwards, I found that the *Peirush* (by *Rabbeinu Yeshaya Mitarani* on *Esther*) makes this very same distinction.

Perhaps we could suggest a practical way of taking a small step in the right direction. Let's make a list of *mitzvos* we want to do that we are currently not fulfilling, including the ones we mentioned above (if applicable). We can put the list on the fridge. At least once a day we can look at it and ask what have we done in order to make that *mitzvah* a reality.

If something was done, we can check it off. A new list can then be drawn up with more specific requirements to be done in order to achieve that goal. We can keep checking off the lists until that *mitzvah* becomes our reality.

May we all be blessed to take small steps in a positive direction, which will enable us to carry out God's Will, and thus deserve that God take the final step in "heeling" us from our difficult situations. May we all be blessed to connect with *batei midrashos,* hear words of Torah, understand them, and merit to live in the Land of Israel in peace and security.

Eikev

Pick Me Up

It is not uncommon to meet people who have stumbled in life. Some have fallen financially, while others have lost their way morally and spiritually. What should our reaction be when we witness such an event? Let us explore what happens when holy objects fall, and find a comparison to people who have fallen to the lowest of places.

One week, I witnessed something in *shul* after *Shacharis* (the Morning Services). About three rows in front of me, a man was taking off his *tefillin* when they dropped to the floor. I found it remarkable that this occurred on the week which looks forward to the portion called *Parshas Eikev*. In chapter 9, Moshe Rabbeinu recounts the episode of the Jews receiving the Torah, and the aftermath sin of the Golden Calf. The verse says, "And I took hold of the two Tablets and threw them out of my two hands and broke them before your eyes" (*Devarim* 9:17). The correlation is striking: on the very week that we read about the Tablets that were cast to the ground, somebody's *tefillin* fell on the floor. Let's analyze what one is supposed to do if, God forbid, this occurs.

The *Magen Avraham* (*Orach Chaim,* chapter 44:5) cites the *Mishpetei Shmuel* who says that the custom is to fast when one's *tefillin* falls on the floor. The same applies when, God forbid, a Torah scroll falls on the floor.

There is a difference however. One should fast when *tefillin* fall on the floor only if they were not inside their case or bag. (If the *tefillin* fell while inside their case, one need not fast; giving a coin to charity suffices.) But if the *tefillin* were in a case that was not closed properly, and a part of the actual *tefillin* box touched the floor, or if the knots which make up the letter *yud* or the letter *dalet* touched the floor, then one would also have to fast. (See

Orchos Chaim Spinka subchapter 1 citing the *Eishel Avraham Butchach*, and see the responsa of the *Sheivet Hakehasi* volume 4:26.)

In contrast, one should fast when a Torah scroll falls on the floor even if it was inside its case. This opinion is cited in the *Mishnah Berurah*, Ch. 40:3 (also see the Talmud *Mo'ed Katan* 26a and the *Ben Ish Chai* on *Parshas Chayei Sarah* #18).

In the responsa *Mahari Bronah* (#127), it says that if the person had not yet eaten that day, he should fast that day even though he had not accepted upon himself that day as a fast day from the previous day. And that person should say the special insert in the *Amidah* at *Minchah* time which is said on fast days, the prayer *Aneinu*. However, if the person had already eaten that day, then the best thing would be for him accept upon himself a fast day starting at *Minchah* time, and fast the entire next day (see the *Kaf HaChaim* 40:6).

If, however, the person is elderly, ill or weak, and finds it very difficult to fast, then the *Chidah* says (in his responsa *Chaim Sha'al* 1:12) that instead he should give charity in place of fasting. He should donate the same amount of money it would have cost him to eat that day. He goes on to say that in today's day and age, since people are generally weaker, the custom has been to fast for half a day and give *tzedakah* in place of the other half of the day.

There are other suggestions for this person to do *teshuvah*, such as a *ta'anis dibbur* (a day without talking outside of Torah study and prayer), and increasing the amount of Torah study that day. This substitution is especially pertinent for people who study Torah all day and would have to stop their Torah study on account of the actual fasting (see the responsa of the *Az Nidberu* 8:20). One should also take upon oneself to guard the sanctity of the *tefillin* and learn the laws of *tefillin*. All this applies to someone whose *tefillin* fell on the floor.

However, if a person witnesses another person's *tefillin* falling on the floor, then the one that saw it happen need not fast. The only time that an observer would have to fast would be in the case that a person witnessed a Torah scroll falling on the floor, even if it was not his own Torah scroll. If, however, one person caused another's *tefillin* to fall on the floor, then the one who caused it to fall needs the atonement; the owner is not required to do anything unless the owner witnessed it falling, whereby the owner would just have to give money to charity (see *Igros Moshe* volume 3, chapter 3).

One should also be careful that *tefillin* straps never drag on the floor, regardless of whether one is wearing them or not. If the straps did drag on the floor, one need not fast or give charity, or do any of the other suggestions mentioned above. In the *Dinim V'hanhagos* (chapter 3, #9), it says that the *Chazon Ish* would always take care to put on and remove his *tefillin* next to a table so that if they fell, they would fall on the table and not on the floor. This would circumvent the whole problem (see *Piskei Teshuvos* chapter 40, which cites many of the aforementioned sources).

We could suggest that every single one of us is connected to a different letter in the Torah scroll (see *Zohar Chadash* 74:4). Moreover, we find that the Torah counts the Jewish people from time to time to determine their number. The Hebrew word for number is *mispar*, and the root of this word can be either *sippur* which means "a story," or *sefer* which means "a book." This comes to teach us that every single Jew is a story unto him or herself, and each Jew is considered to be an entire book. Every single one of us has the sanctity of an entire *sefer Torah*.

Therefore, when one sees a fellow Jew fall down (whether it be literally, financially, or with any other difficulty/tragedy from which one suffers pain), then we should also "fast" because it is as if a Torah scroll has fallen. I don't mean this *halachically*; the point I am trying to emphasize is that we should feel the other person's pain.

The *Yerushalmi* (in *Mo'ed Katan*, chapter 3, Law 7) says that if a person sees a Torah scholar die, it is tantamount to seeing a Torah scroll being burnt. *Rabbi Avahu* says there that he would not eat on the day that a Torah scholar left this world. Although we find a source for fasting only when a Torah scholar "falls" to his demise, we are extending this lesson to include all Jews, who are each a world unto themselves. Although we may not have to *halachically* fast, we should still feel another person's loss and another person's pain.

Just as we pick up a Torah scroll or *tefillin* that fell on the floor, similarly we should "pick up" any person who falls and help out in any way we can. What emerges here is that fasting when an actual Torah scroll or *tefillin* falls is a fulfillment of a *mitzvah* between man and God. However, when we demonstrate that we feel another's pain when they fall, in any sense of the word, we are fulfilling a *mitzvah* between man and man. This is certainly true when we actually help pick the other person up.

May we all be blessed never to drop holy religious items, and may we never even witness such an occurrence. Moreover, may none of us ever fall or stumble in any area of life. But if, God forbid, we witness this happening to somebody, may we be able to walk the walk of *Parshas Eikev*, which literally means "a heel," and feel another person's pain by doing everything in our power to help. And in this merit, may we witness the final salvation when God will pick us all up from the places to which we have fallen.

Eikev

One Hundred Percent

Nobody would be satisfied if their car worked only most of the time. We would not be happy if our eyeglasses allowed us to see mostly clear, but a little blurry. It would not be acceptable if our appliances only worked some of the time. With the aforementioned items we expect 100 percent service.

Are our expectations as high when it comes to improving ourselves spiritually? Let's read on and find out that this is all God asks of us: namely, to be of service 100 percent of the time. This is quite the same demand that we make of the things that serve us in our own lives.

In this week's portion, *Eikev* (10:12), Moshe says to *Bnei Yisrael:* "*Mah Hashem Elokecha sho'el mei'imach ki im l'yirah es Hashem Elokecha* - What does the Lord your God ask of you except to fear the Lord your God?"

It seems, from the language of the text, that *yiras* Hashem (fear of God) is a simple objective, driving the Talmud (*Berachos* 33:2) to ask: is it so easy to fear Hashem? The Talmud responds by saying that, with regards to Moshe (*l'gabei Moshe*), attaining *yiras* Hashem was not difficult.

How does the Talmud answer its question? After all, wasn't the Talmud's question based on Moshe's words of instruction to the people - that they must fear the Lord? If so, how does information on Moshe's *yiras* Hashem help us to understand the challenge that faced the nation of Israel?

We will be able to answer this question once we gain a deeper insight into the words of the *pasuk*. Rabbi Meir in (*Menachos* 43b) tells us that instead of reading the verse as a question, "*Mah Hashem Elokecha sho'el mei'imach…* - What does the Lord your God ask of you…?" we can insert a letter *aleph* into the center of the word *mah* so that the *pasuk* reads like a statement: "*Mei'ah Hashem Elokecha sho'el mei'imach* - One hundred the Lord your God asks of you."

From this *pasuk*, the Talmud derives the law that we are to recite a total of one hundred *berachos* (blessings) each day. Why are we required to say one hundred *berachos* specifically? Before answering this question, we will divert our attention to an interesting insight from the *Torah Temimah* which relates to this topic.

Rabbenu Tam (Tosafos, Menachos, chap. 4, "*Hatecheiles,*" pg. 43b, *divrei hamaschil* "*Shoel*")* points out that there are ninety-nine letters in the aforementioned verse (see *Torah Temimah, Devarim* 10:12). Once we add the extra *aleph* to the word *mah* (in accordance with the Talmud), there is a total of one hundred letters, alluding to the one hundred blessings. The *Torah Temimah* says that this particular verse is a beautiful source for all other instances in the Torah where numbers are rounded off to the nearest ten. He cites the following three examples:

1) Bereishis (46:27): "All the souls of the house of Yaakov that came to Egypt were seventy" (even though we count only sixty-nine).

2) Vayikra (23:16): "You shall count fifty days [of the *Omer*]" (although we count just forty-nine days).

3) Devarim (25:3): "You shall give forty lashes" (despite the fact that only thirty-nine lashes were given).

Thus, Rabbi Meir's interpretation of the verse (in *Devarim* 10:12) serves as a *siman* (sign), that ninety-nine letters in the *k'siv* (the written word) can correspond to one hundred letters in the *kri* (the spoken word), thereby fulfilling the instruction in *Gemara Shabbos* (104a) to create *simanim* for ideas contained in the Torah.

Now we can return to the question posed earlier: why do we say one hundred blessings each day? We could suggest that this particular obligation teaches us an important lesson about how to serve God. The number "one hundred" represents *shleimus*, completeness. If we perform a task with 100 percent dedication, we can safely say that we carried out the task with *shleimus*. Therefore, we learn from this law to serve Hashem with a full heart, mind and soul. We must learn to use 100 percent of our energy in our *avodas* Hashem.

This idea helps us to understand why the verse in this week's portion (10:12) serves as the source for all other cases where numbers are rounded off to the nearest ten (as the *Torah Temimah* explained). Since this verse teaches us about *shleimus* - to give of ourselves fully (100 percent) in the service of God - we can apply this concept to all the other instances.

Thus, regarding our previous examples:

1) Yaakov and his entire family gave 100 percent in the service of Hashem.

2) During the *Omer*, we must devote 100 percent of our energy in preparing ourselves to receive the Torah.

3) Finally, the underlying objective of the lashes is to inspire us to do complete (100 percent) *teshuvah*, so that we will not repeat the same transgressions.

Based on this concept, we can answer our initial question. The *Arizal* comments on the Talmud (*Berachos* 33:2) that the word *l'gabei*, which is usually translated as "regarding," can also mean "surrounding." Therefore, rather than commenting on Moshe's *yiras* Hashem, the Talmud was, in fact, referring to the Israelites who were *l'gabei Moshe*, i.e. surrounding Moshe. Those people who remained close to Moshe were able to draw on his energy - his absolute *yiras* Hashem - and incorporate it into their lives. Moshe inspired all those around him to serve God with 100 percent awe.

It is important to note that the Torah's messages apply to each and every one of us, for all of eternity. We have the opportunity to make one hundred blessings every day - both literally and figuratively. Not only are we obligated to recite the daily berachos, but we must also try to integrate the message of the one hundred blessings into our lives by giving our all, our 100 percent in the service of God. Subsequently, we will succeed in attaining true *yiras* Hashem, like Moshe did, allowing us to "see" or experience God like never before. (The word *yirah*, "awe", is related to the word *re'eh*, "see".)

As we go about our day, let us concentrate on one or two *berachos* that we recite anyway. Let's say them slowly and think about how blessed we are, and try to dedicate ourselves 100 percent to at least one *mitzvah* that day. In this way we are well under way to becoming a complete servant of God.

May we be blessed to give 100 percent in our *avodas* Hashem, putting our might and soul into all that we do, so that we transfer any "**Mah**-ness" (questions and doubts) into "**Me'ah**-ness" (definitiveness and clarity), something of which Moshe would be proud.

Eikev

Firmly Planted, but Freely Flying

In the following *dvar Torah* we are going to elaborate on the previous one. Previously, we mentioned the importance of giving 100 percent of our strength to the service of God. In this next section we are going to further specify where we can concentrate that energy. In addition, we are going to show how we actually benefit from this implementation.

There may be times when we feel that we are not living up to our potential. We may feel that we have fallen short of our responsibilities. This may make us feel distanced from our Parent in Heaven. In this article we will find a way to bridge that gap.

A pretty popular verse found in this week's *parshah* says, "And now Israel, what (*mah*) does Hashem your God ask of you?" (*Devarim* 10:12). Rebbi Meir says that from this sentence, we learn that one is supposed to recite one hundred blessings a day (*Menachos*, chap. 4, *Hatecheiles* pg. 43b).

Rashi (ibid. *Divrei Hamaschil* "*Mah*") explains that this is derived from the word **mah** which is spelled *mem hey*. If one changes the vowels in this word, it reads as **mei'ah**, one hundred.

Of course, it would be appropriate to change the spelling of the word in order to fit the new pronunciation. The new spelling would be *mem, aleph, hey*. These three Hebrew letters spell the word **mei'ah**, one hundred.

After this change, the verse would be read as a statement and not as a question. Instead of "**Mah** (what) does God ask of you," it would be read as "**Mei'ah** (one hundred) God asks of you." In other words, God is asking for each and every one of us to recite one hundred blessings a day.

The *Tosafists* (ibid. *Divrei Hamaschil "Shoel"*) quote *Rabbeinu Tam* who adds a beautiful hint to this idea from the entire verse. He points out that this verse has ninety-nine letters in it. However, when the letter *aleph* is added to the *mem hey* so that it is spelled as **mei'ah,** the verse then has one hundred letters, representing the one hundred blessings per day (see *Rabbeinu Bachya, Devarim* 10:12).

The recitation of one hundred blessings a day can serve as a huge spiritual benefit to a person. We can see this by analyzing the first person created.

Adam HaRishon (the first person) was created so tall that his body stretched from the Earth to the Heavens (*Rav Yehudah* in the name of *Rav, Sanhedrin*, chap. 4, *Echad Dinei Mammonos*, pg. 38b; *Devarim* 4:32). However, after Adam sinned, God caused him to shrink down to the height of just one hundred cubits (*Rebbi Elazar, Chagiggah*, chap. 2, *Ein Dorshin,* pg. 12a; See *Yalkut Shimoni, Va'eschanan, remez* 827; See *Zohar Bereishis* pg. 53b).

The *Ramah* (*Sanhedrin*, pg. 38b) explains that the reason that God created Adam so tall to begin with was so that man would have the capacity of connecting all earthly matters to Heavenly heights. This would elevate the lower world to the higher one. However, once Adam sinned, he "fell short" of this ability.

The *Zohar* (*Bereishis* pg. 35b) and the *Arizal* (*Sha'ar HaPesukim, Parshas Vayigash*) say that Yaakov Avinu was a reincarnation of Adam. It was Yaakov's job to fix what Adam had fallen short of. This explains Yaakov's dream of a ladder that stretched from the Earth up to the Heavens (*Bereishis* 28:12). Yaakov dreamt of the time that he would be able to elevate all earthly, materialistic substances into heavenly spiritual matters, thereby joining the two worlds together.

Perhaps we could suggest that the reason that Adam was shrunk down to a mere hundred cubits was in order to hint to him that through the recitation of one hundred blessings a day, man would be able to rebuild that bridge connecting the Earthly realm with the Heavenly one. Who knows if Yaakov's ladder had one hundred rungs on it?

It is logically sound to suggest that blessings, indeed, have that power. Whether we recite blessings over pleasure, over *mitzvos*, or to give thanks, we are reminding ourselves that everything comes from Above and that we should direct all endeavors to a higher, more meaningful purpose. Does this not achieve the desired goal?

Our Sages have constructed the liturgy in such a way that if we pray daily and recite the appropriate blessings throughout the day, then we will have uttered at least one hundred blessings a day. By doing so, we are bridging the gap between the two worlds.

Obviously, this is accomplished when we actually concentrate on the meanings of the blessings. Mere "lip service" does not really motivate anybody to harness lower level activities for a lofty outcome.

Therefore, a suggestion for a practical exercise is to pick two blessings to focus on this coming week. For three days, say one of the blessings slowly and out loud. Then, for the next three days deliberate on the second blessing chosen. On Shabbos, think of two new blessings to choose for the upcoming week. Keep this up throughout the year, and by the end of the year we will have focused on one hundred blessings properly.

By the way, this would be a good practice to accept upon ourselves this coming *Rosh HaShanah*. By doing so, we will be moving this world of ours towards a more fulfilled and everlasting experience.

May we all be blessed to "score a hundred" this year by climbing the spiritual ladder of success and infusing holiness into the mundane.

Re'eh

The Apple of His Eye

It is part of the human experience for people to crave approval. We should try to treat others with the same courtesy that we desire. Besides, this is the way to stop derogatory speech; mainly by seeing only the good in others. If we never see bad in others then there won't be anything negative to say about them to begin with. Let's explore other benefits that come with this positive outlook.

This week's portion begins with the words, "*Re'eh anochi nosein lifneichem hayom berachah u'kelalah* - See, I present before you today a blessing and a curse" (*Devarim* 11:26). Yonasan Ben Uziel (in his Aramaic translation) renders these words to mean, "See, that I have arranged before you this day blessings and their substitutions."

This translation is seemingly problematic because he should have just said "blessings and curses." What does he mean with "blessings and their substitutions?"

The *Aron Eidus* explains that somebody, who by nature has a bad eye, can transform good into evil. This means to say that such a person can destroy something good simply by gazing at it. This is because there is a current of cursed energy flowing from him which has the power to cause damage.

One example of such a person is Bilaam (the Prophet from Aram). Even though God forced blessings to come out of his mouth, practically all those blessings reverted back to curses (*Sanhedrin*, chap. 11, *Cheilek, Rebbi Aba Bar Kahana*, based on *Devarim* 23:6). This happened because Bilaam, at his core, possessed a bad eye. Therefore, although he blessed the Jewish people, afterwards he turned most of it back into curses just by looking at them with his evil eye. Ultimately, 24,000 Jews lost their lives to the plague, partially because Bilaam gazed upon them with his bad eye (*Bamidbar* 25:9).

This is why the verse says, "One with a good eye, *yevorach*, will be blessed" (*Mishlei* 22:9). The Talmud says that the word *yevorach* (will be blessed) should be read as *yevareich* (he will bless) (*Sotah*, chap. 7, *Eilu ne'emarin*, pg. 38b, *Rebbi Yehoshua Ben Levi*). Meaning, we only give the honor of holding the "Cup of Blessing" for Grace After Meals, to a person with a good eye. This is because a person with a bad eye will wind up injecting poisonous energy into his blessings and transform them into curses.

Obviously, the opposite is also true. A person who possesses a good eye can transform something evil and cursed into something completely good, just by looking at it.

One example of such a person was Moshe Rabbeinu. A verse supporting this idea is the one that discusses Moshe's birth. It says, "And she gave birth to a son and she saw *ki tov*, that he was good" (*Shemos* 2:2). The word *tov* is used to teach that Moshe innately possessed a good eye.

This means that Moshe had the power to transform curses into blessings. A hint to this is found in the words "*Moshe ki tov* - Moshe was good," which has the numerical value of 392. The number 392 shares the same numerical value as the words "*kelalah berachah* - curse blessing." This teaches us that since Moshe was *ki tov* (had a good eye), he was capable of transforming *k'lalah* into *berachah*.

This explains the two sets of curses that are found in the Torah. The first set is found in *Parshas Bechukosai* (*Vayikra* 26:14-44). The second set is found in *Parshas Ki Savo* (*Bamidbar* 28:15-69). When the Jewish people heard the 98 curses in *Ki Savo* in addition to the 49 curses in *Bechukosai*, their faces turned green with fright. The people said, "Who can withstand these curses?" In order to pacify them, Moshe said, "Don't worry; you are all standing here today" (*Rashi Devarim* 29:12 citing *Midrash Aggadah* based on *Devarim* 29:9).

In order to appreciate a deeper understanding of how Moshe appeased them, the *Aron Eidus* says that first we have to clarify where the curses came from. The curses in *Bechukosai* were said in the plural form, and they came straight from God. However, the curses in *Ki Savo* were said in the singular form, and they came from Moshe (*Tractate Meggilah*, chap. 4, *Bnei ha-ir*, pg. 31b, *Abaye*).

This means to say that the curses in *Bechukosai* were harsher because they came down in their raw and bitter state (see *Rashi Devarim* 28:23). However, in *Ki Savo*, Moshe took those very curses from *Bechukosai* and sweetened them.

Moshe achieved this by bringing all those curses into his own essence. This is why the curses were said in the singular form in the second reading, meaning that Moshe took them into his own core. Since Moshe's essence was that of a good eye, he was capable of transforming the curses into blessings. Then, by the time Moshe shared the curses with the Jewish people the second time around, they had already been transformed into blessings.

Moshe pacified them by saying, "Don't worry; you are all standing here today." Moshe meant to say that since today I am the one bringing you the "curses," they have already been transformed into blessings.

This will help us understand the Aramaic translation of Yonasan Ben Uziel when he said, "See that I have arranged before you this day blessings and their substitutions," instead of just writing "blessings and curses." Yonasan Ben Uziel is trying to convey to us the real meaning behind Moshe's statement to the people - that the curses have been substituted with blessings. The blessings are the substitutes.

Moshe explained to them that this is why they have not been destroyed by the curses, even though they have angered God greatly (*Rashi Devarim*

29:12). The reason is because Moshe already sweetened the curses and transformed them into blessings.

There is a hint that shows us that Moshe's good eye already sweetened the curses. When you add the 49 curses to the 98 curses, you get 147, which is, remarkably, the exact numerical value of the words *tov ayin*, good eye. This shows us that Moshe's *tov ayin* transformed all 147 curses into blessings.

Perhaps we could suggest that, in order to be empowered with the capability to transform curses into blessings, we must train ourselves to see good in others. After all, the name of this portion is *Re'eh* (see). The verse says, "*Re'eh* (see) I have placed before you today a blessing and a curse." We have the choice of seeing the blessing or the curse in other people. It all depends on how we view them. The more we focus on the good points of others, and of ourselves, the more we become *tov ayin*.

Granted, this is difficult for us when it comes to certain people that just rub us the wrong way. In spite of that, if we would just write down one or two positive qualities of those people and focus on them, we would begin to appreciate them more.

Then, we would be endowed with the capacity of transforming curse into blessing. Wouldn't the world be a much sweeter place in which to live?

May we all be blessed with good eyes to see the holy spark in each and every person, and thus transform this world from a bitter place into a sweet one. Thereby we will deserve to see - with our very own eyes - the final redemption, which will be a paradise on Earth.

Re'eh

Keeping Kosher

In today's society eating healthy and dieting are trends that have swept the nation. So many articles, magazines, books, medications, and even operations are geared toward controlling what and how much we eat, not to mention relieving allergies related to various products. However, how much time, effort and money is dedicated to ensure that we eat spiritually healthy food? If we invest so much into our physical well-being, which may last eighty or ninety years, how much more so should we invest in our spiritual well-being, which is eternal.

In this week's portion, *Re'eh,* it says, "You are a holy people to Hashem, your God, and Hashem has chosen you to be a people of a select portion to Himself out of all peoples that are upon the face of the Earth. You shall not eat any abominable thing. These are the animals which you may eat: the ox, the sheep, and the goat, the ram, and the gazelle, and the roebuck, and the wild goat, and the pygarg, and the antelope, and the mountain sheep" (*Devarim* 14:2-5).

The *Ba'al HaTurim* comments that the Torah lists three domesticated and seven wild animals that are permitted for consumption, totaling the number ten. These ten animals correspond to the Ten Commandments.

The *Beis Yisrael Tinyana* expounds on the words of the *Ba'al HaTurim* by saying that this correlation comes to teach us that one who wants to succeed in Torah study and fulfill the 613 *mitzvos,* that are contained in the Ten Commandments, should be very careful to avoid eating forbidden foods. Because when a person eats things that the Torah forbids, it stuffs up the heart and the mind, and the person becomes incapable of grasping Torah secrets (see *Tana D'vei Rebbi Yishmael* in *Yoma* 39a). In other words, someone who guards his mouth from consuming forbidden foods, and only partakes from these ten kosher animals, is someone who is now prepared to fulfill all of the 613 *mitzvos* contained in the Ten Commandments.

The *Ma'or Vashemesh* (at the end of *Parshas Shemini*) adds that this is the reason that, in most years, *Parshas Shemini* is read right after Passover. *Parshas Shemini* also cautions us to distance ourselves from consuming forbidden foods. On Passover, the Jewish people are preoccupied with the eating of *matzah*, which is a very holy and spiritual food, thereby sanctifying their mouths.

Accordingly, right after this holiday, we read the portion of *Shemini*, which warns us about eating forbidden food, thus continuing the process of purification that has begun on Passover. We could suggest that Passover, followed by the portion of *Shemini*, begins our journey leading up to the holiday of Shavuos, when we accept upon ourselves the Torah. This shows us, once again, that in order to truly receive the Torah, we have to make ourselves into proper vessels by having our insides cleansed from any source of spiritual filth.

The *Beis Yisrael* goes on to say that if a person is stringent upon himself in the area of *kashrus*, it will help him understand the depths of Torah even more. Not only that, but when a person is careful to make sure that the animals were slaughtered properly, and that the fruits and vegetables are really bug-free and worm-free, then a pure holiness from above descends upon the person, and he or she can now really delve into the Torah's wellsprings.

This is the meaning of the phrase "*zos toras habeheimah*" (*Shemini* 11:46) which means "this is the law of the animal." The words *zos toras* can also be understood to mean that one would be able to understand "this Torah" only through sanctifying oneself with regard to *habeheimah*, meaning being careful with which types of animals we eat (see *Tosafos* in *Kesubos* 104a -

the opening words "*Lo Neheneisy*" citing a Midrash).

Parshas Re'eh continues by saying, "But these you may not eat of them that only chew the cud or of them that only have the hoof cloven; the camel and the rabbit and the rock badger, because they chew the cud but don't have a split hoof. They are unclean to you. And the swine because he has a split hoof but does not chew the cud. He is unclean to you. Of their flesh you may not eat..." (14:7-8).

The Midrash in *Vayikra Rabbah* at the end of *Parshas Shemini* (11:4-7) says that the four animals that were singled out represent the four kingdoms that rose up against the Jewish people. The camel represents Babylon. The rock badger corresponds to Persia. The rabbit symbolizes Greece. And the swine represents Rome. The *Beis Yisrael* explains the meaning behind this Midrash. He says that the Midrash poses an obvious question: once the Torah specifies that a kosher animal needs two signs, split hoofs and chewing of the cud (see *Vayikra* 11:3), then it is obvious that these four animals, which only have one of the two signs, would be disqualified from being kosher. Why then is it necessary for the Torah to go out of its way to mention these four types of animals specifically?

The Midrash addresses this question by stating that there must be more here than meets the eye, in that they represent the four kingdoms. However, it is still perplexing that the four kingdoms would be hinted at in verses that discuss *kashrus*. The *Beis Yisrael* offers an interpretation. He says that in every generation we find that there were righteous Jewish Sages who were held in high esteem in the eyes of the reigning kingdoms.

For example, Daniel, Chananyah, Mishael, and Azaryah were held in high esteem in the eyes of King Nevuchadnetzar during the Babylonian exile. Mordechai was held in high esteem in the eyes of Achashverosh in the Persian exile. Shimon Hatzaddik was held in high esteem in the eyes of Alexander Mokdon in the Greek exile. And Rabbi Yehudah HaNasi was held in high esteem in the eyes of Antoninus in the Roman exile.

This, says the *Beis Yisrael*, is exactly what the Torah is trying to tell us by hinting at the four kingdoms in a verse that deals with keeping kosher. It comes to teach us that in the merit of keeping kosher the nations of the world will not overly oppress us. Only when we are extra careful not to consume forbidden foods will we deserve the respect of the nations in whose lands we live.

This means to say that any person who espouses a philosophy which maintains that if we mix with the nations that surround us, and eat their foods and drink their beverages, then we will be beloved by them, is mistaken. On the contrary, adopting a gentile way of life incites the nations against Israel. However, if we refrain from eating the flesh of camels, rabbits, rock badgers, and swine, then, not only will we not be persecuted by these four kingdoms, but we will even be respected by them.

Let's try to improve our level of *kashrus* a little bit. There are many areas to choose from, for example, blood in fish and eggs, worms and insects, *challah, chalav yisrael, pas yisrael, bishul akum, yayin nesech*, and even food that was left uncovered overnight (thereby coming under the category of food items considered to be dangerous), etc. Let's pick one topic, study about it, and implement our knowledge. In this way, we will create an even greater vessel (ourselves) for receiving Torah.

May we all be blessed to raise the standard of *kashrus* inside our homes and out, which is the process necessary to reach purification, so that Divine holiness descends upon us, helping us explore and probe even greater and deeper secrets of the Torah and its *mitzvos*.

Re'eh

To My "Deer" Parents

Just for the gift of life alone, we could never repay our parents; how much more so we owe them for all the care that we received from them along the way. Surprisingly, in a discussion about *kosher* animals, we can glean an insight into how we can improve our respect and reverence for them.

In this week's portion, *Re'eh*, we read about the animals that we are permitted to eat (see *Devarim* 14:4-5). The *Ba'al HaTurim* points out that of the ten kosher animals listed in these two verses, three are domesticated and seven are beasts. He correlates these ten animals by the order in which they appear in the verses, with the Ten Commandments.

Based on the *Ba'al HaTurim*, the *Torah LeDa'as* (vol. 10) analyzes the connection between the fifth animal, the deer, with the fifth commandment, honoring parents.

He cites the Talmud (*Gittin* 57a) that expounds on *Yirmiyah* (3:19) where the Land of Israel is referred to as *Eretz Hatzvi*, the Land of the Deer. The Talmud asks why this association is made between Israel and the deer, and responds as follows: The actual surface area of a deer's skin is only large enough to contain the deer's body because of its elasticity - the skin stretches itself to accommodate the body. This is evident once the deer dies and its skin is removed, because the area of the skin shrinks. In the same way, *Eretz Yisrael* always has enough space to hold the entire Jewish people. In fact, the greater the number of Jews dwelling in the land, the more the land stretches and expands to accommodate them. Conversely, when Jewish life in Israel diminishes, the land, too, reduces in size.

The *Torah LeDa'as* suggests that the same concept can be applied to the fifth of the Ten Commandments. It often happens when we become a little older and have families of our own, work pressures and so on, that we feel the strain of attending to our parents' needs. However, the Torah hints to us by connecting this commandment with the deer, that if we stretch ourselves - like the skin of the deer - to take care of our parents, Hashem will, in turn, increase our strength and enable us to accomplish all of our goals. This is why the reward for honoring parents, as Rav Saadia Gaon explains, is longevity. In order to properly attend to our parents' needs in addition to all of our own responsibilities, we need time. Therefore, Hashem promises us that we will be recompensed for the time we spend assisting our parents.

It is crucial to emphasize at this point that merely attending to our parents' needs is not sufficient - the manner in which we help them is critical, too.

In *Avos* (5:23), our Sages instruct us to "run like a deer" to do the will of God. In this Mishnah, the deer represents the quality of *zerizus*, eagerness.

Why is the deer selected to symbolize this trait? Isn't the cheetah - the fastest moving animal - a more appropriate representation of zeal?

We could propose two possible reasons why the deer is a more accurate and suitable symbol of *zerizus*:

1) The cheetah is the fastest animal only after building up momentum in its run, whereas the deer is able to move from a complete standstill to a very fast run instantaneously. Thus, the deer teaches us to do God's Will and to respond to our parents' needs immediately, without any hesitation.

2) Unlike the cat family, the deer's run appears to onlookers like a dance; there is a spring and bounce to the deer's movements. Similarly, we are expected to carry out God's Will and to assist our parents with joy and with a "bounce in our step."

Finally, it is important to mention that our obligation to honor our parents exists even once they have passed on. We can help our parents gain credit in the next world by constantly working to improve ourselves, becoming the best we can be and by living life with joy.

So, for those of us whose parent(s) are still alive, let us ask ourselves how we can help them. It may be a good idea to ask them what they really need and try to fulfill their requests to the best of our abilities. For those of us whose parent(s) already passed on, besides observing the *yartzeit* and *kaddish* for them, we can pick one specific area to work on in order to further elevate their souls, as this gives them unlimited *nachas* in the next world.

May those of us with living parents be blessed to respect and appreciate them by always being ready to help, with alacrity and happiness. May those of us with parents in the next world be blessed to continue honoring them by constantly improving ourselves and reaching our potential so that, ultimately, we learn to properly honor and respect our ultimate Parent - Hashem. May we subsequently deserve to be re-united with our entire family in the expanded version of *Eretz HaTzvi*, speedily in our days.

Re'eh

Take It Slow

Rome wasn't built in a day; rather, it was a slow and gradual process that required diligent consistency, determination and hard work. The same formula is necessary in building ourselves into the best people we can be.

This week's portion, *Re'eh*, usually falls just before *Rosh Chodesh Elul* (the first day of the month of *Elul*). We may question the connection between *Parshas Re'eh* and the month of *Elul*? How does this week's portion prepare us for *Elul*?

Parshas Re'eh covers many topics, one of which is the laws of *kashrus* and the characteristics that differentiate a kosher animal from a non-kosher animal (see *Re'eh* 14:4-21). The two signs that a *kosher* animal exhibits are that it has split hooves, and it chews its cud.

Ramban (Nachmanides) writes (*Vayikra* 11:13) that an animal with claws has a cruel nature, as it rips its prey to shreds. It is understandable, then, why split hooves indicate a kosher animal; such animals do not demonstrate cruelty. There is a principle that "we are what we eat" - that is, we are (spiritually) affected by the food we ingest. Therefore, it makes sense that the Torah forbids us to consume wild animals with claws, in order to prevent any negative spiritual effect of cruelty entering our systems.

However, it seems difficult to understand why chewing the cud is a sign of a kosher animal. What does chewing the cud symbolize?

In *Avos* (5:1) it states that God created the world with ten pronouncements. The Mishnah wonder's why ten pronouncements were necessary. Wouldn't one have sufficed? We could suggest that God, by creating the world in this manner, is teaching us a lesson that great things are produced gradually, in stages. Just as God created the world in steps, so must we, a world within ourselves, "create" and improve ourselves, and consequently the world around us, in small, gradual steps. Great people develop themselves through small changes over time. A book is eventually produced by focusing on one page at a time. The ten-step process of Creation, therefore, acts as a guide for our own process of growth and development throughout life.

With this insight we can now understand why chewing the cud is indicative of a kosher animal. The process of chewing the cud is symbolic of a lifestyle that we can mirror. We should take our time and "chew over" our thoughts, review and evaluate our actions and decisions, taking life at a steady pace, one step at a time, in order to effect positive change and genuine growth.

Additionally, we could suggest that the name of the portion, *Re'eh*, which literally means "see," highlights this theme further. We are able to physically see our environment because of the gradual process that turns night into day. An abrupt transition from the pitch-black darkness of the night to the dazzling midday sun would surely be damaging to our eyes. This is alluded to in *Tehillim* (92:3) where it states "*lehaggid baboker chasdecha* - we relate God's kindness in the morning." One of these kindnesses is the gradual progression of sunrise. Thus, we see that even the name of this week's portion, "*Re'eh*," signifies the importance of taking things gradually, step by step.

In the month of *Elul* we begin to blow the *shofar* (*Rema* in *Orach Chaim* Ch. 581:1). The *shofar*, according to the *Rambam* (*Hilchos Teshuvah* 3:4), symbolizes repentance. The Talmud (*Rosh HaShanah* 27b) states that if a person turns the *shofar* upside down and blows with his mouth on the wider end, he does not fulfill the requirement of hearing the *shofar*, even if the correct sounds were produced! The reason for this is alluded to in *Tehillim* (118:5) where it says "*Min hameitzar karasi kah* - From the narrow place I called out to God," indicating that our calling out to God through the blowing of the *shofar* should come from the narrow, smaller end.

The *Ben Ish Chai* adds an even deeper dimension. He explains that the way we blow the *shofar* symbolizes the approach we must take in repenting, in "returning to God." The *shofar*, a symbol of repentance, must be blown from the narrow end. The sound of the *shofar* is produced from a gradual build up, as the waves travel from the narrow mouthpiece, gradually filling the wider cavity to produce the final, powerful blast. Similarly, a person who wishes to repent must begin from a small place, making slight changes in gradual progression, in order to produce real positive change and achieve powerful and lasting results.

It is, therefore, highly appropriate that *Parshas Re'eh* coincides with the Shabbos prior to *Rosh Chodesh Elul*. *Re'eh*, which represents the idea of taking slow, gradual steps to growth and improvement, ties in perfectly with the essence of *Elul,* and prepares us for this awesome month. Each Jew focuses on returning to God, becoming closer to the Creator, precisely through making small, gradual changes at his or her individual pace. The nature of a human being dictates that big, hasty transformations are usually not sustainable and could therefore be counter-productive.

One practical way to implant a small change of improvement would be to give one coin to charity every single day. Before *Shacharis* give a dime, nickel or cent - or a shekel, a half shekel or ten agurot (see *Shulchan Aruch*, *Orach Chaim*, chap. 92:10 and *Tehillim* 17:15). As time goes on, one can increase the amount and the frequency of giving, but this is a good solid first step to increase our attachment to the *mitzvah* of *tzeddakah* and becoming a giver.

May we all be blessed to master the art of patience with ourselves and with others, so that we climb the ladder of spiritual success, one rung at a time, becoming all that we can be in a slow, sure and safe way. This way we will be able to bring the ten-step world back to its original perfect state, and deserve to see the primordial light filter back into this world, and ultimately hear the sounding of the mighty *shofar* blast, ushering in the Messianic era.

Shoftim

Gate Keepers

We have all heard that after *Ne'ilah* on *Yom Kippur* the gates are locked; nevertheless, those gates will always reopen to those who approach God with tearful prayers from the heart.

This week's portion, *Shoftim,* begins with the words, "Judges and officers you must make for yourselves in all of your gates, which Hashem, your God, gives to you for your tribes, and they will judge the people with righteous judgment" (16:18). This verse seems to have been written somewhat out of order. It would have made more sense as follows. "Judges and officers you must make for yourselves for your tribes," and only then should it say, "in all of your gates which Hashem, your God, has given to you." First it should mention that the judges and officers are there to govern the tribes because that is the main idea. Why, instead, does the verse first mention the location of the courts, "in all of your gates," which seems to be the secondary point?

Moreover, according to the *Ramban* (16:18) it appears that each tribe needs to produce judges and officers to govern their own tribe. The judges of one tribe should not decide in cases involving people from a different tribe. This, in itself, is perplexing. It would seem to be better for the judges of one tribe to judge a different tribe to ensure that no bribery takes place. When everything is kept within the same tribe it is more likely for bribery to occur, because there is a tendency for the parties to feel more comfortable with each other. However, when judging a different tribe, it is more formal and the chances of bribery are less.

The *Chasam Sofer* in his *Toras Moshe* says that it is known from the teachings of the *Arizal* that there are twelve gates in Heaven which serve the twelve tribes of Israel. This means to say that each tribe of Israel has a different gate through which their prayers are sent to God. (See the *Magen Avraham* in his commentary to the *Shulchan Aruch, Orach Chaim,* in the very beginning of chapter 68.) Inversely, each tribe receives their specific portion of Torah through that very gate, which acts as a funnel or pipeline through which Divine influence flows.

This is why we often pray to God with the words "*v'sein chelkeinu besorasecha*" which translates as "and give us our portion in Your Torah," since each tribe has a different portion of Torah. This explains the *Ramban's* comment as to why each tribe must produce judges and officers to govern their own tribe and not any other tribe. If the judges of one tribe decide the verdict of a different tribe, it might not be the correct decision for that tribe, considering each tribe has its own Divine way of serving God. (Note: all the tribes keep the same Torah; nevertheless, there are nuances here and there that differ depending on the customs of each tribe, which are dependent on the specific combination of God's Tetragrammaton name to which each tribe is connected.)

This also helps us understand why the verse begins by stating, "Judges and officers you must make for yourselves in all of your gates." The reason we first mention the gates is because it refers to the twelve Divine gates in heaven. Only then, does the verse mention the tribes, teaching us that the various tribes are governed by the different heavenly gates that exist above. Only once this has been established does the verse conclude by saying that "they will judge the people righteously." This means that only when a tribe is judged by their own judges and officers can they be assured that they are indeed receiving the proper judgment for themselves (see also the *Beis Yisrael Tinyana*, which comments on this verse along the same lines as the *Chasam Sofer*).

The various existing *nuscha'os* (texts or versions) of prayer, correspond to the different gates of prayer. It would be advisable to ask a competent *Rav* if we are *davening* with the right *nusach* for us. This way we stand a greater chance of our prayers being answered.

May we all be blessed to witness the ingathering of all our tribes and see the reinstitution of our Torah judicial system, when all the heavenly gates will be opened to receive our prayers and to rain down upon us the holiest of Teachings.

Shoftim

Jewish Superheroes

We all share an affinity for role models. A role model for some people can be an athlete, actor or singer. We can get so caught up in them that we begin to idolize them by hanging their pictures on our walls, and by trying to mimic their behavior, whether in speech or in action. In Judaism, we also have role models; they are our *tzaddikim*. We are supposed to follow their lead by demonstrating sincerity, dedication, sensitivity and loyalty. Let us talk about our Jewish heroes right now.

In this week's *parshah*, *Shoftim*, we are told to act in accordance with our Sages' instructions, and to avoid deviating from their decisions "to the right or to the left" (17:11). The *Sifri* comments that even in situations where the instructions of the Sages are perceived by us as the exact opposite of the truth - meaning that what they see as "left," we identify as "right," and vice versa - we must, nevertheless, heed their order.

This principle is often a source of discomfort for many people who wonder why they have to be guided by the Sages even when their pronouncements seem to contradict common sense. After all, are these Sages not human beings with their own opinions, just like we are with ours?!

In the first blessing of the *Amidah* we find that two expressions are used in relating to God: *Elokeinu* (Our God) and *Elokei Avoseinu* (the God of our fathers). According to the *Dover Shalom*, these expressions indicate two main, distinct paths on which we may embark on our journey to discover God. The first expression, *Elokeinu*, refers to the exploratory path that an individual takes with the aim of recognizing and understanding God in order to create a personal relationship with Him. However, the *Dover Shalom* cautions us not to despair if in the course of our journey we feel "up against a brick wall," unable to continue moving forward because of the unanswered questions that plague us on the way. It is possible that we do not yet have the appropriate equipment to understand and appreciate all the concepts necessary to continue on that specific path.

The *Dover Shalom* advises us, in such situations, to temporarily alter our course and take a different track, that of *"Elokei Avoseinu"* - a path that relies on the wisdom and teachings that have been passed down by the Sages, from one generation to the next, until we hopefully mature and understand on our own. Again, however, the question is raised. Who are these Sages on whom we are told to depend? How can we trust their advice and guidance?

This reminds me of a certain dialogue I once had with someone who approached me and asked, "May I disagree with *Rashi*?" My automatic response was "No!" "How do you know?" he then questioned. I mentioned that virtually every page of the Talmud demonstrates that it is prohibited for us to argue with *Rashi*. He pressed me, "how could that be if the Talmud predates *Rashi*?" I explained to him that often we find a statement made by a Sage in the Talmud. For example, Rav, an Amoraic Sage, says something which contradicts what a Tanaaic Sage said. The Talmud will then question how Rav has the authority to argue against a Tanaaic Sage who preceded him! The Talmud will either answer this by saying that Rav has a different Tanna on his side, or that Rav himself was considered to be a Tanna because he lived during the transition period between Tannaim and Amoraim. The one asking the question thought that Rav was an Amorah, but the one who provided the answer claims that Rav was actually a Tanna.

In any case, it is vital to note that the Talmud does not question the authenticity of Rav's opinion from a logical perspective, but rather exclaims astonishment as to how Rav could possibly argue with a scholar who lived in a previous generation, therefore assuming the principle that later Sages (who are further away in time from the revelation at Sinai) may not argue with earlier Sages.

"So you see, brother," I continued, "You cannot dispute *Rashi*." To which he asked, "Why not?! Perhaps I have a higher IQ than *Rashi* and therefore hold a stronger grasp and understanding of the material than *Rashi* did. My decisions and interpretations may consequently be more precise than *Rashi's*! Are you going to be so bold, Rabbi," he continued, "to suggest that everyone in today's society has a lower IQ than those in the eleventh and twelfth centuries? Even you, Rabbi, would agree that it is possible for someone in today's day and age to be smarter than someone from previous generations! So, why can't I argue on *Rashi*?"

One approach to answering this question can be found in *Avos* (6:6) where the *Beraisa* lists forty-eight ways through which one acquires Torah. Some of the attributes listed seem logical. For instance: studying, listening, articulating, an understanding heart, discussion with contemporaries, tranquility, mastery of the Scriptures, as well as mastery of Oral Law. It is not so clear, however, how some of the other qualities listed assist in the acquisition of Torah. For example: humility, awe, purity, minimizing one's sleeping time, limiting speech, reducing business, minimizing pleasures, possessing a good heart, love of God, love of people, bearing another's load (feeling another's pain). How do these qualities contribute to proficiency in Torah?

We could suggest that this *Beraisa* is purposely teaching us that Torah is not "just another subject," on par with mathematics, the sciences, and the like. One may only need a good brain and sharp intellect to master the latter subjects, but one need not possess moral values. Torah, on the other hand, is the word of God, the sublime word of the Divine. Accomplishment in Torah is dependent not so much on a person's IQ, as it is on a person's piety and character development. Even our great leader, Moshe Rabbeinu, was overwhelmed by the vastness and depth of Torah during the forty days and forty nights on Mt. Sinai. In the end he was given the Torah as a gift because of his diligence, and more significantly, because of his humility. The gift of the Torah was completely independent of his intellectual capabilities.

"So," I continued, "even if you have a higher IQ than *Rashi*, which I doubt, *Rashi* will nevertheless, be more privy to Torah than you because he was an extremely pious person. God will, therefore, reward *Rashi* with Divine intuition and reveal to him the secrets of Torah, some of which you may never be aware! It is a given principle that moral standards decline as we move forward in time and become more distant from the revelation at Sinai. We only have to compare the behavior of our current society with that of our grandparents' generation to see that this is unquestionably apparent! Therefore, based on this information alone, we can be absolutely sure that *Rashi* was more pious than people are today."

I often feel at a disadvantage when attempting to depict to an audience what it means to be a Sage, or even what it means to know a Sage. How is it possible for us to conceptualize our Torah greats from previous generations if we have never even come into contact with the Torah scholars of today? Let's give an example through which we'll be able to understand this.

It is frequently asked why the Torah is composed of an Oral Law as well as a Written Law. Surely it would have been more beneficial for us if everything was written down so as not to leave issues open to interpretation, resulting in much less dispute!? (Although if this were so, *hagbahah* - lifting of the Torah scroll during the prayer service - would be far more difficult!)

Perhaps we can understand the advantages, and indeed the necessity, of an Oral Law, with the aid of the following scenario. Imagine someone (we will name Jonny) approaches you and says "I heard about a sport called basketball. However, I have never even seen a basketball. I have just heard that it is a lot of fun! Will you teach me please?" You have two choices. Either you can send Jonny to the local library to read all the books on basketball from cover to cover, or you could invite Jonny to join you for an upcoming professional basketball game.

Although delving into the literature on basketball would fill Jonny with an immense amount of factual knowledge about the sport (he may even be able to name all the founding fathers of basketball!), attending a game would be far more beneficial if Jonny's ultimate aim is to get onto the court himself and play. By observing a professional game, Jonny would pick up the rules very quickly and, beyond that, he would develop an understanding of the game and its necessary skills and tactics. There is nothing like seeing the real thing! (Please note that I am speaking from experience, having been quite an involved basketball player once upon a time, with never having read a book about it!)

Similarly, if the Jewish people were strictly the "People of the Book," that is the Written Law, we could be filled with knowledge of our history and regulations and all we need to know from a factual perspective; but, we would lack the understanding of what it means to be a Jew, the art of being a Jew. It is to our advantage, then, that when we study, things are often not so clear and easy to understand, because this gives us the opportunity to refer our questions to our Torah scholars, and more importantly, to learn by observing our Sages and appreciating the experience of being in their presence.

To illustrate this point, I would like to share with you two minutes in the life of one of our generation's greatest Sages, Rav Chaim Pinchas Scheinberg *zt"l*, under whom I had the fortune and honor of learning for many years. Two strangers, who had just risen from *shivah* for their mother, approached Rav Scheinberg and asked him a technical question in Jewish Law. Their mother had accidentally been buried in the wrong plot and they wanted to know the *halachah* about re-interring the body in the family plot. One would expect an expert in Jewish Law to simply answer the question.

What I observed, however, was something quite extraordinary. Immediately after hearing the question, Rav Scheinberg had to catch himself on the wall nearby, as if all his energy had been sapped from his body. He began to sob for two full minutes. Why? Because these two strangers had lost their mother the week before.

I hope you will understand why I never bothered hanging around for the answer to the question because for me it was almost irrelevant. I had just learned something far more important than a technicality within Jewish law - I learned more about what it means to be a Jew in those two minutes, than any book could have taught me.

It is Torah giants like these, people who embody such integrity, pureness of the heart, mind, and soul, and have true Divine awareness, who are our Sages of today.

I recall how Rav Scheinberg was once reminiscing about the greatness of the *Chafetz Chaim*, a type of greatness that no longer exists. I cannot fathom the greatness of Rav Scheinberg or the *Chafetz Chaim*, let alone the *Vilna Gaon*, the *Ba'al Shem Tov*, *Rashi*, *Abaye*, *Rebbi Akiva*, *Yeshaya Hanavi*, and Moshe Rabbeinu. These are the types of people who are inspired by God to carry the truth and secrets of Torah from one generation to the next. These are the people regarding whom we are cautioned in this week's portion to listen and act according to their word and not to stray from their instruction. It is true that everyone has a right to their opinion, but that does not make everyone's opinion right.

In order to gain an appreciation of our Torah giants, I would like to suggest reading and sharing stories about them at our Shabbos tables. Although this can never replace having a personal contact with them, at least it can provide a peek into a world with which many of us are unfamiliar.

May we all be blessed to merit meeting the Torah greats of this generation so that the window to an entire world will open for us, giving us some idea of what it means to be a Jew. May we live up to the expectations of our Sages by adhering to their instructions so that, ultimately, we will deserve to witness the coming of the Messiah, resurrection of the dead, and to be reunited with all our Torah greats from over the ages.

Shoftim

Celebration Time, Shalom!

We all crave lasting and meaningful relationships with our spouses and children. The question is how do we create them, obtain them, and maintain them.

One of the many topics in this week's portion, *Shoftim*, is the laws that pertain to a king (*Devarim* 17:14-20). At first glance, it appears that these laws have no relevance to us because we are still living in exile without a king. Nevertheless, beautiful lessons are buried beneath this subject matter that have tremendous significance for us. Let us explore one of those teachings.

One of the verses says, "And it will be that when he sits on the throne of his kingdom, he must write for himself two copies of this Torah in a book" (*Devarim* 17:18). *Rashi* there (citing the *Sifri* 160) says that if he does this, then he will be worthy that his kingdom will be established.

The *Ksav Sofer* says that not only will his kingdom last on account of writing for himself two Torah scrolls, but there is also another quality necessary for this king to be successful. Before we see what that is, let's turn to a seemingly grammatical difficulty with this verse.

It says, "*Vehayah keshivto* - [literally] And it will be *like* when he sits on the throne…" Apparently it should have said "*Vehayah beshivto* - And it will be *when* he sits on the throne…" What does it mean when it says "like he sits?" He is not "like" sitting on the throne; he "is" sitting on the throne.

The *Ksav Sofer* explains that the verse should be read as follows: "*Vehayah* - and it will be if the king conducts himself all the days of his reign; *keshivto* - *like* the first day he sat upon the throne; then his sovereignty will last."

The *Ksav Sofer* explains that on the day of the king's coronation, the king is filled with so much compassion for and commitment to his subjects, that he leads them with kindness and even forgives them for any prior offenses. Therefore, if the king continues to behave this way all the days of his rule, then he will be worthy of his kingdom lasting.

This message is extremely pertinent to us as well, especially when it comes to our relationships. Let's use marriage as an example. It is enormously important to maintain an atmosphere of happiness with one's spouse and uphold excitement at being connected to him or her.

How can one achieve this? A *chassan* (groom) is likened to a king (*Pirkei D'Rebbi Eliezer*, chap. 16). It follows that a *kallah* (bride) is likened to a queen. Just like a king is expected to always reflect on the feelings he had on the day that the royal crown was placed upon his head, similarly a *chassan* and a *kallah* need to be reminded throughout their marriage of how they felt about each other on the day they celebrated their wedding. Those memories and thoughts can help a couple get through the more challenging parts of their marriage. Perhaps we could suggest a practical way of generating these emotions.

Go out on a date with your significant other, and go through the wedding album or maybe watch the video. Talk about how beautiful it was. This can instill freshness into the relationship and encourage a resolve to do anything for your spouse, just like you felt on the day that you tied the knot.

This exercise holds true for any relationship. If parents were reminded how they felt the day that their child was born, it would be much easier for them to get through the difficult parts of child-rearing because their compassion has been aroused.

Since God referred to us, the Jewish people, as a kingdom (*Shemos* 19:6), we can start behaving more and more like aristocracy and not engage in anything beneath our dignity. This means to maintain tolerance, respect, appreciation, care, concern, and love for each other. When we accept this mantle of leadership and carry ourselves with God's vision of kings and queens, we will begin to truly enjoy the people in our lives.

May we all be blessed with a sense of our regal nature and never forget the passion and commitment of our youth, so that we experience true joy with our families and friends.

Shoftim

One, Two, and... Tree

To soar high and yet remain grounded is a much coveted objective. How is this balance achieved?

In this week's portion, *Shoftim* (20:19), the Torah says "When you besiege a city for many days to wage war against it, to seize it, do not destroy its trees by swinging an axe against them, for from it you will eat, and you shall not cut it down." The verse concludes, *"Ki ha'adam eitz ha'sadeh lavo mi'panecha bamatzor* - [for] is the tree of the field a man, that it should enter the siege before you?"

Many commentaries understand the words *"ki ha'adam eitz ha'sadeh"* on a deeper level, as they read the phrase like a statement rather than a rhetorical question. Thus, *"ki ha'adam eitz ha'sadeh"* is translated "[for] the tree of the field is [like] a man."

In what way are we comparable to trees?

We could suggest the following similarity: trees are always attached to the ground regardless of the season. Whether in the bloom and blossom of spring and summer, or in the withering and death of fall and winter, the trees remain firmly affixed to their source. Just like the trees are constantly *davuk la'makom* (connected to their place), so too are we expected to be *davuk la'makom* (cleaving to the Makom) at all times. The word *"la'makom"* not only means "to the place," but is also used to imply God (see *Bereishis Rabbah* 68:9 where *HaMakom* refers to God).

Not only must we attach ourselves to Hashem in the high points of our lives (represented by spring and summer), but also in the dark and low times (symbolized by fall and winter).

Furthermore, we learn about the cyclic nature of life from trees. Trees experience a degree of death in the winter, but are rejuvenated once again the following season. Similarly, when we experience painful lows, we must be mindful of the fact that the dismal times will pass and give rise to new, happier beginnings. Every *yeridah*, descent, always marks the start of the next *aliyah*, ascent. When we reach rock bottom, the only possible direction to proceed is upward.

This idea is alluded to in this week's portion (*Devarim* 17:18). *Rashi* (citing *Sanhedrin* 21b) discusses the obligation incumbent upon a sovereign to write two Torah scrolls - one that remains in his chamber and the other that accompanies him on his travels. We could suggest that these two scrolls represent the dichotomy of a person's life; the "ups" and the "downs." The mobile Torah represents the high points in life because these are times when we venture outside and feel motivated and confident in our desire to "conquer the world." The scroll in the chamber, on the other hand, symbolizes the low periods of life because at times like these, we lack confidence and prefer to stay indoors and not interact with others, thus isolating ourselves from the outside world.

This Talmudic passage teaches us that regardless of our life situation - whether grueling and despairing, or smooth and euphoric - the Torah is there to guide our thoughts, feelings and behavior. When we experience the "highs" of life and feel self-assured, the Torah teaches us to gain perspective and directs us with its laws to continue on the right path. When we undergo "low" periods, the Torah encourages us to never give up and reminds us of Hashem's love for us.

We have the capability to serve Hashem at all times and in all circumstances. God awaits our return to Him and desires our connection, always.

It's not insignificant that each wooden handle used to hold a Torah scroll is called an *Eitz Chaim* (Tree of Life). This signifies the comparison between trees and the Torah itself.

May we be blessed with the strength to march forward so that we achieve an even greater *aliyah* after the long and dark *yeridah* of exile. May we subsequently witness the arrival of King *Moshiach* with his two *Sifrei Torah*, propelling us to the zenith of our existence, a new and wonderful experience for us all.

Ki Seitzei

Virgo

Some people feel trapped inside of their bodies. On one hand, they really feel they could climb to the highest of places; yet, simultaneously, they feel pulled down by various barriers. If only our true selves could break out of the shell, how much more we would be able to accomplish… But how?

Our portion begins with the case of the *yefas to'ar*, a woman of beautiful form. The verses tell us that when we go out to war against our enemies and capture captives, and a Jewish soldier sees a *yefas to'ar* amongst them, he may take her to be his wife.

However, first the Jewish soldier must bring her into his home; she must shave her head and grow her nails long. She must remove the clothing of her captivity, replacing them with more modest attire. She will cry over her father and mother for a full month, and only then, if he desires her, he can have her (*Devarim* 21:10-13).

The *Arizal* and the Maggid of Koznits (Rabbi Yisrael in his *Avodas Yisrael*) explain this whole episode on a deeper level. They say that the *yefas to'ar* refers to a person's soul which is so beautiful spiritually. The captive refers to the soul which is held prisoner inside of the body.

The clothing of her captivity represents the spiritual garb of filth that we created with our sins and surrounds the soul. When it says that he desires her, it means that if the person desires his soul and wants to rescue it from its captivity, then he may do so by crying for a full month. The month of crying refers to the month of *Elul* (see *Zohar, Ki Seitzei*, pg. 72a).

Going to war with the enemy refers to the battle that we wage constantly with the *yetzer hara*, evil inclination. The major battle will take place on *Rosh*

HaShanah, the Day of Judgment. Our main artillery is *teshuvah*, repentance.

Therefore, we must take some time to think about how precious our souls really are. The soul is an extension of God that was carved out from underneath the Throne of Glory. Hashem sent the soul all the way down into a deep pit, the body. When we go about serving Him from the lowest of places, we give God the greatest pleasure, so to speak.

If we really want to connect with our souls, we must do *teshuvah* from the depths of our hearts. However, there are three conditions necessary for this to happen: 1) Refrain from unnessary indulgence in physicality, 2) Become disgusted with sin, and 3) Shed tears in teshuvah. All three conditions are mentioned explicitly in our scriptural verses which discuss the *yefas to'ar*.

1) She must shave off the hair of her head. This means to put up fences protecting ourselves from unnecessary indulgence in physicality for its own sake. Just like hair is not necessary for our survival, so too, excessive materialism is unnecessary for us to exist. Just like the hair is removed, similarly we must remove ourselves from excessiveness, and take from the physical world only what we need in order to live.

2) She must grow her nails long. Just like this is meant to make her unattractive and even disgusting in the soldier's eyes, similarly we have to become disgusted with the moments we spent in sin.

3) She must cry for a full month. This teaches us to shed some tears during the month of *Elul* in order to cleanse ourselves.

The *Sfas Emes* points out that the month of *Elul* is a propitious time to do *teshuvah*. This is because the *mazal* (zodiac sign) of *Elul* is *besulah* (virgin or Virgo). This teaches us that every single one of us has an inner point, or holy spark, that remains pure constantly. No foreign influences can damage or stain that spark in any negative way, even after sinning excessively. That spark is called *besulah*, because just like a virgin is untouched, so too, this spark remains untouched.

Although sin creates distance between us and God, that spark is always connected to God in the deepest way. This is truly who we are. At our core, we are pure, innocent, and holy. It's just that sometimes it's hard to find that spark which lies within us.

However, the month of *Elul* is an opportune time to reconnect with that spark and activate it, because this month is under the auspices and energy of *besulah*, which gives us the ability to get back in touch with who we really are.

The verse "*Ani l'dodi v'dodi li* - I am my Beloved's and my Beloved is mine" (*Mishlei* 6:3), which contains the acronym of *Elul*, is specifically referring to that spark. This means to say that "I," my spark, is always connected to my Beloved, God, no matter what. This month carries within it the energy to locate that spark and return to God from that place.

Perhaps we could suggest an exercise for the remainder of this month. Every morning, upon arising, look at yourself in the mirror, closely. Catch that sparkle in your eyes and say to yourself out loud, "I have a pure and holy spark within me that has never been touched by spiritual pollution. I am special and I am priceless. My spark is unique. Nobody else has a spark quite like mine."

This will increase our self-confidence tremendously. We may not be getting approval from the people in our lives. Therefore, we have to give it to ourselves. We are not fooling ourselves. We are merely reminding ourselves of the truth. Doing this exercise in the month of *besulah* will help us find that *besulah* (purity) within us, wake it up, and activate it. With the renewed strength of self-confidence that we will feel, let's get out there and improve in any area that our hearts desire.

So, this *Elul*, may we be blessed to shed a tear of *teshuvah* and remember that we are so close to Hashem because of that pure virgin spark within our bodies that has been untouched by any spiritual filth from our captivity. May this memory motivate us to reconnect with our inner selves and return to God as one would run back to his beloved.

Ki Seitzei

Ring Around the Mitzvos

Many of us have met people who seem to have an aura around them. This aura is like a peaceful energy that surrounds the person, creating an atmosphere of protection and tranquility. Every single one of us can tap into this light.

This week's portion, *Ki Seitzei,* begins by talking about a *yefas to'ar,* a woman of beautiful form, taken captive by Jewish soldiers during battle. If a Jewish soldier wants to marry her, then he must first go through a process, including the stipulation that she must sit in his house and cry over the loss of her father and mother for a full month (see 21:10-13).

Regarding her crying over her father and mother, there is much interpretation. The Talmud (*Yevamos* 48b) cites the opinion of Rebbi Akiva who says that it really means that she cries over her idolatrous practices, as the nations would refer to their idols as their parents (see *Yirmiyah* 2:27).

The *Zohar* has a different take on this crying. The *Zohar* says that it means that she cries about how far she is from Hashem and how far she has drifted from the Jewish people (see *Zohar Chadash*). These two approaches complement each other. In other words, she cries about how her idolatrous past caused her to be so distant from God and the Jewish people. The difficulty, however, is in understanding how the Torah could expect her to cry, especially about her idolatrous history.

Until she was captured, she was a person immersed in impurity. The whole reason she went out onto the battle field in the first place was in order to seduce the Jewish soldiers (see *Rashi* 21:13). How can we expect such a person to cry over her sinful life? Do not tears need to come from the heart, when a person on his own is aroused to feel such remorse? You can't command someone to cry from the outside, it has to come from within. So how can the Torah expect her to cry?

The *Bnei Yissaschar* (*Tishrei, Tzila D'miheminusa* #7, in the name of Rebbe Pinchas from Koretz), says that when a Jew performs a *mitzvah* in this world, he creates an *ohr makif*, surrounding light, which protects him both physically and spiritually.

Actually, there are certain specific *mitzvos* that are directly connected with this surrounding light because they actually surround us. Some examples are: a *tallis*, prayer shawl (see the text in the prayer book to be recited prior to donning the *tallis*); a *sukkah*; *Eretz Yisrael* (see *Kol HaTor* 1:7); a *mezuzah* in the doorway of a person's house; and *Shabbos*. Even clothing can have an *ohr makif* because certain types of clothing are used in doing a *mitzvah*. For example, wearing a hat and a belt for prayer (see the *Shulchan Aruch*, *Orach Chaim* 91:2), and wearing a jacket for prayer (see *Piskei Teshuvos* there citing the *Toras Moshe* on *Pesach*). Also, in general, when clothing is worn the Jewish way, meaning with modesty, it carries with it an *ohr makif*.

Women are even more connected to the surrounding light than men are, as we find that it is the bride who provides the *tallis* for her groom (see the *Ta'amei Haminhagim* on *Ishus* #947 in the name of the *Ohr Hameir* on *Sukkos*). Since a *tallis* creates surrounding light, and the bride gives the *tallis* to the groom, in effect the bride is providing the surrounding light for her groom. This is evident even under the wedding canopy, when it is the bride that walks around her groom seven times, another act of giving her groom *ohr makif* (see the *Ta'amei Haminhagim Ishus* #961 in the name of the *Tashbats* #467). This is an interpretation of the verse in *Yirmiyah* that says, "A woman shall surround a man" (31:21).

The *Emunas Itecha* says: This is how it is possible to command the woman to cry; because in reality, she has a very high soul inside of her (see the *Ohr*

HaChaim in this week's portion 21:11-14, based on the *Zohar Chadash* in *Parshas Balak* 53:3). It's just that until now she has been immersed in an immoral society with layers of filth and impurity surrounding her, signified by her very immodest clothing. Therefore, she was missing this surrounding Divine light, which subsequently caused her to be callous and insensitive as to just how far she has drifted away from God, the Jewish people, and their holy ways.

Therefore, the Torah commands us to bring her into a Jewish home, which is surrounded with holiness. One example of this surrounding holiness is the *mezuzah* on the doorpost. Additionally, all the other *mitzvos* a person fulfills in his home creates *ohr makif* which permeates the Jewish home. Even the light of a *sukkah* enters into a Jewish home at the end of the holidays (see the liturgical text recited upon leaving the *sukkah* at the end of the *chag*). The Torah also commands that the immodest clothing in which she was captured be removed, and instead she must dress herself in Jewish clothing, which is inherently modest and carries with it a surrounding light.

Now that we've peeled away the layers of filth and replaced them with layers of holy light, that light will begin to penetrate and connect with the holy spark she has inside. She will then start to feel just how distant she is from God, the Jewish people, and their ways, and then she will cry on her own about the idolatrous past which has brought her to the furthest and lowest of places. What comes out of this is that there is no real command for her to cry; rather the command is to surround her in holy light, and then she will cry on her own.

This is our *avodah* in the month of *Elul*: to take off our filthy clothing and engage in doing as many *mitzvos* as we can. This will create a surrounding light that will awaken our true selves deep inside of us. We could suggest that this is the reason why *Parshas Ki Seitzei* is always read in the month of *Elul*. It is because parshas Ki Seitzei has more *mitzvos* than any other single *parshah*. This teaches us that this is a time to involve ourselves in as many *mitzvos* as we can, which will create layer upon layer of light, protecting us physically and spiritually.

Perhaps we could focus on one *mitzvah* this month. For example, let us have our *mezuzos* examined by a competent expert, a suggested practice at this time of year (see *Mateh Efraim*, *Orach Chaim* 581:10 and *Kitzur Shulchan Aruch* chap. 128:3). After reaffixing them, let us try to focus on them once a day. The first time we leave the house in the morning, let us place our right hand on the *mezuzah* and say "May God guard me, shade me, on my right side; may God guard my going out and my coming in for a good life and peace from now and forever; may the almighty *Shakkai* bless me and give me mercy." (see *Rema, Shulchan Aruch, Yorah De'ah*, 285:2; *Aruch Hashulchan, Yorah De'ah* 285:4 and *Tehillim* 121:5.) If we think about the *mezuzah* when we are on the streets, then its sensitivity surrounds us at all times.

May we all be blessed during this season of *Elul* (and at all times) to defeat our enemies, which include the *yetzer hara*, by surrounding ourselves with *mitzvos* in order to get so close to Hashem that one day we will be privileged to see the light that surrounds us all.

Ki Seitzei

Mother Bird

Compassion and harshness need not necessarily manifest themselves in two different people. On the contrary, they can and must live side by side within the same person if he is to achieve completion.

This week's *Parshah, Ki Seitzei,* discusses the well-known *mitzvah* of *shilu'ach haken,* sending away the mother bird. The Torah states (22:6) that on chancing upon a bird's nest on the path, "You should not take the mother bird with her young," but rather, as verse 7 continues, "You should send the mother bird away and take the young for yourself, in order that it will be good for you and that you will have a long life (*arichas yamim*)." This guarantee of longevity is found elsewhere in the Torah with regard to another *mitzvah,* that of honoring one's father and mother (*Shemos* 20:12). We may ask why these specific commandments share a common reward?

Furthermore, we find a Mishnah (*Berachos* 33b) that instructs us to silence a person who prays, "Just as Your mercy, God, has reached the bird's nest, so may it reach us as well," as this is considered an improper way to pray. The Talmud, on the same page, asks why this is so. According to one opinion, the reason is that he is wrongly referring to God's commandments as merciful, when in fact they are simply decrees. Nevertheless, we may ask on this Talmud, why this *mitzvah* is regarded as merely a decree from God as opposed to a merciful instruction from God? Is it not a fact that we are being sensitive by sending the mother bird away prior to taking her young?

The *Vilna Gaon* (*Peninim M'Shulchan Ha'Gra - Imrei Noam, Berachos* 33b) explains that a person's completeness (*shleimus ha'adam*) in serving God is established only when he masters two diametrically-opposed character traits (*middos*), the antithetical attributes of compassion and harshness.

If a person possesses only one of these traits - for example in this case, compassion - it does not necessarily determine his righteousness, because the individual may simply be a naturally kind person and need not have worked on managing the *middah* and directing it appropriately. If, however, he possesses both opposing traits and displays control in utilizing these conflicting *middos* correctly, it proves that he has worked on managing his *middos*, and for this he is considered a righteous person.

There are two *mitzvos* that symbolically represent these opposing traits, one of them is honoring one's parents, and the other is sending away the mother bird. The former *mitzvah* characterizes the quality of compassion, as tending to one's parents, particularly as they become older and require more help, demands much compassion and concern from the caregiver. The latter *mitzvah* of *shilu'ach haken* represents the attribute of harshness, as sending away the mother bird will cause her much distress as she is forcibly parted from her young. (The *Rambam* in two sources [*Peirush HaMishnayos* on *Berachos* Ch. 5, Mishnah 3; *Hilchos Tefillah* 9:7] supports the idea that this *mitzvah* is, indeed, not intended to teach mercy, and remarks that if the aim of the *mitzvah* was for the sake of being compassionate and merciful to the mother bird, God would have forbidden us to slaughter birds altogether!)

Based on this insight, we can understand why the *mitzvos* of *shilu'ach haken* and *kibbud av v'em* share the identical reward of longevity. The *Vilna Gaon* explains that *arichas yamim* symbolically represents *shleimus*, as a long life is often associated with a full and complete life. Thus, through these *mitzvos* a person can reach completeness, as he learns to control and use these opposing *middos* accordingly. A reward of longevity (which symbolically represents completeness) is therefore highly fitting and appropriate!

According to the *Vilna Gaon*, we could suggest that performance of only one of these commandments is insufficient to deserve the promised reward. Only by doing both does a person become *shalem*, complete, as he has demonstrated mastery over contradictory *middos* in order to serve

God with all parts of his being, and therefore merits the reward of *arichas yamim*.

The juxtaposition of two specific verses in *Tehillim* (149:7 and 9) highlights this further. In the first it speaks of taking revenge on the nations (referring to those nations committed to our annihilation), and just two verses later it talks of God's "splendor to all His pious ones." The *Vilna Gaon* explains that this Psalm teaches us that although naturally pious people are kind and compassionate, they, nevertheless, know to take action and act harshly against the nations when the situation and circumstances are appropriate, as dictated by God and His Torah.

It is now obvious why the Talmud considers it improper for a person to call on God to show him mercy the way God displays mercy to the mother bird. A prayer of this nature is suggesting that this *mitzvah* represents a compassionate and merciful act when, in fact, it is exactly the opposite! *Shilu'ach haken* is a harsh, even cruel act, and God instructs us in this *mitzvah* in order to teach us that our actions should all be for the sake of Heaven and not just because we are compelled by our instincts. Compassion and harshness have their place in the service of God and we are expected to work on and use these *middos* appropriately.

Based on all this, the *Vilna Gaon* continues, we are able to understand a verse (*Bereishis* 22:12) which states that at the binding of Yitzchak, the angel said to Avraham that now he knows that he has the fear of God. Although we are aware that the *Akeidah* was the hardest test, why only at this stage did the angel realize that Avraham was a righteous person? Surely this was evident from the hospitality and kindness that he demonstrated earlier?

The *Vilna Gaon* points out that although Avraham did perform righteous deeds, as far as the angels were concerned, his actions may have stemmed from a natural instinct to do kindness. In the final test of the *Akeidah*, however, Avraham was commanded to slaughter his youngest, most beloved son, a truly harsh and cruel act that he would never have naturally dreamed of doing. Yet, he set out to act with all his mind, heart and soul, because God commanded him to do it. It is this mastering and channeling of his *middos*, for the sake of God, that confirmed to the angels how righteous and God-fearing Avraham really was.

May we all be blessed to master the art of balance, demonstrating compassion whenever possible, and harshness whenever necessary. May we merit living a long and productive life, deserving of God's protection, just like a mother bird when protecting her young.

Ki Seitzei

Admit It

When we are hurt by another person, we often cannot tolerate that person's excuses. All we really want is for him to admit that he made a mistake, apologize, and if possible, correct the wrongdoing. This is really the only approach that is acceptable to us, and it is only this type of behavior that can diffuse the tension. As Jews, we must be willing to live by this standard.

The Torah tells us in this week's portion, *Ki Seitzei*, that we may not permit anyone from the nations of *Ammon* and *Moav* to marry into the Jewish people because they did not provide us with bread and water as we came out of Egypt, and because they hired *Bilaam* the son of *Be'or* to curse us (see *Devarim* 23:4-5).

How does this punishment fit the "crimes"? What is the underlying connection between these two specific points (not giving us sustenance, and hiring someone to curse us), and the subsequent result - being denied entry into the Jewish nation? Moreover, what makes *Ammon* and *Moav* worse than all the other nations - so much so, that only they may not join the Jewish people? Even converts from *Amalek* - our archenemy - may be accepted into our nation!

We will be able to answer these questions once we understand the nature of *Ammon* and *Moav*, and how their essence is incompatible with that of the Jewish people.

In *Vayikra* (20:17), we find that the Torah refers to cases of sexual immorality (e.g. a man who has relations with his sister) as "*chessed*," kindness. This type of behavior is labeled as such because it stems from unbridled, unrestrained kindness - *chessed* which is taken to an extreme, to the point that it becomes disgraceful. (The word *chessed*, in such instances, is commonly translated "disgrace" due to this reason.)

We learn that the people of *Moav* promoted promiscuity amongst the Jewish nation as they offered their daughters to the Jewish men. They claimed that their actions were based on the principle of *chessed* and defended their behavior by stating that they lacked a Torah to guide and direct them in channeling their emotions.

However, we may argue their claim as follows. If their inappropriate actions stemmed from an uncontrolled, abundant amount of *chessed*, why wasn't this kindness apparent when the Jews, starving and thirsty, passed by their borders? What happened that they suddenly suppressed their apparently overflowing benevolence the moment the Jewish nation required it?

Ammon and *Moav* could justify their position once again by maintaining that the reason for not offering food and water to the Jewish nation was due to the expense; they simply did not have the funding to satiate the entire people! This claim, yet again, holds no water because we know that they spent enormous amounts of money hiring *Bilaam* to curse the Jews!

The *Emunas Itecha* highlights the reason why *Ammon* and *Moav* may never be granted entry into the nation of Israel, and in doing so, connects the two reasons that are mentioned in this week's portion. The only reason that *Moav* offered their daughters to the Jewish people was to rouse God's anger against us in the hope that He would subsequently annihilate us. Regardless of their true motives, however, they decided to cover their behavior in the guise of "*chessed*."

It is on this point that the Torah elaborates in this week's portion, uncovering the futility of their excuses: if they were so filled with *chessed*, where was the food and water for the starving Jewish nation passing by their land? In response to their second claim, the expense, we remind them of the money they spent in their mission to curse the Jewish people.

The *Emunas Itecha* explains that it is not so much their transgression (promoting harlotry) that was problematic, but the excuses they made to justify and validate their behavior. The problem specific to *Ammon* and *Moav*, which sets them apart from the other nations, is their lack of sincerity and honesty in admitting their true incentives and motivations. The Jewish people can tolerate people who make mistakes, but not those who repeatedly insist on justifying and excusing their wrongdoings.

We learn from this week's portion to always be truthful and honest with ourselves. If and when we stumble, let us acknowledge our mistakes so that we can rectify our shortcomings and improve ourselves, moving forward in our service of God.

Perhaps, we should think about our day just before going to sleep at night to see if we were guilty of any wrongdoing. We should then write it down in a book. This will be a private journal, so there is no point in hiding our true motives. We would only be fooling ourselves. There is nothing strange about making mistakes. After all, we are human. However, our strength is shown when we admit to them. Eventually, our list of mistakes will show a certain pattern of frequency. Once we are aware of the areas in which we tend to stumble, we can then think of strategies to improve in those areas.

May we be blessed in this propitious month of *Elul* to live by the truth, and face up to ourselves so that we are able to sincerely repent for all of our misdeeds and be granted a "clean slate" for the year ahead.

Ki Savo

First and Foremost

When we judge a company's service, much of our opinion is shaped by how efficient they were in getting the job done quickly. Our service to God will be judged in very much the same way.

In this week's portion, *Ki Savo*, we read about the *mitzvah* of bringing *bikkurim*, the first fruits, to the Temple.

The verse states (*Devarim* 26:2), "It will be when you enter the land that the Lord your God gives you as an inheritance, and you possess it and dwell in it, that you shall take of the first of all the fruits of the Earth that you bring from your land... and you shall put it in a basket and go the place that the Lord your God will choose to place His name there (i.e., the Temple)." The *pesukim* then describe the ceremony that was performed by the Israelite and the priest over the *bikkurim*.

Why did God command us to do this particular *mitzvah*? What is the significance of the first fruits, and why are we required to take them to the Temple?

The *Emunas Itecha* provides a beautiful insight into this topic as he illustrates the connection between the *bikkurim* and the *Beis HaMikdash*.

Within the Holy of Holies, in the heart of the Temple, there is a rock called the *Even Shesiyah* (literally, the stone of drinking). The Talmud (*Yoma* 54b) explains that this rock is the foundation upon which the entire world was built; the rest of the world expanded from this first stone. The *Even Shesiyah*, located in the *Beis HaMikdash*, thus marks the first point - the "*reishis*" - of the creation of the Earth.

Now we can begin to understand why God commanded us to bring our first fruits to the Temple, specifically. The *bikkurim*, described as *reishis pri ha'adamah* (the first of the fruits of the Earth), have the same essence as the *Beis HaMikdash* which is *Reishis HaB'riah*, the first point of Creation.

The *Emunas Itecha* then analyzes the symbolism of the *Beis HaMikdash* on a deeper level. He explains that since the Foundation Rock, the initial point of the Earth, is located in the Temple, it follows that the *Beis HaMikdash* represents the characteristics of *hischadshus* (renewal), *ra'ananus* (vigor), and *chiyus* (life). Because all firsts are new and exciting. The *Kohanim* in the Temple were expected to serve Hashem with these attributes (see *Shabbos* 20a). Similarly, the *bikkurim*, the first of all fruits, also teach us to serve God with vitality, enthusiasm and fervor.

Just as the Temple is the original point of Creation, i.e. the *reishis* of the dimension of place, *Rosh HaShanah* is the *reishis* of the dimension of time. The *Emunas Itecha* cites the Talmud (*Rosh HaShanah* 10b the opinion of Rebbi Eliezer), "*B'Tishrei nivra ha'olam* - In *Tishrei* the world was created." This awesome holiday which marks **Reishis** *HaShanah* - the beginning of the year - shares a common message with the *Beis HaMikdash* and the *Bikkurim*. *Rosh HaShanah* reminds us to serve God with enthusiasm and zeal.

Finally, in the same way that the Temple is the *reishis* of all places, and *Rosh HaShanah* is the *reishis* of all moments in time, Adam HaRishon is the *reishis* of the dimension of self. Interestingly, Adam HaRishon, the first human being, was formed on *Rosh HaShanah*, the beginning of time (Although the Creation of the world began on the twenty-fifth of Elul, five days before the Friday of Adam's creation, nevertheless, time was only relevant from Man's perspective. Therefore, the first of Tishrei, *Rosh HaShanah*, is considered to be the first moment in history. See *Zohar* vol.1, p.37, side 1).

The *Emunas Itecha* explains that Adam, by eating from the forbidden fruit, tarnished the *reishis* of self because he caused death and deterioration to enter the world, which is the antithesis of what *reishis* symbolizes - life and growth.

The *mitzvah* of *bikkurim*, therefore, served as a rectification for Adam's mistake, which also involved fruit. As they brought the first fruits to the Temple and imbibed within themselves the message of *reishis* - to serve God with eagerness and passion - the Israelites were, in effect, fixing the dimension of self.

On *Rosh HaShanah*, we, as *Bnei Adam* (which not only means human beings but also implies descendents of Adam HaRishon) accept upon ourselves to serve God with the quality of *reishis* - with excitement and alacrity - and to extend this energy into all places and into every moment of our lives so that ultimately we will rectify all dimensions of existence.

We can participate in repairing the concept of *reishis* every single day. The morning is a time of *reishis*, as it starts the new day for us. We can demonstrate excitement and freshness every morning. Here are a few ideas that we may implement. After reciting the *Modeh Ani*, say "I am so happy and eager to do God's Will today," wash *negel vasser*, and get ready quickly. After *Birchas HaTorah*, start the morning service with the Mishnah "Be bold as a leopard, light as an eagle, swift as a deer, and strong as a lion, to carry out the will of your Father in Heaven" (*Avos* 5:23, *Yehudah ben Taima*). In this way, the whole day is set on a course of alacrity and zeal.

So, first and foremost, may we be blessed this *Rosh HaShanah* by being born again with a youth that is not wasted on the young, maintaining freshness in our Torah and *mitzvos*. May this, in turn, arouse Hashem to respond in kind by bringing *Moshiach* hastily (see this week's *haftarah*, *Yeshaya* 60:22) and thereby transform all of mankind and the entire world to its original form as it existed prior to the sin of Adam.

Ki Savo

Soak It Up

While externalities play a role in Judaism, they simply cannot compare with the priceless value of internal growth.

In this week's portion, *Ki Savo* (28:10), we read that the nations of the world will see that the "Name of God is called upon you [the Jewish nation]," and that the nations will subsequently fear the Children of Israel. Rabbi Eliezer HaGadol (*Menachos*, 35b) explains that the Name of God mentioned in this verse refers to God's Name that is found in the *tefillin* worn on the head (*tefillin shel rosh*).

It may be surprising to find that passersby and the general public are not awe-struck and trembling with fear when they see a Jewish man with the characteristic box and straps on his head, at those times when it is customary to walk through the streets with *tefillin* on. Are we not promised by God through the Torah, as explained by the Talmud, that on seeing the *tefillin*, nations will be filled with fear and trepidation?

An answer to this question can be illustrated by the following story (found in *Peninim MiShulchan Ha'Gra - Kesser Tefilin* and *Zichron Chaim*). The *Vilna Gaon* was once traveling from one village to another and as it became dark he decided to stop at a hotel for the night. When he arose in the morning (however little he had slept during the night!), he put on his *tefillin* and began to pray. (Seemingly there was no available *minyan,* or perhaps he began to pray at sunrise and joined a later *minyan*). Simultaneously, the hotel manager, downstairs in the lobby, also put on his *tefillin*, in accordance with Jewish Law, and began praying the morning service.

Suddenly, a gentile ruffian, in search of money, entered the building and began to beat up the hotel manager. The manager screamed in desperation and was overheard by the *Vilna Gaon* above, who immediately rushed to the staircase to see what was happening. The ruffian, on hearing the hurried footsteps, looked upward, and with one glance at the *Vilna Gaon*, fainted on the spot. The hotel manager, bewildered and confused, asked the *Gaon* why the intruder had reacted so severely after seeing him.

The *Vilna Gaon* explained that what had just occurred was exactly what God promised us in the portion of *Ki Savo*. The gentile, on seeing the Name of God in the *tefillin*, was struck with such fear that he collapsed. All the more perplexed, the manager asked why the ruffian hadn't already fainted on seeing his *tefillin*, as he was also wearing them at the time that the ruffian entered. The *Gaon* pointed out, without judging the manager, that in order to understand why that happened, it is important to meticulously examine the words of the Talmud (*Menachos* 35b). There it does not tell us that the Name of God mentioned in *Ki Savo* (28:10) refers to the *tefillin al ha'rosh*, **on** the head, or *shel ha'rosh*, **of** the head, but rather, that it refers to the *tefillin she'berosh* - the phylacteries that are **in** the head.

In other words, the *Vilna Gaon* was implying, that it is not sufficient to fulfill the *mitzvah* of *tefillin* on an external level by performing the ritual of placing the *tefillin* on the head (see Isaiah 29:13); but rather, the purpose of the *mitzvah* is to affect us internally. Instead of doing the *mitzvah* of *tefillin* by rote, we must imbibe the message of *tefillin* within ourselves. Then, through performing the *mitzvah*, we transform our character, attitudes and behavior, thereby improving our relationships with God and man. This plants God's Name inside of our heads. This is the Name of God that the nations will fear.

For the *Vilna Gaon*, putting on *tefillin* was a life-altering experience. The words of the *tefillin* were not just on the outside, but penetrated his entire being. It was this that caused the ruffian such trepidation, exactly as the Torah and our Sages guarantee! (This would imply that a lack of fear on the part of the nations indicates that we have not yet reached the necessary level of growth as a result of this *mitzvah*).

It is often the case that people are very careful to purchase the highest quality *tefillin* for themselves or for their sons, and will spend vast amounts of money to acquire them. It is really heart-warming that people go to such great lengths to purchase the finest pair of *tefillin*. However, at the same time, I would like to mention that which I told my son: that acquiring a high-quality pair of *tefillin* should not come at the expense of inner growth. A person should not think, once they have gone the extra mile for the "external" pair of *tefillin*, that they have now fulfilled the *mitzvah* and accomplished all that is necessary.

The *tefillin* available at the time of the *Vilna Gaon* were not of such great quality, and some (that I have seen from previous generations) would even be considered *passul* (invalid) *halachically* by a modern day *posek*! Nevertheless, it is also guaranteed that many in the *Vilna Gaon's* generation understood the real meaning of the *mitzvah* of *tefillin* and grew to great spiritual heights because they carried the message of *tefillin* in their minds, hearts and souls.

It is important to realize that the principle of focusing on the meaning behind the *mitzvah* is not applicable only to the *mitzvah* of *tefillin*, but to all of God's commandments. We, as God's People, are expected to approach the *mitzvos* not as technicalities or rituals that we must say or do, but as vehicles for inner growth. We must think about the message that each *mitzvah* contains and recognize how that specific *mitzvah* can improve and refine our life and service of God.

May I suggest, that after *Shacharis*, right before taking our *tefillin* off, we should stop, close our eyes, and think for just a few seconds what *tefillin* means, and how it speaks to us. Carrying that thought with us during the day is part of the process of inculcating *tefillin's* lessons in our systems.

May we all be blessed for our interior to match our exterior, *tocho k'varo* (see *Berachos* 28a), so that the Torah and *mitzvos* are etched upon the tablets of our mind and hearts, and deserve that God restore the world, not just with outer beauty, but with inner beauty as well.

Ki Savo

Gentle Clean Only

Some of our best teachers were the ones who were firm, but also fair and friendly. Maintaining this recipe may just be the secret to success in our lives. Among the many topics contained within this week's portion is the subject of the curses (*Devarim* 28:15-68). Ezra the Scribe instituted that we read about the curses right before *Rosh HaShanah* so that we dump all the curses on the previous year, enabling us to begin a fresh new year of blessings (*Megillah*, chap. 4, *Bnei Ha'ir,* pg. 31b).

The *Tiferes Shlomo* (*Ki Savo, Yesh Lases Ta'am*) explains that even if there is a terrible decree against us, God forbid, just by reciting the curses, it is considered as if we already received all those punishments. Then, there is no need for them to actually happen.

The mechanics behind this system works the same way as the substitution for bringing offerings today in the absence of the Temple. Just by saying the portions of the offerings, we are credited as if we brought those sacrifices. We, thereby, receive the benefits of bringing the *korbanos* (one example of this is atonement) (*Hoshe'ah* 14:3). Similarly, just by saying the portion of the curses, it is as if they already happened.

The *Shvilei Pinchas* says that based on this, we learn a tremendous lesson. This Shabbos we should listen to the reading of the Torah bearing in mind that through the very reading about the curses, it is considered as if we already received the punishments. In this way, we can begin a new year of complete and total blessing.

However, it is interesting to point out that there are two sets of curses in the Torah. The first set is found in *Parshas Bechukosai* (*Vayikra* 26:16-44). The second set is in our portion. Why would God divide the curses into two parts? Why not just lump all of them into one section?

We all know that *Rosh HaShanah* is celebrated for two days, even in Israel. Although the *halachic* reason for this is *sfeika d'yoma* (a doubt about which day *Rosh HaShanah* falls on; See *Rambam Hilchos Kiddush HaChodesh*, chap. 5, *halachos* 7 & 8). Nonetheless, there is a mystical reason behind it as well.

The *Arizal* says that on the first day of *Rosh HaShanah*, God judges with "harsh justice," whereas on the second day of *Rosh HaShanah*, God judges with "soft justice" (*Sha'ar Hakavanos, Rosh HaShanah, Drush* 2, based on *Zohar Pinchas*, pg. 231b).

Righteous people are judged on the first day because they can handle it. The rest of the people are judged on the second day, so that they can also receive a positive verdict. If there would be only one day of *Rosh HaShanah*, it would destroy the world. This is because the judgment would be too harsh and most people would not be able to stand up to such severity (*Zohar Pinchas* pg. 231a). Parenthetically, if a person is suddenly overcome with tears on *Rosh HaShanah*, it is a sign that at that moment his soul is standing before the heavenly Tribunal being judged regarding his fate for the coming year (*Reb Chaim Vital, Sha'ar Hakavanos, Drushei Rosh HaShanah, B'chol Yud Yemei Teshuvah*, citing the *Arizal*).

The *Shvilei Pinchas* suggests that the two sets of curses follow the same pattern as the two days of *Rosh HaShanah*. The first set of curses contains the "harsh" ones, whereas the second set contains the "soft" ones. This is why we need to have two sets of curses, one with which to judge the righteous (harsh), and the other with which to judge the average person (soft).

This explains why God's Name, *Havayah*, is deleted from the first set of curses (Responsa of *Radvaz*, vol. 2, # 769). It is because that Name represents compassion. There is no place for compassion in the first set of harsh curses.

However, that Name of God appears repeatedly throughout the second set because compassion is fitting in a place of soft curses.

This also explains how Moshe, who loved *Klal Yisrael*, behaved so out of character by cursing the Jewish people in *Ki Savo* himself (*Meggilah*, chap. 4, *Bnei Ha'ir,* pg. 31b), even though Moshe was willing to sacrifice his own life for them (see *Shemos* 32:32).

It is because Moshe realized that the first set of curses were harsh, and the Jewish people would not have the capacity to survive them, just like they would not be able to survive with just one day of *Rosh HaShanah*. Therefore, Moshe added a second set of curses which are soft, so that if God has to punish them with curses, let it be with soft ones and not with harsh ones. This is the compassionate Moshe we have all come to love.

One crucial lesson we learn from Moshe is the importance of maintaining a strong sense of compassion, even when there is a need to discipline. We should always try to be firm, fair, and friendly. Even though we may find ourselves in a position in which we have to instruct and guide, we must still treat others with sympathy, care, concern, kindness, and consideration.

If we want God to judge us through the lens of compassion, then we must show Hashem that we are deserving of it by treating others in that very same way. How can we accomplish this?

Firstly, we have to realize that it is not our job to judge, it is God's. Secondly, although we must protect ourselves when we sense danger from other people, we must, nevertheless, never lose sight of the other person's inner self. If we would just stop for one moment and think about the time when that person was a baby, our sense of compassion would be aroused.

We must remember the child inside of that person and try to help him get back in touch with that innocence. By the way, we should also be willing to give ourselves a break by treating ourselves the same way. We should tell ourselves once a day that although we are grown-ups, we are still that child on the inside. After all, we are always called **Bnei** *Yisrael*, the **Children** of Israel.

The mere memory of the child inside will help us treat ourselves and others gently. This does not contradict disciplinary measures that have to be taken. Rather, it just enables us to carry them out with a sense of compassion, and not with cruelty.

May we all be blessed with good eyes, to see that holy spark in each and every one of us, treating everybody with sweetness, so that we merit a year of unlimited pleasantness.

Ki Savo

Chavivus Chabibi

If given the choice of being poor but truly happy, or rich but truly sad, many people would opt for happiness. Being happy is not just an ideal for life, but a crucial ingredient for a Jew in the service of God.

In this week's portion, *Ki Savo*, it says, "God has not given you a heart to know and eyes to see and ears to hear until this day." *Rashi* there says that he heard an interpretation as to what Moshe was talking about.

On the day Moshe gave the complete Torah scroll to the tribe of *Levi* (see *Devarim* 31:9), all the Jews came to Moshe and said to him, "Moshe, our teacher, we also stood at Sinai and received the Torah, and it was given to all of us. So why do you give dominion to your tribe (by giving the Torah scroll just to them)? Tomorrow, do you know what they might say to all of us? They, the Levites, could say that the Torah was not given to the rest of the tribes. The Torah was only given to us, the tribe of *Levi*." When Moshe heard them lodge this complaint, he was very happy and because of this, Moshe said to the people, "This day, you have become a nation" (*Devarim* 27:9). Meaning that, "This day, I understand that you are attached to God and desire God."

The *Toras Avos* asks, why was Moshe so impressed with the Jewish people? Certainly he had witnessed other great heroic feats by the Jewish people, such as:

1) They took the sheep or lamb back in Egypt to bring it as the Pascal offering, thus endangering their lives (see *Shemos* 12:28, *Shabbos* 87b, the *Tur*, and the *Beis Yosef* O.C. 430:1).

2) At the Splitting of the Sea, many Jews jumped into the water even before

it split (see *Yonasan Ben Uziel Shemos* 14:11).

3) When the Jews received the Torah, they died in the process more than once, and had to be resurrected (see *Shabbos* 88b).

These cases demonstrate that the Jewish people sacrificed themselves to do the word of God. So what was it about this story with the Torah scroll that impressed Moshe Rabbeinu so much?

Perhaps we could suggest an answer to this question by first going back to the three scenarios that the *Toras Avos* pointed out. We could suggest that in those three cases, there was an element of fear that propelled the Jews to do what they did. For example, when they took the sheep for the *Korban Pesach*, they were still slaves, and were told by God that they had to do this *mitzvah* in order to deserve salvation. Although it was scary to take the lamb, it was equally frightening not to do so, because that would mean that they would not have deserved to leave and would have been left behind.

Similarly, at the Splitting of the Sea, although we don't want to detract from their courage in jumping into the water before it split, did they have a better choice? They were surrounded by cutthroat Egyptians who were ready to rip them to shreds, limb by limb. Although it must have been scary to jump into the water, the alternative was equally, if not more, frightening. They may as well take their chances swimming to the other side.

And as far as receiving the Torah goes, let us not forget how God held the mountain suspended over their heads, giving them the ultimatum that if they refused the Torah, Hashem promised to turn that place into the largest Jewish cemetery to date.

So in all those cases, we find that the Jews were motivated by fear. However, by this story with the Torah scroll, the Jews were coming from a place of love. A Jew will not be able to acquire an understanding heart, eyes of vision, and ears capable of hearing, until he or she masters the art of *chavivus* (amiability). This means that in all the *mitzvos* a Jew does and in all the Torah he studies, the primary ingredient is the love that goes into it. It is not so much about what we do, as much as it is about how we do it. It is all about attitude.

One way to cultivate love for the *mitzvos* would be to say the following sentences prior to doing the *mitzvah*: "I love learning Torah." "I love *davening*." "I love to do *chessed*." Although at first this will feel awkward, eventually it will become natural and create feelings of warmth and yearning in doing the *mitzvos*, so we don't just perform them begrudgingly, just because we have to.

May we all be blessed to approach God with *chavivus* in our Torah study and *mitzvah* performance.

Nitzavim-Vayeilech - Rosh HaShanah

Making It Stick

Love and respect are two qualities that really make relationships work. This week's portion begins with Moshe's famous words to the people, "*Atem nitzavim hayom kulchem lifnei Hashem Elokeichem* - You are standing today, all of you, before Hashem your God" (*Devarim* 29:9).

The *Zohar* (*Bo*, vol. 2, pg. 32b) says that the word *hayom*, today, in this verse refers to the day of *Rosh HaShanah*. We know this from another verse where *hayom* is used in reference to *Rosh HaShanah*.

That verse is found in *Iyov* (1:6) where it says, "And it happened one day (*hayom*), that the angels came to stand before God, and the Satan also came among them." This verse begins to tell us the story about how Iyov came to suffer so much. One day, God announced that there is no righteous person on Earth like Iyov.

The Satan said to God that Iyov is righteous only because he has a good life. Let's see how righteous he is when he suffers. God trusted Iyov's loyalty and therefore gave the Satan permission to test Iyov with suffering.

The *Zohar* says that this story began on *Rosh HaShanah* when God judges the world. This is why the angels (defending attorneys) and the Satan (the prosecuting attorney) were standing before God on that day. They were conducting a court case.

Just like the word *hayom* in the *book of Iyov* teaches us that the story took place on *Rosh HaShanah*, so too, does the word *hayom* in our portion refer to *Rosh HaShanah* when all of us "stand before Hashem."

The Slonimer Rebbe (*Nesivos Shalom* citing the *Yesod Ha'avodah* in the name of *Rambam* in *Moreh Nevuchim*) says that the way to be saved from harsh judgment is through *d'veikus* (attaching, clinging, cleaving) to God. Once we are *davuk* (connected) to God, then no harm can befall us, just as no harm could ever come to God. The way to achieve *d'veikus* is by constantly thinking about God. We are where our thoughts are. Keeping God in mind means realizing that He exists and is involved in our lives, and also that He is in control and orchestrates everything. When we concentrate on this, we are *davuk* to Hashem.

D'veikus is all about relationships. When thinking about God, we must keep in mind that He is our best friend, our beloved, and our parent all wrapped up in One. When we stand before Him on *Rosh HaShanah*, our feelings should be that of happiness, joy, and excitement that we are so close to our loved One again.

However, love without respect is insufficient. Love without respect will eventually deteriorate. On *Rosh HaShanah* we mention repeatedly that God is the *Melech HaKavod*, King of Honor.

Rebbi Nachman says that although God demands *kavod*, it is not to be confused with honor. *Kavod* is to be translated as "respect." God does not need our honor. Rather, God demands that we respect Him so that the world is filled with respect (*Yeshaya* 6:3). This means that God demands that we find the Divine spark within each other, and respect each other just like we respect God Himself.

The sweetest thing in the world is a relationship where there is respect for each other. Conversely, the most bitter thing in the world is one in which there is a lack of respect. Disrespect is the cause of all corruption and ruination.

Rosh HaShanah is the anniversary of the world's Creation. *Rosh HaShanah* is the world's birthday (*Tefillas* "Hayom haras olam" said in *Mussaf* after the *shofar* blasts). Nobody forced God to create the world. Rather, God did it in order to respect us, because God said that although I am King, there can be no King without a people to govern. In other words, God basically said to us, "I can't do it without you," so to speak. Creation itself was a huge *kavod* for us. The very fact that God asserted that He "needed" us, is unto itself giving us tremendous respect.

Then, God said that He now wants us to respect each other. This is why, on *Rosh HaShanah*, we pray "*uv'chein tein kavod Hashem l'amecha* - and so too, God, grant honor to your people" (*Tefillas Shemoneh Esrei* on *Rosh HaShanah*), because *Rosh HaShanah* is a time of respect.

This, says the *Ishbitzer*, is why we do not ask each other for forgiveness before *Rosh HaShanah* like we do prior to *Yom Kippur* (see *Shulchan Aruch, Orach Chaim*, 606:1). On *Yom Kippur* we are separate people, so if I hurt you, I have to beg forgiveness from you. However, on *Rosh HaShanah* we are all considered to be one.

The reason we are like one on *Rosh HaShanah* is because Adam HaRishon (Adam, the first human being) was created on *Rosh HaShanah* (see *Zohar*, vol. 1, pg. 37a). At that time, all of our souls were wrapped together, included as part of Adam HaRishon. Only later did we break up into separate individuals.

Every *Rosh HaShanah* we go back to that state of being united as one. This is why we do not ask each other for forgiveness before *Rosh HaShanah*, even though it is a day of judgement. My left leg does not ask forgiveness from my right leg because it is part of the same body; similarly, we do not ask each other for forgiveness at *Rosh HaShanah* time, because it is as if we are all joined together as one body.

Therefore, when we respect each other, we are actually respecting ourselves, because we are all connected as one. This could serve as a good way to start the new year.

Let's choose three people that we will go out of our way to respect this coming year. These people can include a spouse, a child, and a person who is difficult to deal with. Write their names down on a piece of paper. They are going to be our "projects" for this year.

Here are some examples of how to treat people with respect:

1) Speak calmly, pleasantly, and with patience.

2) Do not take chances cracking jokes that may be misconstrued as insults.

3) When spoken to, stop what you're doing and give the speaker your undivided attention. This shows them that they are important to you.

May we all be blessed to love and respect each other, and think about God constantly. Thus, we will achieve *d'veikus* of the mind with Hashem, and attach to Him as a friend, a beloved, and a parent, and this will shield us from all tragedies.

Nitzavim-Vayeilech - Rosh HaShanah

About the Words and the Bees

Life is about choices. What profession to pursue, who to marry, and where to live are amongst the most important choices we ever make. We must also choose the motivating factor that propels us in any given direction.

This week's portion, *Vayeilech*, begins with the words, "*Vayeilech Moshe, vayedaber es hadevarim ha'eileh el kol Yisrael* - And Moses went, and spoke these words to all of Israel" (*Devarim* 31:1). Although the Torah shares with us that "Moshe went," it conceals his destination from us.

Most, if not all, the commentaries grapple with this question: where did Moshe go? Although we have come across a variety of approaches which address this question in the past, I have found yet another answer.

The *Aron Eidus* says that Moshe Rabbeinu spent his entire life teaching Torah to the Jewish people in such a way that it would penetrate their hearts and permeate their beings with holy light.

Moshe did not just impart his teachings to the gifted, rather he approached even the simple people, who were not so knowledgeable and who may have been on a low spiritual level. Just as a father "lowers" himself to teach his child, so did Moshe come down to the level of each and every person to help them grow.

Moshe appealed to everybody. He was a master teacher; thus his title, *Rabbeinu*, our teacher. Now, at the end of his life, Moshe wanted to ensure that his teachings would perpetuate until the end of time.

Now, we can understand where Moshe went. He went to each and every person, to instruct them on how to succeed. Moreover, he went down to the level of *kol Yisrael,* each one, guiding them how to thrive.

The *Aron Eidus* points out another virtue of Moshe. As he neared the end of his life, he did not wait for the people to come to him to receive his blessings and insight (as is normally the case); rather, he went to them. Such was Moshe's dedication to the people.

What did Moshe say to them in his final moments? One might think that he said, "I am a hundred and twenty years old today, I can no longer continue," which is found in the very next verse (*Devarim* 31:2). Although this is part of what he said, there must be something more contained in the first verse, "*Vayedaber es hadevarim ha'eileh* - and he spoke these words." Otherwise, the Torah could have just said, "*Vayeilech Moshe el kol Yisrael vayomer aleihem ben me'ah ve'esrim shanah anochi hayom* - And Moshe went to all of Israel and said to them I am a hundred and twenty years old today," skipping over the words, "*Vayedaber es hadevarim ha'eileh* - and he spoke these words."

Says the *Aron Eidus*, there is indeed additional meaning in what Moshe said, and it is hinted to in that sentence. Moshe said *hadevarim ha'eileh*, these words. With a slight change in vowels, the Hebrew word *ha'devarim* (words), can be pronounced, *ha'devorim* (bees).

Moshe's final message to the people was that the "words" of Torah are compared to "bees." When we think of bees, two thoughts enter our minds: they sting and they make honey. A bee's sting is a painful poison, whereas a bee's honey is sweet pleasure.

So it is with the words of Torah. They can either be a potion of life or a potion of death (*Yoma*, chap. 7, *Ba Lo Kohen Gadol*, 72b, *Rava's* statement). It all depends on whether or not we study for the right reasons. Do we want to learn Torah in order to get closer to God and become more compassionate people, or are we only interested in self-aggrandizement? After we study

Torah, have we changed in a positive way, behaving towards others with sweetness, or are our dealings with others conducted with a poisonous sting?

Moshe taught us by example that we must be concerned with every single person, irrespective of his achievements, background or personality. Moshe was considerate with *kol Yisrael*, every Jew, and gently coached each one in how to live a healthy, balanced life. Their behavior made no difference to him. Moshe hoped that it would not make a difference to us either.

What was Moshe's parting lesson to the people he cared for and loved so much? Basically, by comparing the Torah with bees, Moshe taught them that it all comes down to making choices. We have to choose between sweet and bitter. We must choose our words and behavior. We need to choose what type of life we want to lead?

Making the right choices in our lives is what tips the scales of judgment on *Yom Kippur* in our favor! After all, Hashem treats us in the way that we treat ourselves and in the way we treat others (*Sanhedrin*, chap. 11, *Cheilek*, 92a, the opinion of *Rabbi Shmuel Bar Nachmeini* in the name of *Rabbi Yonasan*).

With the taste of honey still on our tongues, may we all merit to make the right choices with regard to how we treat God, others and ourselves, and thereby benefit that the scales of judgment should be tipped in our favor for a sweet year on every single possible level!

Nitzavim-Vayeilech

One For All and All For One

All it takes is one kind gesture. With it, we can reach out to so many people, bringing them closer to living a Torah-committed life.

Often, the combined *Parshas Nitzavim* and *Vayeilech* mark the final Shabbos of the Jewish year. We learn that Shabbos - which culminates six days of work - is *"kollel"* (inclusive of) the previous six days, and has the potential to rectify the week gone by. The *Emunas Itecha* points out that the last Shabbos of the year shares the same essence, but on a grander scale, as it encompasses all the Shabbasos of the past year. This means to say that the final Shabbos of the year has the capacity to fix all previous Shabbasos!

Interestingly, the final Torah portions which we read at the conclusion of the year discuss *mitzvos k'laliyos*, obligations that involve all the Jewish people, in keeping with the essence of the final Shabbos. For instance, we read in *Parshas Vayeilech* (*Devarim* 31:12) about the *mitzvah* of *Hakhel,* when, after the Sabbatical year, all Jews would assemble on the second day of *Sukkos* to listen to the King reading from the Book of *Devarim. Parshas Nitzavim* (*Devarim* 29:9) also contains a reference to this communal *mitzvah* as Moshe declares to the nation, "You stand this day all of you… your heads of your tribes, your elders and your officers with all the men of Israel, your children, your wives, and your strangers in your camp…"

We find another example of a *mitzvah k'lalis* in *Parshas Vayeilech* (*Devarim* 31:19) where we are commanded to write a Torah scroll. The *Zohar Chadash* explains at the end of *Shir HaShirim* (74:4) that the 600,000 letters contained in the Torah scroll correlate with the 600,000 major Jewish souls, hence the acronym of our nation's name "*Yisrael*" (spelled *yud, shin, resh, aleph, lamed*), whose letters stand for the phrase, "*yesh shishim ribu osiyos laTorah* - there are 600,000 letters in the Torah."

Another allusion to the connection between the Torah and the Jewish people is brought by the *Dorshei Reshumos*, who draws our attention to our nation's alternative name, "*Yeshurun*," which, when spelled without the two letter *vavs* (*yud, shin, reish, nun*) forms an acronym for the phrase, "*yesh shishim ribui neshamos* - there are 600,000 souls [in the Jewish nation]."

Although we find hints to the association between the letters of the Torah and the Jewish people as a whole, in what way does the *mitzvah k'lalis* of writing a Torah scroll involve and affect the entire Jewish nation?

The Midrash (*Devarim Rabbah* 9:9) cites the opinion of *Rav Yanai* who said that when Moshe Rabbeinu realized his death was imminent, he wrote thirteen Torah scrolls - one for each of the twelve tribes, and an additional one that was placed in the Ark.

Why did Moshe busy himself with such a task on his final day in *Olam Hazeh*?

The Chernobyler Rebbe, in his monumental *sefer*, *Me'or Einayim*, answers this question as follows: When *tzaddikim* are engaged in Torah study, a lot more is happening than what appears at surface level. While learning and delving into the words of the Torah, they are simultaneously affecting the Jewish souls that correlate to those specific letters with which they are involved at that moment.

On Moshe's final day in *Olam Hazeh*, he wrote thirteen Torah scrolls and in doing so reached out to the souls that connected to the letters of the Torah, drawing them closer to God. Not only did he influence the individuals of his generation, but he touched all 600,000 souls of the Jewish nation throughout history, from beginning to end.

An allusion to this idea is found in *Parshas Nitzavim* (*Devarim* 29:13-14), where Moshe says to the people, "Not with you only do I make this covenant…but also with him that is not here with us this day." Another hint appears in *Parshas Vayeilech* (*Devarim* 31:29), where Moshe refers to *Acharis HaYamim*, the End of Days, alluding to the future Messianic era. The souls of those living during *Acharis HaYamim*, which is our current generation, are rooted in and connected to the concluding portions of the Torah up until the final *lamed* of the Torah scroll.

Let us review the points made thus far: (1) that the final Shabbos of the year encompasses all previous Shabbasos and has the ability to rectify them; (2) that the final portion of the year commands us in *mitzvos* that involve the entire Jewish nation; and (3) Moshe spent his last day on Earth reaching out to all Jews throughout the generations. Based on these points, the *Emunas Itecha* imparts a powerful and practical message that we can incorporate into our lives.

As we approach the final Shabbos of the year, let us be prepared to accept upon ourselves the responsibility to reach out and affect someone else's life, positively impacting those within our circles of influence. Although the professional outreach organizations are doing wonderful work, our help is required. Let us open our eyes and reach out to our immediate family and extended family, our friends, neighbors and colleagues at work, and help draw them a little closer to God. Invite them for a Shabbos meal, set up a time to study Torah with them, and lend a helping hand. All of this will draw them closer to Torah, God and *mitzvah* observance.

So, as I conclude the last message of the Jewish year, may all 600,000 of us be blessed with the ability to fix the entire past year by reaching out to others, so that Hashem reciprocates at the End of Days - reaching out to us by sending *Eliyahu HaNavi* and *Moshiach*.

Nitzavim - Rosh HaShanah

What's Our Strategy?

Before going on a big trip, or prior to making a wedding, we must do a lot of planning in advance to ensure that it runs smoothly and that everybody has a good time. The same is true when embarking on the journey of a completely new year. In order to maximize it's potential, we must prepare in advance. This preparation requires some "time out" to allow for some serious thinking.

This week's portion, *Nitzavim*, always falls out before the Jewish High Holiday of *Rosh HaShanah*, which ushers in a new year. This is hinted at in the very beginning of the portion when it says, "*Atem nitzavim hayom lifnei Hashem Elokeichem* - You are standing today before Hashem your God" (*Devarim* 29:9).

The word *hayom* (today), refers to the day, which is *Rosh HaShanah*, when we stand "before Hashem" in judgment. This idea that *hayom* refers to *Rosh HaShanah*, is supported by another verse that says, "*vayehi hayom…* - it happened one day that the angels came to stand before Hashem, and the Satan, too, came among them to stand before Hashem" (*Iyov* 2:1).

The *Zohar Chadash* (pg. 32b), explains that this verse, in *Sefer Iyov*, is speaking about *Rosh HaShanah* when the two attorneys battle it out. On the one hand we have defending attorneys, the angels, who articulate the Jewish people's positive qualities. On the other hand, there is the prosecuting attorney, the Satan, who points out the Jewish people's negative aspects. Just like in *Iyov* the word *hayom* refers to *Rosh HaShanah*, so too, in our *Parshah*, the word *hayom* refers to *Rosh HaShanah*.

In other words, our *parshah* is speaking to us this Shabbos, reminding us,

"*Atem nitzavim hayom,*" meaning, that you are all standing right before the Great Day of Judgment!

There is an even deeper hint within this portion's opening verse alluding to the judgment of *Rosh HaShanah*. The words, "*Atem nitzavim hayom lifnei Hashem Elokeichem,*" have the numerical value of 1,106. This number is propitious because it is the same numerical value as the words, "*Rosh HaShanah al kisei din - Rosh HaShanah* on the Throne of Judgment." This suggests that on *Rosh HaShanah*, God sits on the Throne of Judgment deciding the fate of all people.

The *Aron Eidus*, teaches that it is for this very reason that the Torah wisely placed a crucial verse juxtaposed to the opening statement of our portion, "*Atem nitzavim.*" At the very end of last week's portion, *Ki Savo*, it says, "*Lema'an taskilu es kol asher ta'asun - So that you should be intelligent in all that you do*" (*Devarim* 29:8).

This adjacency comes to teach us that we must think intelligently about what needs to be done so that we emerge from the Day of Judgment victorious. Just like people brainstorm prior to a court case so that they do not come out liable, so too, must we ponder ways to procure for ourselves a favorable verdict.

This contemplation takes on a certain urgency when the day of our trial is imminent. Such is the situation this Shabbos, which is right before *Rosh HaShanah*.

The *Aron Eidus* suggests that at this time of year it is important to spend a little more time in the *beis hamidrash* (study hall), away from the distractions of this world, in order to explore and probe methods of implementation to secure for ourselves a prosperous year.

Spending this time in the *beis hamidrash* is hinted to as well in our verses. The words "*lema'an taskilu* - so that you should be intelligent," are numerically 956, the same numerical value as the words *beis midrash*. This teaches us that at this time of year it would be wise to set aside some time in a *beis midrash* in order to *taskilu* (deliberate) *es kol asher ta'asun* (all that needs to be done).

Additionally, the *Aron Eidus* proposes that the words "*Atem nitzavim hayom kulchem lifnei*," are numerically the same as the words *Erev Shabbos*, the eve of the Sabbath. Each set of words equals 974 exactly.

This does not only come to teach us that on the "eve" of *Rosh HaShanah* we have a "Sabbath" that precedes it for preparation, but there is another message contained inside it as well.

We all know about the teaching of our Sages which says, "One who prepares on the eve of the Sabbath will have what to eat on the Sabbath" (*Avodah Zarah*, chap. 1, *Lifnei Eideihen,* 3a). This is not referring only to the physical sense, but it is also intended for the spiritual dimension. Meaning, only through proper preparation before Shabbos, can we hope to glean all the spirituality that Shabbos has to offer.

The *Aron Eidus* explains that the days before *Rosh HaShanah* are likened to a "Sabbath eve (the day before Shabbos)." Just like *Erev Shabbos* is meant to be used in wise preparation to obtain the spirituality of the Shabbos, so too are the days prior to *Rosh HaShanah* meant to be used the same way.

We could add that Shabbos is only one day, and therefore we only need one day to serve as its eve of spiritual preparation. However, *Rosh HaShanah* lasts two days, and therefore, we need two days in advance to serve as its eve of spiritual preparation.

In any case, the bottom line is that we need to have a plan! What is our strategy going to be for *Rosh HaShanah*, and for the rest of the year for that matter? Let us share some practical guidance, directing our focus in our preparations during the final hours of the year. The *Aron Eidus* gives instruction here as well.

He says that we will only be able to "stand up" (*nitzavim*) to the ruling of the *Yom Hadin* (Day of Judgment), when we fulfill the rest of our opening verse, which says, "*kulchem lifnei Hashem Elokeichem* - all of you before Hashem God." The word *kulchem*, all of you, is crucial because it comes to teach us the importance of unity!

When we stand united, God loves it so much that the Satan cannot prosecute us. This cohesiveness must thoroughly join all classes of Jews, from the upper echelons right down to the common folk.

This is why the same verse goes on to say, "*rosheichem shivteichem zikneichem v'shotreichem kol ish Yisrael* - the heads of your tribes, your elders, and your officers - all the people of Israel," signifying how imperative it is that all types of Jews get along with each other.

Moreover, when you take the acronym of "*rosheichem shivteichem zikneichem v'shotreichem,*" you get the letters *reish, shin, zayin, vav*. These four letters, when unscrambled, spell the word *shizor,* meaning to twist or bind together, further emphasizing this idea.

Our integration must be so complete that we become like one body. When a person stubs his toe, the pain is registered in the brain and it is felt throughout the entire body. Similarly, we should aspire to become connected on the same level, feeling each other's pain. This is the secret behind the word *rosheichem*, your heads. Namely, that we register each other's aches just as the *rosh* (head or brain) does for the rest of the body.

In conclusion, we are learning here about the importance of camaraderie! Let us be as concerned about the next fellow's judgment as we are about our own. One way to express this would be to pray that the next fellow receive a favorable verdict. This practice trains us to think about others and not just ourselves.

May we all be blessed to utilize the last few days of the year by spending a little extra time in the *beis midrash* contemplating how we can improve, especially when it comes to interpersonal relationships, and thereby secure for ourselves a successful, peaceful, harmonious and sweet year indeed! Amen!

Ha'azinu

Sensitive

Most people enjoy the faculties that God has bestowed upon us. Each and every one of the senses is a gift from God. In fact, the senses can be compared to toys given to a child. However, toys must be used as directed in the manual, because if we abuse the toys given to us, they will either break or be taken away.

This week's portion, *Ha'azinu*, begins with the famous words, "*Ha'azinu hashamayim va'adabeirah, v'sishmah ha'aretz imrei fi* - Listen, Heavens, and I will speak; and may the Earth hear the words of my mouth" (*Devarim* 32:1).

Many commentaries are involved in unraveling the secrets contained in these words, expressed by Moshe Rabbeinu in this song of *Ha'azinu*. The *Aron Eidus* is one who explains and reveals some of these secrets. He suggests that "Heavens" represent a person's soul, whereas the "Earth" symbolizes a person's body.

To further this idea, the *Aron Eidus* points out that the word *hashamayim* (Heavens) has exactly the same numerical value as the word for soul (*neshamah*): 395.

However, the Hebrew word *ha'aretz* (Earth) characterizes the "body" since the body originates from the Earth (*Bereishis* 2:7). (For further analysis and support to this concept that the Heavens and Earth indeed refer to ⌐ul and body, see the Talmud in *Sanhedrin*, chap. 11, *Cheilek*, pg. 91b, `ᵕhi Judah the Prince solves a question that was posed to him by ⌐mperor of Rome.)

ᵗhe relationship between the soul and the body is

unique. He proposes that when we sanctify and purify our souls, then our bodies will follow. The question then arises: how can we purify our souls? Moreover, aren't our souls already pure?

The *Aron Eidus* teaches that, although the soul itself is pure, the place in which it resides is not necessarily so holy. Where in the body does the soul live?

The soul is found in a person's head. We testify to this almost daily when we recite the preparatory paragraph prior to donning *tefillin* (phylacteries). In this liturgical passage we say, "He has commanded us to put *tefillin* upon the head opposite the brain, so that the soul that is in my brain, together with my other senses and potentials, may all be subjugated to His service."

From this prayer, we see clearly that the soul resides in a person's head. The soul is the source of a person's spirituality. So, even though the various parts of the head are physical, their senses are, nevertheless, spiritual. Although the eyes, ears, nose and mouth are physical; the ability to see, hear, smell and taste is spiritual.

For a further discussion supporting the concept that the senses are indeed spiritual, see the Talmud in *Niddah* (chap. 3, *Hamapeles chatichah*, pg. 31a), which mentions that the senses of a person, together with the soul, come from God's participation in the partnership of creating a child.

Therefore, when the *Aron Eidus* said that through purification of the soul, a person will achieve bodily purification as well, he was referring to the sanctification of the senses, which are spiritual in nature and stem from the soul. Once the senses are channeled to holiness, the soul's light can then penetrate the rest of the body, making it holy, too.

Perhaps, the most important sense on which to focus in obtaining this goal is the sense of hearing. Because only when we listen to the words of Torah, with the intention of keeping its commandments, will the soul be abl spread it's purity throughout our entire bodies.

The significance and crucial nature of the sense of hearing is found in *Mishlei*, where King Solomon says, "If one turns aside his ear from hearing the Torah, his prayer, too, will be considered an abomination" (28:9). It seems that a person's spiritual success depends upon harnessing the sense of hearing properly.

This, says the *Aron Eidus*, is what the Torah is trying to convey in the opening statement of this week's portion. "*Ha'azinu hashamayim* - listen heavens" means that we must purify the senses of the soul, represented by the word *hashamayim*. Additionally, we are being told that we have to begin, most importantly, with the sense of hearing, hinted at by the word *ha'azinu*.

Only after we bend our ears to hear the word of God (*va'adabeirah*), and listen to Him, will the rest of our bodies become holy as well. This is why the same verse concludes, "*v'sishmah ha'aretz imrei fi*," meaning, then the body, represented by the word *ha'aretz*, will follow suit.

Practically speaking, we could try to lend our ear to Torah a little bit more by listening to recorded Torah classes while doing chores around the house, or while walking or doing exercise. This will help in purifying our bodies and souls.

May we all be blessed with holy ears to hear, listen and obey God's precepts, and thus benefit by transforming our entire bodies into spiritual entities.

Yom Kippur

The 10th Man

In promoting arts and crafts, we supply our children with the raw materials and let them sculpt their own project. This is basically what God, our Parent, does for us, His children. He provides us with the raw materials, and He wants us to mold them to the best of our ability.

The *Sfas Emes* (*Shabbos Shuvah*) teaches us that the *Asseres Yemei Teshuvah* (Ten Days of Repentance) correspond to the Ten Utterances that God said in order to create the world (see *Avos*, chap. 5, *Ba'asarah Ma'amaros,* Mishnah 1). Therefore, on each and every day during the *Aseres Yemei Teshuvah* we are supposed to be involved in fixing the utterance that is connected to that day.

However, of the *Aseres Yemei Teshuvah*, only the first day (*Rosh HaShanah*) and the last day (*Yom Kippur*) are given the holiness of a *Yom Tov* (holiday), and are in a class all unto themselves known as the *Yamim Nora'im* (Days of Awe). (Even though *Rosh HaShanah* lasts two days, we are focusing on the first day, the Biblical day, for the purpose of this message.) Based on the *Sfas Emes*, it would follow that, of the Ten Utterances, the first one (corresponding to *Rosh HaShanah*) and the last one (corresponding to *Yom Kippur*) are the most important ones. By focusing on the first and the last, we can automatically repair all the others.

Let's concentrate on *Yom Kippur* and its pronouncement. Since *Yom Kippur* is the last of the Ten Days, it parallels with the last of the Ten Utterances (*Bereishis* 1:26) which states, "*Na'aseh Adam* - Let us make man" (see *Bereishis Rabbah* 17:1). This teaches us that on *Yom Kippur* we are supposed to be involved in fixing Adam, meaning ourselves.

After each act of Creation, God said that "it was good," with the exception of the creation of Man. The *Yismach Moshe* (*Bereishis* citing the *Ikarim* 3:2) says that the reason for this is that all other creations were created complete. This means to say that God never expected the other creations to improve upon themselves; they are perfect just the way they are. Thus, the expression "it was good" is very fitting for them.

However, Man was not created complete. God's expectation of Man was for him to improve himself by sculpting and shaping himself into a real Man, or *mentch*. Therefore, at Man's creation God could not have said "it was good," because his future remained to be seen. Man has free will (*Devarim* 30:19), and whether he is likened to an animal or to a *mentch* will depend on the choices he makes.

This is why God said "Let us make man" in the plural, as opposed to "I will make Man" in the singular. Who was God talking to? According to the *Yismach Moshe*, God was talking to Man himself. God said to Man: Let's, you and I, make you into everything you can become. God is basically telling us that He will provide the raw materials and then we (Man) must use them in order to make ourselves into the greatest individuals we can be.

This is why Man is not so much a human "being"; rather, he is a human "becoming." However, we still need to find out what it is, specifically, that we have to do in order to become a Man.

The *Avkas Rachel* (6:4) says that when we pursue the 248 positive commandments, and when we run away from the 365 negative commandments, we are considered Man. We see this from two verses.

The first verse says, "Derech Mitzvosecha Arutz" ("In the way of Your commandments I will run"; *Tehillim* 119:32). This verse speaks about running after the positive commandments, and the Hebrew acronym of this verse spells Adam (Man). This teaches us that being a Man is personified by running after the 248 positive commandments.

The second verse says, "Eshmera Derachai Meichato" ("I will guard my ways from sinning"; *Tehillim* 39:2). This verse speaks about running away from the negative commandments, and the Hebrew acronym of this verse also spells Adam (Man). This teaches us that being a Man is also defined by running away from the 365 negative commandments.

The *Shvilei Pinchas* says that, from all of this, we see that on *Yom Kippur* we are supposed to make a resolution to run after *mitzvos* (good deeds) and run away from *aveiros* (sins). By doing so, we fix the Tenth Utterance on the tenth day, by molding ourselves into Man.

This is why *Yom Kippur* was given the holiness of a *Yom Tov* and was put into a class unto itself, known as the Day of Awe. It highlights the importance of its related Utterance, "*Na'aseh Adam*." Working on ourselves is one of the primary objectives of Creation.

Perhaps we could suggest that on *Yom Kippur* we choose just one positive commandment that we have not been fulfilling, or that we have not been fulfilling 100 percent, and make a resolution (utterance) that this coming year we will adopt that *mitzvah* as our special pet project. Similarly, we can choose just one negative commandment that we have been transgressing, even partially, and say that this coming year we will refrain from it as our pet project.

In this way we will have begun, in a concrete way, the process of shaping ourselves into real *Bnei Adam* (Men).

May we all be blessed to help repair this world by fixing ourselves, so that our Silent Partner will sound the Great *Shofar* that will usher in a new era to which the expression "it is good" will be fitting.

Yom Kippur

Sowing for the Future

Patience is a virtue, because with it we can tolerate the tough times, while looking forward to the happiness that will eventually come.

It is an ancient Jewish custom on the night of *Yom Kippur* to take a Torah scroll out of the Holy Ark, walk around the *bimah* (the central table) and recite the verse, "Light is sown for the righteous, and for the upright of heart, gladness" (*Tehillim* 97:11). What is the significance of this custom?

The Talmud (*Kiddushin* 39b) states that the primary reward for *mitzvah* observance is given to us in the next world. One of the great symbolisms of this idea is the martyrdom of Rebbi Akiva (see *Berachos* 61b). Moshe Rabbeinu, who foresaw what would happen to Rebbi Akiva, asks God, "Is this the reward for Torah?" (see *Menachos* 29b). One answer to Moshe's question can be found in the Talmud, which states that the reward for *mitzvah* observance is not found in this world, but rather in the next world.

We also learn this idea from the verse itself, where it says, "light is sown for the righteous, etc." The *Radak* explains this verse in the following way: when it says "light is sown for the righteous," it means that the righteous sow in this world. When it says "for the upright of heart, gladness" it means that the righteous and upright will receive the happiness and gladness that come with the reward in the World to Come.

Based on all these sources, the *Beis Yisrael* explains why we have this ancient Jewish custom of taking the Torah out of the Ark on the night of *Yom Kippur*. He says that we do this in order to stress that we accept upon ourselves to keep the Torah and its *mitzvos*.

But if a person should ask, "Why should I accept the Torah upon myself, when there have been so many righteous people who have accepted the Torah upon themselves and yet bad things happened to them?" The answer to such a query is the verse that we recite when the Torah is taken out, "Light is sown for the righteous…," which according to the *Radak*, means to say that the real reward is waiting for us in the coming world, just like it was waiting for Rebbi Akiva.

This, in turn, is hinted to in the verse "*Or zarua la'tzaddik u'l'yishrei lev simchah* - Light is sown for the righteous, and for the upright of heart, gladness." If you take the last letter of each word of this verse (*reish, ayin, kuf, yud, beis, hey*), it spells "R' Akiva." This indicates that the light and gladness of heart was waiting for Rebbi Akiva in the next world. The same holds true for every single one of us.

May we all be blessed with the privilege of Torah study and observance, reaping the fruits in this world and the principal reward in the World to Come.

Yom Kippur

What a Team

If we want something done right, we have to do it ourselves. While this rule rings true for those with experience, we must not forget that God Himself set this law into motion.

Sometimes, *Yom Kippur* coincides with a Shabbos. As such, this day provides us with unique benefits, some of which we will now discuss.

The Slonimer Rebbe in his *Nesivos Shalom* points out the inherent difference between *Yom Kippur* and Shabbos.

He explains that the sanctity of Shabbos comes from above, since its holiness is generated by God. However, the sanctity of *Yom Kippur* comes from below because the holiness of the day is generated by the Jews, and by the service of the *Kohen Gadol*, the High Priest.

We find this pattern with regard to the two sets of Tablets. The first set was created by God alone (see *Shemos* 32:16) and therefore it shares a commonality with Shabbos - namely, that its holiness came from above. Regarding the second set of tablets, since Man participated in its formation (see *Shemos* 34:1), it shares a commonality with *Yom Kippur* - namely, that it's holiness came from below.

The Slonimer Rebbe observes that it is for no small reason that the first set of Tablets was given on Shabbos (see *Shabbos* 86a), since it was meant to demonstrate the common denominator between the two. It is equally appropriate that the second set of Tablets was given on *Yom Kippur*, specifically in order to demonstrate their common theme.

Ironically, the first set of Tablets did not last, even though they came from the Almighty One, Who is eternal. It is the second set of Tablets that are still intact today (wherever they are hidden), even though mere mortals participated in creating them. This alone teaches us a very important lesson. That which a person achieves spiritually, on his own, is blessed by God with the ability to endure. This is because our efforts are pleasing in God's eyes.

On the other hand, Shabbos has an advantage over *Yom Kippur*. Precisely because the sanctity of Shabbos comes from Hashem, we can celebrate Shabbos by eating and drinking without being concerned that this indulgence will lead us to no good. However, since *Yom Kippur*'s holiness is generated from below, by us, we cannot celebrate it with eating and drinking, out of concern that such indulgence will lead us into a negative state.

While Shabbos purifies the soul, *Yom Kippur* purifies the body.

Not only that, but on Shabbos we return to God from a place of love, whereas on *Yom Kippur* people tend to return to God from a position of reverence.

Since we require both love and awe of God, it is very special when these two days coincide. It means that we can purify both the body and the soul, and return to God from a place of love and respect, becoming cleansed from above and from below.

May we all be blessed on this combined Shabbos and *Yom Kippur* to be cleansed completely, from above and below, in body and soul, through reverence and love.

Sukkos

Where Are We?

A lthough there may be truth to the adage "You are what you eat," a more accurate maxim would be "You are what you think about." This thought alone might just make all the difference in the world.

Over the last couple of weeks, I had a question about *Sukkos* that was bothering me. I found that, on the one hand, the *sukkah* has the status of *Chutz La'aretz* (any place outside the Land of Israel), whereas on the other hand the *sukkah* has the status of *Eretz Yisrael* (Israel).

There are sources that support both notions. For instance, in the *Yehi Ratzon* prayer said upon entering the *sukkah* it says, "And in the merit of my leaving my house to go out, may this be reckoned for me as if I have wandered afar."

This means to say that if a harsh decree of exile has been sentenced upon us over the High Holidays, then we ask God to consider our departing from our homes into the *sukkah* as some sort of fulfillment of that decree. In this way, we will not have to suffer leaving our homes in a more permanent way.

According to this liturgical passage, going into a *sukkah* is like going into exile. Exile, by definition, means going to *Chutz La'aretz*. So it follows that our *sukkos* have the status of *Chutz La'aretz*.

On the other hand, the *Vilna Gaon* compares the *sukkah* to living in *Eretz Yisrael* since both *mitzvos* are fulfilled with not just one or two limbs, but with our entire bodies (see *Kol Hatur*, chap. 1, para. 7). So according to the Gr"a, going into a *sukkah* is like going into *Eretz Yisrael*.

Herein lies an apparent contradiction regarding the status of the *sukkah*. Is it likened to *Chutz La'aretz* or to *Eretz Yisrael*? Will the real *sukkah* please stand up?

I have not yet found commentaries that address this question directly. However, I did come across some ideas found in various sources that I would like to borrow from, modify, and adapt, in order to offer one approach to resolving this difficulty.

The Talmud shares a Tannaic debate as to what our *sukkos* represent. According to Rabbi Akiva, our *sukkos* commemorate the actual booths that our ancestors built and dwelt in during their forty years of wandering through the desert. However according to Rabbi Eliezer, our *sukkos* symbolically represent the Clouds of Glory that protected our ancestors throughout their journey in the desert (*Sukkah*, chap. 1, *Sukkah Shehi Gavo'ah*, pg. 11a).

The *Piskei Teshuvos* (*Hilchos Sukkah*, 625:1, footnote 3, based on the *Chassam Sofer, Drashos, Drash* 53) applies the rule of thumb, "These and those are the words of the Living God" (*Eiruvin*, chap. 1, *Mavoi Shehi Gavo'ah,* pg. 13b) to this debate between Rabbi Akiva and Rabbi Eliezer.

He explains that in the desert there were two categories of Jews. There were Jews on a higher spiritual level, and then there were Jews on a lower spiritual level. The Jews that were on a higher spiritual level were protected by the Clouds of Glory (like the opinion of Rabbi Eliezer). However, the Jews that were on a lower spiritual level were spat out from Clouds of Glory. What did those Jews do in order to protect themselves from the oppressive desert sun? They built booths for themselves (like the opinion of Rabbi Akiva).

Along these lines, we could suggest the same methodology to answer our original question above. For Jews on a lower spiritual level, who received a harsh decree of exile over the High Holidays, their *sukkos* are likened to *Chutz La'aretz*. However for Jews on a higher spiritual level, who were never sentenced to the harsh decree of exile, their *sukkos* are on the status of *Eretz*

Yisrael.

This is why the holiday is called *Chag HaSukkos*, in the plural, as opposed to *Chag HaSukkah*, in the singular. The very name of the holiday teaches us that there are two types of *sukkos* in which the Jewish people will celebrate. For some Jews the *sukkah* will be the highest level, *Eretz Yisrael*; while for other Jews the *sukkah* will only be on the lower level of *Chutz La'aretz*. The constitution of our *sukkos* depends on our spiritual status.

Two primary aspects in determining the spiritual status of our *sukkos* are our thoughts and intentions. For example, there can be a Jew who lives in Israel and yet pines to be in a different country. All he dreams about are the materialistic advantages to be gained in that country. Spiritually speaking, such a Jew is considered to be living in *Chutz La'aretz*.

This is learned from a teaching of the *Ba'al Shem Tov* that says that a person is really where his thoughts are.

Similarly, you can have a Jew who lives in the Diaspora and yet longs to be in *Eretz Yisrael*. There may be circumstances out of his control that prevent him from making *aliyah*, like illness for example. But, spiritually speaking, such a Jew is considered to be living in *Eretz Yisrael*. It all depends on what our values are and what we wish for.

For Jews whose minds are focused on *Eretz Yisrael* and what it represents, namely *kedushah* (holiness) and *taharah* (purity), their *sukkos* become the embodiment of *Eretz Yisrael*. However, for Jews whose thoughts are constantly on *Chutz La'aretz* and what it represents, namely the pursuit of material gain, their *sukkos* take on the essence of *Chutz La'aretz*.

In order for us to benefit from the spiritual advantages of an *Eretz Yisrael* type of *sukkah*, we could suggest making a wish list. Write down the things we want most in life. What are our goals? Read the list back to yourself to see if your desires lean more towards the spiritual or the physical. Then you can determine where you are and where you would like to be.

If we would like to become the person who dreams more about the needs of the soul than the desires of the body, we can start to study about Creation, the world, its purpose, the *mitzvos*, etc. in order to deepen our appreciation for that which is eternal.

May we all be blessed with a healthy value system, yearning, longing, and pining for spirituality, so that our *sukkos* take on the essence of *Eretz Yisrael*. May we thus merit to have the Seven Shepherds of Israel visit us in our *sukkos*, culminating with another guest, the *Moshiach*, who will build the *Succas David Hanofaless*, the Sukkah of David [The Temple] that has fallen.

V'zos HaBerachah

Heartfelt Tears

There is no comparison between someone who asks us for something, and someone who asks us for something with tears in his eyes. We will be much more inclined to respond to a tearful request than to a tearless one. Let's find out who knew this secret, and put it to good use.

Towards the end of the portion, it says that Moshe died by the word of God (*Devarim* 34:5). How could it be that Moshe died and then wrote that he died? In other words, how did a dead person write that he died? The Talmud (*Bava Basra* 15a) cites the opinion of Rebbe Shimon who says that until that verse, God dictated and Moshe wrote it down. However, from that verse onwards, God dictated and Moshe wrote with tears.

The *Sifsei Chachamim* (#10), citing the *Minchas Yehudah,* points out a dispute in understanding the aforementioned Talmud. According to the *Maharsha*, the Talmud means that Moshe wrote the last eight verses with his tears and not with ink. However, according to the *Maharal*, Moshe used ink to write the last eight verses, but at the time he wrote them, he cried. Either way, Moshe was crying while writing the last eight verses.

There could be many reasons given for Moshe's tears. One could be because he was about to die and would no longer be capable of performing the *mitzvos* (see *Shabbos* 30a). Another could be because he saw that he was not going to enter the Land of Israel. However, the *Beis Yisrael* offers another approach as to why Moshe cried, based on the following story.

A certain *tzaddik* once sat down to learn a book on *mussar* (character development) called *Eis La'asos* which was written in a foreign language. People asked this *tzaddik* why he preferred to study from a book written in a foreign language when so many similar works have been published in the Holy Tongue, Hebrew. The *tzaddik* responded by saying that he knew that the author of the *Eis La'asos*, Rabbi Hillel of Kolomyia, cried as he wrote each and every single sentence, so that his words would fall under the category of "words that come out of the heart will enter into the heart" (see *Berachos* 6b). This *tzaddik* said that he doubts there is another ethical work on par with the *Eis La'asos* due to this heartfelt quality.

The *Beis Yisrael* suggests, based on this story, that this is why Moshe cried as he concluded writing the *sefer Torah*. We know that everything is determined by the way that it ends, like they say, "all's well that ends well" (see *Sotah* 13b). This means to say that the entire Torah depends on the last eight verses. Therefore, at the time that Moshe concluded writing the Torah, he shed tears in order that his words would fall under the category of "words that come out of the heart will enter into the heart," meaning that this would ensure the Jewish people's observance of Torah and *mitzvos*.

The idea that everything depends on the heart is hinted to in the way the Torah ends and then begins. The last letter of the Torah is a *lamed*. The first letter of the Torah is a *beis*. When these two letters are joined together, as when we finish reading the Torah and begin immediately again, it spells the word *lev*, which means "heart," teaching us that our spiritual success is dependent on the sincerity of our hearts.

So, as we conclude this cycle of the Torah, may we all be blessed to be impacted by Moshe's emotional plea, and serve God with all of our hearts, return to Hashem with tears in our eyes, and thus deserve to witness the coming of *Moshiach* this *Tishrei*.

V'zos Haberachah

It's "Kli-r-ly" About the Heart

Uncle Sam may say "I want you," but God more specifically says "I want your heart." After all, that's where it's at.

In most cases, *V'zos Haberachah* is read on a weekday and not on a *Shabbos*.

This itself teaches us a few things. Firstly, it shows us that *V'zos Haberachah* serves as a bridge between that which is holy and that which is mundane. As the only Torah portion to be read on a weekday, *V'zos Haberachah* functions as a bridge that links the holy *Shabbos* with the ordinary days of the week.

Reading *V'zos Haberachah* on a weekday takes the holiness of the Shabbos (on which a Torah portion is generally read), and infuses that holiness into the mundane. This message is pertinent at this time of year, which is the beginning of a new cycle. *V'zos Haberachah* reminds us to take the holiness of an entire month of holidays and *mitzvos* (commandments) that we experienced during *Tishrei*, and imbue that holiness into the rest of the year. The question is, how do we do that?

One specific lesson we could implement is found at the very end of our portion. The last letter of the Torah is the letter *lamed* (*Devarim* 34:12). When the letter *lamed* is spelled out, it consists of three letters: *lamed, mem, daled*. These three letters spell the word *lomed*, which can either mean to learn or to teach. This stresses the importance of a healthy, balanced education. As the tallest of the Hebrew letters, the *lamed* teaches us that learning is the highest Jewish priority!

The question arises as to what is the primary Jewish principle to learn? Here too, the Torah gives us instruction. Although the last letter of the Torah is a *lamed*, the first letter of the Torah is a *beis* (*Bereishis* 1:1). Together, the *lamed* and the *beis* spell the word *lev*, heart. This means to say that it all boils down to ironing out the wrinkles of our hearts (refer to "*Heartfelt Tears*" above, pg. 392, where this issue is explained in more detail). However, what precise aspect of the heart needs our attention more urgently than any other area? Once again, the Torah provides the answer.

The acronym of the Torah's last three words, "*l'einei kol Yisrael* - before the eyes of all Israel" (*Devarim* 34:12), is comprised of three letters: *lamed, kaf, yud*. When unscrambled, these three letters spell the word *kli*, vessel. This teaches us that the heart (*lev*) is the greatest vessel (*kli*) to receive the holy light. And the one thing required to cultivate in our hearts to receive that holy light is unity.

This can be seen from the word *kli*, itself. The word *kli* can serve as the acronym for three other Hebrew words as well: *Kohanim, Leviim, Yisraelim* (Priests, Levites and Israelites).

This teaches us that all classes of Jews need to join together in the service of God. Only when all types of Jews live in harmony and love each other with all their hearts (*lev*), will they develop the proper vessel (*kli*) that will be able to contain the holy light (see "*The Transformers*," vol. 1, pg. 33, for an elaboration on this theme).

It is not surprising to find that the very last of the six orders of the Mishnah states that the greatest *kli* (vessel) that has the ability to hold blessing is *shalom*, peace (Tractate *Uktzin*, at the end of *seder Taharos*, chap. 3, *Yesh Tzrichin*, the opinion of Rebbi Shimon Ben Chalafta, based on the verse in *Tehillim* 29:11). When we live peacefully with each other we will be blessed in every single way. This requires acceptance, tolerance, respect and appreciation.

It is not by coincidence that both the Written Torah and the Oral Tradition conclude with the topic of vessels. Neither is it arbitrary that both stress camaraderie, love and peace as the channels for success. It is about this duty of the heart (*lev*) that we say, "all's well that ends well."

If indeed the greatest *kli* to contain blessing is peace, then the end of our *parshah* (portion), connects with the beginning of the *parshah*. We mentioned that our *parshah* concludes with the acronym "*kli*." The greatest *kli* is in the *lev*, which is also hinted to at the end of our portion. When the *lev* is filled with love, then it becomes the greatest *kli* for blessing. Perhaps this is why our *parshah* begins with the words "*V'zos Haberachah* - This is the blessing," indicating that the biggest blessings come when our hearts go out to each other.

Just as the heart pumps blood throughout the body, so does unconditional love permeate our systems with Divine light. This, in turn, will spread holiness into our new year.

So, this week our *berachah* is echoed by what we are going to thunder together at the end of this portion's reading, "*Chazak Chazak V'nischazek*! - Be strong! Be strong! And may we be strengthened!" May we be strengthened with all the blessings of harmony, peace and love saturating our entire lives.

Shemini Atzeres - Simchas Torah - V'zos Haberachah - Bereishis

Paying the Price at Twenty-One

Sometimes we wonder how it all began. When we look at our current situation, we ask, "What can we do to make it better?" In the following paragraphs we will discuss how an ending should reflect the beginning.

There are four holidays in the month of *Tishrei*. They are: *Rosh HaShanah, Yom Kippur, Sukkos* (*Hoshanah Rabbah* is part of *Sukkos*), and *Shemini Atzeres*. The *Arizal* (*Sha'ar HaKavanos, Rosh HaShanah, Drush Aleph*) says that there is a connection between all of them. He says that ultimately they all come to atone for one sin, and one sin only: the first sin that Man ever committed, eating from the *Eitz HaDa'as*, the Tree of Knowledge.

God began creating the world on the twenty-fifth day of *Elul*. This means that the first *Erev Shabbos* (Friday), when Adam HaRishon was created, was the first day of *Tishrei*. On that day, God commanded Adam not to eat from the Tree of Knowledge. And on that very same day, Adam transgressed (*Pesikta*, #23, *Rebbi Eliezer*; See *Ran, Rosh HaShanah*, chap. 1, *Arba'ah Roshei Shanim,* pg. 16a, pg. 3a of the *Ran's* pagination, *B'Rosh HaShanah*).

Since the first of *Tishrei* is *Rosh HaShanah*, it follows that Adam sinned on *Rosh HaShanah*. On that day God brought Adam to trial, and on that day Adam was acquitted. God said to Adam that since the first of *Tishrei* was used as a day of judgment for him, it would remain a Day of Judgment for all of his descendants. Just as Adam was acquitted on that day, so would his descendants be acquitted on that day.

The *Arizal* (*Parshas Ha'azinu*) says that there is more to this Midrash than meets the eye. It is not just because Adam was judged on the first of *Tishrei* that we are all judged on that day. Rather, we are all judged on *Rosh*

HaShanah for our participation in the sin of the *Eitz HaDa'as*.

You see, when God created Adam, all of our souls were part of his soul, forming one huge soul. So, when the sin presented itself before Adam, there were many voices and opinions arguing inside of him. Since Adam sinned, we are all to blame. It was not so much Adam's spark that sinned, as much as it was the rest of our sparks that either pushed Adam into it, or did not protest strongly enough against it. Hence, are all collectively guilty for the sin of the *Eitz HaDa'as*.

Since that sin occurred on *Rosh HaShanah*, every single year, on the day of that sin's anniversary, we are all judged again. Since rebellion was at the root of that sin, God analyzes whether or not we still have that streak of rebelliousness within us. The sign which indicates that we are truly remorseful, is when we cause a shift in our thinking to become "Yes" people in following God's decrees, whether or not we like them, and whether or not we understand them.

We do not only have *Rosh HaShanah* to atone for the *Eitz HaDa'as*, but we also have *Yom Kippur*. However, if we did not achieve atonement on the High Holidays, then we still have another chance on *Hoshanah Rabbah* to repair the damage that was caused.

Now, *Hoshanah Rabbah* is the twenty-first day after *Rosh HaShanah*. This is important to know, as we will soon see.

Once upon a time, God told Avraham that one of God's names is *Eheyeh*. This name is the one which represents kindness and compassion. The numerical value of *Eheyeh* is twenty-one. God went on to tell Avraham that he was the twenty-first generation since Adam HaRishon. Avraham also represents kindness and compassion. Since the number twenty-one represents kindness, God told Avraham that He was going to give his descendants the twenty-first day from *Rosh HaShanah*, *Hoshanah Rabbah*, as a day of kindness and compassion to finally atone for the sin of the *Eitz*

Hada'as (*Mateh Moshe, Inyan HoShanah Rabbah*, # 957, citing a Midrash).

Of what relevance is the fact that we were given the twenty-first day as an atonement? We are about to find out.

The *Shevilei Pinchas* says that when we sinned with the *Eitz HaDa'as*, the twenty-two letters of the holy Hebrew alphabet were ruined. By definition, this means that the Torah itself was damaged by the sin because the Torah is composed of the twenty-two letters. In turn, all of Creation was harmed by the sin because all creations are outgrowths of the Torah, since Hashem looked into the Torah in order to create all things.

Now, when we say that the twenty-two letters were stained by the sin, we have to modify what we mean, because there is one letter that cannot be negatively affected by sin. That letter is the *aleph*, because the *aleph* represents God. We can see this by spelling out the letter *aleph*: *aleph, lamed, phey*. When the vowels are changed, these three letters spell the word *aluph*, chief. This represents God who is given the title of "*Alupho Shel Olam* - Chief in Command of the World."

Just like God can never be damaged, neither can the *aleph* ever be hurt. So, what was meant by the statement that the twenty-two letters were harmed by the sin? It really means to say that twenty-one of the letters (from the *beis* to the *taf*) drifted away from the *aleph*. By definition, this means that all of Creation, which was created by the letters, drifted away from the *aleph* - *Alupho Shel Olam*, God. This means that we, who are also creatures that were formed from the letters, also drifted away from *Alupho Shel Olam*.

Such is the effect of sin. It created barriers, partitions, and iron curtains between us and God. Therefore, God gave us twenty-one days from *Rosh HaShanah* until *Hoshanah Rabbah* in order to rectify the situation. During each of the twenty-one days, we are supposed to work on fixing one of the letters. We go in reverse order, first working on the *taf*, then the *shin*, and then the *reish*, and so on.

Perhaps we could suggest that this is the reason why this month is called *Tishrei*. It is because *Tishrei* is spelled first with a *taf*, then with a *shin*, and then with a *reish*. The letters go backwards, teaching us that we must rectify the letters in that order. The last letter in *Tishrei* is a *yud*. The letter *yud* often represents God. This hints to us that we must bring the letters back to God. This means to bring all of Creation, including ourselves, closer to God.

I was thinking about what it means to work on a letter a day. Maybe we could propose that each day we should focus on working on what that letter stands for. For example, the *taf* stands for *teshuvah* (repentance), the *kuf* can be pronounced as *kof* (a monkey), teaching us to not just copy what we see other people doing in their service to God, but instead make it personally real and meaningful. The *phey* can be pronounced as *pey* (or *peh*, a mouth) reminding us to work on our speech. The *ayin* means an "eye," prompting us to keep our eyes holy, etc.

By the time we reach *Hoshanah Rabbah*, all the letters, from the *taf* to the *beis*, should be reconnected to the *aleph*. This is why on the next day, *Shemini Atzeres*, we dance with the Torah celebrating *Simchas Torah* (in *Eretz Yisrael*). One of the reasons we are happy is because all twenty-two letters are rectified, which means that the Torah itself, which is made up of those letters, has been mended. Deep down we know that this means that we are also very close to God. This knowledge and feeling causes us to burst forth with song and dance.

We are reminded of all of this when we start the new cycle with *Bereishis*. The Torah starts with a *beis*, not with an *aleph*. This is because the *aleph* (representing God) is beyond this world. Any mistakes we make here can only hurt the letters from the *beis* onwards. The *aleph*, on the other hand, remains unscathed.

As we mentioned, any distance between the twenty-one letters and the *aleph*, and consequently between Creation and *Alupho Shel Olam*, is brought about through sin. But as long as we connect ourselves to those letters through Torah study, we are always given another chance to bridge the gap.

We can keep this idea in mind the whole year round with the following exercise. Each morning, let us say out loud the entire *aleph beis*. Afterwards, let's say that we want to bring the letters, Creation, and ourselves closer to the *aleph - Alupho Shel Olam -* by staying away from sin, and through the study of Torah. This may help us channel each day to the correct service of God.

May we, the descendants of Adam, all be blessed to atone for the sin with the *Eitz HaDa'as*, bringing the twenty-one letters back to the *aleph*, so that we experience oneness with God this *Shemini Atzeres*, this Shabbos *Bereishis*, and this entire year.

Bibliography

The following bibliography provides information on the sources cited in this publication.

Abarbanel (1437-1508):   Rabbi Don Yitzchak Ben Yehudah Abarbanel was a leader of Spanish Jewry. He was also a philosopher, statesman and author of a commentary on almost the entire Tanach.

Abaye (278-338 BCE):   He was a Babylonian Amora, and was the head of the Academy in Pumpedisa. He was a descendant of Eli HaKohen. His father Kaleil died before he was born, and his mother died in childbirth. He was raised by his uncle, Raba bar Nachmeni. Abaye's real name was Nachmeni after his paternal grandfather, and Abaye was a nickname. His famous colleague was Rava, with whom he argued frequently. In only six cases, the law is like Abaye. In all other cases, we follow Rava's ruling.

Abudraham: Rabbi David ben Yosef Abudraham was a fourteenth-century Spanish scholar from Seville. He is known for his commentary on the liturgy.

Admor of Kuvrin (1783-1858):   Rabbi Moshe of Kuvrin was one of the founders of the Slonimer Chassidus, Belerusia. He was known for his dedication to immersing himself in a Mikveh regularly, even in freezing cold water. He is also known for his humility, and for praying with tremendous fervor.

Agra D'Kallah: The title of Rabbi Zvi Elimelech of Dinov's (1783-1841) teachings on the Chumash. He was also the author of the Bnei Yissaschar. (See Bnei Yissaschar & Agra D'Pirka)

Agra D'Pirka: The teachings of Rabbi Zvi Elimelech of Dinov (1783-1841), also the author of the Bnei Yissaschar and Agra D'Kallah. (See Bnei Yissaschar and Agra D'Kallah)

Akavia ben Mehalalel: A first-century Tanna who was a member of the Sanhedrin.

Alexander Rebbe (1879-1943): Rabbi Yitzchak Menachem Mendel Dancyger (Danziger) was a Rebbe in Aleksandrow Lodski, Poland. He was the author of the Yismach Yisrael, and was murdered by the Nazis in the Treblinka extermination camp.

Alshich Hakadosh (1508-1600): Rabbi Moshe ben Chaim Alshich was born in Adrianople, Turkey, and settled in Tzefas where he was a Dayan and teacher. He also authored the Alshich commentary on Tanach. He was ordained by Rabbi Yosef Cairo, his Rebbe. The Alshich was a Halachist, preacher, and Kabbalist, and one of his disciples was Rabbi Chaim Vital.

Arizal (1534-1572): Rabbi Yitzchok ben Shlomo Ashkenazy Luria was considered the most eminent Kabbalist, and primarily resided in Tzefas.

Aron Eidus (1850-1912): Rabbi Shraga Yair of Biala lived in Biala, a city in southern Poland and authored a commentary on the Chumash. He was a grandson of the Yid HaKadosh (Rabbi Yaakov Yitzchok, 1765-1814, who was the student of the Seer of Lublin).

Arugas Habosem (1853-1910): Rabbi Moshe Greenwald was the Rav of Chust, Hungary and the progenitor of the Pupa Chassidic dynasty. The Arugas Habosem is a responsa on halachic issues.

Avkas Rochel: A collection of responsa written by Rabbi Yosef Cairo (1488-1575), the Chief Rabbi of Tzefas. (See Beis Yosef & Rabbi Yosef Cairo)

Avodas Hakodesh: A work by the Chidah. (See Chidah)

Avodas Yisrael: (see Ner Yisrael) A commentary containing thoughts on the weekly portion, teaching people how to serve God properly. It was authored by Rabbi Yisrael ben Shabsai Hofstein, the Koznitzer Maggid. (See Maggid of Koznitz)

Avos: A Mishna tractate in Seder Nezikin devoted to the ethical teachings of the Sages.

Az Nidberu: The author of this sefer, Rav Binyomin Zilber zt"l (1917-2008) was a member of the Moetzes Gedolei Hatorah in Eretz Yisrael, and Mechaber of many sefarim. He was known as "Binyomin Hatzadik" – the name that the Chazon Ish used to refer to him when he learned by him. His name was HaRav Binyomin Yehoshua ben R' Boruch, zt"l. The following are some of his many sefarim: Beis Baruch on Chayei Adam (3 vol), Az NidBeru (14 vol), Bris Olam (hilchos Shabbos) (3 vol), Mekor HaHalacha, Cheshbono Shel Olam, Hilchos Shvi'is and many others published "anonymously."

Ba'al Haturim (1275-1340): A commentary on the Torah authored by Rabbi Yaakov the son of the Rosh - Rabbeinu Asher. The commentary is nicknamed Ba'al Haturim (Master of the Turs) because its author, Rabbi Yaakov, wrote the famous Arba'ah Turim (Four Rows) which codifies all of Jewish law that applies to us today in the absence of the Temple. Ba'al Haturim often derived teachings based on gematria.

Ba'al Shem Tov (Besh"t 1698-1760): Rabbi Yisrael Ben Eliezer was the founder of Chassidism. He settled in Medzibozh in 1740, and revealed himself as a Rebbe. He injected tradition with vitality and joy, making mysticism available to the masses, while emphasizing unconditional love.

Bach (1561-1640): Rabbi Yoel Sirkis lived in Crakow, Poland. He is famous for his commentary on the entire Tur called Bayis Chadash or Bach.

Bamidbar: The book of Numbers, fourth of the five books of the

Torah. It contains various stories about the Jewish people during their wandering in the wilderness.

Bar Yochai: A poetic song written by the kabbalist Rabbi Shimon Levi in which he describes the greatness of Rebbi Shimon Bar Yochai and his teachings. (See Rabbi Shimon Bar Yochai)

Bartenura (1440-1516): Rabbeinu Ovadiyah M'bartenura wrote a classic commentary on the Mishnah. He was an Italian scholar and was buried on the Mount of Olives.

Be'er Heitev: A commentary on the Shulchan Aruch that was authored by various people. Orach Chaim and Even Haezer were written by Rabbi Yehudah Ashkenazy, a German Rabbi (1730-1770). Yoreh Deah and Choshen Mishpat were written by Rabbi Zecharia Mendel ben Aryeh Leib, a Polish Rabbi at the turn of the eighteenth century.

Be'er Mayim Chayim: A commentary on the Torah by Rabbi Chaim Tirer Chernovitz (1760-1816). He was born in Galicia, and died in Tzefas.

Beis Aharon (1736-1772): A commentary on the Torah by Rabbi Aharon Karliner who was a student of the Maggid of Mezritch.

Beis Yisrael Tinyana: A commentary on the Torah by Rabbi Yisrael Toisig (1889-1967) who was the Rav of Meah Shearim, and Rosh Yeshiva of Mesifta Tiferes Aharon from Mattersdorf.

Beis Yosef: A commentary by Rabbi Yosef Cairo on the Tur. Rabbi Yosef Cairo also wrote the Shulchan Aruch and the Kesef Mishna on the Rambam. (See Rabbi Yosef Cairo, Shulchan Aruch & Avkas Rochel)

Belzer Rebbe: The first Belzer Rebbi was Rabbi Sholom Rokeach (1783-1855). He was a disciple of the Seer of Lublin in Western Ukraine. The second Belzer Rebbe was Rabbi Yehoshua Rokeach (1825-1894).

The third Belzer Rebbe was Rabbi Yissachar Dov Rokeach (1854-1926). The fourth Belzer Rebbe was Rabbi Aharon Rokeach (1877–1957). The fifth Rebbe is the current Rebbe, Rabbi Yissachar Dov Rokeach. He was born in 1948.

Ben Azai: He is also known as Shimon ben Azai, and was a second-century Tanna. His love of Torah study caused him to remain unmarried. Ben Azai was one of four people who entered into Paradise, but he died as a result of that.

Ben Ish Chai (1832-1909):   Rabbi Yosef Chaim of Bagdad was a Kabbalist and posek. The Ben Ish Chai Drushim is a commentary he authored on the Torah.

Ben Zomah: A second-century Tanna, who was a disciple of Rabbi Yehoshua ben Chananya. He was one of the four people who entered Paradise, but he lost his mind because of it.

Berdichever Rebbe (1740-1810):   Rabbi Levi Yitzchak was a student of the the Maggid of Mezritch, Poland, and was a passionate defender of the Jewish people. He was an illuy with an unshakable faith in the inherent goodness of all human beings. He would give even the greatest sinner the benefit of the doubt.

Bereishis: The book of Genesis, first of the five books of the Torah. It discusses the stories of Creation, Adam, Noach, the Patriarchs, Matriarchs and the tribes of Israel.

Bereishis Rabbah: The section of Midrash Rabbah on the book of Genesis.

Besamim Rosh: Responsa published in 1793 by Rabbi Saul Berlin (1740-1794). Its 392 responsa are purported to have been written by the Rosh. However, the Rosh's connection to these responsa is a matter of huge dispute. He was the son of Berlin's Chief Rabbi.

Bi'urei Chazon Ish: The works of Rabbi Avraham Yeshaya Karelitz. (See Chazon Ish)

Birkas Peretz: A commentary on Chumash authored by Rabbi Yaakov Yisrael Kanievsky, the Steipler Gaon. (See Steipler Gaon)

Bnei Yissaschar: A commentary on the Jewish months from a mystical perspective, written by Rabbi Tzvi Elimelech of Dinov Poland (1783-1841). He was a nephew of the Rebbe, Reb Elimelech of Lizensk.

Chaggai :   A Judean prophet of the early post-exilic period, and a contemporary of Zechariya. He was one of the three final briefer prophets, and was born in Chaldea during the captivity.

Chaim Sha'al: A work by the Chidah. (See Chidah)

Chanah David: A commentary on the Torah from Rabbi David Berkowitz (Pinsk 1963).

Chasam Sofer (1762-1839):   Rabbi Moshe Sofer was born in Frankfurt am Main, Germany and later became the Rabbi there. He was a student of Rabbi Nosson Adler, and married the daughter of Rabbi Akiva Eiger. In 1806 he became the Rabbi of Pressburg (Bratislava, Slovakia). His commentaries on the Torah, Talmud, and Shulchan Aruch, as well as his sermons and response are classic works. His descendants served as Rabbis in Hungary, Austria and Poland. He vigorously opposed the reform movement, and encouraged Jewish settlement in Eretz Yisrael. He died in Pressburg, Moravia.

Chazon Ish (1878-1953):   He was a Lithuanian Talmudic scholar and posek. He studied under Rabbi Chaim Soloveitchik, and was close with Rabbi Chaim Ozer Grodzinzky with whom he consulted in halachic matters. The Chazon Ish was also knowledgable in astronomy, anatomy, mathematics and botany. He was also well versed in the teachings of Kabbalah. With the help of Rabbi Avraham Yitzchak Kook, he eventually settled in Eretz Yisrael and spent his last twenty years in Bnei Brak.

Chernobyler Rebbe (1730-1797):   Rabbi Menachem Nochum Twersky of Chernobyl, Ukraine. He authored the Meor Einayim, a Chassidic work on the weekly *parshah*. He was a disciple of the Ba'al Shem Tov, and of the Maggid of Mezritch. Rabbi Menachem Nochum also served as the Maggid of Chernobyl.

Chidah (1724-1806):   Rabbi Chaim Yosef David Azulai, lived in Jerusalem, and authored over a hundred books. Many of his works focus on the deeper esoteric aspects of the Torah and Mitzvos. He was a descendant of a famed rabbinic family originating from Castille and Moroco. The Chidah was born in Jerusalem, and was considered the greatest halachic authority of his generation by the oriental and Italian Jews. His huge, multifaceted literary output included halachic rulings, mystical works, commentaries on the Bible and Talmud, a commentary on *Sefer* Chasidim called Binyan Olam, Shem Hagedolim which is a bibliography of books and rabbis, and travelogues. He was involved in communal activities, and also served in rabbinical positions. The Chidah traveled extensively to raise funds for the Jewish community in Israel, and in the course of his travels he visited places such as Egypt, North Africa, and Europe. He became Rabbi of Leghorn, Italy, and died there. In 1960, his remains were brought to Israel and interred in Jerusalem.

Chiddushei Harim (1799-1866):   The title of works by Rabbi Yitzchak Meir Rotenberg-Alter of Ger/Gur, the founder of the Ger Chassidus, Poland. Rabbi Yitzchok Meir was a Talmudic Gaon who became the disciple of Rabbi Simcha Bunim of Peshischa and of Reb Menachem Mendel of Kotsk.

Chofetz Chaim (1838-1933):   This is the title of one of the twenty-one works authored by Rabbi Yisrael Meir Kagan Hakohen of Radin, Poland. Rabbi Yisrael Meir is often reffered to as the "Chofetz Chaim."

He authored works in halachah - Mishnah Berurah, and Biur Halachah (on the Orach Chaim section of the Shulchan Aruch) – and also works on mussar and hashkafah. He founded and headed the yeshiva in Radin. He was famous for his saintly qualities, and recognized as one of the foremost leaders of Jewry.

Chortkover Rebbe (1828-1903):   Rabbi Dovid Moshe Friedman was the first Rebbe of Chortkov, Galicia. His followers comprised one of the largest chassidic groups in Galicia, numbering in the thousands. He led an ascetic life, secluding himself and being preoccupied with study and prayer, day and night. Although he preferred to detach himself from worldly affairs and distance himself from communal disputes, he was nevertheless considered a major leader of Central European Jewry. His teachings have been published in Divrei Dovid, Beis Yisrael and Knesses Yisrael.

Chovos Hal'vavos (Duties of the Heart):   This is a mussar work written by Rabbeinu Bachya Ibn Paquda. He lived in Saragossa, Spain during the first half of the eleventh century.

Chozeh MiLublin (1745-1815):   Rabbi Yaakov Yitzchok Horowitz was the founder of Polish Chassidim, and was nicknamed Chozeh (Seer) because of his ability to see into people's souls. He was a disciple of the Maggid of Mezritch, and also of Rabbi Shmelke of Nilkolsburg and Rabbi Elimelech of Lizensk. After he moved to Lublin, thousands of Chassidim flocked to learn from him. Among his disciples were such Chassidic luminaries as the Yid Hakodesh, Rabbi Simcha Bunim of Peshischa, Rabbi Meir of Apta, Rabbi David of Lelov, the Yismach Moshe, Rabbi Tzvi Elimelech of Dinov, Rabbi Naftali Zvi of Ropschitz, the Ma'or Vashemesh, and Sar Shalom of Belz. He also gained a reputation as a miracle-worker who could accomplish the tikkun, or repair of the soul, of those who sought his assistance and guidance.

Chronicles: The final two books of the Tanach called Divrei Hayamim (the matters of the days), and were composed by Ezra. They begin with the history of humanity, giving the genealogical list down to the Israelite monarchy including Shaul, David and Shlomo. They discuss the kingdoms of Judea and Israel, concluding with the destruction of the first Temple and the subsequent exile into Babylon. The final verses describe how the Persian king Cyrus conquered Babylon, and authorized the return of the Jews to Israel and the building of the second Temple.

Da'as Zekeinim: A collection of comments on the Torah by the Tosafists of the twelfth and thirteenth centuries.

Derech Chaim (Way of Life):   A work focusing on repentance written by the second Rebbe of Chabad, Rabbi Dov Ber Shneur (1773-1827), Rabbi of Lubavitch, born in Liozna, White Russia.

Devarim: The book of Deuteronomy, also called Mishneh Torah (repetition or explanation of the Torah). It is the fifth of the five books of the Torah, and contains 200 laws, seventy of which are completely new. In Deuteronomy, Moshe also warns the people of their potential pitfalls. The entire book was said by Moshe to the people during the last thirty-six days of his life. In Sefer Devarim Moshe chose his own words in order to convey the will of God.

Devarim Rabbah: The section of Midrash Rabbah on the book of Deuteronomy.

Dinim V'hanhagos: An anthology of halachos by Rabbi Meir Greineman (1924-2015) from Lithuania, according to the rulings of the Chazon Ish.

Divrei Chanoch: A commentary on the Torah by Rabbi Chanoch Henach Ehrzan. It is printed in his sefer Gan Razeh. (See Gan Razeh)

Divrei Emes: A sefer on the Torah authored by the Chozeh of Lublin,

Rabbi Yaakov Yitzchak Halevi Horowitz, in 1830, a Chassidic Rebbe from Poland. (See Chozeh MiLublin)

Divrei Yoel: A commentary on the Torah by Rabbi Yoel Teitelbaum, the Satmar Rebbe (1887-1979). He was the founder and first Grand Rebbe of the Satmar dynastry.

Dorshei Reshumos: Talmudic scholars who were known for their expertise in expounding upon verses of the Torah.

Dover Shalom: A collection of speeches and teachings of the first Rebbe of Belz, Rabbi Sholom Rokeach (1779-1855) Galicia. (See Belzer Rebbe)

Drashos Chasam Sofer: See Chasam Sofer.

Eichah Rabbasi: The section of Midrash Rabbah on the book of Eichah.

Eichah: Book of Lamentations, written by Yirmiyahu the Prophet as a eulogy for those who would perish during the destruction of the first Temple. This book is read on the ninth day of Av, which is the Jewish national day of mourning.

Eis La'asos: An ethical work in Yiddish authored by Rabbi Hillel Lichtenstein of Kolomyia (1814-1891), and published in Lvov 1873. He was a Hungarian Rabbi, who was born in Veca and died in Kolomyia, Galicia. He studied in the yeshiva of the Chasam Sofer, and later became the Rabbi of Margarethen. He moved to Kolomyia in 1867, and was the most extreme in religious practice of the Hungarian Rabbis at the time. He admired Chassidus, and used to travel to the Divrei Chaim of Sanz. He authored numerous works, among them Maskil el Dal, Eis La'asos, and Avkas Rochel.

Eishel Avraham Butchach: Rabbi Avraham David ben Asher Anshel

Wahrman of Butchach, Galicia (1770-1840). He was a Talmudist who was won over by the Chassidim. He authored eight works on Gemara, Halacha, Mussar, Aggadata, Chumash, prayer and Psalms.

Elazar ben Chananyah ben Chizkiah ben Chananyah ben Garon: A Tannaic sage who lived during the second Temple era. Elazar arranged the latter part of Meggilas Ta'anis, which lists the national holidays that were celebrated in those times.

Eliyahu Rabba: A commentary by Rabbi Elya Shapiro, on the Levush.

Emes L'Yaakov: A commentary on the Torah by Rabbi Yaakov Kamenetsky (1891-1986). (See Harav Yaakov Kamenetsky)

Emunas Itecha: A commentary on the Torah and holidays by Rabbi Moshe Wolfson. (See Rabbi Moshe Wolfson)

Erachin: Talmudic Tractate in Seder Kodshim.

Esther: A prophetess who became the Jewish Queen of Persia. She was the wife of Mordechai, but was taken by force to be Ahasuerus's wife. Together with Mordechai, Esther was instrumental in saving the Jews from Haman's plot to have them all murdered.

Ezekiel: A Kohen and a prophet who spoke to the Jews after they had been exiled to Babylon. Even though he rebuked them, he also gave them hope that God had not abandoned them, and that life would be restored to them like it was restored to the dry bones in the valley of Dura. He also prophesied one of the most sublime prophesies, the Ma'aseh Merkavah (The Chariot of God).

Gali Razya: An early Kabbalistic work by an unknown author.

Gan Raveh: A commentary on the Torah by Rabbi Chanoch Henoch Ersohn. (See Divrei Chanoch)

Gemara Avodah Zarah: Talmudic tractate in Seder Nezikin.

Gemara Bava Basra: Talmudic tractate in Seder Nezikin

Gemara Berachos: Talmudic tractate in Seder Zeraim

Gemara Chagigah: Talmudic tractate in Seder Moed.

Gemara Chullin: Talmudic tractate in Seder Kodshim.

Gemara Eruvin: Talmudic tractate in Seder Moed.

Gemara Gittin: Talmudic tractate in Seder Nashim.

Gemara Horiyos: Talmudic tractate in Seder Nezikin.

Gemara Kesuvos: Talmudic tractate in Seder Nashim.

Gemara Kiddushin: Talmudic tractate in Seder Nashim.

Gemara Krisus: Talmudic tractate in Seder Kodshim.

Gemara Menachos: Talmudic tractate in Seder Kodshim.

Gemara Mo'ed Katan: Talmudic tractate in Seder Moed.

Gemara Nedarim: Talmudic tractate in Seder Nashim.

Gemara Niddah: Talmudic tractate in Seder Taharos.

Gemara Pesachim: Talmudic tractate in Seder Moed.

Gemara Rosh HaShanah: Talmudic tractate in Seder Moed.

Gemara Sanhedrin: Talmudic tractate in Seder Nezikin.

Gemara Shabbos: Talmudic tractate in Seder Moed.

Gemara Sotah: Talmudic tractate in Seder Nashim.

Gemara Sukkah: Talmudic tractate in Seder Moed.

Gemara Ta'anis: Talmudic tractate in Seder Moed.

Gemara Yevamos: Talmudic tractate in Seder Nashim.

Gemara Yoma: Talmudic tractate in Seder Moed.

Gemara Zevachim: Talmudic tractate in Seder Kodshim.

Gilyon HaShas: Authored by Rabbi Akiva Eiger (1761-1837). Gilyon Hashas is comprised of his notes that appear in the margin of the Talmud. They are masterful because with just one cross reference, Rabbi Eiger asks extremely strong questions that are very difficult to answer. (See Rabbi Akiva Eiger)

Gina D'Pilpali: Written by Rabbi Meshulam Zusha Brandwein, a Chassidic contemporary who studied in Yeshivas Kol Torah and who wrote a commentary on the portions of the week.

Gr"a: An acronym for Gaon Rabbeinu Eliyahu (ben Shlomo Zalman) (1720-1797). He lived in White Russia, and was considered the greatest Lithuanian scholar of his time. (See Vilna Gaon)

Gr"a Imrei Noam: A commentary on Maseches Berachos attributed to Rabbi Eliyahu of Vilna. (See Vilna Gaon)

Hafla'ah (1730-1805):   Rabbi Pinchas Halevi Ish Horowitz, Poland and Germany. He was a halachic authority and Chassidic master. (See the Hafla'ah in his Panim Yafos). The Hafla'ah is his commentary on tractate Kesubos.

Hafla'ah Panim Yafos: The Panim Yafos is a work on the Chumash by the Hafla'ah. (See Hafla'ah)

Hagahos Mordechai: A work by Rabbi Mordechai ben Hillel. He was a descendent of the Ra'aviyah (Rabbi Eliezer ben Yoel HaLevi), and was one of the great Rabbis of Germany (Ashkenaz) at the end of the Tosafos period. Rabbi Mordechai was born circa 1240, and was martyred in 1298 together with his wife (a daughter of Rabbi Yechiel of Paris) and their five children in Nuremberg, Germany. Rabbi Mordechai was a disciple of Rabbi Meir (Maharam) of Rothenburg, as was his relative Rabbi Asher (Rosh), and his brother-in-law, Rabbi Meir HaCohen, author of the Hagahos Maimoniyos. The *Sefer* Mordechai, arranged according to tractates and topics, includes a collection of Tosafos, responsa, Halachic decisions and quotations from various books, mostly from the Rabbis of France and Germany. It is structured around the Alfasi code with additions at the beginning and end of each chapter. However, it includes many things not included in the Alfasi code, and sometimes not even in the Talmud. Apparently, the work did not reach completion due to Rabbi Mordechai's martyrdom, and his disciples added supplementary material to complete it. The *Sefer* Mordechai is found on most of the tractates of the Talmud, and it has influenced Halachic decisions for many generations. It was published in most editions of the Talmud, and through the generations many brief commentaries, additions and notes (some from Rabbi Moshe Isserlis, the Remah) were added and printed in later editions.

HaLeckach V'halibuv: A work on the Chumash and holidays based on Chassidic teachings, authored by Rabbi Avraham Halevi Schorr, a son of the famous Rabbi Gedalya Schorr.

Harav Yaakov Kaminetzsky (1891-1986):   He was the Rav of Tzitevian, Lithuania, and Toronto. He was also Rosh Yeshiva of Mesifta Torah V'Da'as, and considered to be one of the foremost gedolim in his time. He authored Emes L'Yaakov which began on the portions of the Torah and has since expanded to all of Shas.

Hilchos Tefillah (Laws of Prayer):   The portion of the Rambam dealing with laws of prayer.

Hillel: Known as Hillel Hazaken, he was a Tanna who lived about eleven years before the destruction of the second Temple. He was born in Bavel, but moved to Eretz Yisrael when he was forty. He studied in Eretz Yisrael under Shmaya and Avtalyon, and was appointed as Nasi of the Sanhedrin. His disciples became known as Beis Hillel. He was famous for his humility. One of his enactments was the Pruzbul document.

Hoshe'ah: Hoshe'ah ben Be'eri was a prophet. The book of Hoshe'ah is the first of the twelve briefer prophets.

Ibn Ezra (1092-1167):   He was born in Tudella and died in Cordova, Spain. A commentary by Rabbi Avraham Ibn Ezra on the entire Tanach is famous for it's grammatical and linguistic analysis. He excelled in philosophy, astronomy, mathematics, poetry and linguistics. He was also a physician. Rabbi Yehudah Halevi was a friend of his, and became his future father-in-law. It was said that during the Ibn Ezra's travels, he met with Rabbeinu Tam and spoke with him in Torah.

Igerers HaRamban: The legendary letter written by Rabbi Moshe ben Nachman, in which he guides his son to lead an ethical life filled with humility. (See Ramban)

Igros Moshe: Rabbi Moshe Feinstein (1895-1986). He was born in Uzda, Russia, and died in New York. He served as Rabbi in Luban, and became Rosh Yeshiva of Tiferes Yerushalayim. He headed the Moetzes Gedolei Hatorah, and was considered by many as the Gadol Hador and Posek HaDor. Igros Moshe is a classical work of his halachic responsa.

Imrei Noam: See Gr"a Imrei Noam.

Imrei Yosef: A commentary on the Chumash authored by Rabbi Yosef Meir Weiss (1838-1909). He was a Hungarian Rebbe and founder of the Spinka Chassidic dynasty.

Isaiah: Yeshayahu Ben Amotz, a prophet famous for his Messianic prophecies.

Ishbitzer (1800-1854):   Rabbi Mordechai Yosef Leiner founded the Ishbitz–Radzyn Chassidic dynasty in 1839, and acted as it's Rebbe. He was a disciple of Rabbi Simcha Bunim of Peshischa and of Rabbi Menachem Mendel of Kotsk. After Rabbi Mordechai Yosef left Kotsk, he settled in Ishbitz. He was one of the most original thinkers in Chassidism. His teachings were published in his major work Mei Hashiloach.

Iturei Torah: A collection of Chassidic commentaries on the weekly portion by R' Aharon Yaakov Greenberg (printed in Israel in 1985).

Jeremiah: Yirmiyahu ben Chilkiyahu was perceived as a harsh prophet who prophesied about the tragedies that would befall the Jews if they did not improve their ways. He was a Kohen, and authored Eichah and Yirmiyahu.

Job: Iyov was a person whose identity is shrouded in mystery. There are differing opinions who claim that he lived in the times of either Yaakov, Moshe, the spies, the judges or Ahasuevros. Some say he never lived. The book of Iyov describes his suffering, and it is intended to teach us how to deal with suffering in our own lives.

K'motzei Shallal Rav: An array of Talmudic commentaries and responsa, collected by Rabbi Avraham Yisrael Rosenthal.

Kaf Hachaim: (1870-1939) A halachic work incorporating kabbalah authored by Rabbi Yaakov Chaim Sofer. Rabbi Sofer was born in Baghdad, where he studied under Sephardi sages such as Rabbi Yosef Chaim (the Ben Ish Chai). In 1904, he journeyed to Palestine in order to pray at the graves of tzadikim. However, after visiting Jerusalem, he decided to settle there permanently. He studied in the Bet El yeshiva in the Old City of Jerusalem, well known for the study of Kabbalah. In 1909 he transferred to the newly founded Shoshanim L'David yeshiva, and it was there that he composed his works. In addition to the Kaf Hachaim, Rabbi Chayim authored Kol Yaakov on the laws of writing Torah scrolls, tefillin, and mezuzos, as well as focusing on the general laws of tefillin.

Kedushas Levi: Teachings of the Berdichever Rebbi on the Chumash and holidays. (See Berdichever Rebbe)

Keilim: A tractate of Mishnah in Seder Taharos.

Kesser Shem Tov: A collection of the teachings of the Ba'al Shem Tov. (See Ba'al Shem Tov)

Kitzur Shulchan Aruch: A concise work on Jewish law written by Rabbi Shlomo Ganzfried of Ungvar (at that time - in Hungary, 1804-1884). For most of his life he headed the Beis Din of Ungvar. Rabbi Ganzfried is famed primarily for his book Kitzur Shulchan Aruch, a summary of the most important halachic rulings in the Shulchan Aruch, most of which pertain to Orach Chaim, while others deal with other parts of the Shulchan Aruch. The Kitzur Shulchan Aruch also contains ethical admonitions and material about pious conduct. The Kitzur Shulchan Aruch is one of the most popular halachic codes in Ashkenazic communities. Though it is used primarily by common people, even scholars respected its opinions.

Kli Yakar: A dazzling commentary on the Chumash written by Rabbi Shlomo Efraim Ben Aharon Lunshitz (1550-1619). He was born in Poland and died in Prague, where he served as the Rabbi until his death.

Koheles Rabbah: The section of Midrash Rabbah on Koheles.

Koheles Yaakov: A work authored by Rabbi Shlomo Kluger (1783-1869), the Rabbi of Brody. He was born in Poland, and was the chief Dayan and preacher of Brody for more than fifty years. He wrote a great number of works – 160 volumes. His works address all branches of rabbinical literature as well as Biblical and Talmudic commentaries, but only some of these were published.

Koheles: Ecclesiastes is a book written by King Solomon, and describes the vanity of life when void of Yiras Hashem. It is traditionality read on Sukkos.

Kol Hatur: (Voice of the dove): It is a work written by Rabbi Hillel Mishkelov, a student of the Gr"a. It is centered on the Gr"a's teachings, primarily focusing on Moshiach and living in Eretz Yisrael.

Kol Yaakov: A Kabbalistic siddur printed in 1859 by Rabbi Yaakov Kopel Lipshitz, containing the kavanos of the Arizal, and explanations on all parts of the liturgy.

Ksav Sofer (1815-1871):   Rabbi Avraham Shmuel Binyamin Wolf Sofer (Schreiber) was the firstborn son of Rabbi Moshe Sofer, author of the Chasam Sofer. (See Chasam Sofer.) He was born in Pressburg (Bratislava, Slovakia). His mother, the daughter of Rabbi Akiva Eiger, was the second wife of R' Moshe Sofer. In 1839 his father passed away, and thus, at the age of twenty-four, he inherited his father's position as Rabbi of Pressburg, and the head of its yeshiva. He became one of the leaders of Hungarian Jewry and aided the religious settlement of the Holy Land. He authored thousands of responsa to legal inquiries, and wrote commentaries and novel insights to the Torah and the Talmud. None of these, however, were published during his lifetime. He passed away in Pressburg, and his son Rabbi Simcha Bunim, author of the Shevet Sofer, inherited his position. After his death, his Shu"t Ksav Sofer was published during the years 1873-1894.

Lamentations: The book of Eichah. See Eichah.

Leshem: A Kabbalistic work by Rabbi Shlomo Elyashiv (1841-1926). He was a Lithuanian Kabbalist. The full name of this book is "Leshem Shevo V'achlama." It discusses God's emanation of light leading to creation and revelation. The Leshem was the grandfather of Rabbi Yosef Shalom Elyashiv.

Lev Aryeh: A commentary on the Torah by Rabbi Yehudah Aryeh Leib ben Yehoshuah Hushki Willherms.

Levush: Halachic commentary by Rabbi Mordechai ben Avraham Yaffe (1535-1612). He lived in Prague, Czechoslavakia, and Poland, and was a student of the Rema.

Likutei Basar Likutei: An anthology on the Torah written by Rabbi Shmuel Alter (1885-1969).

Likutei Shas: Teachings on Shas by the Arizal.

Likutei Shoshanah: Written by the Noam Elimelech. (See Noam Elimelech)

Likutei Torah Ta'amei Hamitzvos: Teachings on the *Mitzvos* based on the lessons of the Arizal, written by R' Chaim Vital.

Likutei Torah: A commentary on the teachings of the Arizal, written by R' Chaim Vital.

Likutim Yekarim: A sefer which contains a precious collection of Chassidic teachings from the Besh"t, the Maggid of Mezritch, and R' Menachem Mendel from Premishlan.

Machberes Tzamid P'sil: The famed Machberes of Rabbi Menachem Ben Saruk (920-970). He was born in Tortosa, and was an eminent grammarian, philologist and skilled poet. He produced an early dictionary of the Hebrew language, and was involved in both literary and diplomatic matters.

Magen Avraham: A basic commentary on the Orach Chaim section of the Shulchan Aruch by Rabbi Avraham Gombiner (1634-1682).

He lived in Kalish, Poland, and was also a Kabbalist who stressed the opinions of the Arizal.

Maggid of Koznitz (1737-1814):   Rabbi Yisrael ben Shabsai Hopstein of Koznitz was a student of the Maggid of Mezritch, and R' Elimelech of Lizensk. He was a Chassidic master, Talmudist and halachist who authored the sefer Avodas Yisrael. (see Ner Yisrael)

Maggid of Mezritch (1704-1772):   Rabbi Dov Ber Ben Avraham was one of the closest students of the Ba'al Shem Tov, and his successor. He spread Chassidus throughout Eastern Europe. His yeshiva was a training ground for many Chassidic masters such as Rabbi Levi Yitzchak of Berdichev, Reb Menachem Mendel of Vitebsk, Reb Aharon of Karlin, and Rabbi Shneur Zalman of Liadi.

Maharal (1526-1609):   An acronym for Moreinu Harav Rebbi Yehudah Loewe (ben Betzalel). He was Chief Rabbi in Moravia, Posen and Prague, and author of numerous Torah works. He was a Talmudist, philosopher and Kabbalist, and was recognized as one of the greatest figures in Jewish thought.

Maharam (1558-1616):   An acronym for Moreinu Harav Meir ben Gedalyah of Lublin, Poland. He was a Rav and Rosh Yeshiva who wrote responsa, a commentary on the Talmud, and sermons based on the Torah.

Maharam Chagiz (1672-1751):   Rabbi Moshe Chagiz, son of Rabbi Yaacov Chagiz (author of Halachos Ketannos), was born in Jerusalem. Rabbi Chagiz studied under his grandfather, Rabbi Moshe Galante II, and traveled extensively in Europe to raise funds for his yeshivah in Jerusalem. Rabbi Chagiz was renowned for his opposition to Shabbsai Tzvi. In 1738 Rabbi Chagiz returned to Israel and settled in Tzfas. He died in Beirut, and was buried in Sidon. Only a few of his responsa were published.

Maharsha (1555-1632):   An acronym for Moreinu Harav Shlomo Eidels of Ostroh, Poland. He was a Rav and Rosh Yeshiva who authored commentaries on the Halachic and Aggadic sections of the Babylonian Talmud.

Maharshal (1510-1573):   An acronym for Moreinu Harav Shlomo Luria. He lived in Poland, and was a Rav and author of works on the Talmud, Halachah, and *Rashi's* commentary on the Chumash.

Makkos: Talmudic tractate in Seder Nezikin.

Malachi: The last of the twelve brief prophets. It concludes with the prophecy about Eliyahu Hanavi's arrival turning the hearts of all people back to God. We know that he was a part of the Anshei Knesses Hagedolah, the Great Assembly that met in the Holy Temple in Jerusalem at the beginning of the Second Temple era. We also know that he was one of the last three prophets to be included in the era of prophets. The other two were Chaggai and Zechariah. The Biblical commentator, Rabbi Avraham Ibn Ezra (1089-1164), says that it was because there would be no prophets after him that Malachi told the Jews (3:22), "Keep in remembrance the teaching of Moshe, My servant." The prophetic writings close with one of Malachi's more well-known prophecies that Eliyahu the Prophet will herald the Messianic era (3:23): "Lo, I will send you Eliyahu the Prophet before the coming of the great and awesome day of the L-rd." There is a minority opinion in the Talmud that says that Malachi was actually Ezra the Scribe. There is another opinion that he was Mordechai from the story of the holiday of Purim. However, the opinion of the majority of the sages in the Talmud is that Malachi was a separate individual.

Ma'or Vashemesh: R' Kalonymos Kalman HaLevi Epstein (1751-1823) was born in Cracow to his father Rabbi Aharon. R' Kalonymos was a disciple of R' Elimelech of Lizensk, the Seer of Lublin, and other great Chassidic leaders. His work Ma'or VaShemesh is considered one of the foundations of Chassidic thought. It was published in 1842 by his disciple R' Yisrael Hillel Westreich.

Maseches Sofrim: "The Tractate of the Scribes" is a non-canonical Talmudic treatise dealing especially with the rules relating to the preparation of the holy books, as well as with the regulations for the reading of the Law. It belongs to the so-called "smaller tractates," a term applied to about fifteen works in rabbinical literature, each containing all the important material bearing on a single subject. The work is generally thought to have originated in the eighth century. It was finally redacted about the middle of the eighth century. Sofrim is not part of the Babylonian Talmud or Jerusalem Talmud. There are a few points of Halachah which Rabbis have decided straight from Sofrim, since they are not mentioned in the Talmud.

Mateh Ephraim: A Halachic work by Rabbi Ephraim Zalman Margolis from Warsaw.

Mateh Moshe: A work on the laws of prayer and holidays authored by Rabbi Moshe Mos of Premysl (1540-1606). He was a Rav and halachist. The name Mos is thought to be an abbreviation which stands for "Machzikei Torah," or "Marbitzei Torah."

Matnos Kehunah: A commentary on the entire Midrash Rabbah by Rabbi Yissachar Ber HaKohen (1520-1590), a student of the Rema. He lived in Poland, emigrated to Eretz Yisrael, and was buried in Chevron.

Matzeves Moshe: An ethical and homiletic treatise from Rabbi Moshe Asher, the Maggid of Vashilashak.

Me'am Lo'ez: A massive commentary on the entire Tanach written in Ladino. It was begun by Rabbi Yaakov Culi ben Machir (1689-1732). He lived in Constantinople, and was a disciple and brother-in-law of the

Mishneh Lemelech.

Mechilta: Tanaaic, Halachic Midrash on the book of Exodus.

Megaleh Amukos: A Chassidic Kabbalistic work on the Chumash, written by Rabbi Nosson Nota Shapira (1585-1632). He lived in Poland, and was Rav and Rosh Yeshiva of Crakow.

Megillah: A Talmudic tractae in Seder Moed.

Megillas Esther: The Book of Esther, written during the Babalonian exile, describing Haman's plot against the Jewish people and their deliverance from it. This was the last of the miracles to be written down and accepted into the Written Law. What seems at first glance to be a string of mere coincidences is later revealed as Hashem manipulating events in a concealed way.

Meiras Einayim: The preface to "Ba'al Shem Tov Al Hatorah" laying down the fundamental teachings of Chassidus. It was written by Rabbi Shimon Menachem Mendel Gorbachov.

Meor Einayim: A Chassidic work on the weekly *parshah* by the Chernobyler Rebbe. (See Chernobyler Rebbe)

Meshech Chochmah: A commentary on the Torah by Rabbi Meir Simcha HaKohen of Dvinsk (1843-1926). Rabbi Meir Simcha also wrote a commentary on the Rambam's Mishneh Torah called Ohr Somayach. His counterpart was the legendary Rogatchover Rebbe, Rabbi Yosef Rosen. The two had great respect for each other, and would consult each other on Halachic issues.

Mesillas Yesharim (Path of the Just):   A classic work which maps out a step by step process of defeating the yetzer hara, by Rabbi Moshe Chaim Luzzato (1707-1746), otherwise known as the Ramchal, per his initials. He received tremendous praise from the Vilna Gaon who said that the first eight chapters of Mesillas Yesharim have not even one superfluous word. (See Ramchal)

Michah: The sixth book of the twelve briefer prophets in which he prophesied about the Messianic era when "swords will be beaten into ploughshares, and spears into pruning knives" indicating the cessation of war.

Midrash Aggadah: A Midrashic collection based on the works of Rabbi Moshe Hadarshan. He was an eleventh-century compiler of Midrashic anthology, known as "Yedos Rabbi Moshe Hadarshan." He is quoted by *Rashi* on Chumash in a number of places.

Midrash Ne'elam: A section of the Zohar containing Kabbalistic Mid*Rashi*m.

Midrash Psikta D'Rav Kahana: A collection of Midrashim on the Chumash by Rav Kahana. He is believed to be the Amoraic sage Rav Kahana who was the disciple of Rav.

Midrash Shocher Tov: A Midrash on Psalms, also known as Midrash Tehillim.

Midrash Tanchumah: Mid*Rashi*m on the Chumash attributed to the Amora, Rabbi Tanchuma bar Aba. He lived in Eretz Yisrael during the late fourth century.

Minchas Yehudah: A commentary on Chumash by Rabbi Yehudah ben Eliezer of Troyes, written in 1313.

Mishlei: Proverbs; a book of wise teachings written by Shlomo Hamelech.

Mishnah Berachos: A mishnah in the tractate Berachos in Seder Zeraim.

Mishnah Berurah: A commentary on the Orach Chaim section of the Shulchan Aruch by Rebbi Yisrael Meir Hakohen Kagan, the Chofetz Chaim. (See Chofetz Chaim)

Mishnah: The first body of Oral Law, committed to writing by the Tanna Rabbi Yehudah Hanassi. (See Rabbi Yehudah Hanassi)

Mishnas Chachamim: A book on attaining Torah by Rabbi Moshe Chagiz, son of Rabbi Yaakov Chagiz, the author of Halachos Ketannos. (See Maharam Chagiz)

Mishpetei Shmuel: The full title is Teshuvos Mishpetei Shmuel, and it is composed of 134 responsa and treatises of Talmudic commentary. It was authored by Rabbi Shmuel, son of Rabbi Moshe Kalei, who was born around the year 1500, probably in Italy. He studied in Italy at first, and later in Ottoman, Greece. He was a student of Rabbi Shmuel De Medinah (the Maharshdam) and Rabbi David Kohen of Corfu (the Radach). Later, he studied under Rabbi Binyamin son of Matityah Marta (author of Teshuvos Binyamin Ze'ev). He then married his daughter, and eventually inherited his position as Rabbi of the city. He later moved to the city of Vidin, where he accepted a rabbinical position. He passed away around the year 1585.

Modjitzer Rebbe (1755-1856)**:**   Rebbe Yechezkel Taub of Kuzmir, Poland; the first Modjitzer Rebbe. His Rebbe was the Seer of Lublin. His son and succeeder, Reb Shmuel Eliyahu Taub was famous for creating Chassidic song. The Modzitzer Rebbes and their Chassidim are well known for their uniquely inspiring melodies, and for their devotion to serious learning of Torah and Talmud.

Molgenitzer Rebbe: Rebbi Meir Yechiel of Molgenitz, Poland; Chassidic Rebbe and Rebbe of the town.

Moreh Nevuchim (Guide for the Perplexed):   A philosophical work written by the Rambam, Rabbi Moshe ben Maimon. (See Rambam)

Mussaf Rashi: A collection of Rashi's commentaries from elsewhere in the Talmud that pertain to a passage in Tanach or Talmud.

Nachal Kedumim: A commentary on the Torah by Rabbi Chaim Joseph David Azulai (1724-1806). (See Chida)

Navlos Chochmah: A book on emunah, written by Rabbi Yosef Sholom De Lemadigo (Slicia 1631).

Nechemia: A member of the Anshei Knessses Hagedolah. He gave up a prominent position in order to return to Eretz Yisrael with Ezra and thus save the Jewish settlement in Eretz Yisrael.

Ner Mitzvah: A book on Chanukah and its attendant theological issues. Authored by the Maharal. (See Maharal)

Ner Yisrael: Glosses on the works of Rav Hai Gaon by Rabbi Yisrael ben Shabsai Hopstien (1737–1814). He was known as the Maggid of Koznitz, and was one of the more important Chassidic leaders of Poland during the 18th and early 19th century. He was an iluy and student of Reb Shmelke of Nikolsburg, the Maggid of Mezritch, and Reb Elimelech of Lizensk. He wrote many books on Chassidus and Kabbalah, including Avodas Yisrael (see Ner Yisrael) on Chumash and Pirkei Avos. He founded the Koznitz Chasidic dynasty (see Maggid of Koznitz).

Nesivos Shalom: A commentary on the weekly portion and holidays by Rabbi Shalom Noach Berzovsky, the Slonimer Rebbe. (See Slonimer Rebbe)

Netzach Yisrael: A book on exile and redemption. Authored by the Maharal. (See Maharal)

Nezer Hakodesh: A sefer on the Midrash by Rabbi Yechiel Michel bar Uziel (Yasnitz 1719).

Noam Elimelech: A collection of Chassidic teachings on the Chumash, by the Great Rebbe; R' Elimelech from Lizensk (1717-1787), Galicia, Poland. The Noam Elimelech was a disciple of the Maggid of Mezritch. The Noam Elimelech focuses primarily on the role of the tzaddik. His disciples include the Chozeh MiLublin, the Maggid of Koznitz and Reb Menachem Mendel of Riminov. Reb Elimelech's brother was the famous Reb Zusha of Anipoli.

Ohev Yisrael: A Chassidic work on the Chumash by Rabbi Avraham Yehoshua Heschel of Apt, Poland (1748-1825). He was known as the Apter Rebbe, and was known as the lover of Israel because he stressed the importance of loving every Jew. He was a disciple of Rebbi Elimelech of Lizensk.

Ohr Gedalyahu: A collection of teachings by Reb Gedalya Schorr (1910-1979) on the weekly portions and holidays, using Chassidic sources, and heavily based on the teachings of the Sfas Emes. He was born in Poland, and lived and died in the USA.

Ohr Hachaim Hakadosh: A commentary on the Chumash by Rabbi Chaim ben Atar (1696-1743). He was a Kabbalist and Talmudist who lived in Morocco and Italy, but eventually settled in Eretz Yisrael. His massive commentary on the Torah takes its readers through the full gamut of Paradise. One of the Ohr Hachaim's disciples was the Chidah.

Ohr Hameir: A commentary on the Torah, Nach and festivals authored by Rabbi Zev Wolf of Zhitomir. He was a close disciple of the Maggid of Mezritch.

Ohr Torah: Perushim on the Torah from Rabbi Uri Kalmayer, grandson of the Maharsha. (Lublin 1672)

Onkelos: The running Aramaic translation and interpretation on the Torah by the proselyte Onkelos.

Orach Chaim: The first of four sections of the Shulchan Aruch; it deals with the daily laws, Shabbos and holidays.

Orchos Chaim Spinka: A work writtten by Rabbi Nachman Kahane, Rav of Spinka (1905-1976), on the Shulchan Aruch.

Otzar HaMinhagim: A book on Jewish customs written by Rabbi Zev Reichman.

Parashas Derachim: A *sefer* authored by Rabbi Yehudah ben Rabbi Samuel Rosanes (1657-1727), who was born in Constantinople. He was a student and son-in-law of his uncle, Rabbi Avraham Rosanes, one of the Torah scholars of Constantinople. Rabbi Yehudah was considered the greatest Torah scholar of Constantinople in his generation. After his death, his responsa and novellae were collected by his student Rabbi Yaakov Culi, author of Yalkut Me'am Lo'ez, and arranged according to the order of Maimonides' Mishneh Torah under the title of Mishneh LaMelech. Parashas Derachim is one of other well-known works authored by Rabbi Yehudah, which includes twenty-six discourses on a variety of subjects.

Peirush HaMishnayos: A commentary on the Mishnah written by the Rambam. (See Rambam)

Peninim M'Shulchan Ha'Gra: A collection of teachings by the Gaon, Rabbi Eliyahu of Vilna on the weekly portion. (See Vilna Gaon)

Peninim Yekarim: A compilation of thoughts on Sefer Bereishis by Rabbi Shimon Betzalel Neiman (1860-1942), Crakow.

Perisha (1555-1614): Rabbi Yehoshua Volk ben Rabbi Alexander HaCohen (Katz) was born in Poland. He was a disciple of Rabbi Shlomo Luria (Maharshal) and R' Moshe Isserlis (Remah). His father-in-law, the wealthy Rabbi Yisrael ben Rabbi Yoseph, built a study hall in Lemberg for him and aided in publishing his books, and R' Yehoshua named a series of his books Beis Yisrael in his father-in-law's honor. He became famous for his two compilations on the entire Tur: the Prishah (a brief commentary) and the Drishah (an extensive discussion of the Tur and the Beis Yosef). He also made additions to Rabbi Moshe Isserlis' Darkei Moshe, and authored the Sefer Me'iras Einayim (Sema), an important commentary to the Shulchan Aruch, Choshen Mishpat, as well as other works. He was a leader of the Council of the Four Lands, and his disciples were leading luminaries of the next generation.

Pesach Einayim: A book by the Chidah. (See Chidah)

Pesachim: A Talmudic tractate in Seder Moed.

Pesikta: A collection of Midrashim. There are various ones; for example, Pesikta D'Rav Kahana, Pesikta Rabbasi, and Pesikta Zutrasa.

Pirkei D'Rabbi Eliezer: A Midrashic work composed by the Tanna, Rebbi Eliezer ben Hyrcanus. He was also known as Rebbi Eliezer Hagadol. (See Rabbi Eliezer Hagadol)

Piskei Teshuvos: One of the most comprehensive Halachic commentaries to the Mishnah Berurah. It was written by Rabbi Simcha Rabinowitz, Jerusalem, and includes many sources and relevant halachos for today's day and age. It also introduces a host of other minhagim that are not included in the Mishnah Berurah.

Pri Eitz Chaim: A book on the Kabbalistic teachings of the Arizal, written by his chief disciple Rabbi Chaim Vital. (See Arizal)

Pri Ha'aretz: A commentary on the Chumash by Rebbi Menachem Mendel from Vitebsk (1730-1788). He was a student of the Maggid of Mezritch, and a friend of Rabbi Shneur Zalman of Liadi. In 1777 he emigrated to Eretz Yisrael, living at first in Tzefas, and then in Teveria.

Pri Tzaddik: A collection of teachings on the Chumash by the Chassidic sage Rabbi Tzaddok HaKohen (1823-1900). He lived in Lublin, and was known to be a very deep thinker.

R' Simoi: He lived at the time of Rav Gamliel, during the period of the Churban, and was known as "kadosh," due to the fact that he was killed "al kiddush Hashem."

R' Baruch of Medzibozh (1753-1811):   Rebbi Baruch ben Yechiel was the grandson of the Ba'al Shem Tov, and studied with the Maggid of Mezritch. He was the first Rebbe to place an emphasis on living with royalty and regality.

R' Chaim of Volozhin (1749-1821):   He was a leading disciple of the Vilna Gaon, and founded the famous Yeshiva in Volozhin. He was recognized as the non-chassidic leader of Russia and Lithuania. His most famous work was the Nefesh Hachaim on religious philosophy, stressing the importance of Torah study.

R' Levi Yitzchok of Berdichev: See Keudshas Levi or Berdichever Rebbe.

R' Schora: A third to fourth century Babylonian sage who was a disciple of Rav Huna. Little is known about his life and family.

R' Yehoshua ben Levi: A first-generation Amora, and leader of the city Lod. He studied under Rebbi Yehudah Hanassi, and he focused specifically on the Aggada. Rav Chiya and Rabbi Yochanan were his primary disciples. He was one of those who merited entering the World To Come alive.

R' Yitzchak Isaac of Zidichov (1805-1873):   He was a noted Chassidic Rabbi, and the author of Likutei Maharya. He was the son of Rabbi Yissachar Barish, who was the brother of Rabbi Tzvi Hirsh of Zidichov (1763–1831). Rabbi Yitzchak Isaac was a close disciple of Rabbi Tzvi Hirsh of Zidichov until the latter's death. He later studied under Rabbi

Shalom of Belz.

Ra'avad (1120-1197):   An acronym for Rabbi Avraham Ben David of Posquieres, Province, France. He is famous for his critical notes on the Mishnah Torah of the Rambam. He also authored many other works.

Rabbanan: This can either refer to a rabinically instituted mitzvah, or to the consensus of the Sages.

Rabbeinu Bachya (1263-1340):   He was a student of the Rashba, and wrote a commentary on the Chumash that covers many levels, including peshat, Midrash, philosophy and Kabbalah.

Rabbeinu Eliyahu Mizrachi (1450-1525):   He lived in Constantinople, and was the Chief Rabbi of the Turkish Empire. He wrote a super commentary explaining Rashi's interpretation of the Chumash.

Rabbeinu Yeshaya Mitarani (1180-1250):   Rabbi Yeshaya Di-trani ben Mal Hazaken. He was an Italian scholar in Venice known as the Rid. He wrote on almost the entire Talmud and also wrote responsa.

Rabbi Acha: A first-generation Savora sage. Even so, he was recorded frequently in the Talmud.

Rabbi Akiva Eiger (1751-1837):   He was born in Eisenstadt, Hungary. He was an outstanding Talmudic scholar and Halachic authority. He served as Rabbi of Posen, and became the father-in-law of the Chasam Sofer (Rabbi Moshe Sofer, Rabbi of Pressburg), when his daughter Sarah married him as a second wife.

Rabbi Amnon of Maraz/Mainz: He lived in Germany during the eleventh century. He composed the "Unesaneh Tokef" prayer said on the high holidays, after the archbishop cut off his hands and legs as a punishment for refusing to convert to Christianity.

Rabbi Asi: A Kohen and first-generation Amorah. He was a contemporary of Rav, and lifelong friend of Rav Ami.

Rabbi Avahu: He was a third-generation Amora. He lived in Eretz Yisrael, and was a student of Rabbi Yochanan.

Rabbi Chaiya Bar Brei D'Rav Ada of Yaffo: He was an Amorah in Eretz Yisrael, and student of R' Zeira.

Rabbi Chaninah: A first-generation Tanna who lived in Eretz Yisrael. Most of his teachings focus on the area of character imporvemnt.

Rabbi Chiya Bar Ashi: He was a student of Rav, Shmuel and Zeira, and was a man of great piety and holiness.

Rabbi Dustoi: He was a Tanna, and the son of R' Yannai (the Tanna) and Talmid of Rabbi Meir. He was buried in Achbara.

Rabbi Eliezer HaGadol: He was also known as Rebbi Eliezer ben Hyrcanus, a second-generation Tanna who lived after the destruction of the second Temple. He married Ima Shalom who was a sister of Rabban Gamliel the Nasi. He was the author of Pirkei D'Rebbi Eliezer, a Midrashic work.

Rabbi Levi: A third-generation Amorah, he was known as a great orator. He was the official darshan for twenty-two years in the yeshiva of Rabbi Yochanan.

Rabbi Meir Yechiel from Ostrovtsa: A Chassidic Rabbi in Poland at the turn of the twentieth century (1852-1928).

Rabbi Meir: A Tanna who descended from a proselyte, and married Bruria. His main teacher was Rabbi Akiva. He is buried in Teveria, and is commonly known as Rabbi Meir Ba'al Ha-Nes due to his reputation as a miracle worker.

Rabbi Moshe Hadarshan: He was an eleventh-century compiler of

Midrashic anthology, known as "Yedos Rabbi Moshe Hadarshan." (See Midrash Aggadah)

Rabbi Moshe Wolfson: He is the Mashgiach Ruchani of Mesifta Torah V'Da'as, and Rav of Beis Midrash Emunas Yisrael. He is the author of Emunas Itecha.

Rabbi Shimon Bar Yochai: He was among the greatest of the fourth generation of Tannaim, and was the author of the Zohar. He was one of the five students of Rabbi Akiva, and he married the daughter of Rabbi Pinchas ben Yair. Rebbi Yehudah Hanasi was one of his students.

Rabbi Shimon Ben Gamliel: Otherwise known as the Rashbag, he was a Tanna who succeeded his father Gamliel as Nasi of the Sanhedrin.

Rabbi Shmuel bar Nachman: A third-century Amora who lived in Eretz Yisrael. He is one of the most famous Aggadists.

Rabbi Shmuel Bar Nachmeni: An Amora who lived in Eretz Yisrael. He was a student of Rabbi Yochanan ben Eliezer.

Rabbi Yannai: He was an early third-century Amora, and a descendant of Eli HaKohen. He studied under R' Chiah. Rabbi Yannai's daughter married R' Chiya's son. Rav Yannai lived in the upper Galilee and established a yeshiva there. His disciples were Rabbi Yochanan and Reish Lakish. He was a Halachist and an Aggadist. He was extremely wealthy and charitable, and was recognized as being extremely pious and humble.

Rabbi Yehudah ben Teimah: A Tanna, famous for his legendary statement to be "as brazen as a leopard, light as an eagle, fast as a deer, and mighty as a lion to do the will of your father in heaven" (Avos 5:23).

Rabbi Yehudah Hanasi: Rabbi Yehudah the Prince was the primary leader of the Jewish community of Judea toward the end of the second century CE. He was also chief editor of the Mishnah, and head of the Sanhedrin. Rabbi Yehudah was a son of Rabban Shimon ben Gamliel, and was considered to be exceedingly righteous. He was also very wealthy, and had close ties with the Roman Emperor Antoninus.

Rabbi Yehudah: He was a son of Rabbi Ilai, a Tanna, and a student of Rabbi Elazar Ben Azaria and was one of the five students of Rabbi Akiva. He was a contemporary of R' Meir, and is one of the most-mentioned Tannaim in the Mishna. He authored the Safra, known as Toras Kohanim – the B'raisa compilation on sefer Vayikra. "One Pious man" mentioned in Talmudic stories sometimes refers to him. He was known for his extreme devotion to Torah study and its dissemination, despite the great poverty prevalent in his generation.

Rabbi Yochanan: A second-century Amora, and among the greatest of the Amoraim. He studied under Rebbi Yehudah Hanasi, and established a yeshiva in Teveria. He was unusually handsome. He suffered great loss in his life and witnessed the deaths of his ten children. His chief disciple was Reish Lakish, and he had a principal hand in writing the Yerushalmi (the Jerusalem Talmud).

Rabbi Yonasan: He was a late Tanna. He was a friend of Rabbi Chiya and Rabbi Yoshiya, and he compiled B'raisos together with them.

Rabbi Yosef Cairo (1488-1575):   He was born in Toledo, Spain, and died in Tzefas, Eretz Yisrael. He was the Chief Rabbi of Tzefas, and author of the Shulchan Aruch.

Radak (1160-1235):   An acronym for Rabbeinu David Kimchi from Provence, France. He wrote a famous commentary on Tanach.

Radvaz (1479-1573):   An acronym for Rabbi David ben Zimrah. He was born in Spain, and later became Chief Rabbi of Egypt. He attracted illustrious students like Rabbi Bezalel Ashkenazi, author of the Shitah

Mekubetzes and the Arizal. He wrote over 3,000 responsa.

Rambam (1135-1204):   An acronym for Rabbi Moshe ben Maimon. He was born in Cordova, Spain, and died in Cairo, Egypt. He was buried in Teveria, Israel. He was a Talmudist, Halachist, philosopher and physician. He wrote a commentary on the Mishnah, and codified all Jewish laws in his Mishneh Torah, also called Yad Hachazakah. He also wrote Moreh Nevuchim on philosophy.

Ramban (1194-1270):   An acronym for Rabbi Moshe ben Nachman. He was born in Gerona, Spain and died in Eretz Yisrael. He was known as a Talmudist, Halachist, Kabbalist and physician. The Ramban authored numerous works including a popular commentary on the Chumash.

Ramchal (1707-1746):   An acronym for Rabbi Moshe Chaim Luzzato of Padua, Italy. A Talmudist, Kabbalist and philosopher, he authored the Mesilas Yesharim (see Mesilas Yesharim), and Derech Hashem that discusses God's purpose in Creation. He also wrote Da'as Tevunos, among many other Kabbalistic works. The Gr"a said that had the Ramchal been alive in his time, he would have walked from Vilna to learn at his feet.

Ran (1240-1375):   An acronym for Rabbeinu Nissim. He was from Gerona, Spain and famous for his Talmudic commentary. He also wrote Drashos Haran which discusses the fundamentals of Judaism.

Rashbam (1085-1174):   An acronym for Rabbeinu Shmuel ben Meir from France. He was a grandson of Rashi, and a brother of Rabbeinu Tam. They were both leading Tosafists.

Rashbi: An acronym for Rabbi Shimon Bar Yochai, a Tannaic sage who authored the Zohar. The Rashbi was one of Rebbi Akiva's students, and he married the daughter of Rabbi Pinchas ben Yair. One of the Rashbi's students was Rebbi Yehudah Hanasi. (See also Rabbi Shimon Bar Yochai)

Rashi (1040-1105):   An acronym for Rabbi Shlomo Yitzchaki. He is considered the father of all Bible commentary, and wrote on almost the entire Tanach and Talmud. His writings are considered to be the basic way of understanding the text.

Rav Ada: A fifth-generation Amora, who was a great grandson of Shmuel.

Rav Aharon Kotler (1892-1962):   He was born in the Russian Empire, and studied under the Alter of Slabodka, Rav Nosson Zvi Finkel. He married the daughter of Rabbi Isser Zalman Meltzer, the Rosh Yeshiva of Kletzk, Poland and Eitz Chaim, Jerusalem. Rav Aharon Kotler was an illuy and the founder of Beis Midrash Gevoha in Lakewood, New Jersey. He was one of the key figures responsible for building Torah in America.

Rav Ami: A first-generation Amora, a Kohen, and life-long friend of Rav Asi.

Rav Avin: A third-generation Amora who lived in Babylonia. He was a disciple of Rav Huna, and eventually settled in Eretz Yisrael where he studied under Rav Ami.

Rav Baruch Epstein (1860-1941):   A Lithuanian scholar from Pinsk. He was the author of Torah Temima on the Chumash. This work cites the Talmudic pieces relevant to the verses upon which he comments and elucidates. Rabbi Baruch Epstein was the son of Rabbi Yechiel Michel Halevi Epstein, author of the Aruch Hashulchan (see Torah Temimah).

Rav Chanina bar Chamma: A first-generation Amora from Bavel, who came to Eretz Yisrael and studied under Rebbi Yehudah Hanasi and R' Chiya. He was a close friend of R' Yehoshua ben Levi. He became wealthy, and opened a yeshiva in Tzippori.

Rav Eivu: He was the father of Rav, and the brother of Rabbi Chiya.

Rav Gidel: He was a late-third-century Babylonian Amora, and a young pupil of Rav.

Rav Hoshaya Rabba: A Babylonian Amora at the end of the third century to the beginning of the fourth century. He was a pupil of Rav Huna, and lived in Nehardeah and Pumpedisa before emigrating to Eretz Yisrael. He was descended from Eli HaKohen.

Rav Huna: A son of Rebbi Yehoshua, who was a third-century teacher in Babylonia. He was the first Rosh Yeshiva in Sura after Shmuel.

Rav Kahana: He was a student of Rav in Babylonia, and later went to study in the academy of Rabbi Yochanan in Eretz Yisrael.

Rav Masnuh: A Babylonian Amora, and a student of Rav and Shmuel.

Rav Naftoli of Ropschitz (1760-1827):   Rav Naftoli Tzvi Horowitz of Ropschitz, Galicia. He was a disciple of Reb Elimelech of Lizensk. The Ropschitzer, as he was known, was famed for his humor and sharp wit. As a master of mystical interpretation, he wrote the Zerah Kodesh on the Torah and festivals. His closest student was Rabbi Chaim of Sanz (See Zerah Kodesh).

Rav Nassan Bar Minyomi: An Amora, and a student of Rav.

Rav Pinchas: An Amora, and a student of Rava.

Rav Saadia Gaon (882-942):   He was the head of the Yeshiva in Pumpedisa. He authored many works in all areas of Torah, including Emunos V'deos on philosophy. Rav Saadia Gaon was a fierce opponent of Karaism.

Rav Simon: There were two Amoraim with this name. One, Rav Simon Bar Abba, was a colleague of Rabbi Yochanan; and a later one who was a colleague of Rav Ashi.

Rav Yudan: A fourth-century Amora, he was a pupil of Rabbi Aba. Rav

Yudan is quoted only in the Jerusalem Talmud and Midrash.

Rav: A very early Amoraic sage; some say that he was even a Tanna. His uncle was R' Chiya, and he studied under Rebbi Yehudah Hanasi. His real name was Rabbi Aba Aricha (the tall one). He founded a yeshiva in Sura, Babylonia, and was a contemporary of Shmuel.

Rava: A fourth-generation Amora who lived in Bavel, he is famous for his debates with his study partner Abaye (See Abaye). He married the daughter of Rav Chisda.

Ravina: A fifth-century Amora.

Reb Chaim Vital (1542-1620):   He became the closest disciple of the Arizal in Tzefas, and was responsible for recording most of the Arizal's known teachings.

Reb Menachem Mendel of Rimanov (1755-1815):   He was a student of the Maggid of Mezritch, and was known as a pious person and miracle worker. His teachings were published in the Divrei Menachem and Menachem Tzion.

Reb Shmuel bar Nachmeini: A third-century Amora who lived in Eretz Yisrael, and was a famous Aggadist.

Reb Simchah Bunim of Peshischa (1765-1827):   He was a student of the Seer of Lublin and Rabbi Yaakov Yitzchok, the Yehudi HaKadosh. He stressed truth, faith, and humility, and used stories as an important teaching aid. His writings are published in Chedvas Simcha, Kol Simcha and Niflaos Rabbi Bunim. His most famous disciple was Rabbi Menachem Mendel of Kotzsk.

Reb Yehudah HaLevi (1095-1150):   He was born in Todedo, Spain, and died in Eretz Yisrael. He was a philosopher, physician, poet, and composer of liturgy. He was a student of the Rif, and according to some was the father-in-law of the Ibn Ezra. He moved to Eretz Yisrael, where he was tragically murdered by an Arab on his horse, who brutally trampled him to death.

Reb Yirmiya Bar Aba: An Amora, and a student of Rav.

Reb Yitzchak: Where found in Halachic teachings, Reb Yitzchak refers to Reb Yitzchak bar Acha. Where seen in Aggadic teachings, Reb Yitzchak refers to Reb Yitzchak bar Pinchas.

Reb Yoseph: An Amorah at the turn of the fourth century. He was blind, and as a result became singularly proficient in the Targum, as well as in Mishna and B'raisos. He was called 'Sinai' because of his uniquely vast knowledge (in contrast to his friend Rabba, who was unique in his sharp analysis). At one point he forgot his learning due to illness, and his students would remind him of his teachings. He was a student of Rav Yehudah, and a Rebbi of Abaye and Rava.

Rebbi: A title used for Rebbi Yehudah Hanasi. (See Rabbi Yehudah Hanasi)

Rebbe Pinchas from Koretz (1726-1791):   A disciple of the Ba'al Shem Tov who was deeply involved in communal affairs, and collected money for the poor of Eretz Yisrael. He died during his own journey to live in Eretz Yisrael.

Rebbe Yehudah ben Beseira: He was a Tanna during the time of the Beis HaMikdash. He resided in Netzivin, Syria, and was known for his great wisdom. He merited longevity; some even say he lived on after the destruction, and until the early Amoraic period. [There are those who link him with the early Tannaim, the "Bnei B'seira" who were Nesiim before Hillel. In that case he would have a lifespan of some two hundred and fifty years. Others say that he was from those early Tanaaim.] He testified that he was a descendant of the "revived bones" of the prophet

Yechezkel.

Rebbi Aba Bar Kahana: A late third-century Amora, his father Kahana was a pupil of Rav. Rabbi Aba Bar Kahana was one of the greatest Aggadists.

Rebbi Alexandry: A third-century Amora, and a leading Aggadist urging people to do good deeds.

Rebbi Avahu: A third-generation Amora who lived in Eretz Yisrael, and was a disciple of Rabbi Yochanan.

Rebbi Avdimi Bar Chamah Bar Chasah: A third-generation Amora who lived in Haifa, Eretz Yisrael.

Rebbi Binyomin Bar Yefes: An Amora who was a student of Rabbi Yochanan.

Rebbi Chaninah ben Dosa: A first-generation Tanna who lived in Eretz Yisrael prior to the destruction of the second Temple. He was known for his saintliness, and focused intensely on areas on self improvement.

Rebbi Elazar Ben Shamua: He was a Tanna and the last of the Ten Martyrs. He was murdered on Shabbos eve as he recited Kiddush, though he did merit longevity. He was a Kohen, a student of Rabbi Yehudah ben Bava and Rabbi Akiva, and the Rebbi of Rabbi Yehudah Hanasi.

Rebbi Elazar Ben Pedas: An Amora who originated in Bavel but ascended to Eretz Yisrael and became a prime student of Rabbi Yochanan. He was deemed "master of Eretz Yisrael" due to his greatness. He would become engrossed in his learning to the extent that he would forget his surroundings.

Rebbi Nachman of Breslov (1772-1810):   Rabbi Nachman's mother, Faigy, was the granddaughter of the Ba'al Shem Tov. Rabbi Nachman stressed serving God with joy and through meditation. Together with his closest student Rabbi Nosson Steinhartz, he published his major collection of teachings called Likutei Moharan. He lived in Uman during the last few months of his life, and was buried there.

Rebbi Nechunyah ben Hakaneh: He was a Tanna in the time of the Beis Hamikdash; a student of Rabban Yochanan ben Zakai, and Rebbi of Rabbi Yishmael Kohen Gadol. He authored several Kabalistic sefarim, as well as the Kabalistic prayer "Anna B'koach" and the prayer before learning.

Rebbi Nehorai: This is the real name of Rabbi Meir Ba'al Hanes, a third-generation Tanna. (See Rabbi Meir)

Rebbi Reuven: Rabbi Reuven Haitztrobli was a heroic figure who stepped forward repeatedly to help his fellow Jews in the tragic times under the Roman heel.

Rebbi Samlai: An Amora, originally from the city of Lud, who at some point moved to Nahardeah. He was the aide of Rabbi Yanai and of Rabbi Yehudah Nesiah.

Rebbi Shimon ben Elazar: A fourth-generation Tanna, and a disciple of Rabbi Meir.

Rebbi Shimon Ben Lakish (200-275 CE):   He is commonly known as Reish Lakish, and was an Amoraic sage. Originally a robber chief, he repented from his criminal life, and became the chief disciple of Rabbi Yochanan, eventually marrying Rabbi Yochanan's sister.

Rebbi Shimon Ben Yehotzadak: A Tanna, student of Rabbi Meir, and Rebbi of Rabbi Yochanan. (There was another Rebbi Shimon ben Yehotzadak who was an Amora in the time of R' Yochanan and Reish Lakish).

Rebbi Shimshon Mi'astrapoli (1600-1648): A Polish Rabbi who died as a martyr during the Khmelnytsky uprising. He was murdered together with 300 other Jews in the Synagogue while praying. An angel used to come to study Torah secrets with him daily. He wrote a commentary on the Zohar called Machaneh Dan, according to the Kabalah of the Arizal, but it has not been printed yet. He used the name Dan for his writings, because he believed that his soul originated from Dan, son of Yaakov Avinu. His most famous writing is a Kabalistic composition related to Pesach, and is printed in some Haggados. Its readers are promised protection for the entire year if they read it on Seder night.

Rebbi Simon: See Rav Simon above. This refers to the same person.

Rebbi Tanchum: An Amora; the student of Rabbi Yehoshua ben Levi.

Rebbi Yehoshua D'Sichnin: An Amora who lived and was buried in the town of Sichnin, in Eretz Yisrael.

Rebbi Yehoshua Ben Chananya: He was a Levi, the student of Rabban Yochanan ben Zakai and Av Beis Din in the time of Rabban Gamliel of Yavne. He was a contemporary of Rabbi Eliezer. He was a respected Jewish elder in Rome, and would travel there to annul decrees. His mother asked the Sages prior to his birth to pray that her baby would be sagacious. When he was a baby his mother would place his crib by the Beis Midrash so that his ears would hear and absorb the Torah. He was indeed exceptionally wise in the various wisdoms, including astronomy, and he knew the ways of witchcraft and how to counteract it as well.

Rebbi Yirmiyah Ben Elazar: There were two Sages with this name. One was a Tanna quoted in B'raisos, and the other was an Amora.

Rebbi Yossi Ben Zimrah: A second-century Tanna who lived in Eretz Yisrael. He was a Kohen, and his daughter married the son of Rabbi Yehudah Hanasi. He mostly commented on Aggadah.

Rebbi Yossi: This refers to Rebbi Yossi ben Chalafta of Tzippori. He was one of the five students of Rabbi Akiva, and a Rebbi of Rabbi Yehudah Hanasi. He was extremely pious, and Eliyahu Hanavi would regularly visit him. In his arguments with his contemporaries (for the most part, Rabbi Meir, Rabbi Yehudah, and Rabbi Shimon), the ruling follows his opinion. He had five great sons who were each Tannaim in their own right. Upon his death, blood flowed from the drainpipes of Tzippori as a sorrowful heavenly sign.

Rebbi Zeira: A third-generation Amora who live in Eretz Yisrael. He was a disciple of Rav Chisda and Rav Huna, and was known for his ascetic piety.

Reikanti (1250-1310):   Rabbi Menachem ben Binyomin, an Italian scholar who wrote primarily on the Kabbalah. He also authored a volume of Halachic rulings.

Reish Lakish: See Rebbi Shimon ben Lakish.

Rema (1530-1572):   Rabbi Moshe Isserlis of Crakow, Poland. He was a Talmudist, philosopher, posek and Kabbalist, most famous for his work Hamapah, amendments on the Shulchan Aruch. The Rema studied under Rabbi Shalom Shachne, who later became his father-in-law. Among the Rema's disciples are Rabbi Shlomo Luria, the Maharshal, the Levush, the Shela, and the Sma. The Rema is buried next to his shul, which he built in honor of his wife who had died young.

Responsa Mahari Bronah (1400-1480):   A German Rabbi and Posek, also known as Mahari Bronah, whose Halachic positions were well respected and quoted by the Rema.

Ritza: Rabbi Tzvi Hirsch of Ziditchov, Ukraine, a Kabbalist and Chassidic master. (1763-1831) Author of Ateres Tzvi, commenting on the Zohar.

Rokeach (1160-1238):   Rabbi Elazar ben Yehudah ben Kloynymous of

Worms, Gemany. He was a Talmudist, Kabbalist, liturgist and astronomer, and was a disciple of Rabbi Yehudah Hachassid. The Rokeach is a guide to Jewish law and ethics.

Rosh David: A work by the Chidah. (See Chidah)

Ruth/Rus: A Moabite princess and granddaughter of Eglon, who was a grandson of Balak. She was the wife of Machlon and daughter-in-law of Naomi and Elimelech. She lived during the period of the Shoftim. Eventually, she converted to Judaism, married Boaz, and was the progenitor of David Hamelech, who was her great- grandson. The Book of Rus was written by Shmuel Hanavi, and it is read on Shavuos.

Samuel: He was one of the early prophets, a judge, and the son of Elkanah and Chana. Shmuel was a Nazir and was considered to be on par with Moshe and Aharon in certain respects. He wrote the books of Shoftim, Shmuel and Megillas Rus. He would travel to the cities to judge the Jewish people. He was very wealthy, and died at the age of fifty two.

Seder HaDoros: A book of generations written by a Lithuanian Rabbi, Rabbi Yechiel Halprin (1660-1746). It is a chronological work, which gives dates and biographical sketches from Adam Harishon down to the Tanaim, Amoraim, and Rishonim. It was first published in 1678.

Sefer Chareidim: A work on Ethics, focusing on the mitzvos that apply today without a Temple. It stresses not only their Halachic component, but also their ethical and religious dimensions. It was written by Rabbi Elazar ben Moshe Azkari (1533-1600). He was born in Constantinople, Turkey, and died in Tzefas, Eretz Yisrael. He was a Kabbalist who was respected by the Arizal.

Sefer Chassidim: A work containing Halachah, Mussar, customs and Kabbalah, written by Rabbi Yehudah Hachassid Regensburg of Germany (1150-1217). Among his disciples, are Rabbi Eliezer of Worms (the

Rokeach) and Rebbi Yitzchak ben Moshe of Vienna (the Ohr Zarua).

Sefer Hahakdomos (1855-1922):   A sefer authored by Rabbi Yehudah Halevi Ashlag. He was born in Lodz, Poland, emigrated to Eretz Yisrael in 1922, and died there. He is famous for his work "Hasulam", a commentary which systematically interprets the Zohar. In Sefer Hahakdamos, the author lays out a cohesive preface of rules that are needed in order to understand the Zohar.

Sefer HaKavonos: A Kabbalistic work written by Rabbi Chaim Vital, based on the teachings of the Arizal. (See Arizal and Rabbi Chaim Vital)

Sefer HaMitzvos: A book of education which systematically lists and discusses the 613 mitzvos in a legal and moral way, addressing their philosophical underpinnings. It was published anonymously in the thirteenth century in Spain.

Sefer Mitzvas Tefillin: A book about the mitzvah of Tefillin authored by the Sh'lah (an acronym for Shnei Luchos Habris - a different work written by Rabbi Yeshaya ben Avraham Halevi Horowitz.) (See Sh'lah)

Sefer Sha'arei HaMitzvos: A listing of the *Mitzvos* in order, by Rabbi Avraham Tzvi Weinstein (London 1954).

Sfas Emes (1847-1905):   A collection of Chasssidic teachings on the Chumash and holidays by R' Yehudah Aryeh Leib Alter of Ger, the second Gerrer Rebbe. He lived in Poland, and was a grandson of the Chiddushei Harim, who he cites repeatedly in his work.

Sh'eiris Yisrael: Authored by Rabbi Yisrael Dov Ber from Vilednik (1789-1850). He was known as a Tzaddik and miracle worker in the Ukraine.

Sh'lah (1560-1630):   An acronym for Shnei Luchos Habris, which is a work containing a compilation of rituals, ethics and mysticism written by Rabbi Yeshaya ben Avraham Halevi Horowitz. He was born in Prague and died in Teveria, Eretz Yisrael. He was a disciple of the Rema, and was a Halachist and Kabbalist.

Sha'ar Hagilgulim (The Gate of Reincarnations):   This sefer was authored by Rabbi Chaim Vital, and based on the teachings of the Arizal. (See Arizal and Reb Chaim Vital)

Sha'ar Hakavanos: See Sefer Hakavanos.

Sha'ar HaPesukim: A work which views the verses of the Torah from a Kabbalistic perspective. It was authored by Rebbi Chaim Vital, and based on the teachings of the Arizal. (See Arizal and Reb Chaim Vital)

Shach (1622-1663):   Abbreviation for Sifsei Kohen, a commentary on the Yoreh Deah and Choshen Mishpat section of the Shulchan Aruch by Rabbi Shabsai ben Meir Hakohen. He was a Talmudist and Halachist who was born in Vilna and died in Germany.

Shaul: The first king of Israel from the tribe of Binyamin. He was the father of Yehonasan, and father-in-law of King David, and considered to be one of the most righteous people in his generation.

Sheivet Hakehasi: Contemporary responsa by Rabbi Shamai Kehos Gross, Jerusalem.

Shem MiShmuel: Chassidic teachings on the Chumash and holidays by Rabbi Shmuel ben Avraham Bornstein, the Sochachover Rebbe (1856-1920). He was the son of Rabbi Avraham Bornstein, the first Sochachover Rebbe, who was known as the Avnei Nezer after the title of his major work.

Shemos Rabbah: The section of Midrash Rabbah on Shemos.

Shemos: The book of Exodus, second of the five books of the Torah. It discusses the Jewish people's exile, redemption from Egypt, and the building of the Mishkan, its vessels and priestly garb.

Shevilei Pinchas: A work on the Parsha and holidays by Rabbi Pinchas Friedman, a Rosh Kollel of the Belzer Yeshiva in Yerushalayim. The teachings are according to Chassidic and Kabbalistic sources.

Shiltei Giborim: A Halachic work on the Rif and the Mordechai, written by Rabbi Yehoshua Boaz Baruch (1518-1555). He was an Italian scholar also famous for writing Torah Ohr, Mesoras Hashas. He also wrote the Ein Mishpat which cites the relevant verses, Talmudic passages, and Halachic sources to every page in the Talmud. It is printed on the margins of every Talmudic page.

Shimon HaTzaddik: Rabbi Shimon the righteous was a Jewish High Priest during the second Temple. He was a Tanna, and was very pious and benevolent. He was the last Sage of those who comprised the Anshei Knesses Hagedolah.

Shir HaShirim (Song of Songs):   Its words were authored by Shlomo Hamelech. It is a love song describing the relationship between God and the Jewish people.

Shir Hashirim Rabbah: The section of Midrash Rabbah on Shir Hashirim.

Shmuel Hanavi: Samuel the prophet was one of the earlier prophets, and was also a judge. He was the son of Elkana and Chana, and he was a Nazir. (See Samuel for more detail)

Shulchan Aruch (Set table):   A codification of Jewish law, broken down into the following four parts: Orach Chaim, Yoreh Deah, Even Haezer, and Choshen Mishpat. It was written by Rabbi Yosef Cairo. (See Rabbi Yosef Cairo)

Shu't Mahariatz: Responsa written by R' Yehoshua Aharon Zvi

Weinberg, the Av Beis Din of Morgortan, student of the Chasam Sofer.

Shvus Yaakov: Responsa written by Rabbi Yaakov Reischer (1661-1733). He was an Austrian Rabbi and Halachist.

Siddur Arizal: A Siddur (prayerbook) whose nusach is based on the teachings of the Arizal. It is meant to connect any Jewish soul from any tribe of Israel with Hashem.

Siddur Tefillah Yesharah: A famous Chassidic Siddur from Berdichev, with a running commentary on the liturgy called Kesser Nehora.

Sifra D'tzniusah: A Kabbalistic work by Rabbi Shimon Bar Yochai

Sifri: A Talmudic, Halachic Midrash on the books of Bamidbar and Devarim.

Sifsei Chachamim: A popular interpretation of Rashi's commentary on the Chumash. It was written by Rabbi Shabsai Bass (1641-1718). He was born in Kalisz, Poland, and died in Amsterdam. Rabbi Shabsai was a bass singer in the Altneu shul of Prague. This is where he acquired his surname "Bass". He was also involved in printing Jewish books, including the work of Rabbi Shmuel ben Uri, author of the Beis Shmuel (a commentary of the Even Haezer section of the Shulchan Aruch).

Slonimer Rebbe (1911-2000): Rabbi Shalom Noach Berzovsky, author of the Nesivos Shalom, a seven-volume work. He served as the Admor of Slonim for more than twenty years, and is widely known for his teachings, which are published as a series titled Nesivos Shalom. A leading non-Chassidic Rosh Yeshiva has referred to the Nesivos Shalom as the "Mesillas Yesharim of our times." He studied in the the Slonimer yeshiva in Baranowitz, a blend of the Lithuanian Misnaged style and the Chassidic approach. Around 1930, he was appointed by the Rebbe to memorize and later write up the discourses given by the Rebbe on

Shabbos. These discourses were subsequently published as the Beis Avrohom. In 1940 he was appointed Rosh Yeshiva of Achei Temimim, the Lubavitcher yeshiva in Tel Aviv. In 1941, he founded the Slonimer yeshiva in Jerusalem with just five students, and this yeshiva served as the focus for the Slonimer Chassidus which was virtually wiped out in the Holocaust. In 1954, his father-in-law agreed to serve as Rebbe. Rabbi Shalom Noach published his father-in-law's discourses as Birkas Avrohom. He authored many sefarim, and succeeded his father-in-law as Slonimer Rebbe following the latter's death in 1981. He is succeeded by his son, Rabbi Shmuel.

Smag: Rabbi Moshe ben Yaakov of Coucy, a French Tosafist in the first half of the thirteenth century. Smag is an acronym for "*Sefer Mitzvos Gedolos*," a book which discusses the 613 *mitzvos*.

Steipler Gaon (1899-1985):   Rabbi Yaakov Yisrael Kanievsky was born in Russia, died in Bnei Brak, and was a great Talmudic scholar and posek. He was the author of the popular Kehillos Yaakov on Shas, Birkas Peretz on Chumash, and many other publications and articles. Rabbi Yaakov Yisrael married the sister of the Chazon Ish.

Ta'amei Haminhagim: A comprehensive compilation of Jewish customs written by Rabbi Avraham Yitzchok Sperling.

Taharos: The last of the six orders of the Mishnah.

Talmidei Rabbeinu Yonah: The students of Rabbi Yonah ben Avraham Gerondi from Catalan, (1180-1263) and was famous for his ethical work Sha'arei Teshuvah.

Tana D'bei R' Yishmael: The teachings from the Academy of Rabbi Yishmael, a first-generation Tanna.

Tanach: The acronym for Torah, Neviim, Kesuvim (Torah, Prophets and Writings), which make up the entirety of the Written Law.

Tashbats: Rabbi Shimon ben Zemach Duran (1361-1444). He was also known as the Rashbatz. He was a Talmudist, Posek, philosopher, astronomer, mathemetician and physician. He lived in Barcelona, Spain, and authored many works on the Talmud and Halacha.

Taz: An acronym for Turei Zahav (Rows of Gold). It is a commentary on the Shulcahn Aruch by Rabbi David ben Shmuel Halevi (1586-1667), Lodmir, Poland. He was a Talmudist and a Halachist, and married the daughter of Rabbi Yoel Sarkis, the Bach.

Tefillas Hashachar: The fourth chapter of Tractate Berachos.

Tehillim (Psalms):   Five books of prasises to God, ascribed to King David. He co-authored with the following ten elders: Adam, Malkitzedek, Avraham, Moshe, Heiman, Yedusun, Assaf, and three sons of Korach.

Tiferes Shlomo (1803-1866):   Rabbi Shlomo HaKohen of Radomsk, a Torah scholar and Kabbalist from Poland.

Tiferes Shmuel: A sefer on the Torah by Rabbi Shmuel Kaufman of Kaminka (1863-1938). He was born in the Ukraine, and died in the USA.

Tiferes Yisrael: Rabbi Yisrael Lipshitz (1782-1860) from Germany, famous for his classic commentary on Mishnah called Tiferes Yisrael which is considered to be the clearest and most useful commentary on the Mishnah. Rabbi Yisrael led a very ascetic life which included fasting regularly.

Tikkunei Zohar: One section of the Zohar containing seventy explanations on the first word in the Torah, "Bereishis." It is ascribed to Rabbi Shimon bar Yochai.

Toldos Yaakov Yosef: The first book of Chassidus ever written. It was authored by Rabbi Yaakov Yosef of Polonoye (1704-1794), and is often refered to as the Toldos. Originally, he was a staunch opponent of the

Ba'al Shem Tov, until they met. R' Yaakov Yosef was so impressed with the Ba'al Shem Tov that he became a Chassid of his, until eventually he was considered his greatest disciple.

Torah Leda'as: A ten-volume work on the Parshah, holidays and relevant Halachic topics of interest, written by Rabbi Mattisyau Bloom of New York.

Torah Temimah: A commentary on the Chumash by Rabbi Baruch Halevi Epstein, son of Rabbi Yechiel Michel Halvei Epstein, the famous author of the Aruch Hashulchan. The Torah Temimah cites the relevant Talmudic sources to the verses of the Torah, and then offers a commentary elucidating those sources. (See Rav Baruch Epstein)

Toras Avos: A collection of essays by different authors, collected by Rabbi Shalom Noach Berzovsky, the Admor of Slonim (1911-2000). As part of his effort to rejuvenate the Slonimer Chassidus, he was responsible for collecting the oral traditions ascribed to previous Slonimer Rebbes in works such as Divrei Shmuel and Toras Avos. (See Slonimer Rebbe)

Toras Kohanim: Also known as the Sifra; a Tannaic, Halachic Midrash on the book of Vayikra.

Toras Moshe (Alshich): A popular commentary on the Torah by Rabbi Moshe ben Chaim Alshich (1508-1600). He was born in Adrianople, Turkey, and settled in Tzefas. (See Alshich Hakadosh)

Toras Moshe (Chasam Sofer): A commentary on the Torah and holidays by Rabbi Moshe Sofer (1762-1839). He was the Rabbi of Pressburg, and leader of Hungarian Jewry. He was a student of Rabbi Nosson Adler, and married the daughter of Rabbi Akiva Eiger. (See Chasam Sofer)

Tosafos Yom Tov: An extensive, comprehensive elaboration on the Mishnah written by Rabbi *Yom Tov* Lipman-Heller Halevi (1579-1654). He lived in Poland, and was a major Talmudic scholar and a student of the Maharal. He was also well-versed in secular sciences.

Tosefes Zohar: An additonal commentary to the Zohar.

Tosefos: Literally "additions", written by French and German Rabbis throughout the twelfth and thirteenth centuries on the Babyloinan Talmud. Rashi's grandson, Rabbeinu Tam, was the head of the Tosafists.

Tosfos Chadashim: A commentary on the Mishnah by Torah scholars from Amsterdam, Holland. They included Rabbi Shimshon Chassid of Altuna, Rabbi Shaul and the Remaz Hakohen Bloch.

Tur: Literally "row." A Code of Jewish Law written by Rabbi Yaakov, son of the Rosh (1275-1340), Germany. The full title of the work is the Arba'ah Turim (four rows), comprised of Orach Chaim, Yoreh Deah, Even Haezer and Choshen Mishpat.

Tzetel Katan: "A small note" listing seventeen steps to becoming a good Jew written by the Rebbe, Rebbe Elimelech of Lizensk. (See Noam Elimelech)

Tzidkas HaTzaddik: A book written by Rabbi Tzaddok HaKohen of Lublin (1823-1900). Although he was born to a Lithuanian Rabbinic family, he later became a follower of Chassidic Rebbes, such as Rabbi Mordechai Yosef Leiner of Ishbitz and Rebbe Yehudah Leib Eiger (grandson of the famous Rabbi Akiva Eiger). He lived in Poland, and was a Chassidic master, Talmudist and deep thinker. He also authored the Pri Tzaddik.

Uktzin: A Talmudic tractate in Seder Taharos.

Vayikra Rabbah: The section of Midrash Rabbah on the book of Leviticus.

Vayikra: The book of Leviticus, third of the five books of the Torah. It primarily discusses the laws pertaining to Kohanim, such as the offerings

Bibliography

and the service in the Temple.

Vilna Gaon (1720-1797): Rabbi Eliyahu ben Shlomo Zalman Kramer was a genius from Vilna, and considered to be the greatest Lithuanian scholar. He was a Talmudist, Halachist and Kabbalist, and was considered by many to be equal in stature to the Rishonim. His chief disciple was Rabbi Chaim of Volozhin.

Vilna Gaon on Esther: The Gaon's commentary on the book of Esther. (See Vilna Gaon.)

Ya'aros Devash: A collection of sermons written by Rabbi Yehonasan Eibeshitz (1690-1764). He was born in Crakow, and died in Prague. He was a Talmudist, Halachist, preacher and Kabbalist.

Yalkut Divrei Chachamim: An anthology of essays on various subjects, printed in Jerusalem (1948).

Yalkut Me'am Lo'ez: See Me'am Loe'z.

Yalkut Reuveini: An anthology of difficult Midrashim and Kabbalistic works, arranged according to the weekly Torah readings. It was written by Rabbi Reuven Hoshke Hakohen Sofer, a Kabbalist and Rabbi of Prague. He died in 1673.

Yalkut Shimoni: A compilation of Aggados on Tanach written by Rabbi Shimon Hadarshan of Frankfurt am Main in the mid-thirteenth century. This is an extensive and comprehensive collection of the literature of the Sages including the Talmudim, Sifra, Mechilta, Midrash Rabba, Midrash Tehillim, Avos d'Rabbi Nosson, minor tractates, Pesikta, Midrash Tanchumah, and minor Midrashim, some unknown, thus being a treasury of Midrashim arranged according to the biblical verses. It was first printed in Salonika (1521-1526), but the best known publication is that of Warsaw, 1878. The paragraphs are divided into numbered remazim, sometimes a few sentences and sometimes large segments.

Accompanying standard editions is the abbreviated commentary Zayit Ra'anan, by R' Abraham Gombiner, author of the Magen Avraham on Shulchan Aruch, Orach Chayim. A new and corrected edition based upon manuscripts, with the entire Zeis Ra'anan has recently been published.

Yehudah ben Geirim: A Jewish man whose carelessness caused great suffering to Rabbi Shimon bar Yochai. Yehudah ben Geirim leaked information that Rabbi Shimon bar Yochai had criticized the Roman government. This caused Rabbi Shimon bar Yochai to hide in a cave for over a dozen years in order to escape the Roman authories who wanted to execute him.

Yerushalmi: The Talmud composed by the Amoraim of Eretz Yisrael.

Yesod Ha'avodah: A Chassidic work on the Parshah by Rabbi Avraham Weinberg M'Slonim (1804-1883). He was the first Admor of Slonim.

Yesod V'shoresh Ha'avodah: A sefer on Tefillah and festivals by Rabbi Alexander Ziskind. He lived in the second half of the eighteenth century, and was from Horodna.

Yismach Moshe: A sefer written by Rabbi Moshe Teitelbaum (1759-1841), a follower of the Chozeh from Lublin. He brought Chassidic Judaism to Ujhely, Hungary where he was the Rebbe.

Yoel: One of the twelve prophets whose prophecies were brief. He was a son of Pesuel, who according to some was Shmuel Hanavi. His prophecy focused on the famine and plague of locusts which occurred in his own period.

Yonasan Ben Uziel: An Aramaic translation and commentary to the Torah, written by the Tanna, Yonasan ben Uziel. He was considered to be the greatest disciple of Hillel.

Yorah Deah: One of the four sections of the Code of Jewish Law.

Zecharia: One of the twelve prophets whose prophecies were brief. He was a son of Berechia, and his prophecies speak about his own time period until the end of days.

Zerah Kodesh: Kabbalistic discourses written by Rabbi Naftoli Zvi Horowitz of Ropschitz, a disciple of Reb Elimelech of Lizensk. He was from Galicia and known for his humor and sharp wit. He was also a master of the mystical interpretations of the Torah. (See Rav Naftoli of Ropschitz)

Zichron Devarim: A commentary on the Meggilos by Rabbi Moshe Dov Ber of Trashkon (Vilna 1896).

Zohar Chadash: Manuscrips that were not included in the printing of the Zohar, and were added later by Rabbi Avraham Halevi of Tzefas. The Zohar Chadash is divided according to the Parshiyos of the Torah. The Zohar Chadash is also on the Megillos of Shir Hashirim, Rus and Eichah.

Zohar Pinchas: The section of Zohar on the portion of Pinchas.

Zohar: The main body of Kabbalah, written by Rabbi Shimon bar Yochai, and arranged according to the Parshiyos and Megillos. After being hidden for centuries, it was first published in the late thirteenth century by Rabbi Moshe Deleon (1250-1305) in Spain. (See Rabbi Shimon Bar Yochai)

GLOSSARY

The following glossary provides a partial explanation of some of the Hebrew, Aramaic and Yiddish words and phrases used in this book. The spellings and explanations reflect the way the specific word is used herein. Often there are alternate spellings and meanings for the words.

ACHDUS – unity.

ADAM – man; also, the name of the first person.

ADAR – name of the twelfth and final Jewish month (lunar cycle).

ADMOR – acronym for Adoneinu Moreinu V'Rabbeinu – our master, our teacher, and our Rabbi. Usually used as an honorable introductory title for a Chassidic Rabbi.

AKEIDAH – lit. binding; refers to the binding of Yitzchak.

AKEIDAS YITZCHAK – the binding of Yitzchak.

ALEPH – the name of the first Hebrew letter.

AL HANISSIM – lit. for the miracles; a prayer inserted into the liturgy on Chanukah and Purim, thanking God for the miracles that occurred.

ALIYAH – to go up; a term used in reference to being called up to the Torah; also refers to one who immigrates to the land of Israel.

AM YISRAEL – the nation of Israel.

AMIDAH – the silent prayer, composed of eighteen (now nineteen) benedictions, and recited quietly while standing.

AMOS – cubits.

ANEINU – lit. answer us; a prayer inserted into the liturgy on fast days.

ANSHEI K'NESSES HAGEDOLAH – the Men of the Great Assembly .

ARAVOS – willows; traditionally used for worship on the holiday of Sukkos.

ARICHAS YAMIM – longevity.

ARON – ark; can refer to the Ark of the covenant or to the structure in which a Torah scroll is kept.

ASSERES HADIBROS – the Ten Commandments.

ASSERES YEMEI TESHUVAH – the ten days of Repentance from Rosh HaShanah until Yom Kippur.

AV – name of the fifth Jewish month (lunar cycle).

AV BEIS DIN – the head of the Jewish Supreme Court.

AVAK LASHON HARA – lit. the dust of gossip; refers to any gesture of slander.

AVEIRAH – sin.

AVINU – our father.

AVODAH – worship; work.

AVODAS HASHEM – worship; service of God.

AVOS – lit. fathers, often referring to our Patriarchs.

AYIN – the name of the sixteenth Hebrew letter.

AZ YASHIR – lit. then they sang; a reference to the song sung by the Jews after experiencing the Splitting of the Sea.

BNEI YISRAEL – the Children of Israel.

BA'AL TESHUVAH (BA'ALEI TESHUVAH) – repentant(s), or one who has decided to lead a religious life.

BARUCH SHEM – lit. blessed is the Name; refers to the sentence recited right after the Shema.

BEIN ADAM LACHAVEIRO – commandments between man and man.

BEIN ADAM LAMAKOM – commandments between man and God.

BEIN HAMETZARIM – lit. between the straits; refers to the three weeks of mourning between the seventeenth of Tammuz and the ninth of Av.

BEIS – the name of the second Hebrew letter.

BEIS HAMIDRASH (BATEI MIDRASHOS) – study hall(s) of Torah.

BERACHAH – blessing.

B'EZRAS HASHEM – with the aid of God.

BIKKURIM – first fruits brought to the Temple where a ceremony is performed with them.

BIMAH – stage, podium. Commonly refers to the area where the Torah is read from in the synagogue.

BIRCHAS HATORAH – blessings recited prior to the study of Torah.

BISHUL AKUM – lit. food cooked by a non–Jew. Refers to a Rabbinic prohibition that such food may carry.

BITACHON – trust (in God).

BRAISAH – it. outside one; a section of Oral Law that was not committed to writing, l- for it was not part of the Mishna compilation of Rabbi Yehudah Hanasi.

BRIS HAGUF – a covenant made with the body.

BRIS HANESHAMAH – a covenant made with the soul.

BRIS MILAH – the covenant of circumcision; usually refers to Jewish circumcision itself.

B'TZELEM ELOKIM – in the image, likeness or shadow of God.

CHACHAM – a wise person. May refer to the Sages who led/lead the commuity.

CHAF – the name of the eleventh Hebrew letter.

CHAG – holiday, festival.

CHALAV YISRAEL – lit. Jewish milk; milk that was extracted from a kosher animal under Jewish supervision.

CHALLAH (CHALLOS) – the special loaf/loaves of bread eaten on Shabbos or *Yom Tov*; an amount of dough separated from the bread as a tithe.

CHANUKAH – an eight–day holiday which commemorates the miracle of oil lasting eight days. This occurred after the Hasmoneans defeated the Greeks, and is celebrated by lighting the menorah.

CHANUKIA – menorah or candelabra.

CHASSAN – groom.

CHASSIDIM – the different branches of observant Jews who follow the teachings of the Ba'al Shem Tov.

CHASSIDUS – the teachings of the Ba'al Shem Tov and other Chassidic masters.

CHATAS – a sin–offering.

CHAVIVUS – belovedness.

CHAVRUSAH – study partner.

CHAYAV – obligated or liable.

CHAYAV MISAH – one who is liable to the death penalty.

CHAZAL – an acronym for Chachameinu Zichronam Livrachah – our wise men of blessed memory; a title given to the Sages who lived in Talmudic times.

CHEDER – lit. a room; refers to a school dedicated to teaching Torah to little boys.

CHEDVAH – a form of happiness.

CHEISHEK – desire, motivation.

CHELBENAH – galbanum; one of the spices used for the incense offering.

CHES – the name of the eighth Hebrew letter.

CHESHVAN – the name of the eighth Jewish month (lunar cycle).

CHESSED – kindness, acts of kindness.

CHODESH – month.

CHUMASH – the five books of Moses, or one of them.

CHURBAN – lit. destruction; typically referring to the destruction of the Temples.

CHUTZ LA'ARETZ – outside the Land of Israel.

DA'AS – knowledge.

DALED – the name of the fourth Hebrew letter.

DAVEN / DAVENING – pray / the act of praying.

DERECH – way; can also refer to a particular approach to serving God.

DIN – the law; strict justice.

DIVREI TORAH – words of Torah.

DOR HAFLAGAH – the generation that was dispersed after having built a tower from which to wage war against God.

DOR HAMABUL – the generation that was destroyed by the Great Flood.

DRASH – an advanced level of discourse on Torah; can also refer to the third of four levels of Torah understanding. (Pshat (simple), remez (codes), drash (expounding), and sod (secrets)).

EIGEL – lit. calf; usually a reference to the Golden Calf that the Jews sinned with in the wilderness.

EIREV RAV – the mixed multitude of Egyptian converts who joined the Jewish people in the Wilderness.

EIS RATZON – a favorable heavenly moment during which it is propitious for us to ask God our requests.

EITZOS – pieces of advice.

ELIYAHU HANAVI – Elijah the prophet.

ELOKIM – one of the names of God, usually used in the context of strict justice. Also: judge.

ELUL – name of the sixth Jewish month (lunar cycle).

EMES – truth.

EMUNAH – faith; faithfulness.

ERETZ YISRAEL – the Land of Israel.

ESROG – citron; a citrus fruit traditionally used for worship on the holiday of Sukkos.

GALUS – exile. May be used to refer to the time prior to the redemption of the Messiah.

GAN EDEN – Garden of Eden. Can refer to a paradise above in heaven, or to paradise on earth.

GEDOLIM – the Torah leaders of the generation.

GEHINNOM – Purgatory.

GEMARA / GEMAROS – the Talmud / various pieces of the Tamud.

GEMATRIA – numerical value of Hebrew letters and words.

GEMATRIA KATAN – a system of numerical value where all the zeros are dropped.

GEULAH – redemption.

GILGUL – reincarnation.

GIMMEL – the name of the third Hebrew letter.

GLATT – lit. smooth; a high standard of kashrus or a phrase which implies doing something 100% right.

HADASSIM – myrtle branches; traditionally used for worship on the holiday of Sukkos.

HAFTARAH – the section of the Prophets read in conjunction with the weekly Torah portion.

HAGADDAH – the text used at the Seder table on Passover.

HAKHEL – lit. gather; the *mitzvah* for all Jews to gather at the Temple once every seven years to hear the king read from the book of Deuteronomy.

HALACHAH (HALACHOS) – Jewish law(s).

HASHEM – lit. the Name; a reference to God.

HASHKAFOS – outlooks, worldviews or viewpoints.

HAVDALAH – lit. separation; the ceremony on Saturday night which makes a distinction between Shabbos and the weekdays.

HESTER PANIM – lit. concealment of the face; referring to the times that God hides Himself from us.

HEY – the name of the fifth Hebrew letter.

HOSHANAH RABBAH – lit. the great Hoshana; the last day of Sukkos where a special ceremony is perfomed with Aravos.

IKVESA D'MESHICHA – lit. the footsteps of the Messiah, referring to the End of Days.

IMAHOS – lit. mothers; usually referring to the Matriarchs.

IMEINU – our mother; usually in conjunction with a Matriarch.

IYAR – name of the second Jewish month (lunar cycle).

KABALLAH – Jewish mysticism. Also, acceptance of a certain practice or stringency. Also, a piece of knowledge transmitted orally, personally.

KADESH, URCHATZ – lit. making Kiddush and washing the hands; referring to a passage in the preface to the Passover Seder listing its fifteen stages.

KADOSH – holy. Also, removed from physicality.

KAF – the name of the eleventh Hebrew letter.

KALLAH – bride.

KAPPAROS – the atoning ceremony performed prior to Yom Kippur, traditionally using a chicken.

KASHRUS – Jewish dietary laws. Or the Kosher status of an animal or ritual object.

KAVOD – honor.

KAVOD HATORAH – honor of the Torah.

KEILIM – vessels. Also the name of a tractate.

KESHER – knot, connection.

KESHER SHEL KAYAMAH – a lasting knot or a lasting connection.

KETORES – incense.

KIBBUD AV V'EM – respecting a father and mother.

KIDDUSH – a ceremony performed at the onset and morning of Shabbos or *Yom Tov* over a cup of wine.

KIDDUSH HASHEM – sanctification of God's name; giving people a positive impression of God's Torah and the Jewish people.

KIRUV – lit. to bring close; outreach.

KISHKES – intestines. Often used to mean "inner workings."

KISLEV – name of the ninth Jewish month (lunar cycle).

KIYOR – sink, washbasin; usually referring to a specific vessel in the Temple with that function.

KODESH – holy.

KODESH KODOSHIM – the Holy of Holies.

KOHEN (KOHANIM) – priest(s).

KOHEN GADOL – the High Priest.

KOHEN HEDYOT – regular priest (not the High Priest).

KORBAN PESACH – Pascal lamb or kid.

KORBANOS – ritual offerings, usually sacrificed upon the Temple Altar.

KOSHER – description of food that conforms to Jewish dietary laws.

KRIAS HATORAH – the reading of the Torah.

KRIAS YAM SUF – the Splitting of the Sea.

KUF – the name of the nineteenth Hebrew letter.

KVELL – (coll. yid.) to receive tremendous pleasure and pride, usually from a child.

LAG BAOMER – the thirty–third day of the Omer celebrating the revelation of the Zohar.

LAMED – the name of the twelfth Hebrew letter.

LASHON HAKODESH – the holy tounge; biblical Hebrew.

LASHON HARA – lit. evil tongue; refers to derogatory speech about others.

LECHEM HAPANIM – the showbread; the 12 breads exhibited on the Shulchan in the Temple all week.

LEITZANUS – mockery, making fun.

LEVI (LEVIIM) – Levite (Levites).

LIMUD HATORAH – the study of Torah.

LULAV – palm branch traditionally used in worship on Sukkos.

MA'ARIV – the evening service.

MACHLOKES – argumentativeness; fighting.

MACHZOR – prayer book for the holidays.

MAGGID – preacher.

MAKOM – place. Hashem is sometimes referred to as "HaMakom" - the Place.

MALACH – angel.

MALCHUS – sovereignty; kingship; kingly; also refers to one of the Kabalistic spheres.

MANHIGIM – leaders.

MAOZ TZUR – the song traditionally sung after kindling the Chanukah lights.

MASMID (MASMIDIM) – diligent student(s) of Torah.

MATAN TORAH – the giving of the Torah.

MATZAH (MATZOS) – round or square–shaped unleavened bread(s) eaten on Passover.

MAZAL (MAZALOS) – lit. fortune(s), or zodiac sign(s).

MELACH – salt.

MELAVEH MALKAH – lit. escorting the queen; refers to the traditional meal eaten after the Sabbath, on Saturday night.

MEM – the name of the thirteenth Hebrew letter.

MENORAH – candelabra; either refers to the one in the Sanctuary or Temple, or the one we light in our homes on Chanukah.

MENTCH – decent person endowed with refined interpersonal qualities such as respect, appreciation, kindness and friendliness.

MESECHTA – a tractate of Talmud.

MESORAH – the/a tradition; the transmission of our teachings throughout the generations.

METZORA – a (spiritually-caused) type of leper.

MEZUZAH – a parchment containing two sections of Shema from the Torah, affixed to the doorposts of Jewish homes and businesses.

MIDDOS – traits and qualities with regard to ones personality. Also, measures or measurements.

MIDRASH – teachings from the Tannaic and Amoraic Sages on the Tanach.

MIKVEH – a pool used as a ritual bath for purification.

MILAH – circumcision. See Bris Milah.

MILCHEMES HAYETZER – the conflict with our evil inclination.

MINCHAH – the afternoon service. Also, a meal offering. Also, a gift.

MINHAG – custom.

MINYAN – a quorum of ten Jewish men above the age of thirteen, required for the daily services.

MISHKAN – the Tabernacle, Sanctuary.

MISHNAH – the first body of Oral Law that was committed to writing.

MISONENIM – the complainers; refers to the group of Jews in the wilderness who complained about how weary they had become on the journey.

MITZVAH (MITZVOS) – commandment(s).

MIZBEACH – altar.

MODEH ANI – lit. I thank you; the prayer said upon rising in the morning.

MOHEL – circumciser.

MOSHIACH – lit. the anointed one; usually refers to the Messiah. It may also refer to an anointed king.

NAARISHKEIT – silliness.

NACHAS – pleasure, satisfaction; refers to the pleasure a parent gets from a child, or that God receives from His children.

NACHASH – snake.

NASI – prince; a title usually reserved for the Chief Rabbi in Tannaic times who descended from the Davidic dynasty.

NAZIR – nazarite; one who vows to be a nazir, whose laws include refraining from wine, haircuts, and entering a cemetery.

NEFESH – soul, person; can refer to a specific part of the soul.

NEGEL VASSER – lit. fingernail waters; refers to ritual washing of hands upon arising from sleep.

NEILAH – lit. the locking; refers to last service of Yom Kippur where we still have a chance to repent before the gates of heaven are closed and locked.

NESHAMAH – soul; can also refer to a specific part of the soul.

NISSAN – name of the first Jewish month (lunar cycle).

NUN – name of the fourteenth Hebrew letter.

NUSACH – text; refers to a certain version of liturgical or Talmudic text.

OHR GANUZ – hidden light that God stashed away for the righteous in the future.

OLAH – burnt offering.

OLAM HABA – the World to Come.

OLAM HAZEH – this world.

PARAH ADUMAH – red heifer.

PARNASSAH – livelihood.

PARSHAH (PARSHIYOS) – portion(s), as in the Torah portion of the week.

PARSHAS HACHODESH – one of the four additional portions read prior to Passover, discussing the mitzvah of Rosh Chodesh.

PARSHAS PARAH – one of the four additional portions read prior to Passover, discussing the red heifer.

PARSHAS SHEKALIM – one of the four additional portions read prior to Passover, discussing the mandatory contribution of a 1/2 shekel coin donated by every person to the Temple fund for the purchase of animals needed for communal offerings.

PARSHAS ZACHOR – one of the four additional portions, read prior to Purim, discussing the mitzvah of eradicating Amalek.

PAS YISRAEL – Jewish–made bread.

PASSUL – invalid.

PESACH – Passover.

PEY, PHEY – the name of the seventeenth Hebrew letter.

POSEK / POSKIM – authority / authorities on Jewish law.

PSHAT – the plain understanding of the Torah.

PURIM – a holiday celebrating Jewish salvation from Haman's evil decree which called for annihilation of the Jewish people.

RASHA (RESHAIM) – wicked person (people).

RASHB"I – acronym for Rebbi Shimon bar Yochai.

RATZON HASHEM – the will of God.

RAV – a Rabbi; a halachic authority; the Amoraic sage called Rav.

REBBE – Rabbi; usually refers to a Chassidic leader. Also used to refer to a teacher in a Cheder or a personal mentor.

REBBETZIN – wife of a Rabbi.

REISH – the name of the twentieth Hebrew letter.

REMEZ – hint; or the coded level of understanding the Torah.

RISHON – first, or first one. Also used to refer to those authorities living in the Medieval period.

ROSH CHODESH (ROSHEI CHADASHIM) – lit. the head(s) of the month(s); refers to the first day of a month. In a 30 day month it also refers to the last day of the previous month.

ROSH HASHANAH – lit. the head of the year; refers to the High Holiday of judgment which commences the new Jewish year. (Note: the Jewish year consists of many cycles. Rosh HaShanah is the beginning of one of them. For other things, however, the cycle starts elsewhere. The monthly cycle begins at Nissan.)

SAF – the name of the twenty–second and final Hebrew letter.

SAMECH – the name of the fifteenth Hebrew letter.

SANHEDRIN – Jewish supreme court.

SCHLEP – (yid. coll.) to travel or carry in a very tiring and uncomfortable way. Also used to denote anything tiresome.

SCHLEPPING – traveling or carrying things in a very tiring and uncomfortable way.

SEDER – lit. order; a set time for Torah study. Also: the Passover ceremony on the first night, and second night in the diaspora.

SEFER (SEFARIM) – (holy) book(s).

SEFER TORAH – Torah scroll.

SEFIRAH (SEFIROS) – count/countings; the mitzvah of counting the days between Pesach and Shavuos; can be used as a general name for a kabalistic sphere(s) or attribute of Hashem.

SEFIRAS HAOMER – the mitzvah of counting from the second day of Passover (on which the Omer offering was brought) until Shavuos.

SEGULAH – Jewish charm or omen.

SEKILAH – stoning.

SELICHOS – prayers of supplication, begging God for forgiveness for our sins.

SHA'ATNEZ – garment containing a mixture of wool and linen and prohibited to wear.

SHABBOS (SHABBOSOS) – Sabbath(s).

SHABBOS HAGADOL – lit. the Great Sabbath; refers to the Shabbos prior to Passover.

SHABBOS SHIRAH – lit. Sabbath of Song; refers to the Shabbos when we read the song that was sung by the Jews at the sea.

SHACHARIS – morning service. Or morning.

SHALOM – peace.

SHAMASH (SHAMASHIM) – either a helper(s) in the synagogue, or a helper(s) of a great or important person. Also refers to the candle used to kindle the Chanukah candles.

SHAS – acronym for Shishah Sidrei (the six orders); refers to six orders of Oral Law which were committed to writing. May refer to the Talmud.

SHAVUOS – lit. weeks; usually refers to the holiday when Jews celebrate receiving the Torah.

SHECHINAH – the Divine presence.

SHEKEL (SHEKALIM) – monetary currency; in scripture it refers to the currency used in Biblical times.

SHEM HAVAYAH – one of God's names that is spelled: yud, hey, vav, hey. It is not read as spelled.

SHEMA – lit. hear; refers to part of the liturgy containing the sentence declaring God's oneness, followed by three other paragraphs, which is recited twice daily.

SHEMINI ATZERES – the eighth day of Sukkos, technically considered a holiday unto itself.

SHEMIRAS EINAYIM – protecting ones eyes from gazing at inappropriate things.

SHEMITTAH – the Sabbatical year in Israel that occurs every seventh year where the land may not be worked. Also refers to the seven-year period as a whole.

SHEMONEH ESREI – lit. eighteen; refers to the silent prayer that has eighteen (now nineteen) benedictions (see Amidah).

SHEVAT – name of the eleventh Jewish month (lunar cycle).

SHEVET – tribe. Also, stick or staff.

SHIDDUCH (SHIDDUCHIM) – match(es) between a man and a woman.

SHILUACH HAKEN – the mitzvah of sending the mother bird away from the nest, and then taking the chicks or eggs.

SHIN – the name of the twenty–first Hebrew letter.

SHIRAS HAYAM – the song sung by the Jews at the Sea of Reeds after the Egyptians were drowned in it. (See Az Yashir).

SHLEIMUS – completion; referring usually to wholeness either in personality or as a people.

SHOFAR – a horn; typically a ram's, blown on Rosh HaShanah.

SHOVEVIM – an acronym that stands for the six Torah portions Shemos, Va'era, Bo, Beshalach, Yisro, Mishpatim. Some have the custom to fast and add additional prayers to ask Hashem for forgiveness in areas of immorality during the weeks that these portions are read.

SHTEI HALECHEM – the two loaves of breads offered on the holiday of Shavuos.

SHTICK – tricks; usually referring to pranks that are meant to be humorous or clever.

SHUL – a synagogue.

SIDDUR (SIDDURIM) – prayerbook(s).

SIMAN (SIMANIM) – sign(s), or chapter(s).

SIMCHAH – happiness; also refers to a Jewish celebration such as a wedding or a Bris.

SIMCHAS BEIS HASHO'EIVAH – the joyous occasion of drawing the water from the Shiloach spring and pouring it as a libation on the outside Altar during Sukkos.

SIMCHAS TORAH – the joyous holiday celebrating the completion of the yearly cycle of Torah reading which is on the same day as Shemini Atzeres in Eretz Yisrael, but in the Diaspora it is celebrated on the day after Shemini Atzeres.

SIN – the name of the twenty–first Hebrew letter.

SIVAN – name of the third Jewish month (lunar cycle).

SUKKAH – booth or hut, that Jews dwell in for the seven or eight days of Sukkos commemorating the booth or Clouds of Glory that protected our ancestors as they wandered in the Wilderness.

SUKKOS – plural of Sukkah, or the name of the holiday.

SULAM – a ladder.

TA'ANIS DIBBUR – a fast of speech, where people accept upon themselves to remain completely silent for a period of time with the exception of prayer and Torah study.

TAF – the name of the twenty–second and final Hebrew letter.

TAFEL – that which is secondary to something.

TALLIS – lit. garment; prayer shawl worn during the morning service.

TAMMUZ – name of the fourth Jewish month (lunar cycle).

TANACH – acronym for Torah, Neviim and Kesuvim, which comprise the body of the Written Law.

TARYAG – an abbreviation whose numerical value is 613, representing the 613 commandments in the Torah.

TASHLICH – lit. to throw; refers to the custom of saying certain prayers near a body of water containing fish on Rosh HaShanah, thus symbolically demonstrating that we want to cast our sins away.

TEFILLAH (TEFILLOS) – prayer(s); also refers specifically to the silent prayer, the Amidah. One of the Tefillin.

TEFILLIN – phylacteries; black boxes containing four Torah portions on parchment, bound to the arm and head with black leather straps, worn by adult Jewish men daily (except for Shabbos and certain holidays). They remind us of the exodus from Egypt and thereby we subjugate our hearts and minds to God.

TEFILLIN SHEL ROSH – the box worn on the head.

TEFILLIN SHEL YAD – the box worn on the arm.

TES – the name of the ninth Hebrew letter.

TESHUVAH – return, repentance. Also, a response, commonly as a letter responding to a query.

TEVES – name of the tenth Jewish month (lunar cycle).

TIKKUN – fixing; may refer to a spiritual remedy.

TISHAH B'AV – the ninth day of the Hebrew month of Av, marking the Jewish national day of mourning over the Temples' destruction and other tragedies which occurred on that date over the course of Jewish history.

TISHREI – name of the seventh Jewish month (lunar cycle).

TOCHACHAH – rebuke.

TORAH – the Bible; can either refer to the five books of Moses, or to the entirety of Tanach, or can even include the Oral Law. Can also refer to a specific teaching.

TOV – good.

TZADI – the name of the eighteenth Hebrew letter.

TZADDIK / TZADDIKIM – righteous person / people.

TZARA'AS – a (spiritually generated) form of leprosy which can be found on the walls of a home, on clothing, or on a person's skin or hair.

TZE'AKAH – crying out, usually to Hashem.

TZEDDAKAH – charity. Also, justice.

TZIDKUS – righteousness.

TZITZIS – fringes or strings tied to four-cornered garments, reminding us to fulfill the commandments.

USHPIZIN – lit. guests; refers to the Seven Shepherds of Israel: Avraham, Yitzchak, Yaakov, Moshe, Aharon, Yosef, and David who visit the Jewish people in their Sukkos on the holiday of Sukkos.

VAV – the name of the sixth Hebrew letter.

VIDUI – confession.

YAM HAMELACH – lit. the sea of salt; the Dead Sea.

YAM SUF – the Sea of Reeds, usually associated with the Red Sea.

YAMIM NORAIM – Days of Awe, referring to the High Holidays.

YAYIN NESECH – wine that was poured in idolatrous worship.

YEFAS TOAR – lit. beautiful form; refers to an attractive woman that a Jewish soldier is allowed to take during war as a wife.

YESHIVA – lit. sit; refers to a Torah academy.

YESOD – foundation; one of the kabbalistic spheres, or attributes of Hashem.

YETZER HARA – evil inclination.

YETZER HATOV – positive inclination.

YEZTIAS MITZRAYIM – the Exodus from Egypt.

YIRAS HASHEM – awe or reverence of God.

YIRAS SHAMAYIM – lit. awe of heaven; refers to the awe or reverence of God.

YISRAEL – the Jewish people; or another name for our Patriarch Yaakov.

YISRAELIM – Israelites; members of the general Jewish population, excluding priests and Levites.

YOM KIPPUR – Day of Atonement.

YOM TOV – lit. good day; refers to a holiday.

YUD – the name of the tenth Hebrew letter.

ZAKEN – elder; old person.

ZAYIN – the name of the seventh Hebrew letter.

ZEMIROS – songs; refers to holy songs sung at the Shabbos or *Yom Tov* meals.

ZERIZUS – alacrity, care and vigilance in carrying out Mitzvos. Alacrity in general.

First Printing: 2015

ISBN: 978-0-9965158-5-6

Ramot Press

Jerusalem, Israel

www.RamotPress.com

First Printing: 2015

ISBN: 978-0-9965158-4-9

Ramot Press

Jerusalem, Israel

www.RamotPress.com

First Printing: 2015

ISBN: 978-0-9965158-3-2

Ramot Press

Jerusalem, Israel

www.RamotPress.com

First Printing: 2015

ISBN: 978-0-9965158-2-5

Ramot Press

Jerusalem, Israel

www.RamotPress.com

First Printing: 2015

ISBN: 978-0-9965158-1-8

Ramot Press

Jerusalem, Israel

www.RamotPress.com

First Printing: 2015

ISBN: 978-0-9965158-0-1

Ramot Press

Jerusalem, Israel

www.RamotPress.com

CPSIA information can be obtained
at www.ICGtesting.com
Printed in the USA
LVHW052144180319
611031LV00010B/223/P